FROM ORIENT
TO THE
EMIRATES

FROM ORIENT
TO THE
EMIRATES
THE PLUCKY RISE OF BURNLEY FC

TIM QUELCH

First published by Pitch Publishing, 2017

Pitch Publishing
A2 Yeoman Gate
Yeoman Way
Worthing
Sussex
BN13 3QZ
www.pitchpublishing.co.uk
info@pitchpublishing.co.uk

A CIP catalogue record is available for this book
from the British Library.

ISBN 978-1-78531-312-7

Typesetting and origination by Pitch Publishing

Printed and bound in Great Britain by TJ International Ltd, Padstow

Contents

OTHER PITCH BOOKS BY TIM QUELCH

NEVER HAD IT SO GOOD:
BURNLEY'S INCREDIBLE 1959/60 TITLE TRiUMPH
"I thoroughly enjoyed this book." *Programme Monthly*

"A great achievement. Tim Quelch has such feeling for history that the reader lives through the story as if it was happening now." Hyder Jawad, *Soccerama*

"A brilliant exercise, set against a backdrop of a town worried about its economic future and a country grappling with diminished global status." *London Clarets magazine*.

"A superb book" Trevor Meredith, Burnley's title-winning goalscorer in May 1960.

UNDERDOG!
FIFTY YEARS OF TRIALS AND TRIUMPH WITH
FOOTBALL'S ALSO-RANS
"From the Crazy Gang of '88 to Hastings FC, with a political backdrop spanning 50 years, there are stacks of stories to get stuck into." *Four Four Two*

"*Underdog!* is a collection of stories about when the improbable occurs in football. It will give those that buy it a warm glow." *When Saturday Comes*

"*Underdog!* is a riveting mixture of football, social history and popular culture and is an extraordinarily well-researched book." *SportsBookoftheMonth.com*

"This is a major work: erudite, keenly observed social history and an intimately detailed personal odyssey. I was captivated. It is dripping with authentic atmosphere. Quelch writes like a dream and he has an exquisite eye for detail.
Ivan Ponting, *Backpass Magazine*

BENT ARMS & DODGY WICKETS:
ENGLAND'S TROUBLED REIGN AS TEST MATCH KINGS
DURING THE FIFTIES
"An important book, addressing the shameful spills and conspicuous ills of post-war cricket in Blighty. Quelch skilfully sets the pitifully slow death of the Gents-Players divide and 'shamateurism' against a backdrop of a country divided." Rob Steen, *cricinfo*

"Once we thought of the 1950s as a golden age of English cricket. We now look back and find class snobbery, imperial arrogance and racial prejudice. In trying to look at history differently, Tim Quelch should be applauded." *The Cricketer*

"This well written and widely researched book is backed by opinions from many of the great cricketers of the fifties. It is strongly recommended" Cricket Memorabilia Society

STUMPS & RUNS & ROCK 'N' ROLL:
SIXTY YEARS SPENT BEYOND A BOUNDARY
"A most enjoyable investment. I would also suggest that it would be the ideal gift for anyone who has shown sufficient interest in the game to want to learn more about its history. Tim Quelch's entertaining prose might just convert a mere enthusiast into a full-blown cricket tragic." The Cricket Statistician

Tim writes not only very well but humorously and brings back memories of some of the great performers of yesteryear. Tim's descriptive powers regarding players are a treat."
AndrewRobertsCricketStatistics.com

Thanks

THIS book has been written to raise funds for Prostate Cancer UK. All royalties will be donated to this national charity to assist in combating this insidious disease, which sadly took the life of one of the club's heroes, Ian Britton. Led by its vice-chairman, Barry Kilby, Burnley Football Club continues to raise awareness of prostate cancer, also organising screening events at its home ground.

From Orient to the Emirates is primarily an oral history of Burnley's 30-year climb from the brink of extinction in 1986 and 1987 to its present position of strength. It is a collective effort, featuring the views and recollections of past and present players, managers, directors and supporters – taking account, too, of the observations of a range of backroom staff.

I would like to thank former players, including Ian Britton who scored the critical goal in the 1987 Orient game, for their kind assistance in telling this story. I would also like to extend my deep gratitude to chairman, Mike Garlick; vice-chairman and former chairman, Barry Kilby; director, Clive Holt; the late Frank Teasdale, a former director and chairman; former managing director, Derek Gill, club media manager, Darren Bentley, and club historian, Ray Simpson, for their most helpful contributions. I am also very appreciative of Darren's account of his work at Burnley and his terrific support in obtaining the brilliant photos for this book.

I am greatly indebted to the local press, particularly Chris Boden of the *Burnley Express* and Alex James of the *Lancashire Telegraph* in allowing me to use extracts of their press reports and interviews. I am also very grateful to authors, Dave Thomas, Phil Whalley and Ray Simpson for allowing me to reproduce extracts of their excellent work.

In Phil's case, this includes access to his impressive website record *The Claret Archives*. All three have kindly assisted me by checking earlier drafts. Many thanks to you all for your efforts.

Over the last 30 years, the London Clarets have produced a magazine, known now as *Something to Write Home About*. This magazine contains a superb daily record of significant club matters including a vast collection of match reports, interviews with players, managers and directors, plus other observations. I would like to thank everyone who has contributed, including Andrew Firmin, Lee Firmin, Dave McCluggage, Ian Wood, Jane Pike, Peter Pike, Dave Parker, Pauline Pratley, Brent Whittam, Barry Heagin, Steve Corrigan, Andy Waterworth, Michael Bullen, Peter Toner, Mark Pilling, Patrick O'Neill, John Pepper, Danny West, Phil Whalley, Karen Neill, and Dave Thomas, among many others. Without your offerings, it would not have been possible to provide such a wide-ranging, detailed and thoughtful representation of supporters' perspectives during this period.

I am very grateful to Tony Scholes of *Up the Clarets* website in helping my understanding of some of the important twists and turns on this 30-year path and for allowing me to use extracts from his fine article, *My Unshakeable Belief*. His historical records and player profiles on the *Up the Clarets* and *Clarets Mad* websites have been a great aid. Thanks to David Hird, too, for use of his lovingly compiled 30-year video history of Burnley FC.

Some material used is unsourced, particularly historical press cuttings, extracted from national or local papers or club interviews. While I have endeavoured to obtain the prior permission for all material used, this has not been possible in all cases. I hope those who identify any breach in copyright will allow this please, recognising the book's charitable objective, as stated above. Should any concern be raised in this respect please address this to Paul Camillin, my publisher at Pitch Publishing.

May I also thank Paul and all at Pitch Publishing for their excellent assistance throughout.

All but one of the 40 images presented in this book were kindly provided by Burnley Football Club. Author Dave Thomas generously permitted the use of his photo of Roger Eli.

Tim Quelch,
June 2017

Foreword

THIS is a great story. It begins with the once-powerful Burnley football club in grave peril. For in the mid-eighties this club, saddled with ruinous debt, was precariously perched on the brink of oblivion. Yet, thanks to the unstinting commitment and acumen of all involved – directors, managers, playing and backroom staff and supporters – it managed to recover superbly during the ensuing 30 years to become, once again, one of the top clubs in the country. I am proud to have served this club during its rise from rags to riches, initially as one of its directors in the latter 2000s but subsequently as co-chairman in 2012, with John Banaszkiewicz, and since 2015 as its sole chairman.

I was born in Burnley in 1963 when the club was still a leading top-flight side. However, by the time my family and I moved to Blackpool in the late sixties, the Clarets were beginning to struggle to hold on to their First Division status.

Unlike most Burnley fans, my father played little part in developing my love for the club. Apart from an auntie who was a big fan, there was no one else in the family who held a torch for Burnley. My passion was kindled when Rev. David Wiseman, author of several books about the club, spoke at our school in Poulton-le-Fylde during the mid-seventies. I was captivated by his passion for Burnley FC. It was a significant marker in my development as a Claret. I saw my first Burnley game in January 1976. It was an FA Cup tie at Bloomfield Road. Burnley lost to Blackpool and Jimmy Adamson lost his job as their manager.

After our family had returned to Burnley in the late seventies, I developed a closer attachment to the club. This was heightened when I began studying at Bradford University during the early eighties.

In my student days, I frequently returned home to watch Burnley's home games. It was around this time, when I was aged between 18 and 20 years, that I first held the ambition to become the chairman of the club. My family's roots in Burnley go back to the mid-Victorian period. It wasn't just the club that was so important to me; it was the town, too.

The Thatcher years were hard times for the Cotton towns. Their economy was failing with the local unemployment rate remaining around 15 per cent, and even higher in the surrounding districts. I wanted to return something to my home town. I could have opted for charity work but felt that I could offer more in the service of the football club, which apart from that dark period in the mid-eighties, represented such a significant part of the town's identity.

Bob Lord was in charge when I first held this ambition. While I could not see myself emulating his autocratic manner, there was much to admire about his management of the club. It appealed to me too that the position of club director conferred the status of a community leader.

After leaving university I married and moved to London, developing my own business in IT recruitment, which became very successful. During the nineties I was preoccupied with my business and family life so there was less time for football, but I still managed to make a handful of trips to Turf Moor each season, and see all local away games, and some as far afield as Bristol and Exeter. With the kids growing up, and having floated my business successfully on the stock exchange, I had more time to devote to the club. Around 2004 or 5 I approached Barry Kilby, the club chairman of that time, asking whether there might be space for me on the Burnley board. Due to the ITV Digital fiasco, the club was financially stretched. I knew that any money I sunk into Burnley would probably never be seen again. But the club began to prosper, helped especially by Brendan Flood who joined the board at a similar time. I slowly increased my stake.

Owen Coyle then took us to the Premier League in 2009. However, had we failed to win promotion that year, we would probably have had to sell many of the players that had helped take us there. While we stayed for one season only in the top flight and then stuttered when back in the Championship, the turning point in the club's fortunes came with our appointment of Sean Dyche as manager in November 2012.

I live near Watford as my business headquarters is in London. Being so close to Vicarage Road, I gained a good sense of what Sean was offering to the Hornets. One of his qualities stood out – his ability to develop the abilities of both inexperienced and experienced players. This was evident in his work with the youngsters, but also with the first team when he subsequently graduated to assistant and full management roles. We know we cannot just buy our way to success at Burnley. We haven't the resources to do that. But we can develop our players' talents and in this respect Sean represented the best fit for us. Besides, we needed greater continuity after three changes of manager in less than three years.

Sean is rigorous about appointing only those players who meet his requirements. They must be conscientious in pursuit of their developmental targets. They must display maximum effort and application. They need to adhere to his team framework and always display the highest standards of conduct on and off the pitch.

In the last two years, we have doubled the size of our recruitment team to eight staff, led by Head Scout Martin Hodge. They work closely with Sean in identifying his potential targets, undertaking the background research to ensure these players will fit his required profile. It is more difficult to do such detailed research with European players which accounts for their limited numbers on our books. There is more to factor in with signings from abroad, not least of all because we do not know how well they and their families will settle here.

Unlike the situation in the club's glory years during the fifties, sixties and early seventies, few Burnley players now choose to live in or around the town, usually preferring locations nearer to Manchester. It is a big plus that we are situated close to this major city which has so much to offer in terms of leisure, entertainment and shopping opportunities, as well as having a large international airport. This probably grants us greater pulling power than clubs which are more remotely placed, such as Hull or Middlesbrough.

Nevertheless, player recruitment now represents mighty challenges for us because of the huge sums of money involved and the impact that agents have in the process, notably when auctions are created. The reality is that clubs do not own their players anymore. They are leased.

Our chief executive, Dave Baldwin and I have responsibility for landing the targets that Sean and our recruitment team identify, embroiling us in complicated negotiations with agents and other clubs. The summer window of 2016 was particularly hard. As a result, I am now spending much of my work life at Turf Moor. Because of the unpredictability of the recruitment process we always try to present

Sean with more than one suitable option. There always needs to be a plan B, C or D.

I know the fans become very frustrated about player recruitment, as they do about achieving success, but I am not dismayed by this. I am a fan, too. I get their yearning for 'marquee signings' and glory. While we are so much better off than we have ever been, we still need to be careful who we bring in. A few mistakes could see those resources dwindle very quickly.

I remain positive about the club's future despite the area's ageing and declining population. In the 2014/15 season, we made a record profit of £30m. We are expecting to make a healthy profit in the 2016/17 season, too, despite spending a lot more on players. This is a very well-run club. Financially, it has never been in better shape. I don't suffer from sleepless nights. We have shown how well we can compete against richer sides. When we were promoted to the Premier League in 2014 behind Leicester, they had a budget three or four times larger than ours. Now we believe that, slowly but surely, we can compete well with clubs like West Bromwich, Stoke and Southampton all of which have wealthy owners but who do not put huge sums of money into their clubs, surviving largely on Sky's current annual pay-out of £100m plus the revenue gained from lucrative player sales.

In 2009, our objective was to reach the Premier League. Now we believe we have the resources to remain having successfully stayed up last season and having managed to sell our young rising star, Michael Keane for a high fee. Player development is therefore essential in securing our future. The recently re-constructed Barnfield Training Centre is now a base befitting a top-flight club and one that will serve us for generations. The playing surfaces are superb, enabling high quality football to be played all year round. When we were promoted in 2009, the players still needed to change at Turf Moor for training sessions at Gawthorpe, putting towels on their car seats after a muddy work-out. Thankfully, this is no longer the case. The Barnfield Centre has top of the range facilities which is as attractive to experienced recruits as it is to youngsters watched by their proud parents. Our academy has now achieved category two status, granting our youth players better coaching opportunities and higher calibre opposition.

At Turf Moor too, the club offices have had a major upgrade for our hard-working staff, and the Clarets Store is already proving its worth with a much better range of merchandise and leisure wear.

Given how far we have come in these 30 years it is an amazing journey, but one which is far from over in many ways. Maybe it's just beginning. Up the Clarets!

Mike Garlick,
Chairman,
Burnley Football Club.
July 2017

Prologue

ON Saturday 9 May 1987 Burnley Football Club faced the alarming prospect of relegation from the Football League. Burnley was a founder member in 1888. But almost a century later, this status counted for nothing. Its startling successes as FA Cup champions in 1914 and First Division winners in 1921 and 1960 granted no exemption. It was merely a historical curiosity that Burnley was, and still is, the smallest town or city to host England's top-flight champions. Its prestigious victories in European and Inter-Cities Fairs Cup competitions were just cherished memories, as were its impressive FA Cup runs of 1947, 1962 and 1974, and its League Cup feats in 1960/61, 1968/69 and 1982/83.

This roll of honour was of no consequence on Saturday 9 May 1987, other than to remind the football world just how precipitous the club's decline had been. The only detail that mattered on this day was that a threadbare Burnley squad had to beat play-off aspirants Orient in the final game of the season to avoid demotion to the Football Conference, knowing that the club's salvation was also dependent upon results elsewhere. The team entrusted with defending Burnley's proud heritage included both the 'green' and the 'grey' – a pair of 18-year-old apprentices, on £25 per week, plus a quintet of ex-Division One veterans in the late twilight of their careers. If they and their journeymen colleagues had failed in their endeavour, relegation carried the risk of extinction, given that in August 1986 the club was said to be £800,000 in debt and losing £10,000 per week. Liquidation had then only been averted by the narrowest of margins. The stakes could not have been higher for stoical club chairman, Frank Teasdale, his embattled board of directors, and their steadfast team manager, Brian Miller. Miller had once been an England international and a barnstorming midfielder or centre back in Burnley's 1960 title-winning side. How had the once mighty fallen.

The malaise that had gripped the club in the mid-eighties reflected the economic hardships felt throughout the surrounding area. The 'cotton towns' of Burnley, Nelson and Colne and their satellite communities had owed much of their former prosperity to textile and coal production. Indeed, during its Victorian heyday, Burnley became the world's largest manufacturing centre of cotton cloth, thanks to its beneficially moist climate.

The abdications of 'King Cotton' and 'Old King Coal' were presaged during the mid-fifties, but drawn out painfully over the following three decades. Despite the introduction of newer industries such as Rolls-Royce, Michelin, Prestige and EPB, the economic prospects of the 'cotton towns' continued to decline. The last rites of major coal and textile production were administered during the early eighties with the closure of Burnley's last colliery at Hapton in 1981, and the shutting of Queen Street Mill a year later.

During the early eighties, the number unemployed nationally rose to over three million – the highest figure since the 'Great Depression' of the thirties. While 11.3% of British working people were unemployed by the middle of this decade, the proportion of jobless workers in the 'cotton towns' was significantly higher, at around 15-16%, with neighbouring communities such as the Rossendale Valley having 18 or 20% of their workforce on the dole. Even the area's newer industries began to feel the pinch. Dereliction abounded with streets of empty terraced houses, abandoned, boarded-up mills, deserted collieries, rusted and overgrown marshalling yards and a neglected, filthy canal. The desolate, decrepit 'cotton towns' seemed less like a crucible of industrial revolution than its casket.

And just as the local towns were forsaken in this ruinous economic climate, so its residents forsook their once august football team. Whereas home gates during Burnley's League championship-winning season of 1959/60 averaged almost 27,000, in the wretched season of 1986/87 they fell to 10 per cent of that figure. That is until the 'win or bust' final home game against Orient, which, according to official records, drew in 15,696 fans but was probably watched by over 17,000. Five home league games during that season had been watched by fewer than 2,000 hardy fans. Non-league Colne Dynamos, then bankrolled by businessman Graham White, seemed to have a better potential for success than their once mighty neighbours.

No one then could have possibly envisaged that this beleaguered, yet venerable, club would not only ride out this devastating storm but recover spectacularly. During the next 30 years the club would reach the top flight, no less than three times in the space of seven years, attracting average gates of around 20,000 for its Premier League home games.

Saturday 9 May 1987 dawned with an ominously grey haze enveloping the town. Although warm sunlight would soon pierce the murk, leaving an almost unblemished blue sky, this did little to arouse hope of an improbable survival. Instead it seemed like a cruel blessing, intended merely to tantalise the already condemned. For those who had ever held a torch for Burnley FC, the overriding question was 'where did it go so catastrophically wrong'?

1976 – 1986
On the road to oblivion

'Money's Too Tight To Mention'

BEFORE the mandatory wage cap and the feudal 'retain and transfer' system were removed in the early sixties, a talented, tactically astute 'David' – like Burnley or Ipswich Town – could defeat the richer, more fancied 'Goliaths' over the long, rugged haul of an English First Division football season. But even then money screamed. As with Ipswich's championship in 1961/62, Burnley's league title victory in 1959/60 was a triumph against the odds. Thereafter, those odds grew ever longer for a team like Burnley. Situated within a steep-sided secluded valley in a declining area, Burnley's team, like its town, required more resources than it could muster by its own productivity to thrive. The abolition of the footballers' maximum wage in 1961 not only disturbed the balance sheet, it also meant that the club could no longer rely upon attracting the best young talent.

That talent would go increasingly to the highest bidder. As a small-town club with limited means, greater efficiencies needed to be found while facing increasing competition from richer clubs. With the consumer boom of the late fifties unfolding, there were rival leisure attractions to contend with, too. And as that boom unravelled during the sixties with British manufacturing becoming less competitive leading to a worsening imbalance of trade, Burnley FC was forced to consider how it should market itself within the confines of a receding local economy. Its 'sell to survive' policy was born in this climate.

Regrettably, that policy could only work while the club remained in the top flight and seen to give its talented youngsters an earlier opportunity to shine on the big stage. By so doing, Burnley could still hope to compete with and confound the more lucrative enticements offered by larger clubs.

However, it needed its youth policy to deliver at a consistently high rate of productivity to plug the gaps left by its departing stars. By the mid-sixties Bob Lord, Burnley's blunt, autocratic but canny and far-sighted chairman, had been forced to sell at least one of his stars each season at a high return to offset annual revenue losses and the wincing cost of ground improvements. Once the likes of John Connelly (£40,000), Gordon Harris (£70,000) Willie Morgan (£117,000), Ralph Coates (£190,000), Steve Kindon (£100,000), Brian O'Neil (£75,000), Dave Thomas (£165,000), Martin Dobson (£300,000) and Leighton James (£310,000) had departed the 'sell to survive' policy faltered. As Burnley's bumper harvests of young talent withered, its team strength eroded and its support fell away. With the law of diminishing returns biting ever deeper into its prospects the club slid at first steadily, but then rapidly, towards that traumatic day in May 1987.

Relegation from the First Division in 1976 had been disastrous. To combat the fans' swelling criticisms of his financial management, Bob Lord intemperately put the record straight in a match day magazine at the start of the following season. He announced that the club was £400,000 in debt (over £3.4m today), and losing approximately £4,000 per week. The annual loss was revealed to be £146,871. Disaffected, Welsh wing wizard Leighton James, was sold to First Division champions Derby for a then club record fee of £310,000. This did little to allay the club's bleak financial outlook, while ensuring its return to the Second Division. During the 1974/75 season, when Burnley made a bold bid for the First Division title, James had been responsible for around 40 per cent of his side's goals, either directly or by assists. There were none remaining to fill the gaping gap he left. Tony Morley was signed from Preston in February 1976 for around £100,000, in the hope that this promising, young Third Division winger could replicate James' magic. It was expecting too much, too soon.

Despite the economies made by the club following its demotion, in each of the three, largely unsuccessful seasons that followed, the club reported annual losses of over £100,000. Home attendances fell consistently below 10,000 at the start of the 1977/78 season, the lowest Turf Moor gates since the 1930s, and continued falling despite brief upturns in form and interest. Not even the lucrative sale of other young stars such as Ray Hankin (£172,000) and Brian Flynn (£175,000) to Leeds, Terry Cochrane (£238,000) to Middlesbrough and Tony Morley (£200,000) to Aston Villa could halt, let alone reverse, the accumulating debt.

Burnley had established a long tradition of keeping its managerial appointments 'within the family'. This uninterrupted succession had begun during the summer of 1954 when Burnley's former stalwart centre half and captain, Alan Brown, was brought back to the club as manager. Brown had been a pivotal, craggy presence in Burnley's 'iron curtain' defence during the austere late forties. However, Brown was much more than an unyielding, morally censorious stopper. His coaching methods were innovative. His training drills placed greater emphasis upon skill improvement than upon muscular exercise. Meanwhile, his tactical nous spawned an array of bewildering 'dead ball' ruses. It was Brown who established the groundwork for the Clarets' later success, leading a group of first team players in digging the foundations and drains for the club's new 'state of the art' training ground at Gawthorpe. When Brown moved to Sunderland in 1957, having fallen out with the overbearing Lord, he was succeeded by long-serving player, trainer and physiotherapist, Billy Dougall. But Dougall remained in post for only five months before resigning because of poor health. Lord then turned to Burnley's former inside forward Harry Potts who had played under Brown's captaincy in the 1947 FA Cup final.

Building upon Brown's inspirational management, the avuncular and ever-enthusiastic Potts led Burnley to Championship glory in May 1960. But with the sixties game becoming increasingly tactical and defensively-minded, in 1970 he was replaced as team manager by Jimmy Adamson, his astute coach, strategist and 1960 title-winning captain.

Although Adamson was unable to prevent Burnley's relegation from the top flight in 1971, he master-minded a powerful return two years later. But while the family silver needed to be sold to keep the club afloat, team performances suffered. After a wretched run of league form and a stormy FA Cup defeat by Harry Potts' Blackpool side, Lord asked for Adamson's resignation in January 1976. Adamson's assistant, Joe Brown, was invited to take over.

With Adamson's hands prised away from the tiller, and both playing and financial resources dwindling, Joe Brown was left with only a poisoned chalice to hold aloft. Unable to halt Burnley's perilous slide down Division Two, Lord brought back Harry Potts to replace him in February 1977. Potts' irrepressible positivity rubbed off on his downcast squad, prompting a rediscovery of self-belief and, having ushered in a more expansive playing style, relegation was finally averted in the season's final home game with a fluent 3-1 victory over Notts County.

And yet, all was not well, as Potts' side made a dismal start to the following season. Alarmed at the prospect of a further relegation, Lord allowed Potts to re-sign the burly, yet extraordinarily fast striker Steve Kindon who immediately ignited a formidable revival. And with another returning star Leighton James joining him a year later, Burnley embarked upon a promising promotion bid, buoyed by its success in winning the Anglo-Scottish Cup. Alas, the Clarets' performances began to splutter and ultimately stall in the exceptionally cold winter of 1979 which landed the club with a horrendous backlog of fixtures. Burnley's upward momentum halted in that 'winter of discontent'.

This time there was to be no recovery. In October 1979, Harry Potts was sacked following his ageing team's disastrous start to the new season whereupon Brian Miller was asked to take over, immediately replacing many of the ageing stars with the best of the club's emerging home-grown talent. But despite some impressive performances over the Christmas period, relegation to the Third Division duly followed in May 1980. This represented Burnley's lowest position in its 92-year membership of the Football League. The drop also entailed an annual deficit of £300,000, twice as much as had been lost in the 1977/78 and 1978/79 seasons. By then, Bob Lord, the self-styled 'John Bull' of English football, was broken in health and spirit, his meat business apparently foundering. It seemed as if Lord's once proud empire had been reduced to ruins.

In the autumn of 1981, with Burnley languishing in the Third Division relegation zone, and close to bankruptcy, Bob Lord decided to retire, selling his controlling interest to a consortium of four for £52,000. This quartet included local barrister, John Jackson, who had joined the Burnley board of directors in 1976. The shares were divvied out equally between them and Jackson was elected as the new club chairman. The low price paid reflected not only Burnley's calamitous financial state but also increasing public disenchantment with a game scarred with abhorrent hooliganism, crumbling stadia and penal fencing.

Jackson remembered:

'I spent more time trying to persuade Bob Lord to invite me to join the board, than I did in persuading juries that they should accept my clients' version of events... It is impossible to overstate Mr Lord's knowledge of football, and impossible to overstate the precarious nature of the club's finances at that time. Bounced cheques were not unknown... Mr Lord controlled virtually every aspect of the club's affairs. On most important matters, the directors were informed rather than consulted... Mr Lord was content if the club merely stayed afloat... Having replaced Lord as chairman, I in no way controlled the club, indeed my position as chairman depended upon the support of my colleagues... it was my duty to govern by consent. This was later to cause me problems.'

John Jackson requested that Derek Gill, a local businessman and accountant, should undertake a thorough analysis of the club's finances. Gill had been introduced to Jackson by Burnley director, Colin Sanderson. He was evidently a passionate fan of the club, and eager to be of assistance. Gill joined the board in January 1982. He proceeded to serve the club, initially as finance director for all of 1982 and most of 1983, before becoming its managing director between September 1983 and May 1985. Jackson claimed he required a senior executive to manage club affairs while he was preoccupied with his barrister work. Although Derek Gill disputed Jackson's explanation, he was to become one of the club's most conscientious servants, diligently devoting many unpaid hours to his work at Turf Moor, often at the expense of his own business commitments. He immersed himself in various aspects of financial management, also undertaking copious representative duties, at Football League meetings and events, and at first and reserve team fixtures. He was shocked at the shambolic state of the club's finances, during Bob Lord's final years in charge. He found that only the player contracts had been managed adequately. Gill reported:

'Suppliers were not being paid, the position with the Inland Revenue on PAYE and National Insurance was chaotic and the VAT commitment was something to ignore and hope it would go away.'

Derek Gill took issue with Lord's management of team affairs, too. He attributed Burnley's decline during the late seventies to Lord's 'crazy' decision to dispense with Jimmy Adamson's services as manager and head coach. For those unfamiliar with Adamson's career, he was not only a peerless wing-half who was desperately unlucky to miss selection for the England team, he was also an internationally acclaimed coach. Bobby Charlton rated his tactical acumen very highly, having seen him in action during the Chile World Cup finals of 1962. Adamson was then serving as Walter Winterbottom's coaching assistant. His skills captivated the FA so much that he was offered Winterbottom's post after England's World Cup elimination by Brazil. However, Adamson, the 1962 winner of the Football Writers 'Footballer of the Year' award, chose to extend his playing career, opening the way for Alf Ramsey's selection as England's new boss. The rest, of course, is history – at least for Ramsey.

Derek Gill thought that in demanding Adamson's resignation, Lord had scuppered the club's best chance of returning quickly to the top flight, thereby accelerating its footballing and financial demise. And he thought that Adamson, as head coach, had done more to bring about Burnley's success than sublime playmaker Jimmy McIlroy had during the fifties and early sixties. Coincidentally, both McIlroy and Adamson were summarily removed from the club by Lord.

And yet the malaise gripping the club at the beginning of the eighties was suddenly and triumphantly lifted with Burnley's unexpected promotion as Third Division champions in May 1982 under Brian Miller. After a dreadful start to the 1981/82 season, in which Burnley lost six of its opening eight games, a tactical masterstroke was unveiled in the fixture at Portsmouth on 10 October. Martin Dobson was assigned the role of sweeper while full backs, Laws and Wharton, were licensed to push forward, creating extra width. Left back Wharton scored in an impressive 2-1 victory. The impact was dramatic – only one defeat was inflicted in the next 35 league games, resulting in Burnley rising from almost bottom to the top.

Miller's vibrant team represented a brilliant blend of youthful, mostly home-grown, talent and vintage skill and experience. That side included:

Brian Laws a studious, stylish yet gutsy, progressive right back, who would later play 136 games in Division One under Brian Clough, ultimately winning a League Cup winners' medal and an England B cap;

Andy Wharton a combative left back with an enduring passion for Burnley, his local club;

Michael Phelan also a loyal 'Claret' fan, who would develop into a composed and elegant centre back and midfielder. He subsequently played with distinction for Norwich and Manchester United in the top flight, also winning a full England cap;

Swashbuckling Vince Overson a stroppy, strapping, 'no nonsense' centre half who gave no quarter;

Trevor Steven, a central midfielder of precocious poise, perception and power who would eventually play 36 times for the senior England side;

Kevin Young a gifted, deft left-sided midfielder who, on the 18 May 1982, scored a searing equaliser against Chesterfield on a sodden Turf Moor surface to confirm Burnley's promotion to Division Two;

Derek Scott a fierce competitor either at right back or as a box-to-box midfielder with endless stamina and an eye for goal;

Northern Ireland international striker Billy Hamilton – a formidable target man at any level, well supported by fellow forwards the predatory Steve Taylor and Republic of Ireland international Paul McGee.

Their collective efforts were augmented by the classy experience of dependable, long-serving goalkeeper Alan Stevenson, a breath-taking shot-stopper; Martin Dobson, an English international sweeper or midfielder of peerless grace and aplomb; and scrapping Northern Ireland international midfielder Tommy Cassidy.

But Burnley faltered in the higher Division, resulting in the sudden dismissal of manager Miller after his side had suffered its tenth consecutive away league defeat at Bolton in January 1983. Although Miller's assistant Frank Casper, another former Clarets' star, led an encouraging recovery as caretaker manager beginning with a stunning League Cup victory at White Hart Lane and winning seven and drawing four of his 18 league games in charge, it was insufficient to avoid relegation.

Arguably those in charge took too long before realising that Miller's young side required strengthening to compete in Division Two, perhaps deceived by its startlingly powerful start to the campaign in August 1982. But after putting Middlesbrough and Carlisle to the sword in their second and third league fixtures, Burnley lost nine of its next 10 games.

Additions were belatedly made in November. In came pint-sized, former Leeds, Burnley and Welsh midfielder, Brian Flynn, and the ex-Manchester City and Scotland left back Willie Donachie. Nevertheless, the die was almost cast by the time Casper took over in mid-January.

Burnley striker Steve Taylor later remarked:

'We should never have gone down with the players we had.
I still don't understand how it happened.'

Brian Laws added in an interview with Burnley writer, Phil Whalley:

'Yes, the quality was there. Each individual player was good
enough, and so was our team. The players that went down
were definitely good enough to go back up. It only needed
the addition of a couple of players. It was just that we did
very well in the cups that year. You'll find that a lot of clubs
who have success in the cups find that it detracts from their
actual league form. Burnley weren't just the only ones – it
happened to many clubs. I remember Brighton getting to
an FA Cup Final and being relegated in the same year. The
financial gains the club made were enormous. It could have
kept the club in business for many years to come.'

Burnley's brilliant cup runs certainly stood in marked contrast
to their league performances. For while winning only 12 out of 42
league games, the Clarets managed to win 10 out of 16 cup games,
progressing to the sixth round of the FA Cup, and reaching the semi-
final of the League Cup. Having beaten top flight sides Coventry (2-1),
Birmingham (3-2), and Spurs (4-1) to progress to a Milk Cup semi-final
with League champions elect Liverpool they also won their home leg
1-0 while losing 3-1 on aggregate. Sadly, Burnley midfielder Derek
Scott missed two sitters in the first leg at Anfield when the game was
still in the balance. But it was his goal which decided the result of the
home leg.

After Burnley's relegation in 1983, the Burnley board of directors
decided to break with the club's 30-year-old reliance upon 'faithful
retainers'. The caretaking management team of Frank Casper and
assistant Gordon Clayton were not offered the permanent positions.
Chairman, John Jackson explained:

'The production line that had produced Harry Potts and
Jimmy Adamson had come to an end. The board decided
to appoint an outsider.'

Contrary to media speculation, the applicants for the job were not
numerous – John Bond, John Duncan, Frank Burrows and another
un-named North-Western candidate who, according to Jackson,
failed to remember the name of his proposed assistant when asked
at interview.

Bond was flamboyant, outspoken and strongly opinionated but possessed an impressive managerial record. Jackson described him as 'charismatic'. During the early seventies, Bond had transformed struggling Bournemouth's fortunes spectacularly before steering modest Norwich back into the First Division in 1975, having arrived too late to prevent their relegation a year earlier. Second helpings proved more palatable to the Canaries, as under Bond's guidance they thrived in the higher division, reaching a League Cup final in 1976.

Having moved on to Maine Road in October 1980, Bond took his Manchester City team – comprising three of his subsequent Burnley recruits; Gerry Gow, Kevin Reeves and Tommy Hutchison – to an FA Cup final appearance in 1981, where they lost somewhat unfortunately to Spurs after a replay. At his interview, Bond told the Burnley directors that 'he had only one thought in his mind: the First Division.'

Considering Bond's convincing interview performance and impressive CV, Jackson proposed to his fellow directors that Bond was the man to take Burnley forward. Jackson claimed that the decision to offer the post to Bond was unanimous. Derek Gill took issue with this, complaining that he had not been consulted and that he knew nothing of Bond's appointment until he had read about it in an English paper while on holiday in Tenerife. Gill was unhappy about his exclusion from a selection process, which he later considered to be precipitate and cursory. However, upon his own admission, he declined Jackson's invitation to meet with Bond before the appointment was formally ratified. Although miffed at the process he appeared to accept that Bond's appointment was in effect a *fait accompli*.

Looking to achieve a rapid turnaround in Burnley's fortunes, Bond made immediate, radical and expensive changes to the first team squad. This provoked consternation among Burnley supporters loyal to their deposed favourites. Bond hardly endeared himself with his haughty declaration:

> 'If my record at other clubs is anything to go by, it shouldn't take long to put things right.'

Bond stripped Martin Dobson of the captaincy, passing this to veteran newcomer, Tommy Hutchison. It wasn't as if Hutchison was a poor choice. Hutchison had bags of experience as a tricky, hard-working Scottish international winger who defended as resolutely as he attacked. Hutchison was sober, authoritative and totally committed, with an extraordinary degree of fitness. But many Burnley fans could not see past their dismay at the exclusion of club 'elder statesman', Dobson.

Their ire was unfairly re-directed at Hutchison, causing him to dub Burnley 'grumpy town'. Newly recruited England international striker Kevin Reeves wasn't immune either. Eventually, the fans' negativity towards these new acquisitions abated as they began to realise that both players were class acts.

But their anger was re-ignited when it was discovered that popular full back, Brian Laws had left Turf Moor to join Huddersfield. The fee was reported to be £50,000, although Derek Gill maintained it was significantly less, quoting a figure of £35,000. This seemed well below Laws' market value. Bond decided that Laws was 'not a good enough defender' despite being 'quite good' when advancing. And yet Bond had seen Laws in action only in the pre-season friendlies. His assessment seemed neither full nor fair. He later admitted to Burnley writer, Phil Whalley: 'There was more to letting Brian go than me thinking he wasn't that good. I just didn't want him at the football club...' Bond never explained why. Laws reacted to his summary dismissal by stating: 'Mr Bond is entitled to his opinion but I'm determined to make him eat his words... Huddersfield is a family friendly club, the way that Burnley used to be.' Laws' subsequent success at Middlesbrough and Nottingham Forest made his point emphatically.

Laws added:

> 'I was very disillusioned when John Bond came to the club. He was the wrong person for the job. He had his big-time thoughts, having come from a big club, and he tried to make Burnley into a big-time club in a very short space of time. It failed miserably and cost the club dearly. Burnley Football Club wasn't run like that. It was a family club.'

It wasn't as if Bond had a suitable replacement lined up. Future England star Lee Dixon was briefly auditioned for the part, playing in the opening game at Hull where Burnley were thrashed 4-1. Dixon was hastily discarded. This decision appalled Burnley coach, Gordon Clayton. He had been Casper's assistant during the previous season. Clayton implored the club to 'hang on to Dixon at all costs', recognising his huge potential. Burnley's loss would eventually become Arsenal's mighty gain.

Bond was also perversely dissatisfied with Scottish international left back Willie Donachie. Bond told Phil Whalley:

> 'I rated Willie Donachie as a great player at Manchester City, but he wasn't a great player at Burnley. And he wasn't too old'.

Oldham boss, Joe Royle couldn't believe his luck when Bond released Donachie on a free transfer in 1984. Donachie went on to play 169 games for Oldham, helping the Latics win promotion to the First Division in 1991, and to remain in the top flight for three seasons at the dawn of the FA Premier League.

After the bruising defeat at Boothferry Park, Bond claimed:

> 'What amazes me is how simple the solution is – to get better players. Once I have got that team together, I will take full responsibility for what happens.'

What infuriated Burnley fans though was that many of Bond's 'big name' acquisitions – Reeves and Hutchison excepted – appeared to be weakening the club. Neither midfielder Gerry Gow nor centre half, Joe Gallagher seemed fit!

Gow had been a belligerent ball-winner at Bristol City, Manchester City and Rotherham. According to Derek Gill, Gow had 'single-handedly terrorised our entire midfield' when Burnley met Rotherham, at Millmoor during the previous season. But Gow made nothing like that impact in the eight league games he played for Burnley. Bond told Phil Whalley, 'Gerry Gow had done a fabulous job for me at Manchester City but he had very dodgy knees and it just didn't work out for him.' It was a poor return on the £15,000 fee Burnley paid for Gow. The £30,000 fee that Burnley shelled out to West Ham for Joe Gallagher was a more calamitous error, though.

Joe Gallagher had once been a commanding and composed centre half for First Division Birmingham but he no longer had the mobility or pace to fulfil that role. In fairness to Bond, not even a medical specialist from Manchester could find anything wrong with Gallagher's knee other than a degree of retraction. Burnley's medical advisor and director, Dr Iven, was similarly satisfied, having had Gallagher running up and down a flight of stairs to assess his fitness. Following their examinations, Gallagher was awarded a four-year contract, plus a £25,000 ex-gratia payment to be met at the end of his fourth year at the club. What the medical personnel overlooked was Gallagher's limited capacity to twist and turn. This was brutally exposed in his first truly competitive game at Hull. Whenever Gallagher needed to shift direction suddenly, stress was placed upon his damaged knee, causing him to hobble.

The Burnley fans recognised this immediately, quickly dubbing him 'Galloping Joe'. Gallagher did not play another league game for Bond. Burnley were left with a crocked centre-half, sitting on a four-year contract, a loss of well over £100,000 if his wages were considered. Only in his fourth year at the club did he play any meaningful football. With Burnley deeply in trouble, he was patched up and pushed out to play in 44 first team games – 38 more than he played in the three preceding seasons put together. Talk about El Cid!

Bond never passed the buck on Gallagher. He blamed neither vice-chairman, Iven nor the Manchester specialist. Instead, he frankly admitted to the board: 'Gentlemen I have dropped a ricket, Joe Gallagher is not fit.'

Another Bond recruit, Dennis Tueart, also failed to do himself justice due to a lingering Achilles injury. Bond seemed unaware of this problem when he triumphantly announced his signing, claiming: 'You can't get young quality players on free transfers. So, if you want quality, we have got to go for older players. Dennis is a good player – and that's all that matters.' Alas, Dennis was not the formidable, flying winger with an eye for goal that he had been during his Sunderland and Manchester City heydays. He managed just eight starts at Turf Moor, scoring five goals, before calling it a day. He ruefully recognised that his injury no longer permitted him to perform as he once did in his prime, when he won six England caps.

But whereas Tueart's plight saddened Bond, Steve Daley's performances for Burnley frustrated him. Such had been Daley's reputation as a rampaging midfielder, that Manchester City were persuaded to pay Wolves £1.4m for his transfer in 1979. Bond told Phil Whalley:

> 'Me and the chairman flew out to the US to sign him. He was an over-rated player really… he didn't do that well at City. In truth, he wasn't a First Division player, but I thought at the level Burnley were playing, he would do well.'

It was reported that Burnley paid £20,000 for his transfer. But Gill reckoned the true cost was threatening to reach £150,000 as provision was made for Daley to purchase a house for his family.

Derek Gill recalled:

> 'After Daley made his long-awaited debut, in no time the manager was telling us he was overweight and could not play…'

In a desperate attempt to reduce the escalating costs, Gill persuaded his younger son to temporarily vacate his three-bedroomed house to accommodate the Daleys. Gill is incredulous now that such a sacrifice should have ever been contemplated.

Despite scoring a hat-trick at Port Vale in April, giving Burnley their first victory in two months, Daley's contributions were largely undistinguished. Fortunately, Gill managed to negotiate cancellation of Daley's contract, transferring him back to the USA. Although Burnley gained no fee from Daley's return, Derek Gill reckoned that this cancellation saved the club around £100,000 in wages and bonuses.

Bond admitted to Phil Whalley that Southampton central defender, Malcolm Waldron was a 'bad buy' too.

Bond said,

> 'We paid excessively for Waldron. I thought he was a good player and we got him to the club and he couldn't play! You think you know someone and then you get them to the football club and he can't do this or can't do that and you wonder why you bought them. It happens to most managers, but unfortunately it happened to me too often at Burnley.'

Waldron cost Burnley £85,000, only £15,000 less than was paid to Manchester City for Kevin Reeves. To compound the folly, Bond found he had a better centre half on his books in home-grown Vince Overson. As proof of that, Overson and Mike Phelan re-established a redoubtable central pairing leaving Waldron with a succession of filling-in turns before he was off-loaded to Portsmouth in March 1984 for £60,000. It should be said though that initially, Overson appeared still troubled by a groin injury, which had ruled him out for most of the preceding season. Bond decided Overson needed some 'tough love'.

Vince Overson told Phil Whalley:

> 'When John Bond came to the club I couldn't stand the bloke.... I was struggling badly with an injury, and I wasn't physically strong enough to do the pre-season. I'd been out that long. He absolutely slaughtered me... I felt sorry for myself but in the end, I thought "He just wants a reaction from me." I think some people, rather than face him, they backed down, and I think that's the worst thing they could have done with Bond... If you stood up to him, he'd respect you. In the end, I got on very well with him.'

Bond later reflected:

'I suppose my massive mistake was getting too many in too soon… quite a few of them didn't do their stuff and this lumbered Burnley with a few players that weren't up to it… I can be quite an impetuous person and signing players didn't bother me as long as I thought it would make the club better.'

Following an early League Cup defeat by lowly Crewe, a section of the Turf Moor crowd chanted angrily: 'We want our players back'. Derek Gill later admitted that 'the supporters' objections were not without foundation', particularly given 'the bewildering comings and goings.'

Rumours circulated of Bond's supposedly domineering and intimidating manner during training sessions which only exacerbated supporters' dissent. It was alleged that a rift was developing between the highly-paid newcomers and the lower-paid existing players.

In a later interview with the *Lancashire Evening Telegraph* (now the *Lancashire Telegraph*), Martin Dobson took issue with Bond's bullying manner, remarking:

'Every mistake was highlighted. Bond seemed determined to belittle individuals. He would stop play, point the finger and raise doubts as to our ability to play at this level… Young players were low because of the criticism and they didn't have the experience to be able to cope with it… An enormous gulf in the camp had taken place. Senior players and backroom staff arrived from Manchester and there seemed to be a definite ploy to blow away all the traditions and beliefs of the club in one fell swoop.'

In response to increasing supporter discord and declining home gates, the club arranged for fans to meet Bond in a Q&A session. At this meeting, Bond boomed:

'I haven't come here to destroy Burnley Football Club or to be a failure as manager. I have never been sacked as a manager and all I want is a chance. But I have felt less wanted at this club than any other and that disappoints me.'

In his article 'What Went Wrong', written for Paul Fletcher's book 'Burnley FC and Me', Bond ruminated whether the antipathy he experienced was due to his outsider status as a 'southerner.' He said:

'All the previous Burnley managers were northerners, and had learned the way this successful town club survived among the big name, city clubs. Then suddenly this southerner arrives to manage, obviously wanting his own way and using management techniques both tried and tested in the upper division.'

Bond added in a later interview with Phil Whalley:

'I think that the impression I used to give of myself as a person didn't help. I can be brash and I can be flamboyant, but I can be hurt quite easily as well... I'm an entirely different person from the one that used to be depicted in the press.'

Some Burnley supporters still dismiss Bond as a 'big time Charlie' citing his attire as well as his manner. While Derek Gill considered it 'pathetic' that Bond should be criticised for dressing smartly, Dobson's ironic remark about Bond's choice of car seemed to reflect local unease about anyone flaunting their privileged status. Dobson said:

'The first day of pre-season training made an impression, not on the training ground but in the car park. An E Type Jaguar looked a little out of place amongst the Novas and Escorts.'

Bond told Phil Whalley:

'Dobson didn't like the fact that I didn't see him as an automatic choice... All the others have been getting some stick, and he shouldn't just because he's Martin Dobson?... he was an outstanding player and... especially the younger players looked up to him ... but I didn't like the way he played it at Burnley sometimes... I did what any other manager would do; I left him out...'

Despite that, Dobson played regularly under Bond before moving to Bury as player-manager in March 1984.

Midfielder Derek Scott later spoke of his concern about Bond's manner with Dobson. Scott said:

'Dobbo was upset by the treatment of the younger players, all of whom he had taken under his wing and John Bond did not seem to like this. There were some good young players at the time, Brian Laws, Kevin Young, Lee Dixon, they were ordered around like they were in a boot camp... Dobbo defended the kids, he took almost a parental role.'

However, Scott complimented Bond's tactical acumen and coaching skills. Scott said,

> 'Training sessions were excellent and I did learn a lot. Bond was innovative and had many good ideas about how the game should be played. John Bond was very good on the coaching side, but not on the managerial side of things. Being a manager is all about relationships, handling people and he wasn't good at that. His assistant, John Benson, who I have a lot of respect for, was the calm one and definitely the calming influence after one of Bond's outbursts…'

Scott was saddened at the fragmentation of a close-knit team group, although he conceded that divisions between better and lesser paid players were not unusual in professional football. However, he pointed out that Bond's team remained united while on the pitch.

No doubt that unity was fortified by a series of fine home performances during the autumn months. Bournemouth were humbled 5-1, helped by Billy Hamilton's hat-trick of headers. Promotion rivals, Sheffield United were beaten narrowly, too, 2-1 in an absorbing end-to-end tussle. Wigan were overcome 3-0 in an equally entertaining display. In fact, eight out of the nine home games played prior to Christmas were won, keeping Burnley in sight of promotion. But John Bond was far from satisfied with the away form, which featured five draws and four losses.

It was therefore a doleful John Bond who reflected:

> 'Amongst the gloom, every now and then I could see what this team was capable of. We kicked off against Port Vale at 3pm and at 3.30 we were 6-0 up. Brian Flynn was playing as well as at any time in his career. And I knew if only I could combine a few good results with a slice of luck the team would believe … and the directors would believe in me.'

The game, eventually won 7-0, featured a hat-trick by Kevin Reeves.

But a startling 4-1 victory at Wimbledon's Plough Lane restored that elusive belief, arriving on Bond's 51st birthday. Long-standing Burnley supporter, Danny West confirmed:

> 'Two excellent headers by Derek Scott were the highlights, but it was a team performance which suggested that Burnley were getting it right at last. Derek Scott even managed to miss a penalty which would have given him his first senior

hat-trick. Mr Bond was proud of his team's performance
– we all were.'

Bond purred in the Boxing Day match programme:

> 'What a performance at Wimbledon! We beat the division's
> leading scorers at their own game… Now we have our first
> away win I am sure more will quickly follow.'

To cap it all he and assistant John Benson were awarded two-year
contracts. Bond confirmed:

> 'I am really happy here. I love it. It would take something
> really exceptional to remove us from this football club now.'

Sadly, something exceptional did occur. A few weeks later, Kevin
Reeves suffered a career-ending injury. When Phil Whalley asked
what impact Reeves' retirement had upon the team, Bond replied:

> 'Oh a massive loss. He and Billy Hamilton were a tremend-
> ous partnership. Reeves was an international player… as
> good a target man as you could wish to have, and then we
> had Billy Hamilton, who's as honest as the day is long…
> then Reevesy suddenly got this thing, they thought it was
> a tumour at first, but it turns out he's got an arthritic hip
> and that was him out of the game, it was terribly sad, it
> took some stuffing out of the club. If we could have kept
> Kevin and Billy together, we might have been in business.
> Reeves made it tick. That's why a few years previously he
> was a million-pound player.'

As proof of Bond's assessment, before Reeves' injury, Hamilton had
scored fourteen league goals, many coming from near post flicked
headers by Reeves. In the 23 league games that followed, he scored
just four.

Nevertheless, Bond's scout, John Doherty, an ex-'Busby Babe', did
well to find a promising strike partner in Wayne Biggins, who had been
playing non-League football with Matlock Town. His transfer fee was
minimal and his wages low. Biggins did his best to compensate for the
loss of Reeves, scoring eight times in 20 games, including a hat-trick
against the League club which had carelessly discarded him, Lincoln
City. Biggins would ultimately score 30 league goals for Burnley in 78
appearances, but did not have the firepower of Reeves to keep Burnley
on the promotion path.

Burnley's diminishing hope of promotion died following an abject defeat at Newport on 7 April. Eight of the last 10 games were lost with a disillusioned Bond absent from most of these. He claimed that he needed to recruit new players for the following campaign, pointing out: 'Our main problem is in midfield. I have never got it right all season and until I can, we cannot operate properly.' Season ticket sales slumped.

The final game was a rearranged home fixture with Hull. The original game had been postponed, controversially, after Hull had failed to make it through the M62 snow. At the time of the original fixture, the game promised to be a tough promotion tussle but by May it was no contest. Hull needed a 3-0 win to overtake Sheffield United and claim the final promotion slot. Burnley were commended, at least by the many Blades within the crowd, for narrowly thwarting them. By this time, Turf Moor gates had dwindled to little more than 3,000. Thanks largely to outside promotion interest, 8,000 turned up. But all Burnley fans were left with was a marker of how far their club had fallen. For just over a year before, Burnley had beaten Liverpool, one of the world's leading sides, 1-0 watched by a rowdy 22,200 crowd.

As for Burnley's once estimable youth programme, this had become a pale shadow of its former self. The home-grown youngsters that had largely made up the Third Division Championship side of 1981/82 represented the club's last rich harvest of youthful talent. The class of '82 should have provided the bedrock for Burnley's immediate future. Instead, it was fragmented, discarded and dispersed with careless disregard, replaced by players who were largely well past their best. One associated local schoolboy who eluded the attention of the Burnley youth coaches during this period was Padiham-born and Clarets-mad teenager, Andy Payton. He would later become one of the most lethal strikers in the land – at Hull, Middlesbrough, Celtic, Barnsley, Huddersfield and finally at Burnley. According to Payton, youth coach, Arthur Bellamy, released him immediately after John Bond had watched him scoring a hat-trick in a youth game.

Ashley Hoskin, a trainee professional at Burnley during this time told interviewer, Phil Whalley:

> 'A lot of the players used to come from the North East – good players, you know, Trevor Steven, Brian Laws, Kevin Young – and it all just stopped… You can't produce a lot of lads coming through just from an area like the North West – it just doesn't happen. The success they had was with

Geordies, Scottish lads, Northern Irish lads – when they're coming from a bigger net like that you're going to get two, three, four, five lads coming through. Which was what happened with Trevor Steven, Brian Laws, Kevin Young and people like that. But if you're just concentrating on the North West, you're not going to do it... They used to have only three or four apprentices, but as soon as the YTS came in, they went, "Let's have 10, 15. We're not paying for it. If one comes through out of that 15, even better." And I thought that was wrong, instead of having four who were going to be good players. So, there were about 15 or 16 of us, and out of them – all right, I was one of the lucky ones, I'll admit, I played nearly 100 games for them – but some of them lads were never going to make it, it was obvious they weren't good enough. I felt that because of this YTS thing – I mean, you weren't an apprentice, you were a YTS – they just got anyone in, you know...'

So, the club's focus turned to recruiting proven first team performers, which was costlier.

With the club's financial situation worsening, the TSB demanded a reduction in its escalating debt. This meant a sale of the club's prized assets. In August 1984, Billy Hamilton was sold to Robert Maxwell's Oxford United for a derisory fee of £80,000 with ex-Bolton striker, Neil Whatmore offered as an inadequate makeweight. Hamilton had starred in Northern Ireland's plucky performances during the 1982 World Cup finals in Spain. He was worth a lot more than that. Derek Gill believed that had the fee been decided by tribunal, Burnley would have received twice as much. But according to Gill, the TSB would not wait for the more protracted tribunal process to be completed. The TSB had also ended its shirt sponsorship although Multipart subsequently took this on.

Despite the tensions aroused by Bond's appointment, according to Derek Gill, Burnley's financial situation at the start of the 1983/84 season was sound. He wrote in his diary: 'The money coming into the club was considerable, in direct contrast to the final Bob Lord years of near destitution and impending insolvency.'

The Burnley Building Society provided a generous £100,000 in stand sponsorship. The club also took 30 per cent of the £100,000 proceeds from the sale of land, originally belonging to Bob Lord. The land was wanted for the construction of a stretch of the new M65 motorway. The TSB offered extremely favourable banking terms, too, including a £300,000 overdraft. To cap it all, in the summer of 1983, Everton paid over £300,000 for starring, young mid-fielder, Trevor Steven.

Burnley chairman, John Jackson qualified Derek Gill's optimistic assessment, stating: 'Although the finances had improved we were no means out of the mire, and only Trevor Steven's decision to move on made money available.' It seems surprising, then, that he should have allowed John Bond to spend almost £420,000 in transfer fees during that season, when this exceeded the proceeds from Steven's sale by at least £70,000. But it was the inflated wage bill which compounded that deficit substantially. Derek Gill commented: 'We were so committed financially. We'd increased the wages bill enormously; everybody Bond brought in was on top money which was £300 per week. So, we were letting go the likes of Lee Dixon on £140 a week and bringing in Gerry Gow on £300 per week.'

Certainly, the wages Third Division Burnley paid then seem disproportionately high when compared, for example, with those paid by Wimbledon as a First Division side. Wimbledon defender, Mark Morris, stated that he and his team mates were paid 'peanuts, at around £180 per week in 1986'.

On top of the wages issue was that of bonuses. Derek Gill wrote in his diary:

> 'And there was this crazy bonus system we inherited from the First Division days which was very expensive. The £300 maximum wage dated into the heady First Division days and then only for the elite few. The £200 victory bonuses came from the same era. A lot of them had cars, so with salaries plus cars you'd put £100,000 on player costs without them kicking a ball.'

Derek Gill had discovered that 'a home win in a run-of-the-mill mid-table or end of season fixture had the effect of activating the bonus payments which exceeded the net gate receipts'. To his great credit, Gill successfully negotiated a reduction in the bonus scheme to a level more in line with the club's relatively modest status 'without the loss of a single player and with no discernible discontent', allegedly saving Burnley FC 'many thousands of pounds.' Despite Gill's sterling efforts at cost reduction, it seemed as if the mortal damage had been done.

Given the club's high outlay on wages and bonuses in 1983/84, an average home gate of 13,600 was required just to break even. However, the average Turf Moor attendance was less than half that figure. In a situation requiring more checks and balances, there were too many cheques and insufficient balance.

Bond appeared to accept this when asked by Phil Whalley, replying:

'I spent money on what I thought were the right things to enable the club to get back on the right track. If the club cannot afford what you want that's where you need a good strong chairman. Look what's happened at Leeds United. That wasn't down to David O'Leary; it was up to the chairman to tell him that he couldn't have any more players.'

Bond added:

'The club at that time was in the middle of transition. The great Bob Lord era was over and a new, young chairman, John Jackson, headed the board. His inexperience as chairman, a relatively new board of directors, and my determination to have my own way, was a formula for disaster.'

Derek Gill speculated in his diary that had Bond come to Burnley straight from Norwich 'where his record speaks for itself, the outcome might have been different but only if the parameters within which Bond was expected to work had been made much clearer'. Bond seemed to agree with that view, referring to Sir Arthur South, his chairman at Norwich as a 'darling of a fellow'. 'He'd give me an almighty bollocking if he thought I'd done wrong but that didn't stop him putting a hand on my shoulder and saying well done if he thought I'd done something well… If I hadn't had a father of my own I would have wanted him as a father – that's how much I thought about him.'

Derek Gill appeared correct in his estimate that Bond was not as self-confident as he professed, appearing to welcome such patriarchal guidance. Certainly, the lack of unity at board level had not helped, with Bond playing off the chairman and the club's managing director against one another. At least that seemed to be Derek Gill's view.

With the club's debt climbing to £600,000, boardroom tensions rose. According to author Andrew Proctor, the club's accounts for the year ending on 31 May 1984, showed a net loss of £112,515, partially disguised by the £114,500 compensation payment received for Kevin Reeves's injury. Not that this was immediately available to reduce the overall debt. Until Gill persuaded them otherwise, the TSB directed that the payment should be set aside for team strengthening. The large annual loss also reflected a £200,000 drop in match income. Nevertheless, chairman, John Jackson remained convinced that the decision to appoint an outsider was correct, stating:

'The greatest part of the disaster was due to a lack of judgement in its implementation rather than any inherent fault in the policy.'

His managing director, Derek Gill, added:

'While John Bond's management had been an unmitigated disaster for the club and the man himself, it is totally wrong to place all the responsibility for it upon John Bond alone. This is both cowardly and dishonest and regrettably the exaggerated fiction has increased over the years... It was not the money spent on transfers that undermined the club, rather it was the simple fact that we sold and bought the wrong players and that the result of our excursion into the transfer market was to weaken the team.

'Concurrently, the departure of so many crowd favourites [notably Steven, Laws, Dobson, and Hamilton] led to discontent among the supporters who begun to vote with their feet in ever increasing numbers and the income base, necessary to sustain the business was fatally eroded and we got ourselves into a downward spiral which could not be arrested without an introduction of new funds or drastic retrenchment in their absence...'

By the time Hamilton departed in August 1984, Bond had been sacked for a contentious statement, allegedly made by him, in an article printed in a 'red top' newspaper. Bond was reported to have said:

'All I want to do is manage the club in my own way... I am prepared as ever to make Burnley a First Division club again but I am afraid that this is an impossibility for any manager when there is friction between himself and the chairman... it has to be sorted out one way or another.'

Derek Gill remarked:

'A couple of weeks before the new season was due to start, the chairman seized upon a newspaper article written under the name of John Bond which was extravagant to say the least and contained some inflammatory observations. John Jackson was livid and if he had been looking for a reason to sack the manager he believed he had one now... The chairman demanded an explanation from the manager about the offending article and the dismal performance of many of the players he had introduced to the club... [Bond] never put forward excuses, some of which were available to him had he chosen to use them. I am fairly sure he knew that words alone were not going to save him and after... deliberations by the directors he was told he had effectively terminated his own employment. He left the boardroom with dignity...'

But not with good grace, it seemed, for according to club historian, Ray Simpson, in his book, '*The Clarets Chronicles*', Bond declared his intention to sue the club for wrongful dismissal. While this came to nothing, Bond punished Burnley by denying them a late reprieve from relegation to Division Four at the end of the 1984/85 season. The solitary point, that Swansea, took from their final game in May 1985, meant that it was Bond's new side, not his former club, which stayed up.

As for John Jackson's view of Bond he said:

'As the season progressed, the relationship between John Bond and myself deteriorated, if that was possible. Publicly I had to support him and no doubt that is the reason why to this day many people think he was "my man". By the end of the season it was apparent to everyone that the JB appointment had been a mistake and we parted company... My personal view of JB as an individual outside the club was quite different.

Outside the club I enjoyed his company, he was charismatic, loyal to his friends and great fun to be with. My family enjoyed his company on numerous occasions. Another example of problems that arise when business and pleasure is mixed.'

With Bond having departed just days before the start of the 1984/85 season, Burnley had no alternative other than to appoint his assistant, John Benson, as manager. Benson believed the club's hand had been forced because of the unaffordability of his compensation package. Nevertheless, he was totally committed to the task. He was both liked and respected by his players.

In order to replace the half dozen who had left – Billy Hamilton, Willie Donachie, Kevin Young, Dennis Tueart, Steve Daley and Gerry Gow – in came ex-Leeds and Stoke full back, Peter Hampton; former Leicester and Gillingham winger, Neil Grewcock, who had been playing for Southern League, Shepshed Charterhouse; fleet-footed, Hull striker, Alan Taylor, an FA Cup winner with West Ham in 1975; Barry Powell, an experienced central midfielder, formerly with Wolves, Coventry and Derby; and attacking wide midfielder or full back, Kevin Hird, who had moved from Blackburn, his parent club, to Leeds in 1979 for a then hefty fee of £357,000.

With ex-Bolton striker Neil Whatmore bolstering the Burnley attack and experienced professionals, Hansbury, Overson, Phelan, Flynn, Scott, Hutchison and Biggins, still present, Benson should have had sufficient resources to ensure that Burnley retained its Division Three status. Burnley supporters seemed less optimistic, though, as only 4,664 attended the opening day home game with Plymouth. Grewcock excelled, but the Clarets were indebted to Taylor's late goal in salvaging a point. Subsequent results were not encouraging. A Mark Hughes hat-trick at Old Trafford inflicted a humiliating aggregate defeat in the League Cup but more depressingly, in mid-October, Burnley were routed 5-1 at Reading, having led at the interval. This cataclysmic defeat reduced the Clarets to 19th position.

Brian Flynn made his last start for the club at Elm Park. Having been dropped to the bench for the next home game, he submitted a transfer request, moving to Cardiff in November for £15,000. Derek Gill was saddened by his loss, commenting:

> 'I want to acknowledge the super integrity of the player who took a reduction in wages to come to Burnley and was simply "full of it" and bursting to go as soon as the transaction was completed. It was all done in one meeting and there was no question of agents and percentage merchants and associated hangers-on, just simple straight dealing with him… You can go to war with men like Brian Flynn and I am glad to have known him.'

There was a brief upturn in form in late October, but after winning 3-2 at Cambridge on 10 November, Burnley lost six out of the next seven league games with York trouncing them 4-0. Former Claret midfield star Jimmy McIlroy wrote in a headlining *Burnley Express* article:

'To believe that things can only get better is to believe in miracles. I have to concede that nothing short of a miracle can stop the rot and the unthinkable – Fourth Division football at Turf Moor next season.'

Burnley had never stooped so low.

Following a 1-2 home defeat by Wigan on New Year's Day, Burnley were floundering, one place above the relegation zone. London Claret, Michael Bullen concluded:

'The man-to-man marking seems to result in [full backs] Scott and Hampton being drawn all over the place… Phelan is used as a sweeper, having the freedom to push forward whenever he can. [Because the defence is suspect] Kevin Hird often appears in a very deep position. Powell and Hutchison also started the season in midfield until the disappointing Powell was replaced by Brian Miller's son, David, who improved the team.

'Up front Grewcock has been a major influence. When he gets the ball, he goes straight at defenders and often beats them to get into good positions. Unfortunately, his crosses and shots could be better, but now there is no one really to cross to. If only Billy Hamilton had stayed. Wayne Biggins and, at times, Alan Taylor try hard but they do not have the aerial power to cause big defenders problems. Taylor's ball control has let him down too often and the midfield players do not seem to have any understanding with him when they pass. The forwards don't look as if they can do the business.'

Sturdy centre forward, Les Lawrence, was signed from Torquay for a £20,000 fee in November 1984, but Burnley's first black senior player failed to demonstrate the striking threat he had shown at Plainmoor, where he had scored 46 goals in 170 league games.

Neil Whatmore proved no better, scoring once only in nine league games before being moved to Mansfield in March 1985. Apart from two extraordinary thrashings of non-League Penrith (9-0) in the FA Cup and Rotherham in the league (7-0), helped by a hat-trick by Kevin Hird, goals and points remained at a premium.

Desperate to lift his spluttering side, John Benson arranged a 'pay-your-own-way', five-day team break in Majorca at the end of February. It seemed to do the trick. Immediately before departing, fellow strugglers, Preston, were beaten 2-0 at Turf Moor in front of a sparse crowd of 4,768, while another languishing local rival, Bolton, were overcome 3-1 at Burnden Park upon the Clarets' return.

It was a false dawn. Burnley then lost six and drew four of their next ten games including an abysmal 0-2 loss at Wigan on Easter Monday. Although Swansea, then in free-fall, were defeated by an Alan Taylor goal at the Vetch Field on 4 May, Swansea survived, whereas Burnley did not. Their heroic 3-2 victory at Walsall on the final day of the 1984/85 season was in vain.

Once Burnley's relegation was confirmed, John Benson resigned. Derek Gill said of him:

> 'He considered being manager of Burnley to be a great honour and he gave it his very best shot from the first day... Of all the managers with whom I had experience, he spent by far the most time with the reserve players. In between playing with the reserves, and his midweek first team duties, he rarely missed an opportunity to get about and look for free transfers and bargains and I would defy anybody to work harder. A very good number two, it was his misfortune to be thrown in at the deep end of a club in paralysed turmoil.'

At an emergency board meeting, 48 hours before the Walsall game, John Jackson announced his intention to stand down as chairman but chose to retain his place on the board. Derek Gill was expected to bid for the chair but instead submitted his resignation. The in-fighting had proved too much for Gill. He lamented the premature death of former commercial director, Alan Hutchinson, for Gill believed that with Hutchinson's support and wise counsel, the subsequent boardroom discord might have been avoided.

Gill had hoped that the addition of two new directors, Frank Teasdale and former Lancashire cricketer, Jack Simmons, would enable him to successfully challenge Jackson's position as chairman. However, this hope was misplaced. With the board remaining divided, he felt he could no longer hold onerous club responsibilities without having the necessary authority to enact these effectively. Gill was deeply dismayed that his attempt at negotiating a cancellation of Joe Gallagher's contract was thwarted by a fellow director.

According to Gill, not only had this action denied the club significant savings, it left Gill feeling humiliated at an ensuing Football League tribunal where Gallagher's contractual rights were upheld, despite the centre back's unfitness to play any more than a handful of games for Burnley.

Derek Gill wrote in his diary,

> 'I was effectively at odds with the whole board none of whom I regard as fools… But without the power to act as I saw fit, I saw no point in continuing with my enormous personal frustration.'

Nevertheless, he told Burnley author Dave Thomas:

> 'I left the boardroom for the last time with words of real regret… it then dawned on me that without my assistance they could not process the wages… I allowed my business to continue to do this until they got this together.'

Derek Gill attended Burnley's final 'win or bust' game at Fellows Park, Walsall. On a day of high drama, he recorded this surreal ending to the match:

> 'The usual after-match procedure is for directors and guests to gather around the TV for the results service. We were, of course, very eager to get the results of others involved in the relegation struggle… This often involves emotions swinging wildly with each result. There is usually one anorak who can immediately tell you the effect on the league positions… Not at friendly Walsall club who were already safely placed in mid-table! Instead their worthies sat laughing their sides out at a Tom and Jerry cartoon, keeping the results in abeyance for the next 15 minutes. With all the turmoil we were enduring, who is to say Walsall did not have the right idea?'

It was hardly a day for mirth, for 120 miles away at Valley Parade, the celebrations of Third Division champions, Bradford City, were cut short by a raging fire which engulfed their main stand, causing the death of 56 supporters and injuring at least 265 others. Burnley's woes paled into insignificance at this traumatic event.

Following Jackson's resignation as club chairman, and Gill's departure from the board, Frank Teasdale, managing director at Galbraith Holdings plc of Accrington, became Burnley's new chairman. Having sold most of his shares to Teasdale, Jackson retained just enough to maintain his position on the board. Frank Teasdale had been a Burnley director since January 1985, when he joined the board together with former Lancashire county cricketer, 'Flat' Jack Simmons, thereby raising the board number to six.

Teasdale took the opportunity to explain his position, objectives and hopes in a Q & A section in the 'Claret & Blue' match programme of 23 August 1985. He wrote: 'Basically my job is to co-ordinate and ensure that the board's policies are carried out. My job is to liaise between all sections of the club and obviously, the objective is success.' Here, he saw himself as more of a facilitator than a directive leader.

He added in a later club interview:

'I have always been a fan. I was born in Burnley and first went to Turf Moor at the age of 10. I wanted to go to the 1947 FA Cup final but couldn't get a ticket. I also became godfather to two of Adam Blacklaw's children. Adam was such a great keeper. He was a member of the 1960 First Division Championship-winning side. People laugh at me when I say that in the early 1950s Clarets' star, Bill Holden, was my favourite Burnley centre-forward, but I thought he was a brilliant player.

'I started as a fan on the Longside, then as I progressed in life – I began work as a storeman – I moved into the stands, then progressed to the 100 Club, and eventually to the Vice-President's Club where you start meeting the directors. It was then that I became friendly with my immediate predecessor, John Jackson. I sold a lot of vans to Bob Lord for his meat business. My employers, Galbraith Commercials, were the Leyland truck and Sherpa van distributors in Lancashire. So, I had dealings with him both football and business wise.'

Frank Teasdale stated in the 'Claret & Blue' match programme:

'Football is currently facing a massive challenge after what has happened over the last few months [Frank was referring here to the much-publicised incidents of crowd disorder as well as the Valley Parade tragedy]. I just hope that all of the problems can be overcome but I admit that there could be some difficult times ahead for the game in this country. I want to emphasise how important it is for every supporter to show good behaviour. Like other football clubs, Burnley is in the hands of its supporters. Ideally, I want a good and successful team and trouble-free terraces. We have not had all that much trouble in the past, but anyone convicted of trouble-making at Turf Moor will be banned from the ground. I agree with the Birmingham City manager, Ron Saunders, it is the time for people to stand up and be counted.'

The Thatcher Conservative government was threatening to impose greater sanctions upon English football clubs and their supporters, to curb rising football hooliganism. During the 1984/85 season, there had been a rash of serious incidents. There was a reckless charge by a contingent of Liverpool supporters at the Heysel Stadium, Brussels, immediately before the 1985 European Cup final, which resulted in a loss of 39 Italian lives. Previously, a frightening riot, led by so-called Millwall fans, at and outside Kenilworth Road, Luton, had been captured in ghastly detail on national television. And, on the very day of the Bradford disaster, a lethal charge by rampaging Leeds supporters resulted in the collapse of a wall at St Andrews stadium, Birmingham, bringing about the death of an innocent, 15-year-old boy. With English clubs then banned from all European competitions because of crowd disorder, it was unsurprising that Football League attendances continued to fall. The British game was facing an uncertain future.

Scott and Phelan refused to re-sign after relegation. Scott moved to Bolton for £20,000 while Phelan transferred to Norwich for £70,000. Tommy Hutchison left, as well, preferring to join John Bond at Swansea than accept a coaching post at Burnley. With Kevin Reeves departing, too, amid further cost cutting, Joe Gallagher took over responsibility for coaching the youth team.

Derek Gill said of Hutchison:

> 'He always amazed me by his fitness and leadership qualities and went on to become one of the oldest playing professionals, never losing his appetite for football. Eventually, he won over the grumpy Burnley crowd but was unable to erase the Bond association. For Hutchison, the criticism was as unfair as it was uneducated and if I was right on Laws, I was just as wrong on this outstanding man.'

1987 Burnley hero, Neil Grewcock, remarked, after Hutchison's departure, how much the veteran winger had helped him improve his game.

Frank Teasdale received sixty-two applications for the Burnley manager post. The ex-Manchester United, Oldham, Aberdeen and Scotland defender, Martin Buchan, was ultimately chosen, accompanied by experienced, former Manchester United assistant manager, Tommy Cavanagh. In speaking of Buchan's appointment, Frank Teasdale stated:

> 'I am optimistic for the future and I firmly believe the decision to appoint Martin Buchan as our manager was a very good one by the board of directors. The desire to do well is definitely there. Hard work by everyone can lead to success.'

With goalkeeper, Roger Hansbury, transferring to Cambridge, Buchan brought in a replacement keeper, Joe Neenan, from Scunthorpe for £10,000. He also signed central defenders, Ray Deakin from Bolton and Larne-born, Jim Heggarty, from Brighton, both on free transfers, to fill the gap created by Phelan's move.

Frank Teasdale's hopes of a revival were lifted by his team's excellent pre-season form. Rochdale (7-0) and Bolton (4-0) were put to the sword in the Lancashire Manx Cup with Biggins scoring a hat-trick in each game. Biggins also added a brace as the Clarets galloped into a three-goal interval lead in their opening home game with Northampton. However, the visitors fought back strongly in the second half and were unfortunate not to have snatched a draw.

Thereafter, results were erratic. Bury eliminated the Clarets in an exciting League Cup tie, winning 6-5 on aggregate, while the momentum gained from league victories over Aldershot (2-0), Hartlepool (2-0) and Rochdale (1-0) was interrupted by home defeats against Stockport (0-1), Port Vale (1-2) and Colchester (0-2) and hapless losses at Preston (0-1) and Chester (0-4).

After the Colchester game, London Claret, Stuart Pilling, wrote:

> 'The crowd roar as play ebbs and flows, hardly a minute goes by without either side producing something for their fans, be it a delightful chip, timely tackle or dynamic dribble. Goalmouth incidents punctuate these silky professional skills and passionate, exciting football ensues. Unfortunately, I can't write about these things because I was at Turf Moor watching Burnley defeated by table-topping Colchester.'

The crushing defeat at Chester caused *Burnley Express* reporter, Granville Shackleton, to write:

'I have never seen a Burnley side play as badly as this one did at Sealand Road, and neither have I seen Burnley fans as angry with a performance. Burnley were incredibly devoid of ideas, basic skills and lacked concern for their task.'

Only keeper, Peacock, on loan from Doncaster, and Taylor came out of the game with any credit.

Then came the startling news of Martin Buchan's resignation. He been in post for just 110 days. The Chester debacle, which Buchan described as 'suicidal' was his final game in charge. Buchan explained: 'There are certain aspects of the job that I honestly just could not handle.' It was rumoured that Buchan became embroiled in angry confrontation with a Burnley player, after criticising his team's lack of discipline. Buchan continued:

'I could not make the transition from the dressing room to management... the decision is entirely my own. I am heartbroken for the chairman, Frank Teasdale. He has worked unbelievably hard for the club and he tried to persuade me to stay but my mind was made up.'

A shocked Frank Teasdale responded:

'Martin Buchan, in my opinion, is a victim of the soccer rat race and his own integrity. He felt he could not do the job he required of himself. It is a bombshell but we will have to live through it and it is another mountain we have to climb.'

Tommy Cavanagh, formerly Tommy Docherty's assistant at Old Trafford, picked up the reins, claiming: 'This club has got to get down to some straight talking. It needs stability and credibility.' Wayne Biggins was on his way too. After another dispiriting home defeat, this time to champions-elect, Swindon, he joined Michael Phelan at Carrow Road in a £40,000 deal.

With Les Lawrence injured and Peter Devine struggling to match Biggins' striking prowess, Cavanagh was permitted to bring back centre-forward Derrick Parker from Oldham for a £10,000 fee. Parker had netted 85 league goals while playing for Southend, Barnsley and Oldham, but found goal scoring much more difficult on his return to Turf Moor, where he had developed through the youth system.

It was then that Ashley Hoskin, aged 17, signed his first professional contract with Burnley. Manager Tommy Cavanagh told him 'You're on £200 a week basic, and £50 appearance money in the first team.'

Ashley was gobsmacked to receive so much, doubting whether the club could afford this, and feeling a bit guilty about the size of the payment.

Ashley told London Claret, Phil Whalley:

> 'I had been on £32 a week as an apprentice with a tenner appearance money. It was in the contract that if you got into the first team you got an extra £10. There were bonuses as well. It wasn't very much at that time and we had to be in the top six before you got anything.'

Having slipped to 18th position, following a 3-1 home defeat by Southend on 2 November, Burnley produced a better run of form after beating promotion-bound Mansfield 2-1 at Turf Moor. Five more victories were gained in the next eight games. In fact, a late goal from the returning Les Lawrence, gave Burnley a 3-2 win over Hereford, and renewed hope of promotion.

But only one victory was achieved in the next nine games, putting paid to that dream. Meanwhile, the club's already perilous financial situation was worsening. The figures disclosed in the accounts for the year ending June 1985, were ghastly – there was a loss of over £250,000, bank debts totalled £410,000 and a further £240,000 was owed to various creditors.

In mid-February 1986, Jackson resigned from the board having endured unrelenting abuse from a contingent of Burnley supporters, notably from those who had set up a 'Save Our Club' group. If this turn of events gave the disgruntled Burnley fans any cheer, then Frank Teasdale quickly dampened their enthusiasm by calling an extraordinary meeting, announcing that only a new shares issue – lifting the share capital from £8,000 to £50,000 – could avert the club's liquidation.

After a harsh winter came a gloomy spring. A home defeat by Crewe on 15 April was attended by only 1,988 fans. It was Burnley's lowest post-war gate. The new share issue had to be extended, too, after a highly disappointing response. With the directors warning that the club had only a few days left to 'fold or survive', a positive approach by a group of Burnley businessmen forced a further extension. Nevertheless, the number of match day programmes printed for the final home game with Scunthorpe was increased as these threatened to become collectors' items.

The growing threat of administration or receivership prompted Derek Gill to reappear with a rescue package, devised with the help of local businessmen.

Derek Gill told Dave Thomas:

> 'There was never any possibility of Burnley Football Club going out of existence. The nightmare scenario was for the board to bring in an administrator or a receiver whose first duty would have been to find a buyer. Let there be no semblance of doubt that a buyer was ready, willing and able to fulfil all the essential needs of a rescue. My home telephone was red hot with calls from interested parties and others eager to know what was going on and I was flattered to be contacted by more than one capable investor stating that if I return to the club they would be interested in providing finance and support.'

Derek Gill then wrote to the Burnley board setting out his conditions for implementing his rescue package. He demanded that he was elected as chairman with Teasdale becoming vice-chairman. He wanted full responsibility for the club's financial affairs. He professed, however, that he had no wish to replicate Bob Lord's autocratic style, leaving other members of the board with an option of removing him when and if they considered this to be necessary. He said, too, that he had no interest in becoming the majority share-holder. Burnley author, Andrew Proctor, wrote that Gill stipulated that Martin Dobson should be appointed as player-manager. Dobson and his assistant Casper had guided Bury to promotion to Division Three in 1985 and narrowly missed a further promotion despite having a much smaller budget than Burnley had in 1983.

If Derek Gill was confident of his success, he was mistaken. Three days later, Frank Teasdale rang him to say that the club's future had been secured by alternative means. It was a close-run thing. They were within 24 hours of calling in the receiver, when Frank Teasdale's wheeling and dealing paid dividends. Three new directors joined the board: Bernard Rothwell, Bob Blakeborough and Clive Holt. Crucially, the club's bankers, TSB, were persuaded to guarantee the club's existence for another season. The club had been saved by the skin of its teeth.

Clive Holt is now the only Burnley director remaining from these dark days. Before becoming a director at Turf Moor, in the summer of 1986, he had successfully run his own mechanical engineering company. Although a southerner by birth, he moved into the area in 1975. He described his developing interest in football thus:

'When I was young and living in Kent, I watched Gravesend and Northfleet in the Southern League. They later became Ebbsfleet United. And when I was working in Hampshire my nearest club was Aldershot which wasn't ideal. So, when a job came up in Burnley, which then had a First Division team, I couldn't resist.'

He quickly became a Turf Moor regular. Like other current board members, Clive remains a passionate fan of the club he now helps direct.

'But having arrived here, I was very surprised that Burnley was so small. It's hardly Manchester or Leeds, is it? People who live here don't realise, but because of the profile of the football club, people who live in other parts of the country think that the town of Burnley is huge... After years of cheering, jeering and, if I'm honest, criticising everything from Burnley's gameplay to the consistency of its Bovril, I was issued with an ultimatum: either put up or shut up. I chose the former but talk about being thrown in at the deep end...

'When I joined the board, I knew the club was struggling with substantial debts incurred during the John Bond era. It came as a great shock, though, when, at my first board meeting, fellow director, Basil Dearing – a well-respected local solicitor – advised us that the club was trading illegally, and that the only solution was to seek Administration. There was no way I was prepared to agree with this. I had just invested a considerable sum of money in the club. I told Basil: "On your bike, mate! I'm not doing this", knowing that I would lose everything I had invested if we went down that road. Along with other new directors, Bob Blakeborough and the late Bernard Rothwell, we decided that a better way forward was to re-value Turf Moor. This enabled us to bring in further loans on the back of the improved collateral. It averted the immediate cash crisis.

'Each of the directors were assigned a lead responsibility for one of the club's functions. I had catering – I'm not sure why since I had no relevant experience. Someone had responsibility for the commercial functions and another had responsibility for the ground. We had to be very 'hands on' with these assignments. Ignorance was not an excuse. Today, it is so different with specialist club officials taking care of much of this.

'The late Frank Teasdale was chairman. His greatest strength was in keeping the creditors happy. Although tough, single-minded and sometimes stubborn, he was good in getting on the right side of those we needed to influence. He pulled off a major coup by persuading the club sponsors, Leyland to pay their three-year sponsorship up front. That just about kept us going, stopping the utility companies from turning off the water, the power, the heating and the lighting.

'In those days clubs did not rely as much upon "securitisation" as they do today. It is now common practice to balance expenditure against estimated season ticket revenue, for example. Frank was very good at seizing upon such opportunities.'

As a price of their continued assistance, the TSB demanded that the club apply stringent economy measures. The reserve team was disbanded and two of Burnley's better players, Kevin Hird and Alan Taylor were released. Hird went to Colne Dynamos of the North-Western Counties League, with the guarantee of a job outside the game, whereas Taylor joined the large contingent of ex-Clarets at Bury. Cavanagh said: 'We simply could not afford their contracts.' Meanwhile injury-prone striker, Les Lawrence left for Peterborough on a free transfer.

As for centre back, Vince Overson, Burnley's remaining prize asset, he was sold to Birmingham City, John Bond's latest club, for a fee of £25,000. The combined receipts from the sales of Phelan, Biggins and Overson amounted to £135,000, a poor yield compared with the £1m aggregate derived from their following moves. Phelan would join Manchester United in 1989 for £750,000, while Biggins and Overson would command respective fees of £200,000 and £55,000 in their subsequent transfers. Meanwhile, Burnley's average home gate continued to plummet: from around 6,600 in 1983/84, and 4,220 in 1984/85 to 3,203 in 1985/86.

Cavanagh then resigned 'for medical reasons' after being admitted to hospital for a hip operation. He had hardly endeared himself to the sagging Burnley support by habitually sporting a Manchester United track suit but as Neil Grewcock made clear in a later interview, Cavanagh was adept in getting the best out of average players.

Cavanagh was quickly replaced by 'faithful retainer', Brian Miller who was then running a newsagent shop. Martin Dobson had scotched rumours of a return to Turf Moor by signing a further three-year contract as Bury's manager.

Miller chose Arthur Bellamy, a trusted former team mate, as his assistant. Bellamy recalled:

'My former playing mate, Brian Miller, had got me into coaching in the late 1970s when Harry Potts was still in charge. After I retired from playing for Chesterfield, in 1978, I had no desire to stay inside the game, taking on what became a successful milk round in Burnley before turning to a 'chip shop' business. Although I turned him down at first, Brian eventually persuaded me to combine my nightly frying with some daytime coaching of the 'B' team. After Harry was sacked in the autumn of 1979, Brian took the manager's job with Frank Casper succeeding Brian as assistant, and Ray Pointer becoming the reserves coach. I then replaced Ray as youth team coach.

'So, I packed in the "chippy". But it wasn't long before a "bomb went off" with John Bond's and Benson's arrival. They had their own kids' coaching team led by John Sainty, leaving me on the side-lines. And when Tommy Hutchison was asked to help with the coaching, I could see the writing on the wall. Although Benson offered me an alternative job as groundsman at Gawthorpe, the club's training ground, I rejected it at first, but the post came with a house on site. After I discussed this prospect with my wife, I had a change of heart.

'There was so much turmoil in those years. Bond went suddenly, followed a year later by Benson. Buchan then came but quickly went. Cavanagh did likewise. It was incredible. There was no stability whatsoever. Finally, Brian was brought back to steady the ship, having been sacked as Burnley's manager only three years before. Brian summoned me to his office, telling me he wanted me to become his assistant manager. I dare say that a groundsman has never been asked that before. But we knew and trusted one another so I thought I'd give it a go. Brian was told he could sign three or four new players on free transfers. In came Leighton James from Newport, then aged 33 years, for his third spell with the club. James had spent the previous season as player-coach at Somerton Park, Newport. Leighton looked after the kids while Brian and I ran the show, sharing duties on the tractor to roll the pitch.

'Leighton James was joined by a former Turf Moor team mate, Billy Rodaway, who had been a centre-back in Jimmy Adamson's First Division side of the mid-seventies. Brian was also allowed to sign Blackpool's Scottish midfielder, Ian Britton, and Bolton's striker, Wayne Entwistle, both on loan. Joe Gallagher had been medically advised to retire from professional football, but following Vince Overson's departure to Birmingham, he was restored to central defence, having not played any first team football for 18 months. We were that desperate! Here, he was partnered by new club captain, Ray Deakin, who later doubled as the team coach driver. It was a case of all hands to the pump!'

Clive Holt recalls his trepidation then. He said:

'One of my biggest worries was the strength of the team. Before the season started we had arranged a friendly with Wigan who had only recently joined the Football League. The game was an utter disaster. We were thrashed four or five-nil. The side was in disarray. There were only eight full-time professionals – a bit like Blackpool's situation a year or so ago. There were no reserves, so the numbers were made up with trialists. I remember Brian Miller trying to allay our concerns at a board meeting. He assured us: "We won't win the League but we will not be in any danger of relegation!" He believed his side were capable of at least a mid-table position. But we all knew that at the end of the coming season, for the first time, the side finishing in bottom place would be automatically relegated to the Football Conference, and replaced by the Conference champions. The days when the bottom club in the Football League could apply for re-election were over. I dreaded to think that it might be Burnley who would first fall through this trap door.'

9 May 1987

Supping at the last chance saloon

'Livin' On A Prayer'

DESPITE Clive Holt's misgivings about Burnley's prospects, Ian Britton was confident that his new club would be successful. As an irrepressibly enthusiastic, bustling midfielder, he had achieved honours with each of his three previous clubs. His 10 goals and creative energy had played a major part in Chelsea's return to the top-flight in 1977. He had featured prominently in Dundee United's solitary Scottish Premier League success, and he also prompted Blackpool's rise from the Fourth Division in 1985. Despite his impressive credentials, during the summer of 1986 he realised that his days at Bloomfield Road might be numbered.

Ian explained:

> 'I was then in my early thirties. Blackpool manager, Sam Ellis made it clear that I was no longer an automatic selection. I didn't want to be on the bench. I wanted to be playing. Sam told me that Burnley were interested in me. That sounded good. I knew they were a big club. I took part in their pre-season games. I did not realise the extent of their financial difficulties then. They had some good players like

Leighton James and Billy Rodaway. Joe Gallagher had been a successful Division One centre half, too, although he was hampered by a bad knee. Burnley offered me regular first team football. That was good enough for me.

'Maybe the training at Burnley was not the best but it was very similar, in type, to what I had experienced elsewhere. There were the basic fitness drills – the running – particularly during pre-season, with five-a-side games and 'shadow play' to sharpen our ball skills. Tuesday was always the hardest day of training, wherever I played.'

'Shadow play' was introduced at Burnley during the mid-fifties by former Clarets' Sunderland and Sheffield Wednesday coach and manager, Alan Brown. It involves playing against imaginary opponents, a practice which was found to improve momentum, cohesion and positional sense.

Ian continued:

'I was made welcome from day one. Team spirit was good. We started the 1986/87 season reasonably well. We managed to beat Wolves, who had also fallen upon hard times, 1-0 at Molineux. James and little Ashley Hoskin played well in that game as did our back four. After we had beaten Halifax 3-0, at home in the following game, we were fifth, in sight of a promotion place. But then we lost at Tranmere and suffered a demoralising 4-1 defeat by Preston at Turf Moor. Although we managed to win here and there – a 3-1 victory over Lincoln would ultimately prove crucial – the losses began to stack up. By November we were fifth from bottom.'

Leighton James added in a later interview:

'It was a funny season in as much as the side had some useful players. Ian thought we had a really unlucky season. I agree. It started with the very first game at Torquay. We conceded just before the final whistle leaving us with a 1-1 draw, but we played well. Then we came home and beat Scunthorpe and things were looking very promising but for some reason we didn't perform as well as we could and started to struggle. We had some bad games, but when you look at the side we had, you'd think, well, we shouldn't have been where we were. There were a lot worse teams in that league, plus the fact that confidence was at such a low ebb so we didn't really perform as well as we could.'

The already sparse Turf Moor crowd dwindled further. Just 1,692 fans turned up for a midweek league game on the 4 November when first half goals from Neil Grewcock and Ashley Hoskin proved just enough to defeat Colchester. By this time, Burnley had no recognised striker. Parker was injured and Entwistle's loan period had ended. Rookie black 19-year-old apprentice, Bobby Regis, had to be pressed into service up front. Worse still, non-League Telford eliminated Burnley in the first round of the FA Cup, winning with disdainful ease (3-0). There was brief Christmas cheer when a creditable 2-2 draw was achieved at Wrexham on Boxing Day, helped by a goal from Parker on his return. Then two days later, in lashing rain, Crewe were thrashed 4-0 at Turf Moor, assisted by stunning strikes by James and Hoskin, and calamitous errors by a jittery visiting keeper. But languishing Rochdale arrived on New Year Day to inflict a 3-0 defeat on an unchanged side. Worse still, on the 24 January, Hereford United humiliated Miller's men at Turf Moor, brutally exposing the limitations of 18-year-old apprentice goalkeeper, Tony Woodworth. A Red Rose Radio reporter provided this obituary.

> 'Oh, what a sad story it is here at Turf Moor. Many in this crowd of 1,955 were leaving the ground fully 15 minutes from the end. In fact, most of them missed the last two goals. It was Hereford's biggest win since they entered the League in 1972, following their famous FA Cup victory over First Division Newcastle. This day, Tony Woodworth will remember for all the wrong reasons. In the fifteenth minute, he brought down Ollie Kearns in the penalty box and Jimmy Harvey opened the scoring for Hereford with the penalty. Then in the 23rd minute Woodworth failed to catch a high cross and Kearns planted the ball into the net for the visitors' second. Two-nil it was at half-time. Burnley came out in the second half looking as if they might make a game of it. But when Stuart Phillips made it 3-0 in the 56th minute the lights went out altogether and the 'boo boys' really tore into the Clarets. It got worse because in the 72nd minute Ollie Kearns literally walked his way into the Burnley penalty area and crashed in the fourth. Burnley were now torn to shreds and Stuart Phillips added to their misery when he put away the simplest of chances. Five

minutes later the same man completed Burnley's nightmare afternoon when he scored his third and Hereford's sixth. To go down narrowly at home may cause some questions to be asked but to be thrashed 6-0, well, that's beyond any questions, isn't it? And a crowd is gathered outside the offices right now and they're chanting "rubbish!" and "we want football!" Well I can't say anything which will allay Burnley's misery. The players know it. The management know it. And all I can do is to repeat that sad, final score of Burnley 0 Hereford 6.'

Remarkably, a week later at Hartlepool, Miller managed to inspire a much better performance from the same group of players, although a recovered Joe Neenan returned as goalkeeper in place of the traumatised Woodworth. The truth was that Miller had little option as he was down to 13 fit players. Encouragingly, his rejuvenated side managed to dominate their ragged opponents in the first half, taking a 2-0 lead. But on a hard, rutted surface on which the ball bounced awkwardly this proved to be an insecure lead. With Hartlepool reverting to a sweeper system which enabled their full backs to push forward more, Burnley came under increasing pressure. However, it was Deakin's disastrous 77th minute back pass which turned the game. Hogan pounced upon his mistake, rounding Neenan to score. Then in the final minute, Hartlepool's Kevin Dixon was allowed to chase down a long clearance. Despite appearing to lose control, he recovered quickly to hammer the ball past Neenan for the equaliser.

On the following Friday evening, Burnley secured another worthy point at promotion-seeking Swansea. And once again they squandered victory by allowing a late leveller, this time from Swansea's predatory striker, Steve Lovell. Ashley Hoskin, a former apprentice under John Bond, was man-of-the-match after scoring a spectacular goal, good enough to be drooled over by Jimmy Greaves and Ian St John on their Saturday lunchtime ITV show, *Saint and Greavsie*. Hoskin had run virtually the length of the pitch, beating five opponents before unleashing a blistering shot from the edge of the Swansea box that flashed into the net.

The revival was short-lived, though. Wolves arrived at Turf Moor on St. Valentine's Day and unceremoniously ravaged Burnley. Despite being 2-1 up at half-time, the Clarets were blown away in a second half of meek surrender as Wolves scored four times without reply. The rampant visitors had two further efforts ruled out for offside.

Although goals from James and Grewcock salvaged a point at Halifax's Shay stadium on 21 February, a two-nil half-time lead at home, against fellow strugglers, Tranmere, was carelessly frittered away, leaving Burnley with only a point and precariously positioned just three rungs above the bottom. Nevertheless, these two drawn games marked the beginning of a recovery as Burnley established an unbeaten run of six games.

On a raw mid-March night, 2,691 turned up at Turf Moor to watch struggling Burnley take on Northampton, the runaway league leaders. The gate was almost 900 more than for the previous dire 0-0 draw with Exeter. The game seemed to be following a familiar pattern when, in the 15th minute, Charlie Henry exploited some slipshod defending, to volley the visitors in front. But just before the break, Hoskin lashed home an unexpected equaliser after Phil Malley had helped on a short corner. And much to the home crowd's delight, Joe Gallagher, rose to a 70th minute corner and planted his header wide of Cobblers' keeper, Gleasure, to snatch three unexpected points for the Clarets.

The euphoria was quickly dispelled though when Aldershot arrived on the following Saturday, a day of inhospitable wind and faint whisperings of snow. After Aldershot took a 54th minute lead, Burnley's increasingly fretful attacks seemed to founder on the sandy wastelands of the Shots' defence. Burnley's fragile confidence fell apart. The next three games were also lost, leaving them next to bottom.

On Tuesday 14 April, relegation rivals, Torquay, made light of their coach lag, taking a two-goal lead, five minutes after half-time. Ian Britton, restored a smidgen of hope with a 63rd minute goal but with Burnley huffing and puffing ineffectually, Torquay seemed destined to clean up. Then came a 90th minute award of a penalty. The small crowd could barely bring themselves to watch. But ice-cool Leighton James had no such qualms, despatching his shot beyond the Torquay keeper to grasp a precious point. This match was to be Derrick Parker's final appearance for Burnley.

Ian Britton commented:

> 'As the season progressed, results deteriorated and we gradually slid towards the bottom. Eventually, the directors became concerned that we might lose our Football League place and began offering us larger win bonuses. However, we struggled to push ourselves clear of danger, despite gaining important victories as against Northampton. Home attendances were poor. You could

hear the supporters' complaints so clearly in the almost empty ground.'

Four days later, Burnley faced Rochdale away. The 'Dale' were bottom with the Clarets just one place above them. Rochdale had won the reverse fixture on New Year's Day with contemptuous ease (3-0) but had languished since. On a warm, sunny, Easter Saturday afternoon there was to be a resurrection of sorts. With so much at stake, a 3,000-strong Burnley contingent unexpectedly descended upon Spotland, determined to make their presence felt. Fired up by booze and derby bravado, they drowned the home vocal support with their incessant chanting and raucous invective. The away end shuddered under the weight of their furious defiance, reminiscent of better days in Burnley's distant past.

Brawny 18-year-old apprentice, Phil Devaney, making only his second start, replaced the departed Parker. Watched proudly by his Liverpool family, he assumed instant hero status by hooking in Burnley's opening goal in the 13th minute, capitalising upon the Rochdale keeper's inability to deal with Ian Britton's flighted free-kick. It was a bit of a shank, but Burnley had a priceless lead and began to play with unfamiliar confidence with their exultant fans baying them on.

Expertly marshalled by Deakin, Burnley's back four proved redoubtable in defying a side which had just stunned promotion-bound Preston at Deepdale, winning 4-2. Deakin, young Peter Leebrook, Joe Gallagher and Peter Hampton were so commanding that goalkeeper, Joe Neenan, had relatively little to do.

Ian Britton scurried around like an unruly terrier, forever snapping at his opponents' ankles, harrying them into errors, seizing upon the fiercely contested second balls, fetching and carrying, urging his team forward wherever possible. But it was Devaney who was Burnley's star turn, demonstrating the courage, burliness and energetic persistence that had been previously lacking up front. And yet while Burnley were deservedly in front, their lead was still slender. Nerves began to creep in. Much to the relief of all in Claret and Blue, Burnley grabbed a cushion shortly after half-time.

In the 53rd minute, pint-sized, Ashley Hoskin received a short corner from James, and crossed for Gallagher to steal in at the near post and thump his header past Welch in the Rochdale goal. The roar from the delirious Burnley fans was incandescent. At the end, they swarmed ecstatically onto the pitch, taunting their hosts.

Burnley Express journalist, Granville Shackleton aptly headed his report: 'The Corpse Lives On'. He wrote:

> 'The match had all the ingredients of a wake with many of the national media poised like vultures at Spotland, to administer the last rites if the Clarets had been beaten and dropped to 92nd position in the Football League. But all the pre-match hysteria and gloom on radio and television looked rather stupid...For the "corpse" suddenly stirred and the Clarets lived on to fight another day.'

But as sure as the Burnley fans were, that their team was then safe, their celebrations were premature. Just one point was gleaned from Burnley's next three games, culminating in a glum 2-1 defeat at Scunthorpe, after Phil Malley had given his side a 4th minute lead. Director, Clive Holt said:

> 'I remember going to Scunthorpe at the end of April. We were two places above the drop zone and desperate for a victory. I recall that the Lincoln directors were there in force, hoping for a Scunthorpe win to relieve the growing relegation pressure on their side. Much to our chagrin, they went home very happy, sure that their side would survive with only three games left.'

Jimmy McIlroy, Burnley's most feted footballing hero, wrote in his *Burnley Express* column on the 1May:

> 'Burnley have reached rock bottom. Another step down is oblivion. Maybe now it will get through to people that very soon there might not be a Burnley Football Club. Maybe now they will believe that it wasn't a cry of wolf over the past two seasons and that the very existence of one of the founder members of the Football League was on the brink of extinction.
>
> 'Outsiders, especially the Press who for months have seen the decline of this once famous club as a good news story, have all been amazed at the mountain of apathy among the people of the town. And I have been as guilty as the rest of you. Like you, I watched unbelievable mistakes being made and huge sums of money wasted over the years – and like you, I told myself it served them right for the way they ran things. Then, because I like chairman Frank

Teasdale, I agreed to help promote the fund-raising scheme, the Clarets Express, now called Clarets Revival. It was only through this involvement that it gradually sank in just how close the Turf Moor club was to folding up.

'But our appeals, by and large, fell on deaf ears. Very few wanted to know, and certainly didn't feel like subscribing a pound a week to a club that, in their eyes, had squandered hundreds of thousands. Sure, the Clarets Revival is bringing in much-needed cash every week, but it is nothing like the sum I had hoped for. I naively thought that by stirring up interest among the ex-Clarets and showing that virtually every former player was concerned it might just stimulate interest. At every pub or club, we visited, we were warmly welcomed by big crowds who wanted to recall the past great days. Most expressed concern at today's plight – but the stark fact was that the Clarets Revival did not obtain anything like the members Jack Butterfield and the rest of us hoped for.

'Now it may be too late. The club could be three matches away from extinction because it is difficult to imagine a stadium like Turf Moor staging non-League matches and being viable. Should the worst happen, and Burnley finish 92nd, I think this will be the end. But should they survive in the Football League, I think the time is nigh for EVERYONE to get together and discuss ways and means of ensuring Burnley F.C. will never again find itself in such a humiliating situation.

'And I mean everyone – particularly the public. If this dilemma has proved anything, it is that the club need the public more than they need it. So, the obvious answer is to involve the people of the town and surrounding area in some shape or form. Burnley Council should also be invited to become involved, because part of its duty in serving the community is to keep the name of the town on the map – and a successful Burnley F.C. is probably the most effective way to achieve this.

'Right now, all this could be pie in the sky waffle, with everything hinging on three matches. We can do nothing, except turn up at Turf Moor and yell the side on tomorrow and next Saturday. If at 4.40 p.m. a week tomorrow, Burnley is still a Football League side, doesn't it make sense that we all get together with everyone concerned to create interest and make all of us feel part of what was once the town's greatest ambassador?'

Clive Holt said: 'We were given a lifeline, though, one day after this article appeared, when we came from behind to beat promotion-bound Southend at Turf Moor 2-1.' It was a somewhat fortuitous victory with Leighton James equalising with a rasping shot and Neil Grewcock seizing the points with a rare header. However, Burnley were still wobbling in 23rd spot, desperate for a positive result at Crewe on the following Bank Holiday Monday if they were to save themselves.

Clive Holt remembers the occasion vividly. He said:

'The penultimate game was at Crewe. We were losing 1-0 but pressing hard for an equaliser. Then, with what seemed to be several minutes left for play, the referee blew the final whistle. I think he was bothered by the large number of supporters gathering on the touchlines, preparing to rush on at the end. I turned around to the Football League assessor, sat behind me, to complain at this blatant injustice. He waved my protest aside, though, kidding me that he did not have a watch when I could see that his match record of refereeing decisions had their respective timings. Since there was not a clock inside the ground it was obvious that he had access to a watch or a small clock. But he refused to address my objection. From that match onwards, I have always had a stop watch which is now approaching 30 years old.

'Our collective protest that Burnley had been short-timed fell on deaf ears as did a plea to the Football League to reprieve the club from relegation because of its historic founder member status. We were almost out of time and running out of ideas to save our club. We had considered the ruse of buying almost bankrupt Cardiff City and bringing it back to Turf Moor, in what would have been the Football League's first franchise operation. It had looked as if Cardiff would enter Administration. Nothing came of the idea, though.

'So, we were destined to go to the wire, a last chance home game with Orient who were expected to provide stiff opposition as they pursued their play-off ambitions. I am brought to tears whenever I think back on that fateful day. It was like a near-death experience. However, it became the day when local folk reclaimed their team, when 16-17,000 returned to Turf Moor. Before the Orient game, the average League gate had been only 2,800. It was pitiful. In Burnley's heydays of the fifties and sixties, crowds of 40-50,000 had filled Turf Moor. Only the threat of losing their club for ever, caused the local people to return in large numbers. Having said that, had the worst happened, I don't think the club would have necessarily expired. I think I might have been able to keep it alive. In those days, it was possible to buy a club for a few hundred thousand pounds. I was prepared to consider paying that sort of sum to save the club. As it turned out it was not necessary. Ironically, it was Lincoln and not Burnley which fell through the trap door, but then Lincoln staged a return to the Football League one year later. So, relegation might not have been a terminal disaster. If Lincoln could return from the Conference so quickly, why not Burnley?

'Besides, I'm not a pessimist. I held a firm conviction that all would be well. I was sure that if we beat Orient that would be sufficient for survival although salvation was not solely in our hands. I did not expect both of our rivals – Lincoln and Torquay – to win as well. I thought at least one of them would lose and, of course, that's what happened. When we heard that Lincoln had lost their final game at Swansea 2-0, thereby sealing their relegation I had a wry smile thinking of those Lincoln directors who had smugly presumed their side's safety after our defeat at Scunthorpe.'

Burnley's current vice-chairman, Barry Kilby, then just an ardent supporter, was unconvinced that Burnley FC would have survived had Orient won or drawn at Turf Moor. He reflected:

'Had Burnley not won this game, and had Swansea not simultaneously beaten Lincoln, the club would have ceased to exist. I'm sure of that now, having seen the evidence. Its debts were considerable. The utility companies had already threatened to pull the plug at various points during that season. How could we have run a team in the Football Conference with such crippling debts while maintaining a large ground that was totally unaffordable, on the gates we could expect to command? I know there was talk of

Colne Dynamos taking over the stadium, possibly on a ground-share basis – I believe they had a wealthy benefactor backing them then – but the costs involved were prohibitive. It never seemed to be a realistic proposition.'

Others shared Barry's grave misgivings. He continued:

'After we had lost at Crewe, I really thought we had had it. I still went to the final game, of course, desperately hoping we could save ourselves. The prospects were not good. Orient needed to win to try to claim a play-off place. They weren't going to do us any favours.'

Just before the Orient game took place on 9 May, chairman Frank Teasdale and Burnley MP Peter Pike made impassioned appeals to the *Burnley Express* readers. Teasdale said:

'It is now up to the lads on the field to save us, but I appeal to everyone who has the club at heart to back them with the sort of Dunkirk spirit which so many of our fans produced when the team responded by winning 2-0 at Rochdale.'

Meanwhile Peter Pike warned:

'The fortunes of the club have an impact on the town. Its Football League status was one of the factors considered when new industries were attracted to the town. That League status, which has lasted for 99 years since Burnley became one of the 12 founder members of the Football League in 1888, is now threatened for the first time in the club's history… It would mean automatic expulsion from the League with Scarborough replacing them.'

Belatedly, the residents of Burnley awoke. The town's defining industries – cotton and coal – had gone. Only its football club remained as an essential link between its glorious past and its shaky present. But that club was in great peril. On Saturday 9 May, the penny finally dropped, persuading thousands of local people to return to the club they had forsaken, in protection of its and their historic identity. As Joni Mitchell put it, we don't know what we've got 'til it's gone.

Ian Britton, one of Burnley's heroes on this harrowing day, recalled:

'The week before the game the club was inundated with letters from well-wishers, many of which were from bigger sides. TV crews and journalists arrived in the town, realising what a big deal this game was for a club which was once one of the strongest in the country. Manager, Brian Miller managed the media pressure very well, leaving us to concentrate on the game.

'It didn't help that the kick off was delayed for 17 minutes because of the huge crowd that had descended on Turf Moor. We were pent up and raring to go but had to wait, having to go through our pre-match preparations again.'

YTS player, Peter Leebrook, later told a *Lancashire Telegraph* journalist:

'That Orient game was intense, but when you're young you don't really understand it that much. Sitting in the changing room for 20 minutes before we went out, it was silent. I remember thinking then that this must be what it's like to go out as a gladiator.'

Ian Britton continued:

'But once we emerged from the tunnel, we felt strengthened by the huge response that greeted us. The atmosphere was tremendous. It is much easier playing in front of such a noisy crowd where you can't hear the individual gripes. You just focus then on what you must do. Neil Grewcock's goal, coming just before half-time, certainly settled us down.

'Before that it was pretty frantic stuff. It was an important game for Orient, also, as they had a chance of getting into the play-offs. Being in the middle of this battle, the game seemed much faster than it was when I watched it later on video. Of course, football is so much quicker now, so that may have distorted my judgement.

'Shortly after the break, Neil Grewcock produced a wonderfully flighted free-kick from the right wing that I headed home. A lot was made of the fact that, at under five and a half feet tall, I was the smallest player on the field, but I had a decent record of headed goals. This was one of eight in my career, although it was by far the most important.

'The game wasn't over though. Joe Neenan, in our goal, had to make a string of important saves, and then Orient's dangerous striker, Alan Comfort, pulled a goal back. Although this placed us under pressure, knowing how much was at stake, I think it was probably a lot easier for us playing the game than for those watching.'

Some Burnley supporters were so overcome with anxiety that they chose to leave early and pace nervously outside the ground.

Ian concluded:

'Everyone played their part. We had a young lad, Peter Leebrook, at right back. He was only 18-years-old and yet he played with such composure, like a seasoned professional. Phil Devaney, also 18, played up front. He had just come into the side. He looked nervous. A lot was expected of these young lads, taking part in possibly the club's most important game, in front of a baying 16,000 crowd. And yet they did their bit, helped by having 'old heads' around them.

'Eventually the game came towards its end. Referee, George Courtney, warned us that when he signalled, we should be ready to run like hell because it was obvious that there was going to be a massed pitch invasion at the end. The stewards had no hope of keeping the supporters back. But we had no chance of getting off, either. Before we could make a dash, we were immediately mobbed by the fans. It was a brilliant occasion. One of my strongest memory of that pitch celebration, though, was the sight of one of the club's landladies sobbing with joy in the stands. Her tearful relief was captured on the national TV news.

'Once I got back into the dressing room, Neil and I each downed a bottle of champagne. As did Brian Miller. It was a bit of a blur. In fact, the next three weeks was just one long bender. I hardly had to pay for a drink. I still get free drinks on the back of this great escape.

'Frank Teasdale was then the chairman of the club. Although a quiet man, he was Burnley through and through. This result meant so much to him. He was determined that the club would not be placed in this situation again. During the close season, he and Brian Miller brought in some decent players.'

Neil Grewcock, who scored the crucial opening goal reflected:

'I had been desperately disappointed by our relegation to the Fourth Division in 1985. When that Swansea result arrived, and put us down then, it hit me very hard. In fact, I have never felt so low in my life as on that Friday night… Brian Miller did well with what he had. Tactically not the best, but I enjoyed playing under Brian. I probably played my best football at Burnley under him. He did a good job in deflecting all the media attention and pressure from the players prior to the Orient game.

'Most of the Burnley fans we spoke to before the game said they were praying we would not go out of the League. There were hundreds of cards and letters of support… Immediately before the game the noise from outside the dressing room was deafening. The delayed kick off just added to the tension. All we wanted was to get out on the pitch and get the game underway…

'As for my goal, I collected the ball on my right-hand side and cut in on my left foot. A gap seemed to open in front of me, and from about 18 yards, I curled the ball into the bottom corner with my left foot, to the goalkeeper's right. And as for Ian's goal, we had a free kick on the right-hand side in front of the Bob Lord Stand. I didn't necessarily mean to pick out Ian out, just to get the ball into the box. Fortunately, it found his head and he put us 2-0 ahead. When the final whistle blew the relief was unbelievable.'

Phil Devaney later told author Dave Thomas:

'For most of the players it would have been the low point of their careers. It was the high point of mine. I can remember vividly the build-up in the weeks before and the general air of excitement, in the expectation that a founder member may be kicked out of the Football League, and if ever I meet a Burnley supporter when travelling, they all remember exactly what they were doing on that day. I also remember a policeman who was on duty the day of the game advising me that if we were losing near the end of the game, to ensure we were as close to the tunnel as possible on the final whistle as it could be a bit dangerous with a pitch invasion.

'I was a bit concerned when I realised we'd be kicking towards the Bee Hole End, second half. I was fairly sure Neil Grewcock and myself were quick enough to out-run the invading masses at the end, but I wouldn't have put money on Taffy [Leighton James] making it off the pitch alive. Britt [Ian Britton] would also have been OK as well as most of the Beehole End fans were his drinking pals. After the game, we were given a bonus for staying up which was equivalent to about six months wages for me. I was on only £25 a week.'

The only Burnley player unmoved by the euphoria was Joe Gallagher. At the celebratory party which followed, Derek Gill found him sitting alone in a quiet corner, with a subdued expression. Derek explained:

'Joe said he was sad as it was his last match and his playing career was finished. In all innocence, I asked if he had been offered a new contract and if not, there was plenty of time to get fixed up elsewhere. "What me?" says he. "Who the hell will take me with my knee?"

The expensive charade was over, leaving Joe Gallagher with an uncertain future.

Burnley supporter, Dave McCluggage recalled:

'The Longside fence was groaning. I remember thinking they'll never stop the fans getting on. Then, at the precise moment when I wasn't thinking about the whistle blowing, it blew. I delayed my celebrations in case it was a free kick or something. I didn't want to jump around prematurely. Hugs and tears gave way to manly handshakes and backslapping… One Burnley director threw his arms around an embarrassed policeman, hugging him tightly. Thousands swarmed over the pitch and up to the Orient fans. Just for a second it could have been a bit iffy. But in an instant the mood changed. Their fans cascaded down the away end and applauded us. Who could begrudge us the points? The poignancy was not lost on the O's supporters.'

An Orient supporter posted this recollection, 28 years later:

'There was much scarf-swapping and bonhomie at the end. However, no way would this have taken place if we had won. The atmosphere in the ground was frightening to this, then, 17-year-old. To be fair to the Burnley fans, the sheer level of vociferous support they gave to their team was such that I have not witnessed anything like it before or since, despite attending hundreds of games. It's a cliché, but it really was a cauldron.'

The national pressmen arrived in droves at Turf Moor, many convinced they were about to witness a famous burial.

One un-named reporter wrote:

> 'We came prepared to write about a death, but none of us wanted it to happen. Every football fan in the country has a soft spot for clubs like Burnley. We remember the glory days, and who can forget Bob Lord? It would have been a tragedy for them to go out of the League. There was not an empty seat in the box, and 21 photographers were there to cover the most historic day in the club's history.'

Derek Wallis of the *Observer* recorded:

> 'It seemed as if the whole town had turned up, and the team responded with a stirring performance when it mattered most. Next Saturday's FA Cup Final may produce a match of greater quality, but it is questionable whether it will be more dramatic or emotional than this game.'

Rob Hughes of the *Sunday Times* wrote:

> 'Why do grown men become so moved by an apparently trivial sport? If you need to ask, you have no conception of the traditions by which this famous club helped to forge a competition which spread football in its known form around the world. It was not morbid curiosity that brought them all to Turf Moor. It was the dilemma of either seeing a dramatic, last gasp escape from oblivion, or paying last respects to a truly great club which 99 years ago had been a founder member of the League, and which in the 1960's had actually, with great class and culture, ruled as champions and had taken on and beaten the finest in Europe.'

While the *Daily Mail* correspondent, Ian Wooldridge commented:

> 'They were playing for their own careers, let alone Burnley's survival, and the sporting term "sudden death" takes on new shades of meaning when the last pay cheque is only 90 minutes away. I shall never quite determine who won the match: the team or the crowd. The Burnley team were fuelled to 45% talent – which means they played above themselves – and 180% adrenalin. The crowd, in this recently echoing concrete mausoleum at the foot of a

damp Lancashire valley, was as passionate, pro-rata, as I have ever heard.'

Jimmy McIlroy wrote after the game:

'The atmosphere was electrifying. A man tapped me on the shoulder saying, "I was in Texas yesterday, but I wouldn't have missed this day for anything." This is how much the club means to the people of Burnley and the surrounding area. The noise as the players lined up for the kick-off was deafening. There was no way the Clarets would lose through lack of support – but there was fear. For the first time, ever at a football match, I felt my eyes moist. This was my club, on the brink of humiliation, and here were thousands more who felt the same way. Because of what happened all those years ago when I was transferred, I had always imagined something of my feeling for Burnley F.C. had died. But on Saturday afternoon my emotions clearly showed. I was as concerned for the future of the club as the most ardent fan out there.

'At the final whistle, while everyone around was hugging and kissing his or her neighbour, I felt spent and elated, and then sad that the club had to be in its very death throes to awaken interest among its former fans. Now there is some breathing space for the directors to ensure this situation is never repeated. They must work at retaining this new-found interest and to be seen in the next few days to be taking concrete steps to build a team worthy of the support of almost 16,000 very relieved fans.'

Leighton James said:

'The hardest part was the fifteen-minute delay. It heightened the tension although we were better off than the supporters because we had the chance to do something about our predicament. They just had to stand or sit and watch... I had arrived early at the ground that day because I couldn't settle at home. Brian Miller was already there. We started talking and he asked me what I thought. As nervous as I was I told him I fancied us to win. I just thought someone up there won't let this club go. We were helped, of course, in having such a strong, capable and highly experienced referee in George Courtney. Some referees might have buckled under the pressure. Waiting for that final whistle was hell, though... To this day, I still believe that 75 per cent of that crowd came to bury us. You'll never convince me of anything different. I know that I will incur the wrath of a lot of people in saying that, but I don't care, that's what I believe. If that was not the case then why did they turn up on a day like that, when they hadn't turned up all season when we could have done with their support?'

Brian Miller told the Granville Shackleton of the *Burnley Express*:

'That's the longest 90 minutes I have ever sat through... the last 20 minutes were agonising but we've done it, and now we have to strengthen the side while keeping within our financial limits. The town of Burnley responded today and the backing was fantastic. Now the club should make sure that the mistakes of the past are never repeated... Today has been a victory for the team, the fans and the town of Burnley. Let's take it from there.'

Brian Miller was widely respected for his display of dignified composure in the lead up to, and during, this harrowing game but as Clive Holt pointed out: 'You didn't want to be in the way when Brian was angry!' For the generally genial Miller tended to incubate his frustrations, before suddenly exploding with anger. These outbursts were usually short-lived, though, and without lasting rancour.

Orient's manager, Geordie Frank Clark, sportingly remarked,

'I never liked the idea of the bottom club in the Fourth Division going out without even the chance of a play-off. Just look at this ground. It's magnificent, and yet this great old club had one foot in the trapdoor when we began this game... I think the enormous crowd affected the Burnley's players more than ours.

What a sight, wasn't it? To see nearly 18,000 packed into this great stadium. My only criticism of my own players is that we made the mistakes we have made all season – in their penalty area and in our own. How on earth can the smallest player on the field – Ian Britton – be allowed to have a free header from a set piece and score the goal which eventually clinched it?'

As the final whistle blew, a relieved Frank Teasdale told a BBC TV reporter:

> 'I can't find the words to describe it. Put simply, we deserved it. The crowd was marvellous. Of course, I feel for those at Torquay who are going down instead of us. I wouldn't want this to happen to anyone.'

Teasdale hadn't known that there had been late drama in the game between Torquay and Crewe. Here, a patrolling police dog had broken free of his handler and bit Jim McNicholl, the Torquay right back, on his thigh. Torquay were then losing 1-2 and, with little time remaining, looked destined for the drop. But the protracted delay, that followed the dog bite, enabled them to re-group and force a late equaliser to stay up. It was just one of those days!

Frank Teasdale then told Granville Shackleton of the *Burnley Express*:

> 'Several people have asked me these last few days, "What has it been like on Death Row?" It has been dreadful. I couldn't sleep at all on Friday night. I was listening to the radio at four o'clock in the morning. But now we are safe as far as our League status is concerned. The battle begins all over again to make sure we never find ourselves in this position again. We have all got to work together to revive this club, and, with the backing of the town which we had today, we can do it. I was inundated with messages before the game wishing us good luck. The crowd's backing was fantastic and if only we can get a good proportion of them back next season, this club can stride forward.'

It was fitting that the final game was sponsored by Frank Teasdale's employer, John Gilbraith, chairman of Gilbraith Commercials. It was the fifth game sponsored by him during this season. Without their financial support, the club would have been in greater jeopardy. Frank Teasdale and his board of directors were quietly confident that the TSB, the bank which purportedly 'likes to say yes', would back Burnley for a further season. It would be the club's centenary as a Football League member.

In casting his mind back, Clive Holt concluded:

> 'It was a wretched time. It was very much hands to mouth, with a threadbare squad, one physio, Jimmy Holland, and

a "bucket and sponge" trainer in former player, George Bray. I remember George getting very fed up with one of our players who kept going down claiming injury. George's patience finally snapped in one game resulting in him emptying the bucket of cold water over him. It was a rare funny moment.'

However, not everyone saw the season quite as unhappily as Clive did. Ashley Hoskin told Phil Whalley:

'We were getting back to Burnley being a family club. We thought we were good enough to hold our own. I respected Brian Miller. Brian brought back Billy Rodaway and Leighton James, and there were people there who obviously loved the club… The team spirit was good. There were never any groups of players on their own, whispering about the others. We used to have a laugh. On Mondays, we'd talk about what we'd done on the Saturday night. We were all together. Until the last five or six games of the season, it never entered my head that Burnley would be fighting on the last day to stay in the League. The reaction from the changing room was the same – it didn't dawn on anyone, I don't think, until it got to the stage when we were thinking, "We could do with winning this one", because if results don't go for us…'

'Brian was doing a good job with no money. If a player came up for twenty quid I don't think we could have afforded it. That was the reality. At one time, without any option, Brian put Jason Harris in, who was only 16, Peter Leebrook, 17. There was Darren Heesom, at left-back, 17, myself, 17. When you put that many youngsters in, it didn't do us a lot of good… But there was no indication whatsoever that we'd be where we ended up – no chance! But the team who went down instead of us – Lincoln – we played them away at the beginning of January and lost 2-1, and they hardly won another game after that. They were second in the Division Four after beating us. So that goes to prove how it happens.

'And, you see the fans – it never happens now – and they're on you and on you. But at that time, Brian never got any stick because people realised that there was no money in the pot; he'd got what he'd got and we'd either sink or swim. There was the odd barracking – I mean, sometimes I couldn't go out of the house in Accrington – but Brian never seemed to get that as much from what I hear now. Fortunately, we managed to swim – just!

'Before the Orient game, the police came into our dressing room. We knew that if we lost, they couldn't guarantee our safety. If you go back to the Hereford game, we weren't allowed outside of the dressing room, so God knows what would have happened… Through knowing what the passion is like in the town – I mean some of the players who weren't from around this area didn't believe it, but I was telling them, "You come out with me round Accrington one night." When we'd won, it was brilliant, you'd end up on someone's shoulders. But when we'd lost it was curtains shut, door locked, don't answer it. And that's what it got to.'

Unknown to Ashley and his team mates, the police had issued a bomb warning earlier on the day of the Orient game. According to Turf Moor groundsman, Roy Oldfield, he was told to scour the ground for potentially suspicious devices. It transpired that it was a hoax call. But given the Irish sectarian terrorism of the time, it seems incredible that a groundsman should be assigned such a risky operation.

The Player-of-the-Year award went deservedly to Clarets' skipper Ray Deakin, the only ever-present player during the 1986/87 campaign. Deakin received his award modestly, ignoring all calls for a speech. He told Granville Shackleton afterwards: 'I've never known support like it. We have not done anything to deserve the sort of fanaticism that was shown out there by our fans today. We have given no-one any reason to come and watch us and yet, in the end, they kept us alive.'

29 May 1988
Wembley Way

'Never Gonna Give You Up'

A NEAR-DEATH experience normally draws a family together. This was evident at the emotionally charged Orient game and, continued into the next season. For 5,419 fans turned up for the opening home fixture against Colchester. Leaving aside the 'do or die' Orient match, this was the largest home league gate in three years. Unfortunately, Colchester ignored the script, ruthlessly exploiting a casual Burnley defence to win 3-0. Things were about to get a lot better, though.

Burnley Director, Clive Holt commented:

'Thanks to Frank Teasdale's successful "wheeling and dealing" and, of course, the healthy receipts from the Orient game, which enhanced creditor confidence, we had the scope to spend more on the 1987/88 Burnley team. Manager, Brian Miller, brought in some good additions including: Paul Comstive, a tall, skilful, midfielder from Wrexham; Steve Davis, an imposing, young centre back from Crewe, who had been capped for the England Youth team; and George Oghani, a pacey striker from Bolton with a good average strike rate of one goal in three games.

'The wage bill for this improved first team squad was about £5,000 per week, which, of course, is a fraction of the current weekly cost of employing just one first team player.'

George Oghani became the first black player to represent Bolton Wanderers after his 1983 transfer from Hyde United. In moving to Burnley in 1987, he became only the third black player to represent the Clarets – behind Les Lawrence and Rob, or Bobby, Regis.

George said:

> 'I was ready to leave Bolton. The previous season had not been that great. So, when Brian Miller approached me, I was interested. I knew Burnley had been a big club in years gone by. Brian admitted that the club's recent survival had been a close shave, but he was so positive about the future that this rubbed off on me. It felt like a proper club again. The ground was impressive and it was clear from the Orient game that its fans had not lost their passion.'

Only four incoming players required transfer fees: Steve Davis, a £15,000 purchase from Crewe, after he had served a successful loan period; the Wrexham pair, Paul Comstive and goalkeeper, Chris Pearce, for a combined fee of £12,000; and Andy Farrell, a utility player from Colchester who cost £5,000. Five other recruits joined on 'frees' – strikers, George Oghani and ex-Claret, Steve Taylor, experienced defenders, Peter Daniel and Peter Zelem, and young midfielder, Shaun McGrory. Brian Miller retained eight members of his 1986/87 squad: Deakin, James, Britton, Leebrook, Grewcock, Hoskin, Malley and Devaney, but strengthened his team in eight positions, spending less than £35,000. This was impressive.

Burnley's first league victory came at Somerton Park, Newport on the 22 August 1987. Here, Neil Grewcock set up George Oghani for a second half winner in a game which Burnley had dominated after the 30th minute dismissal of Newport's experienced defender, Phil Brignull. An ultra-defensive Wrexham side was then overwhelmed by three late goals, in the second leg of the League Cup, setting up an attractive tie with high-riding First Division side, Norwich City. Although Burnley lost 2-1 on aggregate, pride was restored with two battling performances, the first of which was watched by a Turf Moor crowd that was only marginally below 8,000.

Meanwhile, league form remained promising. Carlisle were defeated 4-3 in a Turf Moor thriller on 29 August, and following three successive 1-0 wins over Swansea, Tranmere and Wrexham, Burnley rose to the dizzy heights of third place. A fallow period ensued, during which Cambridge (0-2), Crewe (0-0) and Rochdale (1-2) were battered but not beaten, and League newcomers, Scarborough, proved resolute in defence of their solitary goal. But with a brace of away victories, at blustery Exeter (2-1), just after the 'Great Storm', and at radiant Torquay (3-1), third position was reclaimed on 24 October. Then, at a cold, foggy Wolverhampton, in early November, Burnley were out-muscled and out-classed (0-3). The game was described sardonically by a BBC reporter as 'a battle between two arthritic giants'. Fourth Division leaders Wolves had Steve Bull and Andy Mutch up front, the best goal-scoring partnership in the bottom two divisions. Burnley fell to 10th place.

In attempting to improve his side's strike-rate, Miller brought in young Sheffield Wednesday forward David Reeves on loan. Reeves scored on debut, helping defeat Bolton 2-1 in a home league game, watched by almost 11,000 fans. This win avenged Burnley's earlier FA Cup loss to Wanderers. Thereafter, league results were up and down. A 5-0 battering by Peterborough, at London Road, on 28 November was corrected by a 4-0 drubbing of Rochdale on Boxing Day, while another pulsating 'goal-fest', at Carlisle, on New Year's Day, gave cause for further festive celebrations (4-3). It seemed as if Reeves possessed the silver bullet. However, having scored eight times for Burnley in 16 league appearances, Reeves was recalled by Sheffield Wednesday. His last appearance was in a 3-0 home win over Exeter on 5 March which took Burnley briefly into a play-off position. Reeves signed off with a pledge of loyalty to Burnley, refusing to join any other Fourth Division club on loan that season.

In February, Burnley had set up experimental double-priced turnstiles to raise money for purchasing players. Burnley historian, Ray Simpson remembered:

> 'In the 1987/88 season, the club introduced an optional admission charge of £5 for some games. The standard home entrance fee was £2.50. The optional charge was introduced to raise funds for team strengthening. We were very keen to keep loan player, David Reeves. 7,841 fans chose to pay double which raised around £20,000. Unfortunately, Sheffield Wednesday would not let him go.'

Clive Holt was frustrated at the club's failure to land Reeves permanently. He said:

'When Reeves's loan spell expired, the board agreed to make funds available for Miller to attempt to sign him permanently. But when I told Brian Miller this, he looked dumbfounded, saying that Frank Teasdale had said the club could not afford Reeves. I was angry. It had been a collective board decision that we should attempt to sign Reeves, and yet Frank had reversed this unilaterally. The thing about Frank Teasdale was that he was terrific in keeping the wolf from the door but at heart he was a very cautious man. In his time in charge I think we missed important opportunities to progress because he was too risk-averse.

'With the club's financial position healthier than 12 months before – our losses had been slashed by over £100,000 to a manageable £40,000 – I confronted Frank concerning his lone stance on Reeves. This was a player that went on to score well over a hundred more league goals for lower division sides. I was angry with Frank Teasdale and wrote him a letter, stating my intention to increase the size of my shareholding stake, proposing to pay £50 for each share – instead of the existing price of £15 – posing a direct threat to his position as chairman. This caused a hell of a row. The aggravation was too much for Basil Dearing who feared that his professional reputation was becoming tainted with the controversies besetting the club. Basil had been badly shaken by the fans' vociferous protests during the previous season. Consequently, he resigned. Although we managed to patch up the boardroom squabble, Burnley's promotion challenge faltered, not helped by our failure to sign Reeves.'

However, Burnley's progress in the Sherpa Van Trophy was startlingly successful. Following a victorious penalty shoot-out with Halifax, the club qualified for a two-legged Northern final with Preston. The victor would meet their Southern equivalent at Wembley.

Club historian, Ray Simpson recalled:

'The Sherpa Van competition of 1987/88 was so important in bringing about Burnley's revival. League form had been OK and gates had doubled, but that cup-run provided the catalyst for the club's eventual success. We had been drawn to play at Third Division Bury in the Northern Quarter-finals. It was a foul night with the rain sheeting down. We were drenched on the open Gigg Lane terracing, but when Paul Comstive scored with a penalty, right in front of us, putting Burnley through to the Northern semi-final, we instantly forgot our discomfort. On our way home, we were ecstatic to hear that Sunderland had been eliminated. It was then when we realised that a Wembley appearance might just be possible.'

Clive Holt added:

'At the celebratory meal after the Orient game in May 1987, I had euphorically proclaimed: "There will be no repetition next season. In fact, we might even get to Wembley!" As it turned out that's exactly what happened!'

The improbable dream was achieved after victory in the second leg of the Northern final on 19 April 1988. The game was played at Preston's rickety Deepdale ground, still featuring its famous, if flaking, Edwardian structures. It was a balmy spring evening. The trees in adjacent Fulwood Park were coming into leaf. Above us was a pallid, pastel sky. From the tinny public address emerged the pop sounds of the day. 'I Should Be So Lucky' squealed Kylie. We wondered and hoped. For how better to celebrate Burnley's Lazarus-like revival than at Wembley in the Football League's centenary year?

But the odds were against the Clarets. Preston's plastic pitch gave them a clear and arguably unfair advantage. It was no coincidence, surely, that North End had remained undefeated at home since 12 December 1987. Besides, Preston had been the better side in a tense, goal-less first leg at Turf Moor. Burnley were also without their talismanic right winger, Neil Grewcock. A horrific tackle in the Halifax tie side-lined him for nine months, ultimately blighting his remaining career.

Pugnacious North End manager, John McGrath, fashioned his team in his image. As a tough Newcastle centre back, McGrath recalled being told by his equally abrasive boss, Joe Harvey: 'I want to see how fast their centre forward can limp.' George Oghani, Burnley's lithe, mobile striker, needed to take note.

15,680 fans had turned up for the first leg. Two thousand more made it for part two. Even a half hour before kick-off, the caged Town End was heaving with boisterous Clarets, clamouring for a morsel of restored glory and trading jibes with their mocking adversaries. The febrile atmosphere was stoked well before kick-off.

Clinging shirts and skimpy shorts were the contemporary fashion but Burnley's keeper, Chris Pearce, preferred tracksuit bottoms to counteract the risk of 'Astro burns'. On the mullet front, Preston's Brian Mooney was just ahead of team mate Tony Ellis and Burnley's Paul Comstive.

Preston made one change to their side. Jones replaced 'Big Sam' Allardyce in central defence. Brian Miller's son, David, had played in midfield at Turf Moor, but this time he slotted in at right back. He had come closest to breaking the deadlock in the first leg only to be denied by 'Whooshy' Deakin's goal line clearance. Another Claret in waiting, Warren Joyce, took over Miller's midfield role. Burnley were unchanged with George Oghani partnered up front with Steve Taylor.

Preston started brightly – Mooney testing Burnley's defence with his quick feet, pace and strength. Clarets' left back, Shaun McGrory, was about to have a very difficult evening. Chris Pearce didn't do much to calm Claret nerves when, after only five minutes, he fumbled a free kick right in front of the horrified Burnley fans. However, he made amends from the resulting corner by plucking the ball from the heads of the foraging Preston pack. Two minutes later, George Oghani released midfielder Paul Comstive, but with the ball zipping across the artificial surface Comstive failed to control it and the opportunity vanished. Back came Preston and the now alert Pearce had to save well from Mooney after another forceful run.

The Burnley defenders were guilty of conceding possession too easily. A limping Steve Gardner at right back was the worst offender. It seemed strange that Brian Miller did not substitute the former Manchester United apprentice with a bandaged knee. Centre half, Steve Davis, an absolute steal from Crewe at £15,000, was rock-like though with Deakin giving rugged assistance. But with Farrell, Britton and Hoskin frequently brushed aside in midfield, a lot was being asked of Comstive. He had to combine the roles of suave creator and gnarled bouncer with an emphasis on the latter. Up front, George Oghani and Steve Taylor had little to work with as they doggedly pursued the high, wayward punts from Burnley's besieged defenders. 'Whooshy' Deakin demonstrated the aptness of his sobriquet with a succession of thumped long clearances. Nevertheless, Oghani did his best with the meagre service, constantly harrying Preston defenders Jones, Wrightson and Atkins, scurrying from one to another with the intention of forcing an error and disrupting North End's forward momentum.

With dusk descending and Preston well on top, Mooney seemed to sparkle in the artificial lighting. It was if the Irishman was invigorated by the floodlights' glare; his dashes along the right flank, intensified, his twists and turns even more bewildering. In the face of his marauding menace, the back-pedalling Burnley defenders were at full stretch in containing the mounting threat. Prompted yet again by Mooney, Tony Ellis volleyed just over. Then Ellis turned provider, putting left back Gary Swann through on goal. Pearce raced to his right to block Swann's surging advance, but Comstive was there just before him. The resulting pile-up left Pearce with a nasty blow to his thigh, preventing him from taking any further goal kicks. But adversity suddenly turned into advantage. The ensuing clearance found Britton. Belying his previous anonymity, he curled an exquisite pass around Jones to release Oghani in the unguarded inside left channel. George made no mistake with a rasping left-foot drive that evaded Brown's dive and found the far corner. It was completely against the run of play but the elated Burnley fans did not care, breaking into song: 'Que sera sera, whatever will be, will be, we're going to Wem-ber-lee, que sera sera!'

Incensed by the injustice, Preston poured forward again. In the 40th minute, Pearce was again smart in denying Ellis and although Swann netted four minutes later, after Ellis had sold his markers a dummy, the goal was ruled out for off side. So, half-time arrived with Burnley ahead. A combination of spoiling tactics, obstinate defending, brilliant goalkeeping, and one moment of sublime opportunism, had given the Clarets an unexpected advantage.

The second half started like the first. Mooney dispossessed McGrory and flashed a low centre across the box. Fortunately, neither Ellis nor Brazil could quite convert the cross. Then Davis's last-ditch interception thwarted Mooney just as he was about to shoot. Moments later, Preston were awarded a free kick on the edge of the box but Atkins squandered the chance by chipping straight at Pearce. Comstive briefly lifted the siege when he put Steve Taylor in behind the Preston defence. Frustratingly, the veteran striker, now shorn of his former pace, was forced to settle for an inconsequential corner. The action returned quickly to the other end with Pearce fumbling a cross, Mooney had the goal at his mercy. Luckily for the Burnley keeper, Mooney shot over. Pearce was quick to atone for his mistake by pushing Mooney's next powerful drive away for a corner. For all the pressure Preston exerted, though, Comstive had the opportunity to seal the game in the 55th minute. Having capitalised on some sloppy defending by Joyce and Wrightson, he advanced into the box but drove the ball across Brown though just wide of the right-hand post, much to the frustration of the Burnley fans in the crushed Town End pens, but to the delight of their adversaries who gleefully derided the squandered opportunity.

Stung by Burnley's temerity, Preston proceeded to force two quick corners, both of which were repelled. Mooney continued to roast McGrory at will and, in the 62nd minute, his neat exchange with Miller opened the right flank for the him to fire across the face of goal – but once again fractionally in front of Ellis and Brazil. Ellis had been getting little change out of Davis who was playing out of his skin while Brazil was struggling to dominate Deakin. Nevertheless, with Preston camped around Burnley's box, it was inevitable that the odd opportunity would come their way. One of these arrived in the 64th minute. Ellis squeezed a pass between Davis and Deakin, putting his strike partner through on the left of goal but, like Comstive, Brazil dragged his shot wide of the far post. It was the Clarets' fans turn to jeer contemptuously.

Burnley's reprieve lasted just 60 seconds. Atkins flicked on Wrightson's long, lofted free kick allowing Brazil to sneak behind Davis and Deakin and tuck away a simple finish. The Preston supporters were merciless, scornfully parodying the visitors' songs, mocking their premature Wembley claims. The Clarets' fans were not to be subdued, though. Just because their team remained under the cosh they refused to be cowed and came back in strong voice. On the pitch, a more cautious approach was adopted. George Oghani was drawn back to help his embattled defenders leaving the labouring Taylor alone up front.

Now Preston were switching play from flank to flank with Ronnie Hildersley inflicting upon Gardner what Mooney had on McGrory. This public humiliation eventually became too much for McGrory for in the 70th minute Burnley's beleaguered left back was booked for illegally redressing this unequal contest. The problem wasn't just with the Clarets' full backs, though. With his midfielders frequently overrun, Miller replaced the ineffectual Andy Farrell with Phil Malley. He had few options. Burnley attacks were becoming as rare as ospreys, although Oghani's 84th minute flick almost put Taylor clear but keeper Brown was a shade too quick for him. However, Preston ended the second half as they had begun. In the 88th minute Brazil was given far too much time and space to turn and shoot at goal. Fortunately, his shot whistled past the right-hand post. And then right at the death, Davis' muscular block stopped Hildersley in his tracks. It was to be extra time.

Brian Miller strode onto the pitch, formed his players into a circle and began haranguing them in what appeared to be a frenzied tactical instruction. His team had given everything. They looked done in, barely able to take in Miller's demands. Surely, this was Preston's game?

To Burnley's surprise, though, the game turned in the second minute of extra time. Up until that point, Brian Miller's son had kept tiny Ashley Hoskin tucked inside his pocket. Burnley's diminutive winger had hardly managed a kick. However, in the 92nd minute he suddenly sparked into life, earning his team a free kick on the left-hand edge of the Preston box. Deakin pumped the ball high towards the far post. Under pressure from Davis, Brown palmed the ball away towards the right touchline. Malley seized upon the loose ball, and rapidly made for the by-line before crossing hard and low into the crowded penalty area. First Davis and then Oghani deflected his cross, momentarily wrong footing the Preston defenders but leaving Hoskin, six yards out, with just enough space to get in a right foot shot. His first effort was charged down but with the ball luckily rebounding to him, he hammered it high into the net with his left foot. As the net bulged, the Burnley fans behind went berserk, screaming, leaping and clawing at the wire fencing with animal joy. With jabbing gestures of defiance and a roar of vindication they taunted the silenced home support, challenging them to deny their Wembley dream. 'And now you *got* to believe us and now you *got* to believe us….!' The ancient Town End stand with its creaking timbers rocked, rolled and buckled under their exultant exuberance.

Preston were far from finished, though. Mooney almost made an immediate riposte, having left two Burnley defenders for dead. But as before, Ellis was so near, yet too far, from converting the winger's sharp, low cross. Despite his thigh injury, Pearce continued to pull off a succession of brilliant saves, denying Mooney, Ellis (twice) and Atkins in the next 10 minutes. Nevertheless, Preston could not turn their supremacy into goals leaving Burnley to kill off the game with just two minutes remaining, McGrory being the jubilant instigator. With fatigue, and growing desperation, compromising Preston's defence, McGrory coolly slipped a simple ball to the unmarked Comstive in the inside left channel. Burnley's playmaker spotted George Oghani in space to his right, the striker having broken free from his minder. With Oghani collecting the ensuing pass, the pair suddenly found themselves two on one with Atkins, Preston's remaining defender. Oghani seemed certain to score but unselfishly shifted the ball to Comstive for a simple tap in. The linesman flagged furiously for off-side but referee Barrett over-ruled him deciding that Atkins' deflection of Oghani's pass had played Comstive's onside. Burnley were indeed going to 'Wemberlee'.

At the final whistle, hundreds of Burnley's ecstatic fans scaled the perimeter fencing, swarming onto the pitch to mob their heroes. Oghani was among those to be garlanded with a Burnley scarf. Despite having little to work with, he had run tirelessly in Burnley's cause, playing a crucial part in all three of their goals. He was the Clarets' leading scorer, too, with 17 goals thus far. 'Renaissance man', George, had done as much as anyone to turn around Burnley's flagging fortunes.

Of course, everyone had worked their socks off on this glorious evening. Despite being outplayed for long periods, Miller's courageous team had refused to wilt. It was a stubborn, dogged, gritty, heart-warming triumph. Burnley were back with pride!

George Oghani recalled:

> 'The Wembley final was definitely the highlight of my time at Burnley – a time I remember with great warmth. When I came out of the tunnel to face that huge crowd I felt so proud I felt 10-foot tall and thought my heart would pump out of my chest. Wolves were the stronger side, of course. Steve Bull and Andy Mutch were such good strikers and their defenders were strong as well, but that made no difference to our enjoyment. We were second best, but we gave them a good fight especially in the second half when Leighton James came on. He was a quality player and made a big difference. I should have scored from one of his pinpoint crosses, so should have Paul Comstive, but it wasn't to be.'

> 'Brian Miller was a good judge of a player. He made some good signings that season – Paul Comstive, Steve Davis, Andy Farrell. But he probably wasn't given enough resources to have put together a promotion-winning side. David Reeves would have made an important difference had we signed him permanently. I rated David Reeves – quick, strong, sharp in seizing an opening and a clinical marksman. I played with him at Carlisle as well. He's the only member of that team that I still see occasionally... With Brian, you knew where you were. He would wear his heart on his sleeve. If he wasn't happy he'd let you know it whereas Frank Casper, who took over from him, tended to be more introverted.'

He added:

'Yes, the Preston goal was crucial but my goal against First Division Norwich in the League Cup was probably my best for Burnley. That game proved that Burnley were on the up once more.'

When asked whether fans' criticisms ever got on top of him, George answered obliquely, saying:

'I think the fans have a right to express their views. They pay their money. And in any event, the Burnley crowd were brilliant. Like Bolton where there was a similar proud tradition, the Burnley fans appreciated their football. I would love to see them in the Premiership.'

Clive Holt remembered George with a smile. He said:

'George Oghani took a lot of ribbing from his team mates over an incident with an ironing board. On one trip, a team mate presented him with one found in a hotel bedroom, suggesting he might need it. We fell about with laughter. George took it in good heart. He had little choice really. You have to cope with a lot of banter at a football club.'

On 29 May, all manner of transport was commandeered to take Burnley's supporters to Wembley. All available coaches were chartered, leaving one group of fans to hire a furniture van. Many Clarets donned 'Burnley on Tour' T-shirts, listing their side's various Sherpa Van conquests – Tranmere, Rochdale, Chester, Bury, Halifax and Preston. These fans weren't averse to a dash of irony. As for the abundant Wolves fans, they had their horned headwear and old gold shirts emblazoned with 'Beware of the Bull'. Beware indeed! During the 1987/88 season, Steve Bull, the Tipton predator had scored 52 goals in 58 appearances in all competitions. This was a Dixie Dean-like strike-rate.

This event was rightly known as the 'friendly final'. On the day before, 102 'fans' were arrested at Stamford Bridge for violent offences. There was none of that nonsense here. Burnley and Wolves supporters drank together in pubs all over North West London, enjoying good-natured banter while basking in the sun's warmth. Whatever the result, we knew we would remember this day for the rest of our lives.

Burnley fan Mark Pilling was one of around 30,000 Burnley supporters at Wembley. He had this to say:

'The Baker Street tannoy trilled: "The train on platform four is for the Wembley extravaganza". The sarcasm was misplaced as 80,841 people converged on the land's premier stadium to witness the finest moment in the recent history of Wolverhampton Wanderers and Burnley football clubs.' This attendance was 10,000 higher than for England's home Rous Cup game with Scotland, eight days earlier.

'The preliminary match, dominated by Ray Pointer and Peter Noble, of 'the Vintage Clarets', manufactured a 2-0 Burnley win. When Leighton James trotted into the real thing as a 61st minute substitute, one couldn't help wondering whether he'd joined the wrong game.

'The pitch was in gorgeous condition, perfect for playing sweet, controlled football. However, as good as their approach play was, Burnley were not really hurting Wolves, although Farrell's first minute diving header went narrowly wide. Robertson and Streete were dominant at the heart of Wolves' defence giving Oghani and Taylor very few opportunities.

'Wolves first demonstrated their threat after 11 minutes when Pearce tipped a fierce 25-yard free-kick from Garry Bellamy against the bar, and Peter Daniel cleared. Then the mighty Bull – a future England centre forward – shot viciously wide as Wolves bared their teeth in an open game. There were moments of real skill, too, like Comstive's cheeky flick to Pearce over the charging Bull.

'It took 22 minutes for the inevitable to happen. A corner was floated over from the right. It was only partially cleared. Bull scooped it back and Pearce could only palm in Mutch's header. It was a soft goal and Pearce rightly berated himself for not doing better. The header lacked power and Pearce should have turned it aside.

'Wolves then seized control but up until the break they were unable to turn their greater possession into further goals. Davis was marshalling Bull superbly although he was booked in the 37th minute as their tussle heated up. However, our spirits were lifted when Wolves captain, Ally Robertson, was substituted within five minutes of the restart. We wondered whether this would help our strikers to have more of a look in. But Streete rose above his considerable stature to breach the gap.

'Shortly after half-time, Steve Davis met Deakin's free-kick but his header was directed straight at Mark Kendall in the Wolves' goal. It was dead ball situations which would win this day. Wolves' second goal in the 51st minute came from a free-kick, leaving us merely fighting for pride. Dennison slotted it neatly into the left-hand corner with Pearce nowhere. Wolves fans went wild. After the game, Wolves' manager Graham Turner told the journalists that Dennison had been practising free-kicks all week and making a mess of each one. He said he had considered instructing him not to take any in this game. If only he had!

'Burnley refused to lie down. On the hour, Steve Taylor finally had a good chance to open Burnley's account but his header, from McGrory's cross, cleared the bar. Shortly afterwards, Leighton James came on for McGrory and immediately turned the clock back with some sparkling wing play. Oghani provided a superb cross for Comstive on 62 minutes, but his header clipped the top of the bar. Then Andy Thompson cleared off the line in the 67th minute from Comstive after James had set up the midfielder. As the game drew to a close, Oghani and Comstive had further opportunities but so did Wolves on the break with Mutch and Bull very close to adding to their lead. Oghani ran valiantly and Comstive drove forward from midfield but the killer touch was lacking. Looking back, Wolves were in a different class.'

Ian Britton remarked:

'Coming out in front of that huge crowd gave me goose bumps. It was a terrific day. Everyone enjoyed the occasion. There was no trouble at all. It was such a friendly affair. We were disappointed to lose, of course. Admittedly, Wolves were a very strong side. They scored a brilliant goal from a free kick, but we helped them by conceding a soft opening goal from a corner that should not have been given. We also missed a number of good chances in the second half, largely set up by Leighton James' brilliant wing play. We weren't downcast, though. A year before the club was on the brink of extinction. We had come a long way in a short time.'

The *Daily Telegraph* correspondent wrote:

'It's not every day that two Fourth Division teams emerge as a greater box office draw than an England international.'

The *Times* reporter added:

> 'Burnley's spirit was undimmed and they played a full part in an enjoyable spectacle. They deserved better reward in the second half when Leighton James came on to offer a nostalgic reminder of happier days at Burnley.'

On their return to Burnley, 5,000 people lined the streets in heavy rain to hail their team's efforts. Chants of 'We'll support you ever more' roared out from everywhere. The town's team had lost but the club had redeemed itself. Never has that chant been made with greater sincerity. Captain, Ray Deakin said:

> 'I felt more emotional when we reached the Cat's Whiskers' roundabout than when I stepped out at Wembley. With the rain and the fact, we lost, I thought who would have blamed them if they hadn't turned up. But the fans are superb. They never cease to amaze us.'

Chairman, Frank Teasdale remarked on it being a moving occasion. He added:

> 'The fans are unbelievable – we never thought they would turn out in such numbers. Their behaviour at Wembley was a credit to everyone and this is a wonderful way to round off a great weekend for the club.
>
> 'John Gilbraith, the club's main sponsor agreed saying: 'The players did Burnley proud. This is once again a family club and it wasn't for some time.'

The Sherpa Van competition netted over £150,000 for the club, creating an overall £210,000 profit for the season before tax. Director Clive Holt remarked: 'The money from that Wembley final helped keep the club going for several years after.'

When asked whether he would have preferred promotion from the Fourth Division to a Sherpa Van final at Wembley, Brian Miller replied:

> 'In some ways, yes, but what really matters is the long-term future of the club and, if I'm totally honest, I would have to say that Wembley could be better for us. If you're going to move up from one division to another you must be ready for it. There's no point in going up to come straight down again. I'm not saying that would have happened to

Burnley but I know deep down we need to be stronger for the Third Division.

'As it is, our profit from Wembley should enable me to go out and buy three or four new players in the summer; the type of players who can help us to become genuine promotion contenders... Don't forget, this club nearly died. It was almost the end. Fortunately, I could bring in eight new players to make sure we didn't get ourselves into that situation again...

'Burnley may have survived the drama of a penalty shoot-out against Halifax to squeeze into the Northern Final, but we were at Wembley on merit. In the decider against Preston we only managed a draw at home and everybody thought Preston were going to Wembley. But we won 3-1 at Deepdale... We sold all our tickets and I can't tell you what it's like to see Burnley alive and buzzing again!'

1988 – 1991
'Claret Blues'

'Domino Dancing'

HOPES were high at the start of the ensuing season. The average Turf Moor league attendance had doubled during the 1987/88 campaign to 6,281, emphatically reversing a four-year decline. The coffers had expanded, not only with the substantial Wembley booty, but also with season ticket sales doubling. The club were therefore delighted to announce a £210,000 annual profit, its first in over a decade. And to cap it all, the bookies backed Burnley to win the Fourth Division championship. Brian Miller's restrained response was: 'That's very flattering... Hopefully that confidence will rub off on us.' Not all Burnley fans shared this confidence, though, some rebuking Frank Teasdale for not splashing out more on new players, although Miller was awarded a new two-year contract.

Recognising the need for team strengthening, the Burnley board permitted Miller to bring in three 'free' signings before the 1988/89 season started: 21-year-old striker, Brendan O'Connell, from Exeter; 26-year-old midfielder, Paul Atkinson from Oldham, who had once commanded a £175,000 transfer fee; and experienced 31-year-old midfielder, Gary Rowell, formerly with Sunderland and Carlisle.

But the team's poor showing in the pre-season Lancs Manx Cup did little to satisfy the critics. Burnley were defeated by Preston and Blackburn at home and by 10-man Blackpool away, causing Miller to reproach his players' lack of focus and poor finishing. Nevertheless, the Clarets started the new season strongly, topping the Division by early September having beaten Rochdale 2-1 at home, defeating Halifax 2-1 at the Shay and, most impressively, thrashing York 6-0 at Turf Moor. As autumn approached, Burnley remained promotion bound, making light of a 2-0 defeat at Torquay, with successive home wins over Colchester (2-0), Rotherham (1-0), and Exeter (3-0), which restored them to pole position on 8 October.

Miller was purring. Commenting on the Rotherham victory he enthused:

> 'Games don't come any tougher than that on Tuesday when we kept our 100% home record while ending Rotherham's away run of three successive wins. And what a great sight it was to see a crowd of 9,283. It was easily the best in the Fourth Division this season, and beat the 7,510 figure for our opening game against Rochdale. With Steve Davis ruled out because of injury and skipper Ray Deakin still out of action, our options were reduced, but Peter Zelem came in, after missing much of the previous season through injury, and performed magnificently. I was so proud of the way our team battled against such confident opponents.'

Also, the current League Cup champions, Luton, were held to a 1-1 draw in the first leg of a Littlewoods Cup tie at Kenilworth Road. While the First Division side prevailed in the home leg, albeit by a solitary goal, a Turf Moor crowd of 14,036 fans witnessed a highly competitive performance by the Clarets. Miller concluded: 'I thought our football over the two legs with Luton was as good as any we have played this season.' Then came a rude awakening at Peterborough where Burnley lost 0-3. Miller commented: 'It all went wrong at London Road. Posh went through our midfield too often and too easily. After seven attempts in 23 years we are still trying to achieve our first win over them. Having five key men out of action did not help, but hopefully our injury situation will soon improve.'

Frank Teasdale reacted by loosening the purse strings, allowing Miller to sign Colchester's pacey wide-man, Winston White, for a £17,500 fee. White made his debut in the top-of-the-table home clash with Leyton Orient on the 22 October. Although two goals down after an hour's play, Burnley recovered well to earn a point. Leading goal scorer, Brendan O'Connell levelled in the 70th minute after Comstive had coolly dispatched a penalty.

A 0-0 draw at Carlisle was then followed by a comfortable 2-0 home win over Cambridge United, with goals from Oghani and O'Connell, lifting the Clarets back into top spot at the end of October. This was as good as it got, though, as five out of the next seven league games were lost with the other two games resulting in disappointing 0-0 draws. Chester also eliminated Burnley from the FA Cup at the first hurdle (0-1). Miller strove hard to arrest the slide, adding Cambridge right-back, Ian Measham, to his squad following the loss of Peter Daniel, to injury.

Measham was thrilled to join Burnley saying:

> 'The size of the club and its support were much bigger than Cambridge, although I will always be grateful to them for giving me the opportunity to play League football. I enjoyed my two years there, but when I signed for Burnley I knew I was joining a real football club... I started my career at Huddersfield as a right winger but I seemed to spend most of my time tackling the opposing winger. The Huddersfield coaches spotted this and I was quickly converted into a right full back.'

With Burnley often laborious in attack, Measham's foraging speed along the right flank was a welcome shot in the arm.

Ex-Claret, Villa and England star, Tony Morley, was also drafted in on a short-term loan from West Bromwich to inject further zest into the attack. But he was a pallid imitation of the tricky, tearaway winger who had helped Aston Villa win the First Division in 1981, and the European Cup a year later. He lasted for five games.

It seemed as if Miller's team was no longer capable of breaking down sides who defended doggedly, and counter-attacked swiftly. White had pace in abundance but tended to interrupt his forward momentum by running around in circles, vainly seeking a killer pass. As Christmas approached the fans' early season optimism had soured. The gate for the abject 0-0 home draw with Hartlepool on December 3rd was just 6,289, representing a 3,000 fall from that for the splendid 'blood and guts' tussle with Rotherham in early October.

Christmas was overshadowed by the horrific disasters at Lockerbie and Clapham. The Boxing Day fixture at Turf Moor did little to lift the Clarets' solemn mood. An aspiring, vibrant Wrexham side came, saw and ultimately conquered with disdainful ease, winning 3-1. Future Burnley forward, Kevin 'Rooster' Russell was the star of the show, heading Wrexham's opening goal and dumbfounding his opponents with twinkling footwork, sinuous movement and crisp passing.

To add to Burnley's woes, the game was marred by crowd disorder. The match officials complained that they had been abused and spat at by home 'fans' in the Cricket Field stand as they left the field. A notice was placed in the match day programme for the following game warning anyone exhibiting such anti-social behaviour would have their stand membership cancelled immediately.

Despite national concern about football crowd disorder, Burnley MP Peter Pike and three other local MPs, voiced their opposition to the introduction of a compulsory membership scheme. They argued that the scheme would do nothing to prevent hooliganism outside football grounds, while imposing ruinous bureaucratic costs upon smaller clubs, and penalising law-abiding citizens. They criticised this measure as a scatter-gun attempt to curb the misbehaviour of a tiny minority. Ultimately, common-sense prevailed and the Thatcher Government ditched the scheme.

Back on the pitch, George Oghani scrambled an 88th minute goal to defeat ultra-defensive Grimsby on New Year's Eve (1-0), but after a subsequent loss at Tranmere on the 2 January 1989, Miller fell upon his sword, announcing: 'It is the right time for me, it is the right time for the club and it is the right time for the fans who, I believe, wanted it this way.'

Sixteen years later, former managing director, Derek Gill provided this testimony:

> 'Brian Miller served the club long and faithfully to the best of his ability beginning as a player who gained England honours and subsequently in every imaginable post, culminating in the uneasy crown reserved for the manager... Brian had much to offer and his integrity was as unquestionable as his real love for Burnley... He was such a nice and friendly guy that he would go to great lengths to avoid internal confrontations, probably being too loyal to his staff when ruthlessness was needed. When rattled, though, his pent-up anger could suddenly explode. I was not sure whether he could control it very successfully.'

Frank Teasdale dismissed a bid made by Graham White, the Colne Dynamos owner, to takeover Burnley FC, describing it as a 'laughable proposal.' He then enticed Frank Casper back to Turf Moor to replace Miller as manager, just as had happened in January 1983. Before Teasdale's call, Casper had been assisting Martin Dobson at Bury, helping guide the Shakers to promotion to Division Three in 1985.

Meanwhile, Miller, the supreme loyalist, became Burnley's Chief Scout.

Frank Casper wrote in the Burnley match day programme for the Halifax game:

> 'It came right out of the blue when the Burnley chairman and his directors said they wanted to see me last Monday, 9 January. And now, here I am, back at Turf Moor which has so many happy memories for me as a player, and, yes, in an earlier spell as assistant manager and then caretaker manager just over five years ago... It is a great feeling to be back here at Turf Moor and I am delighted to have Brian Miller in our team in a new role for him as chief scout. It is a position which is vital to any club and I wish Brian every success in it. I have spent about five happy years with Bury... It is a nice club but it has not got the following this club has... Despite the disappointments this club has had over the past two months, I believe we still have a chance of going up... If we all pull together we have every chance. LET'S GO!'

Derek Gill thought Frank Casper's coaching skills were stronger than his managerial capability. He remarked:

> 'Frank Casper is the perfect example of the coach who should never be called a manager... He had seen his playing career cut down in vicious circumstances just as he was reaching his peak, and international honours should have been his... Whilst I can sympathise and to an extent understand it, I cannot describe him as other than bitter, as one shocking foul act had taken away his playing career, decimated his wage packet and seen the culprit escape scot free and even gain England recognition. It was such a pity but Frank did seem to carry a chip on his shoulder for some time... But to me at least, Frank Casper was a coach par excellence..."

By way of an illustration, Derek Gill told Burnley author, Phil Whalley:

> 'Before the Milk Cup semi-final with Liverpool in 1983, Frank Casper generously shared with me his game plan for the first leg at Anfield. As I sat watching in the stands I was astonished to see how effectively this plan was working

against such mighty opponents. Frank had observed how slow Graeme Souness had been in tracking back in previous games, and therefore instructed Derek Scott, our attacking midfielder, to exploit the gap this left. Doing as he was bid, Scott twice found himself one-on-one with Bruce Grobbelaar, the Liverpool keeper. Alas, he squandered both opportunities. But the plan was brilliantly devised, if disappointingly executed.'

Club historian, Ray Simpson, commented:

'I'm not sure whether Frank Casper was a better coach than a manager because in those days they had to be both… But when Frank Casper returned as Burnley manager in January 1989, I had the sense that he was delighted to be back at the club where he had "arrived" as player in 1967, after signing from Second Division Rotherham. He gave me the impression that this was where he felt he belonged, where he felt truly comfortable.'

Frank Casper started well enough. Having been given a warm reception at the start of his first game against Halifax, Burnley played with renewed zest, immediately swarming all over their reeling opponents, and taking a two-goal lead. However, Halifax fought back determinedly, and but for a phenomenal save by Pearce, would have certainly left with a point. After the game, Frank Casper ordered his players to undergo a series of physical exercises. It wasn't clear whether this was a 'warm down' or a punishment for a slack second half display.

His appointment of Michael Docherty, a former Burnley team-mate, as his head coach gave a clue for he said:

'I am sure Mick is going to be a great asset to the club. He is a disciplinarian and he will, I am sure, get the very best out of any player under his guidance… So, we've got a backroom team of ex-Clarets who are determined to contribute a lot of hard work into putting this club right again.'

Although Burnley lost 1-2 at Rochdale, they beat both Stockport and Torquay by 1-0, raising hopes of a late promotion bid. However, the previous malaise returned after the Clarets blew an early two-goal lead at Colchester (2-2). They were subsequently thrashed 3-0 at Exeter. And after a tame 1-1 home draw with Peterborough, Burnley performed dismally at a sunny Brisbane Road on 4 March, losing 0-3. Here player-coach Leighton James played as sweeper.

The following home game against Scunthorpe was partially covered in a Channel Four TV documentary entitled 'Claret Blues'. It was difficult to understand the club's reasons for participating in such a shoddy production, unless it was a naïve attempt to keep pace with the MTV generation. All this disheartening film appeared to do was to deride the club and its frustrated fans.

Other than devoting excessive footage to a fictional couple, comprising a fatuous fan named 'Dave' and his put-upon girlfriend, the film contains 'fly on the wall' sequences shot in the Burnley dressing room and pitch-side. Frank Casper is shown preparing his players immediately before the match. He is also captured while berating them at half-time and afterwards as his team slid to a demoralising 0-1 defeat. In his pre-match briefing, Casper stated that promotion was possible, but at the end of the game, the subject was sullenly dropped. It was clear from the brief match action and the close-ups of the fans' exasperated expressions, that the game was a stinker, settled with a soft far post header.

Frank Casper is portrayed as surly and stressed, angrily pushing aside a truculent fan who confronted him. At the ensuing press conference, he distanced himself from this disappointing performance. Meanwhile, the fictional 'Dave' caricatured Burnley fans as dim losers with flat caps and inflatable bananas.

Long-standing Clarets' supporter, Tony Scholes, recalled:

> 'I was in that film. I wished I hadn't been. I thought, we all thought, that Channel Four were intending to make a serious documentary about the club and its supporters. We were horrified with what they produced.'

Ian Britton said:

> 'I liked Frank Casper. He and his assistant Mick Docherty were prepared to join in the fun with us and share a laugh, especially when we were taken away for a few days' break, but Frank was strictly professional when it was time to knuckle down in readiness for the next game. It was always clear then who was boss. Frank never minced his words, being as direct with his opinions as he was as a player.'

Sadly, the Channel Four film failed to do justice to Ian's estimation of him.

When Hereford arrived at Turf Moor on 1 April Burnley were facing a possible reprise of 1987. Supporter chants of 'Sack the Board' grew in intensity both inside and outside the ground. Gates were continuing to fall to around 5,500. Meanwhile, with Colne Dynamos pressing hard for a Conference place, their chief, Graham White made a further takeover bid but this was also rejected.

Casper's programme notes for Hereford game were evidently framed to draw the disgruntled fans' fire. He wrote:

> 'As you are all aware now, our search for a new face or two to boost our playing staff before the transfer deadline was not successful. Not, as I have said before, because we didn't try hard enough, or that our board of directors were not prepared to give me money to spend on the right type of player, but simply because the whole system, just before the March limit for signing players, seems to have changed completely from a few years ago... We have found clubs asking silly money for players who are probably coming to the end of their contracts, and at the end of the season will be available at a reasonable fee fixed by tribunal...'

While George Oghani left the club in April 1989 after a regrettable training ground incident involving goalkeeper, Chris Pearce, Neil Grewcock made a welcome return after a 12-month absence due to injury. But he was unable to prevent three successive defeats which left Burnley in 17th position, six places above the drop zone. Belatedly, Burnley rediscovered the knack of scoring goals. On 29 April, Doncaster were beaten 3-0 at Turf Moor with a brace from O'Connell and then Lincoln were defeated 3-2 at Sincil Bank on Bank Holiday Monday, Burnley's first away victory since the 3 September. Despite humiliating defeats in their final games, at Crewe (0-4) and at home to Scarborough (0-1), safety was duly secured, albeit in sixteenth place, six rungs below their 1987/88 position. Although the average home gate rose to 7,062, this was largely on the back of the team's promising start. There was little cause for cheer, but what happened at Hillsborough, on 15 April, put these concerns into perspective, leaving deeper misgivings about the entire British game.

In June 1989, Ian Britton bade farewell to the club he had helped save. He later commented:

> 'The 1988/89 season was my last at Burnley. I thought it was possibly my best for the club. However, Frank Casper

told me at the end of the season that much as he wanted me to stay, there was not enough money to extend my contract. Although disappointed, I had no hard feelings. I enjoyed my time at Burnley. After leaving the club, I remained in the Burnley area. I did not want to go back to my native city of Dundee or to any other part of Scotland. I liked Burnley and felt at home here. The country around is so beautiful.'

Frank Casper recruited five new players during the long, hot summer of 1989. In came: the versatile 24-year-old Roger Eli, from Northwich Victoria, on a 'free'; Peter Mumby, a 20-year-old striker or midfielder from Leeds, also on a 'free'; John Deary, an experienced, combative, box-to-box midfielder from Blackpool for £30,000; Tony Hancock, a promising 20-year-old striker from Stockport for £50,000; and midfielder or full back, Joe Jakub, who was a free agent, too. Jakub had played 42 games for Burnley during the late seventies and early eighties, before joining Bury and Chester. Crucially, Casper persuaded his existing utility player, Andy Farrell, to stay. Farrell would play an important part in Burnley's later promotion successes.

John Deary explained the reasons for his move to Burnley thus:

'I had been at Blackpool for 10 years and I felt ready for a change. Blackpool manager, Jimmy Mullen offered a contract and a testimonial but Frank Casper's assistant, Mick Docherty, persuaded me to have a look at Burnley. Mick had previously been coaching at Blackpool. When I met Frank Casper and Mick at Turf Moor, I liked what they had to say but the clinching moment was when I walked out onto the Turf. I decided to sign there and then. I had a feeling that this was a right move and wanted to be part of taking the team forward.'

Frustratingly, the 1989/90 season panned out in a similar vein to the one before. A dismal opening day defeat at Rochdale (1-2) was followed by a turgid 0-0 home draw with Stockport, watched by 6,537 unimpressed fans. Much to their surprise, though, Burnley then embarked upon an eight-match unbeaten run. The 1-0 victory at Chesterfield on September 2nd, which kick-started their revival was accompanied by ironic chants of 'Teasdale in!'

Goal-scoring was still a problem for Burnley, despite winning five, drawing three and losing only one of their opening nine league games, a run of form which lifted the Clarets into the play-off places. A barren phase ensued, interrupted by a solitary 3-2 win, at Doncaster. This prompted Casper to sign the nomadic, veteran striker, Ron Futcher. Futcher's goals helped Burnley progress to the Third Round of the FA Cup for the first time since 1985, and re-ignite promotion hopes. But his impact was diluted by his side's lack of pace. The brief upturn in form, over Christmas and New Year, coincided with the arrival of loan-signing, Junior Bent, Huddersfield's ultra-fast, goal-scoring winger. In a reciprocal deal, Burnley's misfiring striker, Brendan O'Connell, went to Leeds Road. In March 1990, O'Connell moved on to Barnsley for £45,000. Here, he made a successful transition to a midfield role. George Oghani spoke well of O'Connell, his former striking partner:

> 'I know the fans got onto him after a while, but there was no criticism of him in the dressing room. I can assure you of that. He did an important job for the team. The fans might not have seen that but we did.'

Having had two takeover bids snubbed, Colne supremo, Graham White, offered the Burnley board £1m in exchange for a ground-sharing deal. Almost simultaneously, a wealthy Burnley shareholder demanded that 35,000 un-issued shares should go on sale at £30 each. With the prospect of a £2m windfall, Frank Teasdale allowed Frank Casper to buy John Francis, a lightning quick striker from Sheffield United for £90,000, having accepted £50,000 from Preston for the goal-less Tony Hancock. Neither a cash windfall nor an improvement in form came about, though. The season fizzled out with Burnley no better off, mired once more in sixteenth place. Demonstrations re-commenced outside Turf Moor with up to 500 fans calling for the heads of the board members and the manager.

Frank Teasdale confronted his critics combatively, stating: 'We understand patience has been sorely tested but we will not succumb to the foul abuse hurled at us by an uninformed and disruptive minority.' He maintained that during his time in charge, the club's stability had been improved but recognised that the team had not progressed as well as had been hoped, with continuity badly hampered by a succession of significant injuries. Frank Casper stood firmly alongside his embattled chairman, stating: 'It takes a couple of years to sort out who you want at the club and who you don't want. We have got those we don't want out and in the next 12 months we will be sorted completely.'

While the Burnley board and manager exhorted patience, this did little to assuage the fans frustrations at an apparent lack of progress. One disgruntled London Claret who typically travels around 20,000 miles each season in support of his team, penned the following entries in his diary.

19 August 1989, Rochdale, away (1-2): 'A good day is spoilt by the football. Still the Cemetery Arms was good.'

11 November 1989, Scunthorpe, away (0-3): 'Eli gives arguably the worst performance of central defending I have ever witnessed.'

22 November 1989, Stockport, away, FA Cup (2-1): 'Wonders never cease. The Clarets score an FA Cup goal in open play. After countless attempts, I have finally seen Joe Jakub play well.'

26 December 1989, Carlisle, home (2-1): 'My brother earns a gold star for driving me to the best performance of the season. He earns another by driving us home again.'

6 January, Blackpool 1990, away, FA Cup (0-1): 'Third Round day and Burnley are actually in the cup. The bad news is that they adopt a depressingly defensive attitude and are sunk by a late goal.'

13 January 1990, Stockport, away (1-3): 'The Clarets surrender a goal lead with just 15 minutes left.'

20 January 1990, Rochdale, home (0-1): 'Despite the opposition being down to nine men we still manage to lose. It's enough to turn you to drink.'

20 March 1990, Hartlepool, away (0-3): 'A nightmare. With no trains available, I am forced onto the National Express. The overnight coach is full, with some people talking all the way to London. The heaters are on full blast. Absolute hell! The team gives a pathetic display.'

24 March 1990, Peterborough, away (1-4): 'Even Chris Pearce joins in the dross giving his worst performance in the annual destruction at Peterborough. After the game, I consider giving up altogether but feel much better after a session in the Boys Arms. The Burnley supporters again demonstrate against Frank Casper who later derides them as not being proper Burnley supporters. If that's so, what the hell were they doing there, Frank?'

31 March 1990, Doncaster, home (0-1): 'David Jones, hitherto the worst ever Burnley player, comes back to haunt us, scoring the winning goal.'

10 April 1990, Southend, home (0-0): 'Despite Southend having a player sent off after just 15 minutes, the Clarets hang on for a goal-less draw. It is the seventh goal-less draw this season. Hardly the stuff to drag supporters out.'

24 April 1990, Halifax, away (0-0): 'Chris Pearce earns us a point
at Halifax in front of only 2,556 people. Jason Hardy misses two
sitters and then suffers the embarrassment of assuming he is being
substituted. To his horror and ours he finds he must complete the
match. Frank Casper smiles contemptuously at the supporters. We
do help to pay your wages, Frank!'

1 May 1990, Exeter, away (1-2): 'We run a night trip to the rearranged match at Exeter and sit in rabid jealousy as the Grecians
are presented with the Fourth Division championship trophy. We
lose although John Francis did put us in front. The train home is
not until 2am so we kill time in an Indian restaurant much to the
disgust of the staff.'

5th May 1990, Colchester, away (2-1): 'The season comes to an end
with a victory at doomed Colchester. The whole season has been a
shambles. The best part has been the camaraderie of the support,
not just from Clarets' fans but those I met from other clubs.'

Burnley's average home attendance figure during the 1989/90 season
was 6,222, 12 per cent lower than that for the previous season. It
seemed as if the post 'Orient' revival had slipped into reverse.

Roger Eli, a versatile player, recruited by Frank Casper in the
summer of 1989, has happier recollections of this season, though. In
his book '*Thanks for the Memories*', written jointly with Dave Thomas,
he said:

> 'After scoring two goals in the 5-0 FA Cup win over
> Scunthorpe in December, for the first time ever I'd heard
> a crowd chanting my name. Roars of 'Eli, Eli, Eli,' rolled
> down from the Turf Moor terraces... With mass chanting
> like that I felt like a gladiator.
>
> 'Commercial manager, Joyce Pickles had Roger Eli T
> shirts produced. I still have one. "Clarets secret weapon" it
> says on the front. But the picture of me is so unflattering.
> I looked like a criminal...
>
> 'I didn't want the Eli chants to stop. Supporters don't
> grumble at players who always give 100%. I saw supporters
> who were passionate. It was the least I could do to show it
> myself... When the offer came of a new contract, despite
> the troubles [the fans' angry demonstrations], I signed.
> I'd played 30 games, the fans had taken to me, I'd struck
> up a good partnership with Ron Futcher up front, but

when needed, I could play anywhere… I never liked the description "utility player". It was almost demeaning…

'Chairman, Frank Teasdale got a rough ride from the supporters. He was a true Burnley supporter with claret and blue blood but took some flak for the club's demise over the years. In truth, the club had been dying since before he took over but supporters need someone to kick and in this case, it was Frank Teasdale. He had some awful stories of the abuse he suffered. Fans saw it as his fault that the club had no money… He was good company off the field but in the boardroom, he was a businessman and it always seemed to us that he had a hard streak when it came to settling players' wages.'

Frank Teasdale had another worry to contend with during the 1989/90 season – combatting the spectre of rising football hooliganism. In the 27 August 1989 match programme, Frank Teasdale declared:

'As well as the playing side, we must look also to the future of membership schemes, closed circuit television, ground safety, and everything connected with football hooliganism… With immediate effect, any person convicted of a public order offence or assault prior to, during, or after a football match will be banned from Turf Moor for life… Government measures are at present under consideration… any crowd misconduct could bring the club into disrepute with serious consequences such as heavy fines and ground closures.'

The 1990/91 season was accompanied by crises in the Gulf and the Balkans. It was the time when Margaret Thatcher was deposed amid vociferous protests over the proposed Poll Tax and internecine squabbling over Britain's place in Europe. Frank Casper's countenance began to resemble that of the under-fire Mrs Thatcher. By the end of the 1989/90 season his team was spluttering. Although still respected by his players, he had lost the confidence of many supporters. He became increasingly defensive, often bearing a haunted expression. He was not helped by the loss of Mick Docherty, his running mate, during the summer of 1990. The former full back accepted Stan Ternent's offer of an assistant manager post at Hull.

After Docherty left Turf Moor, Frank Casper chose former Blackpool boss Jimmy Mullen as his new assistant. The former

Sheffield Wednesday centre back had been dismissed at Bloomfield Road following the Tangerines' relegation to Division Four. Mullen had previously captained both Rotherham and Cardiff to promotion.

Young Burnley striker Peter Mumby was particularly sad to see Docherty depart, stating in a later interview:

> 'I loved that man. He was a terrific coach. Although recurrent injuries stopped me from establishing a regular place in the first team, Mick always had time for me and the other reserves, too. This was quite unlike Jimmy Mullen who replaced him. He had no interest in the reserve players. But it is no good being bitter and twisted about that. After all, Jimmy Mullen led Burnley to successive promotions once he took over from Frank Casper in 1991.'

Although Frank's teams too often flattered to deceive, his signings of Steve Davis Mark II, Ron Futcher, John Deary, Steve Harper, Roger Eli, John Francis, Joe Jakub and John Pender paved the way for Burnley's subsequent promotions in 1992 and 1994. 'Captain Fantastic', John Pender, was signed from Bristol City for £70,000. He had previously been a stalwart central defender with Wolves and Charlton. He was a key member of the Molineux side which won promotion to the First Division in 1983. Pender was physically and mentally strong, commanding, and very consistent. He also chipped in with crucial goals, mostly headed efforts from set plays, such was his aerial dominance at both ends of the pitch.

The performances shown by Casper's team in 1990/91 were much more to the liking of Burnley supporters. London Claret Andy Waterworth observed:

> 'The Clarets' football has had greater purpose, greater aggression especially in midfield and, most of all, now displays more variety and imagination than in previous seasons. The home victories over Halifax (2-1) and Cardiff (2-0) were clear examples of this in which they overcame first half frustrations and, by maintaining their shape and good football, they eventually succeeded. Last year that would not have happened.
>
> 'John Pender has proved an excellent buy and added a lot of strength and composure to the defence. John Deary has run himself daft in all the games I've seen. He has formed a good partnership with White and Jakub, and importantly,

scored a few goals. John Francis has added steadiness to his speed and power. He is now looking a first-rate striker. Ron Futcher doesn't deserve all the stick he gets, particularly given his strong hold-up play and excellent strike rate [he scored 25 goals in 52 league starts in his two seasons at Burnley]. But he seems too slow [Futcher was affectionately known as 'Rocket Ron'] and with his niggling attitude, he appears in danger of being sent off. The other doubt concerns Burnley's away form. It would help if they stopped handing their opponents an early three-goal lead.'

Despite their various away dazes, in late March and early April, Burnley put their disappointing away form behind them, winning at Scarborough (1-0), Scunthorpe (3-1), and Aldershot (2-1) and putting themselves in with a great chance of automatic promotion. However, a woeful 0-1 defeat by Maidstone at Dartford put paid to that, not helped by Futcher's dismissal. Despite accumulating 79 points – a tally that was usually sufficient to guarantee promotion – Burnley were left with the lottery of a play-off place which meant contesting a two-legged semi-final with Torquay.

In his book, Roger Eli recalled:

'[Before the first game at Plainmoor] we were on the coach waiting impatiently for Frank Casper. Jimmy Mullen had remained in his seat with more than a few wondering: "Should he not be going in to find the boss?" Some of the players were becoming quite angry at both the delay and Jimmy Mullen's disinclination to find him. As the directors, too, began to ask each other what was happening, Frank finally appeared. He looked ill. That never happened before. It was out of character. We felt protective... He dashed through the doors of the hotel and hauled himself up the steps of the coach before taking his seat and telling the driver to leave. This produced a strange atmosphere on the coach. The Board members looked a little bemused; the players were taken aback and exchanged puzzled looks across the aisles. [Midfielder] David Hamilton was cursing under his breath at the delay. It was not exactly the best start to the afternoon and left us in a strange mind-set... We lost the game 2-0. The fans and the reports say that we were dreadful in that game. That was down to us, the players. But why were we so poor?'

London Claret, Ian Wood, offered his view on what happened in a piece written for their magazine, *'Something to Write Home About'*. He stated:

'What transpired at Torquay could only be said to bring shame on Burnley Football Club. With Futcher suspended, Casper decided to leave out winger, Neil Grewcock, and include Ray Deakin, out of position, in a sort of central midfield position. Within five minutes we were behind. Pearce made "a nonsense" of coming for a long throw and Dean Edwards swept home. Bookings mounted as both sides indulged in some nasty challenges that produced bad feeling. The longer the game continued at 1-0, the more defensively the Clarets played. Time wasting had been the order of the day from the first minute. The Clarets got what they deserved when Matt Elliott's shot trickled home with seven minutes left (0-2).'

Current director, Clive Holt added:

'Because Torquay could only grant us a few hundred tickets, we decided to beam television coverage of the game to a large screen set up at Turf Moor. But when I saw Frank Casper follow his team out onto the pitch, I feared for our chances. He didn't look as if he was in the right frame of mind to lead the club in such an important game.'

Roger Eli continued:

'On the way back to Burnley, as ever the knee was swollen [It was a niggling injury which would eventually bring his career to a premature close]. The knee was tender and throbbed all the way home along mile after mile of featureless motorway. We talked about winning at Turf Moor but mostly we were down and quiet; we knew full well we'd played badly. A bit of management-inspired geeing-up before the game might have helped. Remember the Al Pacino speech in that American football film "Any Given Sunday"? These things work in a dressing room. But there was nothing that set us in the right frame... If Frank Casper was ill why did Jimmy not step in? It seemed to us no-one was steering the ship.

'Burnley battered Torquay in the second game. How they held out we'll never know. Even the goal Burnley scored in the final minute was an own goal... [Torquay had] two unbeatable centre halves who dealt with most things. One was Matt Elliott who went on to have a fantastic career with Leicester City. We trudged off at the end so disappointed, heads down, shoulders slumped... It was also the game when Blackburn Rovers supporters hired a small plane to fly over Turf Moor. [It trailed a banner which read] "Staying down 4ever, luv Rovers, ha, ha, ha."

'Frank Casper was someone I had a massive regard for. He was instructive. He'd stop a practice game and tell you how to do things, where to go, how to make a run. He and Eddie Gray [formerly of Leeds and Scotland] had several similarities. Frank was the manager who had faith in my ability in whichever position he played me. He was a top-quality coach and for me was a big loss to the game when he turned his back on football and was replaced by Jimmy Mullen later in that year. He was the sort of boss you could talk to when you needed to, or share an opinion with. Some of the abuse he endured was downright vicious and cruel. These are people that do their best and being a manager means sticking your head above the parapet. That takes guts. Frank felt enormous pressure from success-starved fans. It got to us, too.

'Jimmy Mullen was different. His coaching and tactics were simple. He never over-complicated things. He was helped that he didn't have to experience the screams of abuse that Frank Casper endured. But Mullen was someone I never really took to. He had the managerial ability to win two promotions. You can't take that away from him but in the dressing room, he wasn't well liked with his brash and sometimes intimidating manner. Maybe they're qualities a manager needs to be successful; the ability not to get too close to players, to be distant, ruthless and impersonal. But we were wary of him. There was a groundswell of opinion in the dressing room that Mullen wanted Casper's job. That's football you say and shrug it off. There's always someone who wants the boss's job and thinks they can do better.'

For the time being however, embattled Burnley chairman Frank Teasdale retained faith in Frank Casper, allowing him a further season to make good what was narrowly missed in the 1990/91 season.

As for the FA Cup and Leyland DAF Trophy competitions, these featured promising performances but disappointing exits. For Burnley progressed to the third round of the FA Cup, having seen off non-league Stafford Rangers (3-1) and Third Division, Stoke City (2-0) but then appeared to lose their nerve against First Division Manchester City when an upset seemed possible. Colin Hendry's goal settled the tie. As for the Leyland DAF Trophy, Burnley's early progress suggested another Wembley appearance might be feasible before they encountered a vengeful Preston at Deepdale (1-6). At least the Manchester City home defeat secured a lucrative pay day, with 20,331 supporters attending. This was the largest Turf Moor crowd since the 1983 sixth round, FA Cup tie with Sheffield Wednesday which was watched by 23,184 people. Burnley's Ground Director, Bernard Rothwell, deserved great credit for securing an improved capacity, after tight restrictions were imposed in accordance with the Taylor Report, which followed the 1989 Hillsborough disaster.

Bernard Rothwell proudly explained:

'The Licensing Authority, Lancashire County Council, reduced the capacity on our Safety Certificate to 13,301. Some may have said that, with an average gate of around 7,000, this was acceptable. The revised figure was not acceptable to the Board, though. We were determined to get the ground capacity restored to a more realistic level. Turf Moor gates were rising once more. The average home gate for League games had reached 7,882, 27 per cent higher than during the 1989/90 season. My job as Ground Director was to secure a licence allowing a higher capacity. The packed stands and terraces surrounding you, now, are clear evidence of what we have done.

'Since July we have spent more than £50,000 on ground improvements, giving us a new capacity of 20,900. The increase has come from raising the Cricket Field Stand capacity from 1,280 to 4,200 – the final increase of 600 was approved just last week. The permitted size of the home section on the Longside terrace was lifted from 3,360 to 4,750, while that on the Beehole terrace was raised from 3,000 to 6,000... There is much more to do: a new police box, new gents toilets, additional turnstiles... We are constantly striving to make our ground suitable and safer in the higher leagues...'

1992 – 1994

'Jimmy Mullen's claret and blue army'

'Things Can Only Get Better'

MUCH to Eli's and Mullen's disappointment, Ron Futcher moved on, having failed to agree a new contract. Roger described Futcher as 'a real professional with an exceptional knowledge of football.' Eli remembered Futcher's exasperation at the service he received from some team mates, yelling, 'To feet, f***ing feet!'. Roger said:

> 'Ron had been brought up with the right coaching and playing values at Manchester City. He had a real passion for the game and taught me the art of finishing. On the pitch, we'd look out for one another. We had many scraps with opposing defenders. We'd take it in turns to leave an elbow in when challenging for a ball. If one of us took a hit, the other would sort out the offender. Ron could moan for England but he was a joker too, with forthright views about how the game should be played, often being the first to say, "That's not right" to Casper and Jimmy Mullen.'

But in pacey Scottish striker, Mike Conroy, Casper found an improved model. Conroy had lost his mojo at Reading and had been wastefully assigned a full back role. His transfer fee of £35,000 represented a snip as Conroy powered Burnley to promotion with 24 goals in 38 league starts. Similarly, Steve Davis, who moved to Barnsley for a £180,000 fee, was replaced by a better Steve Davis Mk II, a bargain £60,000 signing from Southampton. The identically-named defenders had briefly played together for Burnley, prompting the memorable chant: 'There are only two Steve Davises!' Steve Davis Mk II's centre back partnership with John Pender provided the lynchpin in Burnley's spectacular rise between 1991 and 1994.

However, this was just a pipe dream as Burnley and Rotherham United met one another at Millmoor in the opening fixture. Rotherham, like Burnley, was a town of lost industrial prowess. London Claret Ian Wood reported lugubriously:

> 'Pre-season results hardly inspired confidence. A dour defensive performance was to be expected, with new signing, Steve Davis Mk II operating as sweeper. Most of the team played so deep that goalkeeper Chris Pearce had plenty of company. The negativity became more marked after one of the new boys, Mike Conroy, stabbed in John Francis's pass late in the first half. Eventually a lack of fitness took its toll as the Millers pounded the Burnley goal, with two goals in the last 20 minutes proving decisive. Davis was the best Claret on display, but another ultra-defensive performance brought back bad memories of last season. I was able to visit five pubs in the town, the pick of which was the Kingfisher serving Old Mill Bitter. Splendid!'

Hapless Aldershot were beaten easily at Turf Moor. They had only seven months left before being wound-up. Wigan ended Burnley's interest in the League Cup, winning 6-3 on aggregate. Then, on 31 August, came a startling change of fortune as the Clarets won 4-1 at Doncaster without playing as well as the result suggested. Ian Wood explained:

> 'With 20 minutes to go and the score at 1-1, it seemed another frustrating afternoon was in store. This was despite the dismissal of Doncaster's, Billy Whitehurst, a legendary hard man, on the stroke of half-time after giving as bad a rendition of centre half play as it is possible to see. Then, as if by magic, Casper awoke from the dug-out, and brought on fleet-footed left winger, Steve Harper, a recent

free signing from Preston. Clearly needed much earlier, Harper dismantled what was left of the Doncaster defence. Another new signing, Mark Yates, a £40,000 midfielder from Birmingham City, scored a fine individual goal, while goalkeeper, Andy Marriott, a loan acquisition from Nottingham Forest, made the first of 15 highly impressive performances.'

With Mike Conroy and Roger Eli looking good up front, Chesterfield were then turned over at the Turf (3-0) with Eli netting a hat-trick, Burnley's first since 1985. High-riding Crewe proved to be a tougher nut to crack, though, despite the dismissal of ex-Claret, Ron Futcher (1-1). Whereupon the run ended abruptly, with the next three games lost, the 1-3 defeat by 10-man Scarborough being the worst of the three. Five days later Frank Casper resigned, leaving his assistant, Jimmy Mullen in temporary charge. The match day programme for the ensuing home game against Carlisle contained Frank Casper's last words and his chairman's testimony.

Frank Casper wrote:

> 'I thought the performance at Scarborough last weekend was the worst I have seen since coming back to Turf Moor. It is a mystery to me why things should have turned so sour after such a promising start, but things will come good… very soon. I know the players train properly and I know the team is good enough to mount a serious promotion bid… but once they cross the white line and get into action, it's up to them and there's nothing more I can do for them.
>
> 'I could make excuses by saying the side has been badly hit by injuries and suspensions. We had first choice players like Mike Conroy, John Francis, David Hamilton and Steve Harper missing last week. Having so many key players out certainly unsettles the team and other players sometimes lose their rhythm when regular partners are missing. But the team we fielded on Saturday should certainly have been good enough to beat Scarborough, and the players know my feelings about how they performed.'

Having accepted Casper's resignation, Frank Teasdale stated:

> 'Our manager, Frank Casper tendered his resignation on the 3rd October. He feels, after careful consideration of this position and recent team performances, that it is

time for him to step down. Having met with him at his request to discuss the situation, we accept that he has made this difficult decision with the best interests of the club in mind. Although things have not gone right on the pitch over the past weeks, there can be no doubt that our professional squad, youth squad and scouting policy have been strengthened during his time at the club. The game must go on as they say, Jimmy Mullen knows the score and will take charge of Saturday's game versus Carlisle United. Hopefully our fans will remember the good times that Frank Casper gave us as a dedicated player, and sympathise with him now he is another casualty of football's demand for success. He deserves that!'

The transformation was immediate and sensational as the next nine league games were won with some terrific performances such as the 6-2 thrashing of Wrexham at the Racehorse Ground where audacious teenager Graham Lancashire scored a hat-trick. Mullen was not required to present a CV or to attend a competitive interview. He was duly confirmed as permanent manager, also winning the Fourth Division Manager of the Month award for November.

Roger Eli remembered:

'Frank Casper called us together and told us very briefly he was leaving... He was clearly choked. He thanked us and with huge dignity wished us luck... We learned later that he'd been deeply upset by the death of a good friend, Gordon Clayton, his assistant manager in 1983... I'm pretty sure the funeral was the same week... I guess he didn't want to go the same way as his friend... He said it wasn't just the abuse he endured at Scarborough. To this day, I regret we didn't do more for Frank Casper. Footballers don't play badly on purpose or not try...

'The shape of the team was beginning to emerge. Marriott was damned good in goal. The defence, Measham, Davis, Pender and Jakub was ominously hard to beat. Andy Farrell and John Deary were skilled and competitive in midfield. Steve Harper and John Francis played wide. Up front was Mike Conroy – scoring all the time, the prodigy that was Lancashire and me, bustling, all action, head going in where it hurt, chase anything. The next games couldn't come soon enough. It was becoming a side that people wanted to watch. The average home attendance for league games rose by 33 per cent to 10,521, the best at Turf Moor since the mid-seventies… The dressing room was a great place to be… after every win there was jubilation; hugs, high fives, shouting, towels tossed around, huge smiles… A win is the ultimate collective high in the game. The group is everything.'

By 21 December, Burnley were top, having defeated Aldershot 2-1 in a howling gale at the Recreation Ground. Fierce promotion rivals, Mansfield, had already been beaten 3-2 at Turf Moor in a pulsating, cut and thrust display of full pelt football. Mullen's rejuvenated side seemed unstoppable. Even a late Northampton equaliser at the County Ground, was instantly brushed away with a ruthless, lightning counter-attack, led by the speedy Harper and finished decisively by Conroy, to the uncontained joy of the many leaping Clarets behind the goal.

Despite Burnley's surge to the top, Jimmy Mullen did not rest on his laurels, bringing in reinforcements such as gifted, attacking midfielder, Adrian Randall, for £40,000, from subsiding Aldershot, and Robbie Painter a wide midfielder, from financially troubled Maidstone for £25,000. Both played important supporting roles during the run-in to the championship.

Chants of 'Jimmy Mullen's Claret and Blue Army' were bellowed incessantly wherever Burnley played. No longer harangued for his supposed failings, Frank Teasdale basked contentedly in the beaming adulation his club now received. Even when paired with Second Division, Derby in a third round FA Cup tie, Mullen's side rose admirably to the occasion, rattling their stronger opponents with the intensity of their attacking play. Burnley gained a deserved replay after Roger Eli powered a bullet header past Peter Shilton in the Rams' goal. The replay featured one of the proudest displays of support ever witnessed in the English game.

Over 4,000 Clarets' fans descended upon the Baseball Ground for the replay, initially in vain, as fog caused an abandonment. Undeterred, they tried again, providing one of the loudest, sustained dins ever encountered by the watching journalists. The Clarets' fans' hollering of 'Jimmy Mullen's Claret and Blue Army' was as deafening as it was relentless. Over and over they bawled the refrain, on and on they clapped and stamped, pounding the advertising hoardings with percussive power. Undaunted by Chris Pearce's catastrophic blunder, their chanting became even louder, their defiance more intense. The game was lost but not in their hearts. The bedlam persisted, past the final whistle and for 15 minutes afterwards. These fervent fans were not to be subdued.

Burnley historian, Ray Simpson remarked:

> 'How can I forget that FA Cup-tie with Derby in 1992. After a drawn game at Turf Moor we were losing the replay at Derby until the fog rolled in, causing the Burnley fans to chant: 'C'mon You Fog!' Absolutely hilarious! And when the game was re-arranged, there was the incessant chanting of 'Jimmy Mullen's "Claret and Blue Army". It continued throughout the second half and for 15 minutes or so after the game. I'd never heard the like before. It gave me goosebumps to be part of that passionate support.'

As journalist John Sadler put it:

> 'I wanted others to hear and see this. Big men, important men who are making important decisions that could alienate the game from ordinary working folk. I wanted Graham Kelly to be there to prove to him that those who talk of Super Leagues should not underestimate the passion of so-called little clubs... I urged the club's chairman to get his manager and players to return to the pitch and wave their appreciation.
>
> 'These were real fans; genuine football people with a deep love of their club, no matter the result of a single game. They had nothing to do with the executive box brigade and corporate hospitality merchants to whom football is pandering in the modern era.'

Manager Jimmy Mullen gasped: 'In all my 23 years in the game I've never witnessed anything like that. It left my players feeling they were prepared to die for those people.' Derby won the tie, but the Clarets' fans won the plaudits.

With copious praises heaped upon him, Mullen modestly attributed his team's success to a mere tweaking of Casper's tactics. London Claret, Dave Parker, took issue with this, commenting: 'The team was unrecognisable from that run by Frank Casper. It had pace, power and an indomitable desire to attack whether playing at home or away.'

Right back, Ian Measham agreed, reflecting:

'Brian Miller and Frank Casper liked to play football the Burnley way, that is, a passing game, building progressively from the back and playing through the lines. Jimmy was more direct. He realised that to get out of the lower divisions, it was necessary to get the ball out of defence quickly and hit opposing defences at their thinnest. He wanted us to play more in our opponents' final third of the pitch. Of course, you need very swift players to play that way and in Francis, Harper, Conroy, Eli and Lancashire we had some of the quickest around.' Ian was no slouch, either, when breaking from defence.

Presenting the case for the defence, Steve Davis added:

'John Pender was the best player I played with during my long career at Burnley which spanned three divisions. He was a great leader and man. We complemented each other so well and enjoyed two promotions together. He was a skipper who led by example.'

Roger Eli identified John Deary as an important box-to-box midfielder who was also a battling ball-winner. Roger remembered an iconic picture of Deary snarling over a fallen Bryan Robson who was hardly a shrinking violet.

'John had everything and the fans loved him and what he brought to the team; bravery, physical toughness, the team mate you'd want next to you in a real scrap.'

In turn, Deary complimented Andy Farrell, his central midfield partner. Both were often forced to battle against greater numbers when Burnley's 4-4-2 formation morphed into 4-2-4. Deary said:

'The player I connected with most was Andy Farrell. I could rely on him to be there when I was out of position or needed help. We always supported each other and worked well as a unit but we had our falling outs too. I remember "Faz" once winning a terrific header in the middle of the park. I went ballistic with him. He looked bewildered why I was giving him so much grief.

So, I told him straight that he had strayed onto my side of the pitch, telling him to "eff-off" to his side. He was really pissed off with me, refusing to discuss the subject as we walked off at half-time. I finally got him really riled leading him to tell me to "eff-off" too. We both laughed about it after the game, though.

'That 1991/92 team made up the best dressing room I have ever known. It could be mental at times, a real mad house. You couldn't discuss anything without around 15 players demanding a right of say, screaming and shouting their point of view all at the same time. Although we had some seasoned, hard pros there among us who hated to back down, arguing their point for all they were worth, I cannot remember any serious falling out. Most of the time we accepted it when we were in the wrong. But that was hard because you would never hear the last of it... The pre-season trip to Russia had brought us closer together. Mind you, it was grim. There wasn't much food and we became dehydrated in the 40-degree heat. We lost a stone or so there. It wasn't an ideal preparation for the new season, leaving us a bit jaded, but the bonding that took place there, made us into the successful team that we were to become.'

Mullen biggest headache was finding a reliable goalkeeper after Marriott returned to Forest at the end of November. Having lost form and confidence, Pearce became persona non-grata for much of the season, restricted to brief filling in turns. Short-term replacement, Mark Kendall, proved no better. He was at fault for at least two of the goals Burnley conceded in a heavy defeat at promotion rivals, Blackpool (2-5). Third replacement, Nicky Walker, was patently a gifted keeper, but was recalled to Hearts after just six appearances. And yet Burnley lost only five of their 35 league games under Mullen, winning 23 and drawing seven. Twice they recovered from two-goal deficits, at Walsall and Scunthorpe. The championship was duly won on a heady night at Bootham Crescent on 28 April when John Francis's late scrambled effort gave Burnley the points, promotion and the championship in front of thousands of ecstatic Clarets' fans.

London Claret, Ian Wood concluded:

'Quite simply this will go down as the season when Jimmy Mullen transformed the club from a shambles, into Fourth Division champions. Mullen was like a breath of fresh air, mostly playing an attractive, attacking style using two wide players. The forwards led by the always improving and clinical Conroy revelled in the many chances created. Eli at his marauding best was outstanding in many games,

115

Lancashire even more so, particularly during October. The wide players, Francis, Harper and latterly, Painter, delivered consistently dangerous balls, with Francis's pace a constant threat to the opposition while his lack of a good first touch was a constant threat to my blood pressure. In midfield Deary and Farrell, often outnumbered, were industrious and scored crucial goals in the closing games. Measham and Jakub were rock solid at full back, Pender equally so at the heart of the defence. We also had the opportunity to witness the excellence in goal of Andy Marriott and Nicky Walker, sadly both only on loan. Against this was the complete deterioration in the form of Chris Pearce. But most of all we had Steve Davis, arguably the best player in the division. His confidence on those long, surging runs, his strength and assurance in defence, his overall calmness under pressure made him a class act. Once again, we can be proud to be a supporter of Burnley Football Club. This is not just because we won the Fourth Division, but because we did it well and undoubtedly, we have one man more than any other to thank for this. I drink to Jimmy Mullen.'

Club historian Ray Simpson added:

'Although some found him volatile, I found Jimmy Mullen to be always warm and welcoming. He was the sort of person you would like to have as your next-door neighbour, someone to share a drink with. He was so proud that he managed to drag this famous club back into better days... There are some football managers who show very little emotion, no matter how things are going. But Jimmy Mullen isn't one of them!

'I have been watching Burnley since the 1950s, when they were one of the best teams in England and yet I rate that promotion season under Jimmy Mullen in 1991/92 as one of my favourites and most enjoyable. After the disappointments and despair, we had endured, culminating in the dark days of 1987, it was exhilarating to watch the side Jimmy Mullen fashioned, mainly from Frank Casper's signings. After that dreadful defeat at Scarborough, Jimmy Mullen guided basically the same team to nine consecutive victories, playing fast, attractive, attacking football. We went to games, home and away, expecting to win everyone. It was fantastic.

'I remember we were playing at Scunthorpe towards the end of that season. We had been losing 2-0 before their debutant goalkeeper, Chris Marples, got tangled up with Mike Conroy behind the by-line. It looked like the loan keeper threw a punch. Anyway, he was instantly dismissed. With a rookie in the home goal we got a goal back. Things then got very feisty, not helped by the Conroy incident. There was an enormous amount of added time. In fact, we were still playing just before the Sports Report jingle struck up. It was ridiculous, but thankfully there was just enough time left for Steve Davis to snatch an equaliser with a thumping header.'

The other good news was that the club made a profit of £291,250 during this promotion year, bettering that gained in the previous year by over £200,000.

At the dawn of the FA Premier League, promoted Burnley joined the Second Division of the Football League's rump. With the economy labouring and unemployment continuing to rise, civil unrest returned to the 'mean streets' of Britain during the summer of 1992, to estates in Bristol, Huddersfield, Salford, Stockton, Luton and Burnley. Once again, a lack of work, cash and hope seemed to provide the tinder, while a breakdown in family discipline and abrasive relations with the local police probably supplied the sparks. On Burnley's Stoops and Harghar Clough estates there were five consecutive nights of rioting. Here, the male unemployment figure stood at 26 per cent while youth unemployment was stuck at a dreadful 60 per cent.

By contrast, the Clarets enjoyed a season of quiet consolidation in the higher league. They began by winning the pre-season Marsden Lancashire Cup and, notwithstanding a rash of injuries to key players – Davis, Conroy, Deary, Harper, Eli and newcomers, Penney and Clayton – they proceeded to establish themselves securely in mid-table, recording notable victories over upwardly-mobile, West Bromwich (2-1), Fulham (5-2) and Chester (5-0). However, the season was not without its disappointments, notably a barren run of results in early spring.

John Francis had left surprisingly, in the summer of 1992, to join Cambridge United for a £95,000 fee, only to return on transfer deadline day, 1993, for £25,000 less. Chris Pearce, Peter Mumby, Jason Hardy,

David Hamilton and Ian Bray also departed. But in came several key signings, headed by former Stoke, Everton and Manchester City star, Adrian Heath on a 'free' transfer, and Marlon Beresford, a brilliant young goalkeeper from Sheffield Wednesday for a bargain figure of £95,000.

Edward Lee, then the *Burnley Express* Sports Editor, provided an assessment of Burnley's 'Class of 1992/93'. Here a few excerpts:

Adrian Heath:

> 'Heath scored on his debut at Stockport and simply went on scoring. He scored 20 league goals and three crackers against Sheffield United in the FA Cup. In doing so he passed 100 league goals in his illustrious career and joined a very select band of Clarets to pass 20 for a league season. Heath scored some outstanding goals. He scored with volleys. He scored with free kicks. He scored with diving headers. He scored with 20-yard chips and he scored from the penalty spot – itself an achievement for the Clarets in the 1992/93 campaign! Named as the supporters' clubs' player-of-the-season, Heath proved he had lost none of his class as he went on to record his most prolific season in goal-scoring terms. Boundless enthusiasm and unending energy made him an ideal leader of the Burnley front line.'

Marlon Beresford:

> 'During the previous season, Burnley used no fewer than five goalkeepers on their way to the Fourth Division title. The 1992/93 campaign was a completely different affair as Marlon Beresford stole the show. Signed from Sheffield Wednesday just after the start of the season, he made an excellent debut against Rotherham and went on to write his own headlines throughout the season as he made a series of breath-taking saves. Beresford, chosen by his fellow professionals as a PFA award winner and the best keeper in the Second Division, earned rave reviews wherever he went and installed himself as the best Burnley goalkeeper for three decades. A great favourite of the fans, the Lincoln-born Beresford came to Burnley to play first team football and, in doing so, took the first step up the ladder to future stardom. It would be difficult to pick his best game of the season. His debut was outstanding, his performance against

Plymouth Argyle breath-taking, and his role in a 1-1 draw at Huddersfield beyond comparison.'

John Pender:

'A skipper who led by example throughout the season. Pender simply never gave up. A two-goal hero at Plymouth in one of only four away wins, Pender continued his almost unbeatable partnership with Steve Davis for much of the season as the pair earned star billing in countless matches. Battered and bruised on more than one occasion, Pender simply refused to give in, as witnessed by everyone at Bournemouth where he was knocked unconscious, but returned to the field 10 minutes later and immediately won a header!'

Not that Jimmy Mullen's team selections necessarily won the fans' approval. Some were bemused by his lack of faith in midfielder, Adrian 'Spaceman' Randall, who appeared to possess the skills to become a class act, as emphatically demonstrated in his dominant display against table-topping Stoke in the final game of the season (1-1). Pushing forward, Randall could be unstoppable, confounding top defenders with a feint, a step-over, a sudden change of direction or a dab on the accelerator. At his focused best, Randall was a composed and well-balanced attacking midfielder with an array of raking passes, having also the deft footwork to create space around him in crowded situations. However, the former England Youth international remained an enigma – brilliant in one game, anonymous in the next. He wasn't much of a scrapper, either, particularly when the chips were down. Perhaps that's why Jimmy Mullen was initially hesitant of using him regularly. Perhaps, too, Randall didn't want it enough. When asked what his career ambitions were, he replied casually: 'to stay fit and free of injury' and when asked how he saw his future beyond football, he said with a smile: 'just relaxing.'

Arguably, Burnley's best performance of the season was against Premier League Sheffield United in the third round of the FA Cup which ended as a 2-2 draw. This followed what many Clarets considered to be a particularly satisfying round two victory over John Bond's Shrewsbury Town. Forgive and forget? Not a bit of it.

Jimmy Mullen wrote in the match day programme for the FA Cup replay against the Blades on the 12 January:

'I thought we did enough to win the original tie, and when you are two goals ahead with less than 10 minutes to go and your opponents have just hit the upright, things look to be going your way. I thought we adapted well to the conditions, and Adrian Heath showed all his experience to fire us two goals ahead in the first half. Steve Davis was unlucky not to send us three-up when his header hit the crossbar and Mick Conroy was unlucky not to be able to clinch things from the rebound – the conditions just getting the better of him. But all credit to Dave Bassett and his team. We knew they would never stop trying and that was just the case as they pulled a goal back with nine minutes to go, and snatched an equaliser with only seconds remaining. Despite the hard, icy pitch I thought both teams did everything they could to provide an entertaining match… It's nice to be back at Turf Moor after such a long break. We last played here on 12 December. It was great, too, to see so many of you at Bramall Lane and the 8,000 or so Burnley fans at the game were a great credit to the club.'

Unfortunately, Burnley had blown their chance, and in front of a 19,061 Turf Moor crowd, the eventual semi-finalists prevailed helped by a hat-trick from Brian Deane. Although the most distressing outcome of this defeat was the reckless surge by Burnley fans on the Longside that nearly resulted in the death of an 11-year-old boy. This charge followed Adrian Littlejohn's recriminatory celebrations after tucking away the Blades' fourth goal. Having suffered shameful racist abuse during the game, Littlejohn was understandably delighted to land the knock-out blow.

The other great regret of this campaign concerned the fate of Burnley cult hero, Roger Eli, who played his last first team game for the Clarets in January, having seemingly lost his battle to overcome persistent knee injuries.

London Claret, Jez Wilson, gave this tribute:

'He had a hairstyle not unlike the Jamaican chanteuse, Grace Jones, and as he ran at defenders he must have seemed nearly as frightening. The record books of the time indicate that he stood 5ft 10in tall and weighed 11st 3lbs. He certainly made the most of what he had got. Incredibly strong and with an awkward, angular gait, he was very difficult to knock off the ball and he routinely out-jumped taller defenders. He was brave and a great chaser of lost causes. His attitude rather than his natural ability saw him perform way above expectation time and time again. Burnley fans traditionally warm to a brave centre forward. I was brought up on the stories of Andy Lochhead's heroic performances against Napoli when he had a set of Italian studs scraped across his balding pate. That is why I will be eternally grateful to Roger Eli, a goal-scoring hero I can tell my kids about.'

With the average Turf Moor league attendances remaining over 10,500, and the two FA Cup third round games alone attracting 42,000 people, chairman Frank Teasdale was well satisfied. Once the club accounts for the 1992/93 season were revealed, his satisfaction was even greater as a £302,939 annual profit was announced, four per cent up on the promotion season.

In the club's official yearbook, Frank Teasdale wrote:

'Although we didn't win promotion, I am sure most fans would have to agree that the club is in good shape after a season of consolidation in the new Second Division. We knew that the challenges were going to be tough, that is why we were keen to invest in a very talented goalkeeper, Marlon Beresford, and a highly respected goal-scorer, Adrian Heath. Nobody could argue that those two players were anything but major successes, and their efforts alone earned the club headlines across the country. Later in the season we continued to strengthen the squad which seemed to be hit by injuries almost every week… It would be remiss of me to write anything about last season without mentioning our loyal supporters. We are all aware that you didn't have as much to cheer about as in the previous season, but everywhere we went you turned out in great numbers to cheer the lads on. Once again, thank you for your support.'

And yet some fans had grown impatient. The Burnley board of directors were once again accused of having 'insufficient ambition'. Such was the pressure exerted by these criticisms that Jimmy Mullen and Frank Teasdale set out their positions in the *Burnley Express*.

In a joint article entitled 'Please Show Patience', Jimmy explained:

'It has come to my attention, through rumour on the terraces and whispers around the town, that my professional ambition may lie away from Turf Moor, having supposedly not received support from my directors.

To those concerned, my ambition and desire to succeed at this club has not altered from the day I arrived, and I repeat it is an honour to manage Burnley Football Club.

'Supporters will have disappointments during the season, as I and my players do. Unfortunately, this disappointment has surfaced from the assumption that new faces with large price tags have not been introduced through a lack of finance from the directors. The reason why no "big names" have joined our dressing room is simple [Didn't Adrian Heath count?]. I will not introduce players to Burnley Football Club who would not contribute fully to the cause and more importantly, I will not allow this club to pay excessive amounts of money for such players.

'From the day I arrived, the support that this club has provided, through its chairman, Mr Frank Teasdale, and his fellow directors, is beyond belief. On a personal note, gentlemen, I wish to say a very big thank you.

'The directors' philosophy at Turf Moor is simple – "the manager manages all football affairs". On no occasion during my time here have I had to question that view. As a player, and now as a manager, I require from my colleagues two things: LOYALTY and PATIENCE.

'About "loyalty", at the beginning of the new season we arrived in the Football League Second Division as Champions of the 'old' Fourth Division and, may I add, achieved this with some style. These players were applauded for their efforts and achievements, and in return they deserve our loyalty and an opportunity to play at a higher level.

'Regarding "patience", very few teams achieve successive graduations to "premier status", but those who spring to mind such as Carlisle have suffered similar downward trends, a result of not having made a sound base to build a team from as progress is made.

'Team building is an ongoing process with no simple solutions. Money will not necessarily provide the answer to the team building programme I have in mind. Patience is a requirement that I now ask for and is so important to Burnley Football Club and its continued success. Expressed vocal dissatisfaction proves counter-productive with the players beginning to take note more of the crowd noise than my own instructions.

'With the support and encouragement of Mr Teasdale and his fellow directors I see no reason to look towards pastures new. We as a club are moving in the direction we and every Claret supporter wishes to see and with the same loyalty you, the supporters, have shown over the years. I look towards a long and distinguished association with Burnley Football Club.'

Frank Teasdale then added his view, stating:

'Once again we find ourselves criticised for a lack of ambition. It has been clearly stated at every possible opportunity that our manager governs all aspects of team management. This obviously includes team selection and all transfer activities in and out.

'There is also a suggestion that Jimmy Mullen will get disgruntled with a lack of finances from the board. This is totally unjustified and could not be further from the truth. Jimmy Mullen has publicly stated that he knows what the job entails and is not prepared to spend money for the sake of spending, which would prove counter-productive from the club's point of view.

'Everyone connected with the Football Club wants success and I would ask each and every one who supports the Clarets to be patient, allowing Jimmy Mullen to get on with the job. He has our confidence. Let him have yours.'

Frank Teasdale, his board of directors and club manager might have thought that, having achieved a glorious promotion, they would be spared such cantankerous carping at least in the immediate aftermath of that triumph.

But the editor of one Burnley fanzine was unimpressed with this criticism of the fans, feeling it smacked of 'the pot calling the kettle black'. He remarked:

'Jimmy is starting to experience crowd frustration... He doesn't realise that the Burnley crowd is not renowned for its patience and that his histrionics week in, week out, on the bench (sorry, off the bench), are similar to the frustrations we show. Three wins from the last 12 games in March and April tell their own story. Wasted words Jim, I think. Time for Frank Teasdale to tell Mr Mullen to calm down methinks...

'A lot has been made in the press that we are not spending lots of dosh to strengthen the team... But in addition to the signing of Beresford for £95,000 and Heath, Paul Wilson has been bought from Halifax for £90,000 to replace Joe Jakub. Now the priorities seem to be to find a midfield schemer... The failure of Heath and Conroy to strike up any sort of understanding may be due to a lack of creativity in midfield...

'My own view is that the accounts are not as rosy as people seem to think [He was wrong.] Teasdale gets a lot of stick but it must be recognised that the directors are not multi-millionaires and that they are seriously attempting to build this club up again. If you know anyone with pots of money who wants to help, then I am sure the Board would be very interested... Plans for an all-seater stadium at Turf Moor have now been announced and for the first time, and after the crowd surge at the Sheffield United Cup tie, I am not completely against it. The injury to the little lad made me think: "Thank God he has fully recovered".'

Nevertheless, it seemed as if Jimmy Mullen could no longer count upon the unanimous approbation of the Burnley fans. Despite improving his squad in readiness for the 1993/94 season, adding: goal-scoring Blackpool wide man, David Eyres for £90,000; creative striker, Kevin 'Rooster' Russell for £150,000, and battling midfielder, Warren Joyce also for £150,000, his call for patience was ignored by the sceptical tendency. Their doubt then turned into discontent as three popular players: Mike Conroy, Steve Harper and Ian Measham were allowed to leave.

Ian Measham recalled:

'My departure from Burnley was entirely down to the new contract I was offered. I thought I was worth more than they did. Doncaster really wanted me to play for them and offered Burnley £40,000 to let me move to them. I guess their enthusiasm persuaded me to think it was time for a change. I have no grudge against Burnley. I still look out for their results. Their fans were terrific and I will always remember with fondness the many letters of support I received from them after sustaining a serious neck injury in one game. Besides having five good years at Turf Moor, capped by that brilliant promotion season, my family and I had 10 fantastic years living in the town. Part of my heart belongs there. Both of our children were born there, too. I will make sure they never forget their roots.'

In an interview held with London Claret, Brent Whittam, just after his £85,000 move to Preston in August 1993, Mike Conroy said:

'I didn't want to leave Turf Moor... There was no animosity between me and the Burnley management, although Jimmy Mullen was quoted as saying some things in the press which were not true. Certainly, in the two years I was there, I had a good relationship with Jimmy. Sometimes I feel he could've done more for me regarding a new contract... Look, if someone is asking you to take a pay cut and someone else is giving you a considerable rise, what would you or anyone else do? The sheer professionalism of Preston under John Beck impressed me. Working for him has given me a new outlook and everything you hear about him isn't always correct. [John Beck gained notoriety because of his apparently ruthless use of the 'long-ball game'.] Plus, I didn't have to leave the Burnley area... However, had the deal not gone through it might have been difficult for the Burnley management but not for me. I knew I would be in the side sooner or later. I would have been where I wanted to be but would I have been where the club wanted me to be?'

In response to a question concerning his disappointing goal scoring record in 1992/93 – seven goals in 38 league starts – Mike replied:

'Strikers are never happy. I could have had 35 the previous year. I am not one for excuses. The team didn't do as well, so strikers don't do as well. Many times, I found myself crossing instead of being in the middle. 'Inchy' Heath had never scored twenty goals before and I'd like to think I had a big hand in him getting that amount. Injuries and suspension didn't help but obviously I was sick, but that's football...

'In the year before, if I missed a chance I knew I'd get another. I can't say the same last year... There were a lot of crosses that didn't come in to me when I was centrally placed or went behind the goal. Besides, you can't be crossing balls, heading balls down and scoring at the same time. I'd like to look at every game and find out how many chances I had; you'll find not that many... Every goal gives me immense pleasure, even in training. I remember every single goal of my career. It's difficult to single any one out as my best, although I enjoyed scoring the winner in an FA Cup tie against Shrewsbury, John Bond and all. Then there was the goal against Cardiff in 1992 which gave me 20 goals for the season, the first Burnley player to do that in 27 years.'

Mike Conroy also told a local journalist:

'I look upon the North West as my second home. It was great. There is only one side that can compete with the loyalty of the Turf Moor support and they're Scottish. The Burnley supporters are very passionate about the game and it is an honour to have played for such support and such a club... I loved living in the town and made a lot of friends.'

The pre-season chuntering was dispelled quickly after an impressive home victory over much-fancied Port Vale. All three new signings excelled, with Warren Joyce scoring both of Burnley's goals in a 2-1 win. The football glittered as much as the scintillating sunshine. The slick exchange between Heath and Joyce for the first goal was top-drawer football. Although visiting Leyton Orient were then out-classed by Burnley's fluency (4-1), the Clarets' first three away games, at Reading, Rotherham and Bournemouth were all lost, with the dismal 0-1 defeat at Dean Court possibly their worst performance under Jimmy Mullen. Not even a dazzling display at Premier League Spurs, which ended with Burnley's undeserved elimination from the Coca-Cola Cup, could prompt a better run of league results on the road.

London Claret Dave Parker summarized the schizoid pattern when he wrote:

'The contrast between home and away performances has been startling; at home, confidence abounds, the ball is passed to feet, space is found, with wonderful crosses and superb goals. Away, there is no space, long balls are hoofed out of defence to 'Rooster', John Francis and 'Inchy' Heath, and the opposing strikers are allowed glaring gaps.'

Try as he might, Jimmy Mullen failed to find a solution. Even as late as 19 March 1994, he was still spitting tacks at Burnley's away failures, the latest of which had occurred at relegation-bound Fulham. Here, Burnley had surrendered a 2-1 interval lead, to lose 3-2. Jimmy Mullen could barely contain his frustration, exclaiming:

> 'Sorry to repeat myself, but it was yet another case where the Clarets had taken over the game, only to let it go. It's much, much more than simply disappointing to see this kind of thing happening repeatedly. Annoying, frustrating, downright ludicrous? You find the words! All I know is that it is very hard to bear. It seems to be that every goal we score away from home, we have to work damn hard to achieve. On the other hand, opponents are able to pick up easy goals from our mistakes.'

Burnley supporter, Peter Toner opined:

> 'I personally think Mr. Mullen should shoulder the blame. He seems unable to find a formula for winning away. He locks the players in, shouts at them, but picks the same team, no matter how badly they play. When we defend, the forwards become too detached from the midfield and the defence is too deep. Consequently, the midfield becomes isolated. Most home teams pack their midfield, and just charge through. We cannot play 4-2-4 home and away and not go out to attack… If we don't then we may as well change to 4-3-3, as we are left with two wingers who do not reinforce the midfield.'

And yet, despite their continuing shortcomings on the road by New Year, Burnley were in 4th position with a good chance of making the play-offs, primarily because of their excellent home form. London Claret Dave Parker gave this mid-season review:

> 'Up front the players seem to be taking it in turn to have superb spells. John Francis has been outstanding recently, as in turn have David Eyres, Adrian Heath and Kevin Russell. In the middle of the park, things seem quite solid, although I feel Adrian Randall has been somewhat unlucky to lose his place.
>
> His form while Warren Joyce was injured earmarked him for a longer run, at least to this observer. Marlon Beresford continues to inspire in goal. He has now clocked up five penalty saves for Burnley and has often made

crucial saves at vital moments. Which leaves us with the back four. Davis and Pender seem close to their best again, and Les Thompson at left back must be the most improved player in the Division if not the League. The worrying position to most fans is right back. Central defender, Mark Monington, has filled the vacancy left by Ian Measham's transfer and has undoubtedly done his best. To me and others, though, he does not look to be a full back, and on several occasions, has missed tackles or been caught out of position. This has now been added to by his two recent sending offs. It's time for either a signing or for bringing in one of the youngsters.'

In an interview with Phil Whalley and Karen Neill, Burnley's star striker, David Eyres commented:

'When we played at home it was almost a foregone conclusion that we would win, but away from home for some reason we couldn't get a draw, never mind a win. However right up until the final month we still felt that we were good enough to go straight up. Our away form, cost us, though, as we slipped down to sixth.'

To plug the gap at right back, Jimmy opted for experience, bringing in Bolton's Gary Parkinson for £80,000. He became a crowd favourite, noted for his strong tackling, astute covering and superb distribution. A glorious destiny awaited him at Wembley. With Kevin Russell leaving, in a £125,000 deal, for Bournemouth because of domestic issues, Mullen signed much-travelled striker, Tony Philliskirk, from Peterborough and veteran Scottish winger, Ted McMinn. While McMinn lacked pace, he had hypnotic ball skills, also possessing lethal crossing and set-play acumen.

Burnley's poor away record comprised just four victories, six draws and 13 losses. This was worse than that of relegated Fulham. Only one point was taken from their visits to the four demoted clubs, and yet Burnley's home form was the best in the Division. The 55 points won at home, an 80 per cent success rate, enabled Burnley to squeeze into the final play-off place, 12 points behind Plymouth their semi-final opponents. While Burnley were crumbling to a 1-4 defeat at already relegated Exeter, in the final game of the season, Peter Shilton's Plymouth were thrashing Hartlepool 8-1 at the Victoria ground. Their semi-final looked a lost cause.

The first leg was played on a damp, grey, cold Sunday afternoon on 15 May 1994. It was an abrasive, attritional game in which Burnley were fortunate to remain unscathed in terms of goals conceded and injury. Despite the dismissal of Plymouth's Adrian Burrows, the huge travelling support were sure their side would prevail, bellowing repeatedly: 'We'll score in a minute!' Dwight Marshall had the opportunity to vindicate their faith after breaking through, and finding himself one-on-one with Beresford. However, disconcerted by the Burnley keeper's dash from goal, Marshall screwed his shot wide. Unabashed, the Pilgrims' fans chanted: 'We only need 10 men!' Certainly, their depleted team scrapped for everything, targeting Burnley's danger man, McMinn, for rough treatment.

At Home Park, Jimmy Mullen had no need to motivate his team. David Eyres told Phil Whalley and Karen Neill:

> 'We got one of the local papers down there and stuck it on the wall before we went out. It was saying that Plymouth had sold 40,000 preliminary tickets for the final and that they had booked all the local coaches to travel to Wembley… And the way they celebrated when they came out onto the pitch, it was like treating the game as a little warm-up for Wembley. We thought: "Right, we'll show you!" We were determined to spoil their party.'

The monkey chants then directed at John Francis only sharpened their resolve. Despite taking an early lead, Plymouth were undone by Francis's pace and power. He quickly turned the game on its head, twice bursting through Plymouth's ranks to slot the ball past their advancing keeper. Francis celebrated his first goal with a recriminatory ape-like gesture, before being engulfed by his exultant team mates. His second, however, was greeted with a partying gesture, a sinuous wiggle followed by a bark of delight. The Home Park racists had their bile stuffed down their throats. Burnley duly wrapped up the game just before the close. McMinn punished Plymouth for their brutal treatment of him at Turf Moor by sweeping past two home defenders and taking a pot shot, leaving Plymouth 'old boy', Warren Joyce, to bury Nicholls' resultant spill. Joyce shook his fist at the Plymouth fans who had berated him.

Four years later, Warwick University lecturer, Lincoln Allison interviewed Home Park hero, John Francis, together with Roger Eli. Allison was interested to hear of their experience of racism, particularly in football. Francis said he hadn't encountered much of this while growing up in Morley, although aware of it sometimes in Leeds centre.

However, he recalled being hit by a banana when he made his debut for Halifax at Darlington. He said:

> 'The centre half kicked me calling me a "black bastard". I was intimidated by the thought of all those people hating me. It affected my game quite badly. It got so that if a marking defender didn't call me a black bastard for the first half hour, but eventually did, I'd say "Oh, you've noticed at last." At Plymouth, the crowd were making monkey noises to me even though they'd got two black players... On the other hand, I got off to a good start after signing for Burnley. Here, once they consider you as part of the family, race is forgotten. One night I went into a pub in Burnley and everybody started singing "Super Johnny Francis". They seemed to keep it up for ever. It was very embarrassing. You don't know what to do...'

Roger Eli added:

> 'When I was a 17-year-old apprentice at Leeds they had the most racist element you could possibly imagine. They did Nazi-style salutes in unison and direct monkey chants at black players with a passion. I was on £25 a week at the time and would spend around £15 of that on taxis to avoid meeting them at the bus station... Like John, though, the Burnley fans seemed to take to me straightaway... I hardly went out at night in Burnley, not because of the racism but because the adulation was so embarrassing.'

Both John and Roger agreed that despite improvements brought about by initiatives such as the 'Kick It Out' campaign, racism was still prominent in the game, even during the late nineties. John cited an incident in a junior game where a black Burnley player was subjected to a torrent of racial abuse by an opponent. Although the opposing coach took the offender off, he restored him later in the game. While acknowledging the growing number of black players, Roger referred to the paucity of black administrators and managers. Almost 20 years later, that deficit remains.

Sadly, for John Francis, the Plymouth game was his last taste of glory. At Wembley, he sustained a severe injury, early in the game, which curtailed his remaining career. Roger was released at the end of this promotion season. He complained of being excluded by Jimmy Mullen, despite recovering from his knee injury.

While their memories of Burnley's success at Wembley are tinged with regret, Burnley fans remember this day with unalloyed joy. London Claret Andrew Firmin wrote:

> 'I had insisted upon club shop Wembley crap as a birthday gift and I was now wearing a new scarf and (oh dear) a rosette. My only excuse was that this was a special day. The Wembley song formed the other part of my spectacularly tasteless present. It was terrible, but I had suspended my normally clinical musical judgement and was playing it to death. Both sides. We gave it a last spin before we set off along with The Fall's "Kicker Conspiracy".
>
> 'The tube was full of Clarets. My stomach started to churn with the regularity of a washing machine. Then we stepped out of the train and saw Wembley in the distance. So, what? It's a crappy, clapped-out Empire relic. What made the hairs on my arms stand on end was what was between. Everyone described it as a sea of claret and blue and I see no reason to differ. We stopped a moment to look and remember. I won't forget it. This is a great club we support.'

David Eyres remembered:

> 'The preparations couldn't have been better. We went down south a couple of days beforehand. We had the best of everything, a fantastic hotel, we even had a game of golf. We prepared as if we were Manchester United. It made us feel like top Premier League players. We knew the atmosphere would be great with 40,000 Burnley fans there. It was just unbelievable though. It still gives me goose pimples watching the video.'

Andrew Firmin continued:

> 'Inside the ground we sat high, looking down on a pitch bathed in sunshine. At least our £24 had bought us a reasonable view. We had over 30,000 seats there and looked magnificent. Stockport had a smattering, spread thinly around the seats in the opposite corner. The team then stepped out dressed entirely in claret. We roared.
>
> 'With less than two minutes gone we made a shoddy show of defending and went a goal down. A free kick close

to the corner yielded a truly terrible cross, but fortunately for Stockport it was met by even worse defending. The marking disappeared and Chris Beaumont scored with a free header. Such was our numerical superiority, Wembley fell still. You could almost see the confidence evaporating. Was it going to be like any old away game, after all?'

David Eyres' version of this event was:

'We were all given a man to pick up and the man who scored was mine! I was disappointed at that. I marked the space at the near post rather than the man, so if I'd done my job properly I would have probably stopped that cross coming in. It was sickening going a goal down but the lads came back well.'

Andrew Firmin observed:

'After that, we were shaky with the normally reliable pairing of Davis and Pender looking vulnerable and Beresford showing his nerves at every cross. This was when it started to get physical. As in the first leg against Plymouth, Stockport were paying Heath and McMinn the considerable compliment of kicking them every time they had the ball. We were awarded a string of free kicks, as the game stopped more than it started. Less than half of the first 20 minutes was taken up with football. Perhaps if the referee had started booking people it might have calmed down.

'It hinged on the sending offs, of course. That was Stockport's gripe. Their grievances really started when John Francis wasn't sent off for a wild challenge but, as he was the one on the stretcher, we hardly benefitted, particularly as we were forced to tear up our game plan. But when their bloke got sent off all hell broke loose.

'McMinn went down the right wing, was body checked by Michael Wallace, and as he lay on the floor, appeared to be kicked. We later found he was spat at. After Wallace's dismissal people started to sense the tide might turn. We gradually asserted ourselves and it started to look like a more even game. Francis's substitution enabled Andy Farrell, club stalwart and sole survivor of Wembley '88 to get a game, which was fitting.

'After 29 minutes, the great David Eyres picked up the ball to the right of the Stockport penalty area. He ran across the box, beat one man, beat the next, beat a third, shot with his left foot and the ball flew into the back of the net. My powers of description take me no further. It was magnificent. The place erupted. At the time, it seemed as if no finer goal had been scored at Wembley.'

David Eyres confided to Phil Whalley and Karen Neill:

'I probably wouldn't have been in that position to pick the ball up, but John Francis was injured early on and the gaffer pushed me up front and I played as a spare front man alongside 'Inchy'. I picked up the ball on the right-hand side. I wouldn't have been on that side if John Francis had been on. It was just one of those tricks that I had always done, feint to shoot and cut inside, go past a couple of players and then get a good strike on goal. When it hit the back of the net, I headed straight for the Burnley fans at the other end who just went up. I'm getting goosies now talking about it. It was fantastic! I think it was the first time I had cried on a pitch! It could have been an even better day. I went around the goalkeeper but it had fallen on the leg I only stand on – my right... Then I had a header against the bar. I could have had a hat-trick.'

Andrew Firmin recalled:

'In the second half we started on top. Our next goal seemed imminent. Heath messed up a good chance when clean through and Eyres again went close. The second sending off offence occurred while Eyres was chasing a ball down the left wing. It seemed a mile from the action and everyone missed it except the linesman. Apparently, Beaumont had stamped on Thompson, who could have retaliated or allowed justice to take its course. Rather surprisingly, he chose the latter. The Stockport supporters went crazy at Beaumont's dismissal, blaming the referee for their decimated team rather than their own unruly players.

'After that we thought we were bound to win, trying to forget that we had lost against nine men before. The pressure mounted on the Stockport goal. Joyce was put through with only the goalkeeper to beat. He took aim.

We rose. But he shot wide, bringing about the hands-on-head thing, the universal gesture of an agonising miss. Still Burnley piled it on. It was the clearest indication of the space that was then available that Parkinson should have scored the crucial goal. Having provided the overlap for Eyres, he was then surprised to find himself in the box with only the keeper to beat. He panicked, tried to control the ball, failed, saw it running away from him and poked at it, hoping for the best. The keeper who'd had a good game until then, dived, got a hand to the ball, but it somehow eluded him, bouncing off at an angle before rolling into the net. The record told me this happened in the 66th minute.

'The place went mad. Parkinson, a man possessed, ran to the Burnley hordes, hurdling the anti-hooligan moat at a single leap. Throwing himself at the fence he was embraced by the delirious crowd. Chaos, joy, then I looked at my watch. There was an age to go. Just assume at this point I am looking at my watch at least twice per sentence.

'Now Stockport started to attack. We have never looked comfortable playing against Kevin Francis and we started to give away free kicks. They brought Andy Preece on, whom I feared, but thankfully he wasn't fit. Jim Gannon then missed two excellent chances before giving way to David Miller, who, of course, has Claret and Blue blood in his veins.

'Stockport had at least two other clear-cut chances. We had more. David Eyres hit the bar for the second time. Every time the ball went out of play we thought it must be the end. We actually played about eight minutes of stoppage time. It seemed longer. The whistling kept going for more than 10 minutes. Then, right at the end, Steve Davis picked up the ball deep in his half and started running. He beat most of the remaining Stockport players as he ran down the middle, cool and oblivious to everything. We all stood sensing something special. He just kept going. An easy pass would have made a certain third but he decided to shoot. What a goal this would have been. Sadly, he remembered he was a defender and scuffed his shot, sending the ball hopelessly wide.

'David Miller got a final kick just as the referee blew for time. Bedlam ensued. There were the familiar celebrations, the laps of honour, the bouncing team photo calls, the medal presentations, the donation of scarves and hats and the trophy head balancing. For any other team, it would seem corny. Not for us, though. We don't get as much of this as we deserve. The rest was all hugging and some tears. There is no point going on. If you weren't there you'll just have to regret it for the rest of your life.'

Frank Teasdale said:

'Winning promotion twice in three seasons is tremendous progress for a club that has spent such a long time in the doldrums. As a Board of Directors, we always believed that things would go our way in the end – and to win the play-off final at Wembley was just the icing on the cake for us.

'To win the final means that we are now right back at the business end in football. The ground will have to be transformed with full houses becoming a regular feature as some big-name clubs come to town. It promises to be a very exciting period in the history of the club and a period in which we all will have to come to terms with some major changes. We must convert Turf Moor into an all-seater stadium while making sure the manager has the right players to meet the new challenges. It's a time when we will need your full support – and I'm sure we'll get it.'

Frank Teasdale must have been pleased by the rising home attendances. The figure for 1993/94 was 11,327, an annual rise of seven per cent. However, a 29% rise in employee costs took the total outlay to £1.2m, contributing to an annual operating loss of £16,518 before tax, compared to a £219,546 profit in the previous season.

But not all Burnley directors were sure that Jimmy Mullen was the man to take the club forward. Clive Holt said:

'During the 1991/92 season, Jimmy Mullen's infectious enthusiasm seemed to spur the team on as we deservedly took the Fourth Division title. However, after Jimmy had guided his side to a further promotion, two years later, I became worried whether he, like Frank Casper before him, was losing his grip. A chance remark made by one of his senior players, Adrian Heath, gave me cause for concern. Heath had spent most of his career playing at the highest level. So, when he said to me, following Burnley's success at Wembley, "We went up despite Jimmy", I began to wonder how we might fare under Mullen in a much more challenging second tier.'

Unlike Eli and Heath, David Eyres had no doubts about Jimmy Mullen's worth. He told Phil Whalley and Karen Neill:

'He's unique, Jimmy. I'll always be indebted to him, the fact that he brought me into professional football at Blackpool and improved my game. I couldn't speak too highly of him. He had the same team talk. He made you feel like you were a top player. He never really talked about the opposition. He just encouraged you to go out and express yourself, have the confidence to believe in what you can do and you'll win the game comfortably. He didn't really say a lot. He motivated you by making you feel you were a lot better than the team you were playing. He did snap sometimes, which he had every right to do because we did have a few poor games. I thought he was a top manager.'

Vindicated by the Wembley triumph, Jimmy remained unchallengeable for another eight months, but thereafter, the doubts about his management returned.

1995 – 1998

'Burnley were back'

'Bang and Blame'

THE Burnley board certainly did not leave their manager short of funds for team strengthening. For Jimmy Mullen was granted an unprecedented £1.3m 'war chest' for incoming transfers. The disparaged John Bond received only a third as much. Even if the £240,000 worth of outgoing moves are considered, Mullen was backed with over £1m of new money as he sought to keep his team in the second tier of English football. Unfortunately, his various forays into the transfer market met with limited success. Had Mullen managed to recruit a robust, yet creative midfielder, such as ex-Liverpool and Republic of Ireland star, Ronnie Whelan, who joined fellow strugglers, Southend, and a free-scoring striker, such as Aston Villa's Guy Whittingham or Barnsley's Andy Payton, feasible additions, perhaps, given the resources at his disposal, Burnley might well have survived. For despite impressing with their attractive play, Mullen's Clarets often lacked a cutting edge. Apart from emphatic home wins against Sheffield United (4-2), Southend (5-1) and Derby (3-1), goals were at a premium all season.

Ex-Bury forward, Liam Robinson, epitomised the lack of penetration up front. Robinson was signed from Bristol City in July 1994, for a then club record fee of £250,000. Given Robinson's successful career at Bury, where he had scored 89 goals in 248 league starts, Jimmy Mullen thought he was the bustling goalscorer Burnley needed, notwithstanding Robinson's poor return at Ashton Gate, where he netted only four times in 31 Division One starts. Some Burnley fans speculated that Mullen had gone in search of Bristol City's powerhouse target man, Wayne Allison, but had been palmed off with Robinson. Perhaps it should have come as no surprise when Robinson struggled up front, despite working his socks off. He would jointly comprise a Heath-Robinson strike force, remarkable for its lack of stature, for Robinson was only five-foot seven inches tall while Heath was an inch shorter.

Although sturdily built, Robinson had neither the skill nor the physical presence, particularly in the air, to trouble most First Division defences. Admittedly, he scored the winning goals in each of Burnley's notable victories at Luton (1-0), Millwall (3-2) and Charlton (2-1), during an encouraging autumn interlude, but these strikes were either fortuitous, as at the New Den, or laid on a plate by a colleague's pass. In general, his finishing lacked precision and composure. Having slid in a late fifth goal against Southend on 31 December, he managed just one more – an explosive, late equaliser against West Bromwich on the 4 March. In the wretched New Year period, his confidence and effectiveness waned substantially, to the extent that he was relegated to the bench after a dispiriting 0-2 defeat at swampy Watford on 11 February. This was Burnley's fifth successive defeat in a losing sequence that extended to eight league games, equalling an unwanted club record established 100 years before. His season's tally of seven league goals from 29 starts was no better than that of Burnley's imperious centre back and captain, Steve Davis.

In a remarkably candid interview, conducted by London Clarets Brent Whittam and Dave McCluggage, Jimmy Mullen dismissed the suggestion that Robinson had been an unsuccessful signing. He retorted:

> 'I just think that the lad has been very unlucky, so far, this season, very unlucky. I think he's got seven or eight goals so far. If he had the just rewards for his endeavour, he'd have about 40 bloody goals… People may be getting at him for his goal-scoring but surely never for his work rate?'

Robinson's plight might not have been so marked had Heath and Eyres not lost their scoring touch. Heath's goal standard had been declining steadily since his stellar first season at Turf Moor. Although he retained the nous and skill to produce a 'killer' pass or cross, he found the net on only two occasions in 1994/95, both goals coming in

FA Cup ties against lower division opposition. Before injury brought 'Inchy's' season to a premature end, he was scoreless in 21 league starts.

The loss of Eyres' potency in front of goal was felt more sharply. His 26 league and cup goals during the 1993/94 season were largely responsible for maintaining Burnley's promotion challenge. As a wide, left-sided midfielder he had the ability to 'ghost' into space at the near post to convert chances created by Heath and others. His sudden acceleration enabled him to arrive late and decisively. After making a sluggish recovery from injury, Eyres found that the canny First Division defenders were generally alert to this stratagem, leaving him often neutralised, at least as a potential goal-scorer. His eight league goals from 38 starts included three penalties. As for the remaining strike force: John Francis was side-lined by his Wembley injury, while Tony Philliskirk, Graham Lancashire and Nathan Peel were not considered good enough for this division, although 'Phyllis' was allowed a late reprieve, scoring the opening goal against Bolton, his former club, in the last game.

Former apprentice John Mullin played well against Liverpool in the FA Cup, almost snatching a late winner in a highly creditable 0-0 draw. But apart from rifling in a vital equaliser in a 2-1 home victory over Luton, Jimmy Mullen considered him too raw for regular league action. In conversation with Whittam and McCluggage, Jimmy explained:

> 'I think John Mullin could be a very, very good player. He's forced his way into the team now, and held his own, certainly against the likes of Liverpool, and done very, very well... he will be given games if he performs to these standards. It's up to him now.'

Unfortunately, Mullin was introduced into a side low on confidence, immersed in a long, losing streak. When asked which players he looked to, to turn their fortunes around, Jimmy Mullen replied:

> 'Well, your most experienced players... Winstanley, Davis, Pender, Parkinson, Harper, Eyres and Heath. They've got 2,000 games between them, so they're the sort of people I would look to...'

It must have been apparent to Mullen in the opening 0-2 defeat at Middlesbrough, that his newly-constructed strike force lacked the physical strength to dominate uncompromising, battle-hardened opponents, such as Bryan Robson, Nigel Pearson and Neil Cox. To address this deficit Mullen recruited giant, black target man, 'Big Bad John' Gayle, from Coventry for £75,000. Although not a prolific goal-scorer, Gayle caused havoc in the opposition's box with his heavyweight 'bump and grind' style. If given the penetrative aerial service that Ted McMinn could supply, he represented a threat on goal, while his proficiency in barging defenders aside or in pulling them around, created space for other attackers. Even a sturdy centre half like ex-Claret, Vince Overson, had difficulty in subduing him.

Having no other target man with Gayle's physical strength, Mullen seemed to discard him too quickly, transferring him to Stoke in January 1995 for a £70,000 fee, just after the muscular colossus had scored against Southend with a thunderous scissor kick. While not blessed with pace, Gayle had a better touch that his hulk-like physique suggested. Instead, Mullen experimented dismally with Paul Stewart in this role, having signed him on loan from Liverpool. But Stewart seemed incapable of emulating Gayle's presence. To the layman's eye he appeared overweight and unfit, and, if the rumours were correct, on cringingly high wages. Jimmy Mullen explained to Whittam and McCluggage:

> 'I'm looking for Stewart to give us his full experience at the highest level with Tottenham and Liverpool, to hold the ball up a lot better than we have been doing. When the ball goes up to the front men, it's just coming back too easily. It's important that the ball stays in the opposition's final third for a bit longer, for our other players to get up there in support, allowing us to get the ball out wide to cause them problems... We've battered Reading and Swindon... We've proved we can do this very, very well. You don't go to the likes of Luton, Millwall and Charlton and win on merit without doing than sort of thing...'

Regrettably, Jimmy was to be disappointed. Stewart returned to Liverpool after only six goal-less appearances, having been sent off in his penultimate game, the debacle at Oakwell (0-2), for an intemperate outburst at the referee. Burnley completed that heated affair with only nine men, with Parkinson also dismissed for a push on ex-Claret, Brendan O'Connell. The Burnley fans chanted vociferously 'Two-nil to the referee'. But Burnley's disciplinary record was dire. Apart from Stewart and Parkinson, Beresford had seen red twice, as had Hoyland, while Davis, Eyres, Vinnicombe, Dowell and Harrison completed the red card 'rogues' gallery'.

As relegation woes intensified in the New Year, Mullen belatedly cast around for a proven goal-scorer. He told Whittam and McCluggage:

'I rang Celtic about Andy Walker and Willie Falconer but Tommy Burns said at this moment they were not available... I made a bid for Guy Whittingham who had moved from Portsmouth to Sheffield Wednesday. But Trevor Francis, the Owls' manager, was very happy with him, and, reading between the lines, I think there'll be people moving on there and Whittingham will become number one... I went back to Villa about Graham Fenton but they'd just turned down a million and a half bid for him. Now there's no way I can go with that. Let's be realistic. But make no bones about it, if the right player became available at £300,000 to £350,000, I've no doubt that the chairman would say, right, if that's what you want it will be done.'

As proof of this, at the end of February 1995, Jimmy signed Brighton striker, Kurt Nogan for a new club record fee of £300,000. Nogan had been a prolific goal scorer at the Goldstone Ground, having netted twenty goals in each of his first two seasons there. But in the 1994/95 campaign his supply of goals had dried up. He had not scored in any of his previous twenty-six league appearances. It was no surprise then that he was slow to make his mark at Turf Moor. In sharp contrast, Paul Shaw, a 21-year-old loan signing from Arsenal, arrived on transfer deadline day, and proceeded to play with verve and confidence, scoring four league goals in only eight starts, briefly raising faint hopes of survival.

Mullen did better with his defensive strengthening. He did well to recruit former England Under-21 left back, Chris Vinnicombe from Glasgow Rangers for £200,000. Although more proficient on the overlap than in dogged defence, Vinnicombe slotted in comfortably before sustaining a horrific jaw injury at Reading, in early November, for which the perpetrator, Andy Bernal, was dismissed.

Jimmy Mullen recalled:

'I saw him go out like a light before he'd even hit the ground. I immediately ran to him with Andy, our physiotherapist. I knew Chris was in trouble, his eyes were rolled back and what looked like black tar was coming out of the side of his mouth. I was saying Andy, Andy, Andy for f***'s sake! And he was saying to me "don't worry boss, he'll be alright", explaining to me that when it's a really, really deep problem, wherever in the body, it won't be like the blood you'd get if you stuck a pin in your finger… I was accused of trying to get the game stopped. All I was trying to do was to get attention to Chris as soon as possible. Nothing else mattered.'

This injury ruled Vinnicombe out for 15 crucial league games. As a stark reflection of his loss to the team, Burnley descended from a position of relative comfort – fifteenth place on 20 November – to bottom at the end of February. Despite auditioning several stop-gap replacements, including young reserves, Wayne Dowell and Chris Brass, Mullen failed to find adequate cover, leaving the team with an onerous task in avoiding relegation.

Recognising that John Pender was no longer the sturdy partner that Steve Davis needed, Mullen paid Bolton £150,000 in August 1994, for their experienced centre back, Mark Winstanley. He performed well as a robust and quick stopper, astonishing the Clarets' contingent at the New Den by heading two goals, turning the game on its head. Although his distribution was often wayward, Winstanley's whole-hearted displays won him runner-up in the London Clarets' player-of-the-season ratings, with his esteemed partner and skipper taking the trophy. In fact, the Burnley defence was well-regarded in this poll, with Vinnicombe and Parkinson taking fourth and fifth place, midfielder, Randall squeezing in just above them.

Realising that he needed reinforcements to increase his tactical options, in October 1994, Mullen signed Sheffield United's versatile defender, Jamie Hoyland, initially on loan, but then permanently for a £130,000 fee. He started well, knocking the ball around in midfield with calm assurance, helping Burnley to play progressively from the back, but it soon became clear that he was too slow for a midfield berth. Hoyland recalled:

'It was a great move. Things were not working out for me at Bramall Lane so I was delighted to come to Turf Moor. It was immediately clear that Burnley were playing brilliant football under Jimmy Mullen. The problem was in not scoring enough goals. We could have done better by bringing in Nogan earlier. I got off to a good start, though, scoring the winner against Notts County (2-1) and then buried a belter against my former club in November. I really preferred to play at centre half but with Davis and

Winstanley playing so well, I was prepared to adopt other positions, in central midfield or as a sweeper... 'Parky' (Gary Parkinson) was a fantastic footballer. So was David Eyres. It was a real footballing side in which everyone got on. When I arrived, Jimmy had just introduced a diamond. It worked like a dream in the victory at Charlton at the end of October.'

Here, the Addicks' back four were guilty of playing too deeply. Their midfield had to retreat to link up with them. As Charlton forward, Gary Nelson pointed out in his book *'Left Foot Forward'* this granted Burnley acres of space in the middle of the park. Midfielders, Adrian Randall and Hoyland revelled in the resulting freedom. Not even referee Bailey, who had unaccountably ruled out three Burnley 'goals', could save Charlton as Davis stabbed the Clarets into a 52nd minute lead, from a corner, while Robinson added a second with a lunging poke, having chased down Davis's long clearance. Neither Whyte's late goal nor Hoyland's dismissal, allegedly for foul language, could save the home side.

As uplifting as this victory was, Burnley's frailties in midfield soon re-surfaced. Alan Harper came to Turf Moor in August with a wealth of top flight experience, having won a League championship winners' medal with Everton in 1987. Although he gave occasional glimpses of his former ability, as in the Elm Park rain, at Reading, he seemed too ponderous in thought and movement. He was constantly in danger of being dispossessed, a weakness accentuated by his erratic passing. Jimmy Mullen thought that Harper was ideally suited to a holding midfield role, helping protect the Burnley back four. It was a position that he had fulfilled successfully at Luton, his previous club. His sluggishness meant that it was Burnley's attack which was held up, though. He played in 27 games before succumbing to injury.

Given Burnley's problems in midfield, it seemed odd that John Deary joined Rochdale in January 1995 for £25,000. Mullen explained:

'John asked for a transfer first and foremost. Bear in mind John is 33 years-old. He was offered a long contract by Rochdale; a lot longer than I would have been prepared to give him come the end of the season... I don't think that in the long-term John's going to get us out of trouble because you need the legs, the stamina and strength... John used to get us six or seven goals from midfield but this season he has got only one against Bolton and one in the FA Cup at Shrewsbury where we were stepping down a level…I brought Jamie Hoyland in to do a similar job, in terms of getting his foot into midfield and setting up play. John in his first and second season with the club spent as much time in the opposition's box as any of our strikers did, but in the last 12 months he seemed to be happy to sit in that midfield area.' As for John, he had no regrets about leaving, saying some years later: 'It was a pleasure playing for Burnley – great memories of a great ground, great fans and great people.'

With Hoyland struggling to fulfil the central midfield role Mullen had intended for him, Farrell moving to Wigan, and Joyce being passed over, the Burnley boss was given permission to sign Steve Thompson from Premier League side, Leicester City for £200,000. Thompson was a pass master and a dead-ball specialist, but like too many of Mullen's players, he lacked the necessary speed to hurt the opposition. This collective lack of pace not only held Burnley back, results-wise, it probably contributed to their appalling disciplinary record. Thompson was yet another Burnley player to be troubled by injury, missing five critical games at the end of the 1994/95 season and most of the following campaign. He made only 44 starts at Burnley before joining Rotherham in July 1997.

Randall, however, was a notable success in midfield, scooping up several of the player-of-the-season awards in 1995. He attributed his improvement to a better work-rate stating:

> 'When I first came to the club I thought the game would come to me. I would hang around in the middle of the park waiting for the ball. Now I tend to work harder to get the ball. I also work harder on the defensive part of my game as well, leading to an increase in confidence around the midway point in the season… I'm the sort of player who needs to be told I'm playing well… I'm very honest with myself and never truly happy with my game. However, everything went exactly to plan in the Swindon away game (1-1). I was really fired up for it because I come from the area and there were a load of family and friends watching which helped me to have a very good game.'

Unfortunately, Randall's career fell away, moving to York for £140,000 in December 1995 and thence to Bury on a free transfer, a year later.

Twenty-one-year-old Gerry Harrison made a positive impression in Burnley's midfield, too. He had failed to establish himself at any of his six previous clubs, but soon won favour among the Burnley fans with his driving power and rugged competitiveness, suggesting that he might go far, providing he could control his volatility. He played in 16 league games during this season in a variety of defensive and midfield roles, but it would be in subsequent seasons that he would emphasise his worth.

Jamie Hoyland was deeply disappointed that his new team failed to capitalise upon the promise it displayed upon joining them. He concluded dolefully:

> 'We were naïve and perhaps a little too adventurous... We went bombing forward thinking "we'll be alright, we'll score", but we didn't. We didn't take enough of our chances. Meanwhile other sides were punishing us when they had theirs... If you don't concede you have a decent chance of winning, but we couldn't stop conceding silly goals. The fact is that in Division Two, teams might put away only one in six chances whereas in the First Division that ratio improves to two or three in six, while in the Premiership it is higher still at four or five out of six.'

As for 32-year-old Ted McMinn, he was aware that age was catching up with him, reflecting:

> '[In Division One] the full backs were that bit quicker and harder to get away from... My time was almost coming to an end. I was becoming increasingly troubled by injuries. I could no longer play regularly. But I'm so grateful that Jimmy brought me to Burnley. It's left me with such brilliant memories, particularly the play-off games and the chance to play at Wembley.'

During this season, it was rumoured that Jimmy Mullen had fallen out with McMinn and was disinclined to pick him. Jimmy discounted this, insisting: 'Ted did his calf. So, when he told me he was knackered, he was not saying he was out of breath, he was explaining he was out because of injury.' When fit to play, though, McMinn was a threat on either flank.

Had Burnley managed to field bigger and better strikers, Ted's sublime crossing might have reaped greater reward in the 17 games he started.

It was a disappointing campaign for Burnley's star keeper, Marlon Beresford. He made his eighth penalty save, out of 13 faced while at Burnley, denying John 'Mr Penalty' Aldridge a winning goal for Tranmere (1-1). But he was unusually error-prone. His twin blunders at Middlesbrough gifted John Hendrie both goals. He was also critically twice at fault in a home defeat by Grimsby (0-2). Against a dire Notts County side at Meadow Lane, he changed the course of the game when his clearance hit their waiting centre forward and ballooned into the net (0-3), while his reckless charges at Oldham (0-3) and Portsmouth (0-2) resulted in his dismissal.

He commented:

> 'The new back-pass rules have made decision-making more difficult for goalkeepers. You see more of them having to get involved in play as they are left with a dilemma when to stay on their line and when to come out of their box. This is probably the hardest part to grapple with. You have to practice the different situations in training. It's not too bad in summer, but when the pitches cut up and the ball begins to bobble, mistakes can be made… You must decide whether to race out to prevent an opponent getting his shot away, but at the risk of causing injury and being dismissed, or to stay at home and risk conceding a goal. The clamp-down on professional fouls and handling outside the area has made this very difficult.'

Put simply, Burnley were not good enough. Even a massive outlay of £1.3m paled by comparison with Wolves who splashed out £3.5m on Neil Emblen, David Kelly, Steve Froggatt and Tony Daley – presumably offering much higher wages, too. Nevertheless, Burnley derived limited value from their £1.m investment. Less than £250,000 was recouped as Mullen's 1994/95 signings moved on. It was deeply frustrating too that they could not emulate modest second tier clubs such as Southend, Port Vale, Luton and Grimsby in retaining their hard-won second tier status. Despite their impressive victories over Derby (3-1) and Sheffield United (4-2) – the latter showcased live on Granada TV – there were a long line of abject performances, as at a freezing Fratton Park; at relegation-bound Notts County; and at Tranmere (1-4). Even during their 10-match unbeaten run, Burnley could only manage three victories. In too many games parity was the best they could achieve. So, it came to pass that on a grey, gusty, cold and wet Saturday at the end of April, time was called on Burnley's brief stay in Division One.

London Claret Andrew Firmin graphically described the glum occasion:

'After a two-month beaten run our fate had been sealed in all but name… It boiled down to the game against a poor Portsmouth side at home, where only a win would keep the mathematicians amongst us happy. Predictably we capitulated… No one was shocked; it had for a while been a question of when rather than whether. I left the ground wanting no part in the applause and made my usual furious strides up the steep hill to Manchester Road station, knowing that if I was quick enough there was a sub-10-minute pint to be had before the train came.

'It was raining; you really need the rain on the walk up that hill to ram home the futility of it. Walking ahead of me I saw one of our most frequent travellers (I will spare any blushes), an ever-present that season, taking big steps, head down, not looking in front of him or to either side. Concerned about his welfare I went to catch the fellow. I undoubtedly said something ridiculous like 'cheer up'. This got no response, not even a look in my direction. Then, he suddenly said: "Tell you what, Firmo, shall we kick the shit out of my umbrella?" Uninformed visitors to Burnley might have been perturbed at the sight of two large men taking runs in the rain at the umbrella, kicking it with fury. It was soon a wasted mess of metal and man-made fibre, black and ruined in the drenched gutter. We then hurried on for that swift pint.

'I can't say I can recall the journey home, probably the same mixture of arguments, songs and absurd conversations. When I got home, however, I cried like a baby. I can admit it… I woke the next morning feeling very hung over and thoroughly ashamed. But not to have wept bitter tears would be like not dancing on the picnic tables outside Ye Olde Swiss Cottage after the Wembley triumph less than a year before. I am glad I marked relegation, our relegation, as emotionally as I marked our promotion… So now, when I see these sobbing fans on TV I try to curb my smirking and find it in my heart to feel some sympathy. And next time you see me leaping about on a picnic table outside a pub, which I hope will be soon, don't look on me too harshly. I shall just be making the most of an all too brief moment of glory.'

Some months before relegation became inevitable, the Burnley fans' anger was turned on Jimmy Mullen. Their once fervent chants of 'Jimmy Mullen's Claret and Blue Army' were replaced by snarling denunciations of 'Down cos of Mullen!' At Southend on 8 April just as Burnley were sliding to another ignominious defeat, one Burnley fan broke the sepulchral silence gripping the away end by giving a hoarse yet earnest rendition of 'My Way', ending with a bitter finale, 'I did it my way, the Jimmy Mullen way, the f***ing relegation way!", releasing gales of gallows laughter.

When asked by Whittam and McCluggage how he coped with the flak he received during his final months at Burnley Jimmy was philosophical, believing that many of the accusations levelled at him were stirred by false rumours and mischievous innuendos which he felt largely powerless to rebut. He saw this as part and parcel of living in a 'goldfish bowl'.

He explained:

> 'What I've had to understand, having moved into the area, was what Frank Casper taught me when I first joined the club. He said: "You're joining a big club in a tiny village". Now that hit home very, very quickly. When I was here, and Frank Casper was manager, I had to travel between Blackpool and here because it was difficult selling my house... I'd get back to Blackpool at the end of the day and I'd hear fanciful stories about what was supposedly happening at Burnley Football Club. I'd say, "Hang on a minute, where have you heard that?" "Oh, a couple of friends at the game today told us." I'd then say, "Well you'll never be so far from the truth with that story." Then they'd say something like "Yeah, it's a big club, but one based in a tiny village." Never, ever, has a truer thing been said.'

Despite growing demands for his head, Jimmy Mullen remained resolute, determined to avoid the drop and hold onto his job. In both respects, he was backed wholeheartedly by his chairman, Frank Teasdale. When questioned on the dreaded vote of confidence, Jimmy admitted:

> 'Yes, I did wonder what the board were thinking about things, once relegation was confirmed. But to be fair to

my chairman, all along he said: "No, don't even think about it, you've got a job to do just get on with it." No, I never thought my job was at risk, not with this chairman... I work for a board and a chairman who reflect not just on a six-month period, but on a four or five-year period. In their opinion, the club is a lot better off than it was four years ago, so they are not going to make rash decisions based on a few months. The fact that the club is in a better position is something I take a lot of pride from, despite accepting that the buck stops with me for this relegation.'

Astonishingly, though, Jimmy Mullen then divulged to Whittam and McCluggage that he had been 'tapped up' by other clubs. After initially stating he "would rather not say" which clubs had head-hunted him, he suddenly had a change of mind, revealing:

'Alright, the one this time around was the Leicester thing. A press guy rang me and said he had to do a story on my background. I replied, "What do you mean?" And he said that if Mark McGhee says no to the job, they are going to make an official approach. I said: "I don't know where you got that from". And he replied: "I'm telling you it's true." It's nice to know but I'm not interested.'

Jimmy Mullen remained to fight another campaign, but not one that he would complete. As if the despondency surrounding Turf Moor was not oppressive enough, richly bankrolled Blackburn Rovers won the Premier League.

But one member of the Burnley board did not appear to share his chairman's endorsement of Mullen. Current Burnley director, Clive Holt concluded:

'The solitary season Burnley spent in Division One was a disaster. Jimmy seemed to struggle with the extra pressure. It was said to me that on one occasion he had absented himself during a home game, only to be found later fast asleep in a Turf Moor toilet cubicle. It gave cause for further doubt whether we had the right man in charge. But at least that "one season wonder" allowed us to avail ourselves of a Football League Foundation grant which met 50% of the costs of erecting two badly-needed, all-seater stands on the sites occupied by the Longside and Bee Hole End terraces.

'To go back a bit, when we started planning the redevelopment of Turf Moor, six years before it started, we had five MPs here as guests of the club. They were on a fact-finding mission for Margaret Thatcher's doomed ID card scheme. At half-time we learned of the Hillsborough disaster. Things slowed down after that. It wasn't until 1993 that a suitable design and workable financial plan came through that seemed viable. We still didn't have much money so we concentrated on coming up with a scheme that was self-financing, and that takes time.

'This capital project was estimated to cost £5.28m. We could not have afforded it had we not been promoted in 1994. Our one year stay in the second flight allowed us to qualify for that grant, which was allocated to help all clubs at this level, to build all-seater stadia in compliance with a recommendation in the Taylor Report. The report had emerged from the first Hillsborough enquiry. We were certainly in the right place at the right time, but not all board members were enthusiastic about the capital project given that the club had to find £2.64m from its own resources to supplement the Football League grant.

'Fellow director, Bernard Rothwell suggested putting seats on the Longside terraces as a cost-saving measure rather than building a replacement stand. I opposed this suggestion. I thought we needed two new, purpose-built stands on a larger footprint to accommodate the revenue-earning functions that a modern club was expected to provide, such as banqueting and conference facilities, and executive boxes. We could not do that if we retained the Longside and Beehole End terracing.

'I am not a constructional engineer but I am a very experienced mechanical engineer, having successfully run my own company. This experience has taught me that, whenever it is necessary to embark upon a development of this size and importance, it is imperative that the client is totally conversant with each of the project details, being integrally involved in drawing up the specification, and in the appointment of the contractors, ensuring throughout the project that the contractors are held accountable for the delivery of each specified item and that the required quality standards are met. While these stands were being constructed I scrutinised each aspect of the development, making sure that if the contractor attempted to depart from the original specification that prior approval was sought, and that it was done on the understanding that each variation incurred no extra cost to the club. I maintained a comprehensive record of each of the written communications with Linpave, the contractors.

'Despite that, at the end of the construction, Linpave attempted to add around £0.5m to the final bill. So, I went through every item listed in that bill with a fine-tooth comb to ensure no unauthorised extras had been slipped in. As it happened there were several. Therefore, we disputed the charge. Linpave tried to take us to court but thanks to our rigour throughout the process, including the maintenance of a comprehensive record of all communications with the builders, the High Court judge determined that the final bill should be £0.28m less than the original estimate and that the £0.5m of unauthorised additions should also be deleted.

'Some people expressed disappointment with the new stands, regarding them as "too clinical and unadventurous". Maybe that's true. What we have, though, was what we could afford at the time and they have helped set up the impressive club we have today. I'm proud of what we managed to achieve here. It's so important to get the infrastructure of the club on a sure footing, so that when we do get success on the pitch we can stay there. Not every club can have benefactors like Jack Walker and if, Blackburn hadn't, they'd have been in a similar position to us.'

The reconstruction began with the demolition of the much-loved Longside. This work started following the home fixture with Hull City on 16 September 1995. Although the match programme and various Burnley fanzines contained many supporters' stories of fond, glorious or stark occasions spent on these hallowed terraces, the farewell ceremony seemed flat and insipid. The awful quality of the game did not help – a 2-1 victory over the toothless Tigers. All around were disengaged fans with blank expressions. Meanwhile the lunchtime beer soured in our bellies.

Relegation was certainly to blame for the disaffection. Those expectations of restored glory, aroused by a sunny victory at Wembley had been brusquely cast aside. It seemed harder to be re-enthused about starting over, as reflected in the 25 per cent fall in Turf Moor's average attendance during 1995/96.

Frank Teasdale attempted to rally the Clarets faithful in a pre-season address, set out in the new Burnley FC magazine. He wrote:

> 'It's unfortunate that we launch this magazine in the wake of relegation but I prefer to look at it as an indication of our resolve to bounce back. It's obviously a blow to be relegated but life goes on and we just must get on with the job in hand, all of us.
>
> 'It's the manager's job to get us back into Division One and it's the job of the board to back him. I have every confidence in Jimmy Mullen… I must say to people that we have had good times and I honestly feel that it's better to have been there and failed than not to have been there at all… I know we have had our critics but I personally felt, right to the end, that we wouldn't go down. Unfortunately, we had some bad luck, some bad decisions and we contributed to our own downfall. Perhaps at times there were also wrong selections and I think Jimmy would admit to that.
>
> 'I have been a supporter for more than 50 years… I've seen the good times and the bad… We, the board, are passionate and relegation hurts us as much as anyone else. But I will say this. I'm ready for Division Two and as we proved last year, by spending more on players than ever before, we are ready to support the manager and he picks the team. We've done our bit. The rest now depends on the trials and tribulations that the game throws up… There's been a lot written and said over the summer about players moving out of Turf Moor.'

As expected, Steve Davis moved on, although it was surprising that his destination was Luton Town, after a £750,000 deal was agreed, while bright prospect, John Mullin joined Sunderland for what seemed a cut-price fee of £40,000.

Frank Teasdale continued:

> 'I'll put on record that when a player is out of contract and wants to play in the Premier League [as Mullin did] how can we stand in his way? There might be any number of

reasons for him wanting to move: family reasons [as was the case with Davis], a better team, higher division or more money [as was the case with both Davis and Mullin]. At the end of the day it may just be that the man sees his future somewhere else. Good luck to him.

'As a fan, I would ask you, the Burnley fans, to keep supporting. I know everybody has had a disappointment but we have to prove to people that we can come through this… I'm told that we are favourites for promotion… I'm not sure whether that's a burden or not. I suppose it's better to be thought of in that way rather than regarded as candidates for relegation… But what we must do as a club is to give it our best shot… I don't think we will fail.'

As proof of Frank Teasdale's continuing support of Jimmy Mullen, he allowed him to bring in ex-Leeds, Hull, Port Vale and Plymouth centre back Peter Swan for £200,000 to replace the departed Davis. Ultra-hard man, Swan, could also play up front where he had scored 36 first team goals for Leeds and Hull. Although his preferred position was in central defence he was a towering presence in either box. Swan took few prisoners. He tackled with shuddering intensity and headed with visceral force, as evidenced by his crucial, crashing winner against Peterborough in April 1996. On the other hand, swifter, more nimble opponents troubled him. Swan took his place as a third defender in Mullen's new 5-3-2 formation in which Parkinson and Vinnicombe exercised their progressive credentials as wing backs. Meanwhile, John Pender became surplus to requirements, joining former team-mate, Andy Farrell, at Wigan in a £40,000 deal.

Upon arrival at Turf Moor, Swan claimed:

'I am a 100 percenter. This club has real potential otherwise I wouldn't have come… Camaraderie is 90% of the battle and we have that in abundance here. There are no cliques, unlike other places. Everyone gets on well and they look after each other. They may not be the best of mates off the park but on the field, we are a team and the team spirit is first class.'

So, while many fans were unconvinced, still highly critical of the manager and the board who backed him, in Swan's view, at least, the dressing room held together.

Swan added:

'I saw a few games when I first came here. I thought they needed a bit of organisation, on the pitch, some man management and psychology if you like. I think I can bring that. Some players need a kick up the backside, others will only respond to an arm around the shoulders or a joke. I think I can sort out who needs what.'

It sounded as if Swan had designs on the captaincy, held then by Hoyland.

Irrespective of Frank Teasdale's expressions of faith in Jimmy Mullen a vocal section of Burnley fans continued to denounce him, even after his side had scrambled into fourth place in early December 1995. His team's lofty position, at the start of the festive season was hardly robust, though, being largely reliant upon Nogan's goals. Sure enough, after beating Stockport 4-3 in an error-strewn home match in mid-January, Burnley nose-dived. Just one point was taken from their next seven league games, causing the Clarets to fall 11 places to sixteenth. Some fans doubted the necessity of the new stands. For the Crewe home game on 10 February a '3.33' protest was organised which attracted the attention of the national media. A group of disaffected Burnley fans decided that at 3.33pm they would turn their backs on the action, urging others to follow suit in demonstrating their dissatisfaction with the club's management. Burnley lost 0-1, a fourth successive defeat. Within 48 hours of the game ending, Jimmy Mullen had gone, prompted by a distressing incident at a local restaurant.

Frank Teasdale was invited by BBC Radio Lancashire to clarify what had happened. Teasdale said on air:

'Well, obviously, the results have not been going well but more importantly the abuse got too much, and following the incident at the weekend it was obvious that we had to part company with Jimmy, for his sake and his family's sake… Apparently some 'supporters' had verbally and physically abused him and his wife at the weekend… The unrest had been going on for weeks, demonstrations etc. but when it goes from football to his house and restaurant, enough is enough. The details were confirmed when I met him and his wife at my house after the latest incident. Regrettably, it was then mutually agreed to bring his contract to an immediate end…

'We've got to remember what he's done for this club… I will never forget the Wembley trip… Regrettably some of those who were cheering and throwing flowers at the coach are now throwing other things which says a lot for football fans doesn't it? I accept they are entitled to their opinions but when it becomes physical there has to be something wrong...

'As for the supporters' criticism of me, that has been because of our lack of doing anything with Jimmy... We must hope that they will now get behind the club and we'll go in the right direction... We have engaged a PR consultant to hopefully take some of the criticism off our backs and arrange talkbacks or whatever... We know that fans judge a club by results on the field... We are now advertising for someone to replace Jimmy. We, of course, want the very best man for the job.

'Jimmy Mullen is a friend of mine and will always be so because he is that type of guy... I've no doubt at all that there'll be no arguments between Jimmy and the club regarding his future and what he is entitled to. We're not that sort of club...

'My message to all those who were involved in the restaurant incident, think about it and ask yourselves in all conscience would you do it again? Because if you would there is something sadly wrong with you.'

David Eyres expressed similar sentiments at Jimmy Mullen's departure, feeling that a couple of his bigger buys may have let him down. They were un-named. After Jimmy had gone, the protesting fans got their wish. Several candidates were considered, allegedly including Steve Coppell, Mike Walker, Michael Phelan and Brian McClair. However, it was the fans' favourite, 'Inchy' Heath, who was appointed as player-manager. Heath had left Burnley earlier in the season to assist his mentor and former Everton manager, Howard Kendall, at Bramall Lane.

He explained:

'Howard has been an integral part of my footballing career. When I was a young boy at Stoke, before I got into the side, I used to clean his boots. He used to wax lyrical about Everton Football Club, and talk to me about the great games and great nights at Goodison Park that he'd been involved in, and my dad used to speak so highly of the Harvey, Ball and Kendall midfield partnership. So, when

I got the opportunity to go to join Howard again, firstly as a player at Everton, and then as his assistant at Sheffield United, I jumped at it.'

Turning to his return as manager, Heath said:

'I want to get Burnley back to the top. It is a big challenge but I am confident I can take that challenge head on and make Burnley great again. In the immediate future, I want to help Burnley climb the table first, but the long-term aim is to reach the Premiership inside five years. I have a great deal of affection for this club, and simply could not say no. They are an ambitious club and I feel I'm ready for the task in hand. I had an unbelievable rapport with the fans as a player and hopefully that will be a big plus in turning the fortunes of the club around.'

But those fans who expected an immediate turnaround were sorely disappointed. Having snatched an outrageously lucky 1-0 victory at Bristol City, in Heath's first game, helped by the 'hand of Nog' [Nogan], Burnley quickly reverted to type. Oxford smashed five past them at the Manor Ground (0-5), Wycombe trounced them 4-1 at Adams Park, and even beleaguered Brighton, on the brink of oblivion, proved too good for them at the decrepit Goldstone Ground (0-1).

However, some gutsy displays at promotion-bound Swindon (0-0), Notts County (1-1) and, most importantly, at Wrexham (2-0), helped stave off a further relegation. The hero of the vital victory at the Racehorse Ground was the almost forgotten Liam Robinson. He put Burnley ahead with an astonishing long-range, chip shot. But it was Nogan's 20 league goals which were primarily responsible for averting Burnley's return to the basement. He was duly selected as the London Clarets' player-of-the-season, followed closely by Mark Winstanley, who performed consistently in a ragged side. Winstanley celebrated his commendation with a cracking goal in the final home game of the season – a 2-1 victory over Shrewsbury. Encouragingly, former apprentice, Paul Weller, starred in a wide midfield role. Paul Smith, also a home-grown wide midfielder graduated to the first team too. With young Andy Cooke, a Mullen recruit, demonstrating his prowess as a gutsy, battling centre forward, the future seemed a little brighter.

Heath's first full season in charge was a more upbeat affair. Burnley headed the Second Division table after a 2-1 win at scorching Luton, where Beresford saved another penalty, and a home victory over Walsall. Nogan was once again Burnley's hot shot, but subsequent results were frustratingly erratic. Heath was permitted to purchase a proven goal scorer, Paul Barnes of Birmingham City, for a new club record fee of £400,000. Barnes remained goal-less in his first eight games, but on 5 October 1996, he scored all five goals in a 5-2 home victory over Stockport County. He became the first Burnley player to score so many in one game since Andy Lochhead performed this feat in the mid-sixties. It seemed then as if the Barnes – Nogan pairing was the best strike force in the Division, and yet there was never a time when both front men scored in the same match. Twenty-two-year-old target man, Andy Cooke, a bargain £40,000 signing from Newtown, appeared to be a better foil for either player. Nogan then became embroiled in a row with Heath over a new contract, believing he was worth more than he was being currently paid. After being demoted to the reserves, Nogan moved to Preston for a cut-price fee of £150,000, half his purchase value. Nogan had scored 33 goals in 87 league starts at Burnley. Surely, his sale warranted a higher figure? Robinson and Thompson also left at the end of this season as free agents, as did Vinnicombe and Winstanley over the next two seasons. Only £150,000 was recovered from the £1.1m spent on these five players.

Nevertheless, Burnley maintained a play-off challenge for most of the 1996/97 campaign. Gillingham (5-1) and Peterborough (5-0) were put to the sword, with both Barnes and Cooke scoring freely. Impressive victories were achieved over champions elect Bury (3-1) and promotion-chasing Wrexham (2-0). But it was successive away victories at high-riding Brentford (3-0) and Walsall (3-1) in March which suggested that Burnley might seal a play-off place. It was not to be. Four out of the next five games were lost with the humiliating 0-5 defeat at Wycombe the worst of the lot. Jamie Hoyland attributed the collapse in form to the departure of Heath's running mate, John Ward. He explained:

> 'John was a superb coach. It was he who got us playing as well as we did that season. When he left towards the end of the season to take over the managerial position at Bristol City, we lost our main tactician and organiser. Adrian was a good man-manager but it was Ward who had the ideas to make things tick on the field.'

A season which had promised much, ultimately delivered little. Even a brave display against Liverpool in the FA Cup resulted in a 0-1 defeat, despite Burnley mounting a brilliant defensive display with young Chris Brass performing admirably as Steve McManaman's marker.

Adrian Heath concluded:

> 'I'm the first to admit that it's been an extremely disappointing turn of events. I honestly thought last summer we could be looking at automatic promotion come April. Even in the last couple of months we were all set for the play-offs. But in reality, it's fallen far short of my expectations, and I know that we have fallen far short of yours, the fans... Our lack of consistency has cost us all season.
>
> 'We probably have the worst record against the bottom five sides in the league. The likes of Peterborough (2-3), Rotherham (0-1 and 3-3) and York (0-1 and 1-2) have been a thorn in our side. The top sides have managed maximum points against these sides, yet we have managed just four. I recognised we had a few problems in the make-up of the squad and I thought I could work through them as the season progressed. But these re-surfaced and caused the problems which could account for our inconsistency. I realise that I have not been very open at times. I can't always afford to do that. In retrospect, I'd have liked to contain things more, to keep certain things quiet.'

What Heath was referring to here were the contractual disputes he had with Beresford and Nogan, leaving him at loggerheads with both players. He admitted that this had been particularly difficult because they were former team mates and, in Beresford's case, a previous room-mate too. He also felt compelled to drop Peter Swan for what he considered to be a 'poor attitude' although he later restored him after a successful heart-to-heart discussion.

Heath confessed to a national journalist that making the transition from player to manager was tougher than he envisaged, regretting the loss of dressing room banter and high jinks. He said rather sadly, 'Whenever I enter the dressing room now it just goes quiet.' He also found just 'how bloody infuriating footballers can be', citing his frustration at their inexplicable inconsistency. Here, he referred to a home defeat by York. He said: 'After having a great week of training, the players did not perform on the day. When it came to the match I could have picked 11 people off the street who'd have given York a better game.'

David Eyres saw Heath differently, telling Phil Whalley and Karen Neill:

> 'As a manager there has to be that little gap between you and the players, but 'Inchy' more or less stayed pally with the lads. If we had nights out he'd come with us and people used to think, you know, he's the manager, he shouldn't really be coming out with us. But he was a good manager in that all he wanted to do in training was to play football. It was probably my best pre-season when he was in charge – five-a-sides, short, sharp running. It was a player's dream. I was about 31-32 years-old at the time. It was exactly what I wanted as a footballer.'

Like Hoyland, Eyres felt Ward's absence keenly, particularly as his departure coincided with a critical dip in form. Before Ward left, a play-off place was there for the taking.

On balance, though, Heath was satisfied with his first full season in charge, stating:

> 'We've made tremendous progress in the last 12 months and I'm confident that next year will be a big one for us… Several of our young players have made excellent progress – Smith, Weller and Brass, for example. Glen Little will also be a welcome addition to the squad, having signed from Glentoran in November 1996, and assuming he keeps improving at the same rate, he will have a great year.
>
> 'During the summer, you can expect to see the playing staff change quite significantly. There are around nine or 10 players who are out of contract. Although I can't say now who'll go and who'll stay, it at least gives us the opportunity to change ranks.'

Burnley director Clive Holt remembered:

> 'Adrian Heath seemed like a breath of fresh air. I thought we might get somewhere under his leadership but then he was courted by Howard Kendall, his former boss at Everton. He left us believing that he would assume the reigns once Kendall retired or moved on. It didn't happen, though. I tried hard to persuade Heath to stay, pointing out that his experience as number one at Burnley was better than a further spell as an assistant manager, in enhancing his

career prospects. It was to no avail, so we turned to former Newcastle, Spurs and England star Chris Waddle in the summer of 1997. Chris was top of our list from day one. On the one hand Burnley gained a manager with the best back-up in Glenn Roeder, and secondly Chris was still a useful player.'

Waddle arrived at the club in a blaze of national publicity. He brought with him ex-QPR and Newcastle centre back Glenn Roeder as his assistant, plus former Aston Villa and England midfielder Gordon Cowans and ex- Norwich and England goalkeeper Chris Woods as coaches. Expectations soared. Many fans believed Waddle could emulate Bryan Robson's feats at Middlesbrough and restore Burnley quickly to the top flight.

David Eyres was initially very positive about the appointments of Waddle and Roeder. He told Phil Whalley and Karen Neill:

'I got on fantastically with Roeder. His training was like Inchy's. It was all football-based. Waddle made me captain which was a great honour. So, it started well. But although the training under Waddle and Roeder was very good, you'd never come off the training field absolutely knackered. Perhaps it wasn't the best then, because in that division there are a lot of hard, tough sides. We really struggled at first and looked likely to go down.'

Although the club was not nearly as well-off as in 1994, Frank Teasdale allowed Waddle to bring in three expensive signings; Mark Ford, a midfielder from Leeds for £275,000; central defender, Steve Blatherwick from Nottingham Forest, for £200,000, subject to appearances; and Lee Howey, a centre half or striker from Sunderland for £200,000. It seemed strange that Waddle should choose to invest so heavily in Howey after the equally versatile Peter Swan had been allowed to move to Bury in August for a mere £50,000. It soon became obvious that his signings had not strengthened the side. Howey was a poor substitute for Swan. As for Blatherwick, he made just 13 starts. Ford, too, proved to be a major disappointment. Although slight in stature he was reputed to exhibit the feisty qualities of Leeds' 'enforcer' David Batty. However, at Burnley he was largely anonymous, being too easily brushed aside in bruising midfield tussles.

Burnley made a dreadful start, failing to score in any of their first six league fixtures, and not recording a league victory until their

'Livin' on a Prayer'. A pensive Burnley manager, Brian Miller, hemmed in by press photographers before Burnley's 'do or die' final game against Orient on 9 May 1987.

'Pint-sized' Ian Britton celebrates his improbable headed goal against Orient. The result was that this once powerful, yet beleaguered club, would not only survive but thrive.

Brian Miller and captain Ray Deakin lead out the Burnley team at
Wembley, on 29 May 1988, to contest a Sherpa Van Trophy Final, watched
by a massive 80,841 crowd.

Mike Conroy scoring against Wigan in a League Cup defeat in August
1991. But his 24 league goals would help power Burnley to the Fourth
Division championship in April 1992.

Burnley manager, Jimmy Mullen, celebrates with a bottle of champagne, after his side seize the Fourth Division championship with a 2-1 win at York on 28 April 1992.

Roger Eli, a cult hero of the 1991/92 promotion-winning team, now enjoys a successful commercial career beyond football.

'Super Johnny Francis', on the right, bursts past Plymouth defender, Steve McCall, in the 1994 Second Division play-off semi-final. Francis's two goals took Burnley to Wembley.

David Eyres, on the left, and Gary Parkinson celebrate the latter's match-winning goal against Stockport at Wembley in the play-off final on 29 May 1994.

Randall and Heath celebrate the latter's spectacular winner in an FA Cup tie at Chester. Despite spending over £1 million on new players, Mullen's Burnley were relegated in April 1995.

Popular Burnley goalkeeper, Marlon Beresford, here defying Premiership Fulham, in an FA Cup tie in February 2003, which Burnley won 3-0 after a replay. Marlon was a Wembley winner in 1994.

Paul Barnes scoring one of his five goals which helped Burnley defeat Stockport 5-2 on 5 October 1996.

Chris Waddle became Burnley's player-manager after Adrian Heath resigned. Despite the hype, his side only narrowly avoided relegation by beating Plymouth 2-1 in his final game in May 1998.

Andy Cooke was a combative target man, who led the line in Stan Ternent's promotion winning side of 1999/2000 and headed the two goals that kept Burnley up on 2 May 1998.

Stan Ternent, on the right, transformed Burnley's fortunes, guiding them back to Division One in 2000, and challenging twice for a Premier League place in the early 2000s.

'Padiham Predator', Andy Payton scored 81 senior goals for the club he had supported since boyhood. After saving them twice from relegation his goals took them back to the second tier.

Ian Cox, on the left, was a 'Rolls-Royce' central defender, who was signed from Bournemouth in 2000 for £500,000, playing a significant part in Ternent's successes.

Ex-England international, Ian Wright, on the left, was signed in February 2000 to boost Burnley's promotion bid. Here, he is helping achieve that at Scunthorpe on 6 May 2000.

Ian Moore, on the right, became Burnley's first £1 million signing, while higher bids for home star, Glen Little, on the left, were refused in the hope of winning a Premier League place.

'Hard man' Kevin Ball in typically battling mode. Stan Ternent regarded Ball as his 'best signing'. They seemed kindred spirits for both men were fearsome midfield 'enforcers'.

'Gazza', on the left, preparing to take a free kick. While not at his best, he came within a whisker of taking the Clarets into the play-offs at the end of the 2001/02 season.

Robbie Blake, to the right of goalscorer Gareth Taylor, was Ternent's second £1 million signing. He served Burnley bosses Stan Ternent, Steve Cotterill and Owen Coyle with distinction.

Steve Davis was renowned for his powerful surges from the back. Here, Norwich's Malky Mackay is hard pressed to stop him. Davis achieved three promotions with Burnley.

Steve Cotterill in trademark belligerent mood. Having replaced Ternent in 2004, he kept a cash-strapped club, still reeling from the ITV Digital collapse, in the Championship.

Steve Cotterill signed several quality players for low or no fees. Central defender, John McGreal, on the left, was one of these, a composed, elegant, yet resolute centre-half.

Richard Chaplow, on the left, was one of few youth players to play for the Burnley first team, making his debut in 2003 but was sold to West Bromwich for £1.5 million in 2005.

Wade Elliott, on the right, was a promising winger when signed by Cotterill, but developed into a thrusting midfielder who scored a fine, promotion-winning goal at Wembley in 2009.

Brian 'Beast' Jensen, a keeper who was erratic under Ternent, better under Cotterill but flourished under Coyle. Here, he is beating Chelsea in 2008 with a penalty shoot-out save.

Ade Akinbiyi is congratulated after the Clarets' stirring comeback at QPR in February 2008. Burnley won 4-2 helped by a hat-trick from England international, Andrew Cole, second right.

Graham Alexander was signed by Cotterill for £200,000. His pugnacious midfield displays and deadly spot kicks played a leading part in returning Burnley to the top flight in 2009.

Centre-back, Clarke Carlisle was another crucial signing by Cotterill. His dominant display at Wembley, in May 2009, won him both a winners' medal and the 'man-of-the-match' award.

The Burnley team celebrate their club's return to the top flight after 33 years. Owen Coyle, the architect of their success, is top left with operational director Brendan Flood to his right.

Owen Coyle's sudden departure to Bolton in January 2010 left the club in disarray as reflected in Barry Kilby's sombre expression. Brian Laws, on the right, became the new boss.

Ex-Bournemouth boss, Eddie Howe, on the right, replaced Laws as Burnley's manager in January 2011. Here, he is congratulating Jay Rodriguez, Burnley's young, rising star.

Howe signed Charlie Austin from Swindon for £1 million in January 2011. Austin scored 41 goals in 82 senior appearances before being sold to QPR in 2013 for around £4 million.

Sean Dyche became Burnley manager in November 2012 after Howe left for 'personal reasons'. Here, Dyche is being held aloft having guided Burnley into the top flight in 2014.

Despite being relegated from the Premier League in 2015, Dyche masterminded an immediate return. Here, record-signing, Andre Gray, equalises at rivals Brighton.

After an unbeaten run of 23 matches, Burnley won the Championship in May 2016 after a 3-0 win at Charlton. With the trophy not on site, the Burnley players made do with inflatable ones.

Burnley made an impressive start to the 2016/17 season by beating Liverpool 2-0 at Turf Moor. Here is Sam Vokes (centre) celebrating his early goal.

Record signing Jeff Hendrick (number 13) is congratulated by his team-mates after scoring with a 'world class' volley against Bournemouth in December 2016. Burnley won 3-2.

New record signing, Robbie Brady, equalises against Chelsea in February 2017 with a sublime free kick. Like Hendrick and Ward, Brady is a Republic of Ireland international.

eleventh game in mid-October. Even Waddle's presence failed to provide the openings upon which Barnes and Cooke could thrive. The arrival of Gerry Creaney, an ex-Celtic, Portsmouth and Manchester striker, on loan, heralded a brief upturn in results. But with Waddle then lacking the resources to sign him permanently, another barren run ensued once Creaney returned to Maine Road.

Waddle told a *Burnley Express* reporter some years later:

'I was really disappointed we didn't keep Gerry Creaney. It wasn't wages. The board had heard he liked a drink. He loved it at Burnley, we played football, got it into his feet, and he was scoring goals – eight in 10 appearances – he had a new lease of life, but the chairman said 'no', and that was the end of it.

Muscular, free-scoring Halifax striker, Geoff Horsfield, also interested Waddle, but the club could not afford his fee. Horsfield later went to Fulham for a fee of over £300,000.

Given the absence of creativity, it seemed perverse that Waddle should ignore the merits of 22-year-old right winger, Glen Little, for whom Heath had correctly predicted a bright future. Glen Little recalled:

'I was totally bombed out. The only people who knew why were Waddle and Roeder. Waddle didn't even speak to me for three months. I never trained with the first team. Players who had never played a professional game in their life were ahead of me. It was a nightmare. I was close to leaving… I used to ring my mum a lot and she told me to pack it in and come back to London… When the fans challenged Roeder to pick me, he said I wasn't fit to lace Chris Waddle's boots… Training was a joke. Waddle would often say on a Monday, "See you guys on Wednesday". His team-talks on Friday would last for five minutes, then we got the footballs out, and on match days he'd just say, "Go out and play". It seemed there was no game plan.'

David Eyres became quickly disillusioned too. He recalled:

'It began to go a bit sour around the time of the Preston home game. I missed a penalty and Waddle dragged me off. I wasn't happy. Even the Preston players said to me that they were glad I had gone off as they thought I was doing all right. So, I had a bit of a bite and it didn't go down too well. There was a bit of an argument in the dressing room. We didn't fall out but you could see that things weren't the same. And then I came into training one day and Waddle said, "Preston are interested in signing you." I said that I didn't want to go anywhere. I'm happy here. He said, "Well, they've offered £80,000 for you and we've accepted it." I had to go to speak with them. I could have stood my ground but there was little point if you are not in the manager's plans. Thankfully, it turned out OK for me and Burnley. But it was such a sad way to leave.'

Emerging youngsters, Chris Brass and Paul Weller, built upon the start that Heath had given them to become first team regulars, although Paul Smith fared less well. Despite coming from behind to beat promotion contenders, Northampton (2-1) on 29 November, the next three league games were lost. The nadir was reached after a 0-2 defeat at Gillingham on 3 January. This loss left Waddle's men in bottom place. It was to be misfiring Paul Barnes last game for the Clarets. He was about to be transferred to Huddersfield in exchange for Andy Payton, bringing the Padiham-born striker back to the club he still loved, despite being rejected by them as a youngster, 15 years before. It was a deal that would favour Burnley. Whereas Barnes netted just twice in 30 league appearances for the Terriers, Payton scored 69 league goals in 115 starts for Burnley. Not only did Payton help Burnley evade relegation in 1997/98 and 1998/99, his 27 goals, in 1999/2000, powered the Clarets to automatic promotion.

Andy Payton recounted to a *Burnley Express* reporter:

'Once I got the £30,000 signing-on fee I was owed by Huddersfield, I was ready to sign for Burnley. I really wanted to join them but was scared I might flop. That would have been terrible. This was the team I had always supported. It was the team all my mates supported...

'I have a lot to thank Chris Waddle for in bringing me back to Turf Moor, although Burnley's situation was desperate when I signed. We were four points adrift at the bottom with four clubs going down... I made my debut against Southend and – much to my relief – scored the winner, getting ahead of my marker at the near post to fire a low cross past Neville Southall. I was worried I wouldn't last for 90 minutes because I knew how important it was to run your bollocks off to show you care. Andy Cooke was brilliant at that and in getting stuck in. The fans love that.

'The trouble was the team didn't have enough winners. Gerry Harrison was a hard worker so was Paul Smith and Paul Weller. I should say too that Chris Waddle played a big part in getting us out of the mess. He worked his balls off in the games he played – a real classy player as well... We had a run against several teams near the top and beat the lot, even Fulham with all that money they had and big-name players like Chris Coleman. To be fair we were hanging on in these games but I still managed to score the winner in each one of them. I ended up with nine goals in 19 appearances.

'We knew money was tight. But it was a shock to find Marlon Beresford leaving while we were travelling to Walsall. Apparently, he had signed for Middlesbrough. We were stunned. Coach Chris Woods had to play in goal. Amazingly we came away with a 0-0 draw, although I will never know how. We ended up having to beat Plymouth at home in the final game of the season and hoped that another result went our way. Thankfully, we won and stayed up but we knew Chris Waddle wouldn't stay.'

In a candid interview, he held with a *Burnley Express* journalist, more than 10 years later, Waddle recalled:

'The first five months were hell, but you couldn't have written a better script for the last day. I felt I needed a few players then, and I saw the chairman and he, more or less, said we needed to sell people like Glen Little, Andy Cooke, Paul Weller. It was frustrating because we had a good second half of the season, and I knew if we could add a bit of experience, we had a fair chance of getting out of the division. I had a meeting, and it was all about cost-cutting and selling players. I felt I was banging my head against a brick wall and decided to get out, and give someone else a fresh start and let them get on with it.

'I had to sell Marlon Beresford, and David Eyres moved on. It was just one of those things, I suppose. Whoever I bought was going to be well-scrutinised, £30,000 was like £3m, and every penny was well-accounted for. But a couple of the buys didn't fit into how we played. There was expectation on people like Mark Ford, and he couldn't handle it. It was difficult. At Leeds, he was used to winning the ball and then giving it to Gary McAllister, but I said to him that he could pass the ball as well – that was what I bought him for.

Ford commented:

'I thought Burnley was a great move for me and I really enjoyed myself there, although not as much in the season which followed when I suffered a broken ankle. Chris brought me here for my aggression and distribution ability and I think my strength lies in holding the ball up and laying it onto the likes of Glen Little, and in the season after, Branchy, who can run with it.'

Chris continued:

'Who knows what would have happened the season after? I wanted a central midfielder, another player at the back, maybe two or three players, and I think we would have been a match for most teams. I wish I had had more money to spend, but I don't begrudge Stan Ternent the funds he got. Soon after Stan took over, I spoke to him six or eight weeks in, and he said: "How did you get this team to survive?"

'In the boardroom after Plymouth, there were a lot of glum faces, and I thought they didn't really want me there anymore. The experience put me off a bit, to be fair, and I would think it is highly unlikely I will go back to that, but you never say never. I'm enjoying my media work with 5 Live and Setanta Sports but, if I did get back into it, I don't think I could find a harder board to work with. I'll always remember that year the pressure on me was silly. We were 25/1 and then favourites after I took over, and expectation levels were ridiculous. You have to enjoy your work, and I was just banging my head at the end, and probably made the right decision to walk away.'

Waddle added:

'Andy Payton was an unbelievable deal. It felt like Paul Barnes wanted away with how he was talking, and I went to see Payts in the reserves at Huddersfield. I remembered him from Barnsley, Celtic and Middlesbrough, and I saw Peter Jackson after the game in his office. He came up with what I was about to say, "How about swapping Barney for Payts?" I had thought there would be no chance. Barney wasn't firing for us, and I thought Jackson would have said "no chance, you can't be serious!" In the end, it was like I was doing him a favour! We eventually got it sorted, and he was a great signing, he got nine goals in 19 games, Andy Cooke finished with 16 goals, and they hit it off well.'

Waddle remains proud that his team showed the strength of character to beat Plymouth, and avert relegation. He remembers the club fondly:

'I always keep an eye out for Burnley. I had a funny year, but I enjoyed it. It's a football-mad town, with a great history. I think we were scrutinised more than anyone else because I was a bit of a name, but the lads were great, and over the second half of the season, if we had matched that form over the first half, we would have finished seventh. People only remember we finished fifth bottom after beating Plymouth on the last day of the season, and we took a lot of criticism, but we were under a lot of pressure, and a lot of players in that team hadn't played a lot of first team football.

'We were always confident that day against Plymouth, in front of a big crowd, and we were good at home – we had beaten Bristol City and Fulham. We felt we had turned it around after January, and were playing football the way we wanted to play. But the players really stood up that day, there was a real hunger, despite their lack of experience.'

Waddle still comes across Burnley fans on his travels, and enjoys the banter:

'Some fans still give me a bit of stick when I see them, but that's part and parcel of football. A lot say they enjoyed the football we played, and that's the thing about Burnley, they want their teams to play good football. Owen Coyle certainly did that, playing the right style of football. The fans have been brought up on good football, and they will be patient if you are trying to do that.'

Burnley director Clive Holt's perspective upon what transpired that season varies from that put forward by Chris Waddle. He said:

'Waddle was still a useful player but not a good manager. He seemed preoccupied with his media interests, often leaving the running of the team to his assistant Glenn Roeder.

'As the relegation worries intensified in the New Year, we became increasingly exasperated with the often absent, Waddle. There was one occasion when he was required to report to the board on how he proposed to overcome the growing danger of the drop, but he sent Roeder instead while he attended some media event. Roeder had already made himself very unpopular with the supporters at a preceding fans' forum, when he disdainfully dismissed their calls for Glen Little's inclusion. Little was an unconventional but hugely talented winger.

'At that board meeting attended by Roeder we did something that, as far as I know, has never been done before or since at the club – we demanded that he pick Little and Weller, who was an impish wide midfielder, for the next game. It wasn't a suggestion, it was a direction. We considered that the club's desperate position called for desperate measures. Waddle was furious, of course. But we were insistent and rightly so, for Little played a leading part in Burnley's recovery as did Payton, of course, and Weller and Gerry Harrison.'

The Plymouth game on 2 May 1998 will remain long in the memories of those who were there, whether players, coaching staff, directors or supporters. The occasion was huge. It was a dog eats dog scrap. Unsurprisingly, 18,811 attended, many from Plymouth. This attendance figure was almost twice the average home gate for that season. As the Plymouth manager, Mick Jones rightly said: "It was like a bear pit out there". Gerry Harrison played in Burnley's defence on that nerve-shredding afternoon. His never-say-die attitude and willingness to give his all for the cause played a critical part in Burnley's recovery and eventual salvation. He was prostrate on the turf at the final whistle, drained physically and emotionally.

Gerry recalled:

'It was out of our hands after we drew 3-3 at Oldham in midweek after being 3-1 up. We had to beat Plymouth who were fighting for their lives, too, while relying on other results. Andy Cooke put us ahead with a splendid header, and although Plymouth equalised with one of their own, Cookey thumped in another header shortly before half-time. We had chances to put ourselves out of sight. Paul Weller hit the woodwork, but we couldn't get that crucial third goal so it was a matter of hanging on. We had the luck. The Plymouth centre forward missed from six yards in the closing stages. He may have been put off by Mark Winstanley's air shot, but it was a huge relief when he prodded the loose ball gently into Chris Woods' midriff. From the fans' point of view, it was a great match to be at [No, it wasn't Gerry, it was utter torture!].

'The atmosphere at the final whistle was incredible. I was on the floor, hurt, after blocking a shot but it didn't matter. It was such a relief to know we were safe, although the other key result didn't come through for five minutes or so. We were getting information from the side-lines where someone had a radio. We knew the Brentford game was going our way. I think we deserved to stay up. We had a dodgy start that season, losing games while still playing well. Chris said before the game to go out and give it all we had. I think everyone did. I can't express how much that game meant to me and everyone involved. It would have been hard for Burnley to come up again from the Third Division. I played in that Division when I was on loan to Hull. It's a difficult one to get out of.' [We know, Gerry!]

Clive Holt continued:

'Having averted relegation by the skin of our teeth, my fellow directors and I were undecided about whether Waddle should be retained. I wasn't completely averse to the suggestion that he be given a further season in which to prove himself. We recognised that management had represented a steep learning curve for him, but that perhaps he had learnt from his mistakes. However, when I discovered that both he and Roeder were tied up with the England World Cup squad during the summer – Waddle as a media pundit and Roeder in some junior coaching capacity – I became very concerned about who would take care of the club's preparations for the new season. As it turned out, Waddle took the decision out of our hands and resigned shortly after the Plymouth game. It seemed as if he had lost his appetite for the job.

'Our short list of candidates to replace Waddle comprised: 'Big Sam' Allardyce, then manager of Notts County; Stan Ternent, who had taken Bury into the second tier and Neil Warnock who had won many admirers by helping some modest sides to punch above their weight. Sam seemed interested, but his chairman scotched the idea, reminding him and us of his contractual obligations. We weren't prepared to break with protocol but Phil Gartside, chairman of Bolton Wanderers, was not so coy, taking Allardyce to Burnden Park in the face of Notts County's protests. Allardyce has a tough, combative reputation but he is much more of "thinking manager" than his image suggests, basing his team plans upon forensic scientific analyses. Of the remaining two contenders, we thought that Stan was the better candidate because of his coaching expertise in the top flight, his remarkable record of success as Bury's manager and his Burnley background.

'Bury tried to bully us into paying compensation but I knew Stan was then out of contract at Gigg Lane and quickly quashed that suggestion, only for Stan – unbeknown to us – to appoint Sam Ellis as his deputy. Ellis was then under contract to Bury so we were forced to shell out £15,000 to secure his services. But as I pointed out, £15k isn't too much to pay for two important acquisitions. Fifteen years later we received £1m from Bournemouth for releasing manager, Eddie Howe and his assistant, Jason Tindall, from their contracts at Burnley. That deal we struck for Ternent and Ellis seems some bargain when compared with that.

'Buttressed by several new signings, Stan was about to transform our fortunes. But his first season at the club in 1998/99 was at first inauspicious and then disastrous, before a magnificent revival during the last three months lifted us well clear of the relegation zone. Board members were understandably concerned about the club's plight but Stan wasn't easy to deal with, being insistent that he should be left to run things his way. He once refused to speak with me for three weeks. It hadn't helped when he took it upon himself to tell three of Chris Waddle's signings – Blatherwick, Howey and Williams – plus Mark Winstanley, that they would never play for the club again. It hardly assisted us in securing decent transfer fees for them.'

Although Chesterfield coughed up £50,000 for Blatherwick and Northampton paid the same for Howey, this represented a miserly 25 per cent return on what Waddle had paid for them 12 months before. Scunthorpe tried to return loan signing, Mark Winstanley, having failed to impress the Iron's manager, Brian Laws. Stan would have none of it.

Burnley were then carrying considerable debt following the construction of two new stands. According to the annual accounts, published on 7 December 1998, the club was £3,936,800 in debt. This total had risen by £807,484 during the 1996/97 season. It was also stated that the club was losing between £40,000 and £50,000 per month. Teasdale and his fellow directors realised that additional investment was imperative.

Two contenders came forward; Fylde-born, Ray Ingleby, who owned a large American company specialising in renting audio-visual equipment; and Burnley fan, Peter Shackleton, the principal of Derby City Technology College which he had funded, run and built from scratch. According to Clive Holt, Frank Teasdale preferred the Shackleton bid, which not only promised a £12m investment via various un-named backers, but also assured Teasdale that he would remain as club chairman. Ingleby's bid was substantially less – he subsequently bought £1m worth of club shares. Ingleby also envisaged a change of chairman which appealed to many supporters who despaired about the prospects of improvement under Frank Teasdale.

However, Clive Holt was sceptical about the credentials of Shackleton's backers. He explained:

'Before we would allow discussions to go any further, we insisted that each investor deposit £1m with our club solicitors as an act of faith which is not unusual in this kind of deal. As for Shackleton, no money arrived. There were a lot of promises but nothing came. After the second failed promise, I started looking in other directions but Frank Teasdale just kept on hoping it would come. Unbeknown to Frank, Bob Blakeborough and I talked with Barry Kilby who emerged as the most likely candidate to take over. The change took place just before Christmas 1998. Frank

Teasdale wasn't keen to go, though. Despite what was said at his funeral, he fought hard to retain his position.'

Club historian, Ray Simpson, felt it important to qualify any impression that Frank Teasdale was unduly swayed by self-interest. Ray said:

'Frank Teasdale was a very decent man. He was Burnley through and through. He was so thrilled to become club chairman, regarding it as a supreme honour. He endured awful abuse at times but never relented in his efforts to take Burnley forward, which he certainly did. He lived alone. Burnley FC seemed to be his family. At his funeral, it was revealed that he wished to have his ashes scattered at Turf Moor. How appropriate!'

Barry Kilby recalled:

'When I became the major shareholder in late 1998, Waddle had gone and Stan Ternent was in charge. But the team was struggling. Heavy defeats at Preston, Bournemouth and Fulham, left the club only two places clear of the relegation zone at Christmas. Stan was refusing to speak with the board.

'The financial situation was not clever. Ray put some money into the club after a rights issue, but it was the £5m that I invested which clinched the deal. My investment was the product of the sale of my G-Tech company. I realised that the money was probably lost as soon as I put it into the club but that didn't deter me. I immediately paid off the overdraft on the stands, only to find that the bank was not prepared to offer the club a further one. I thought then that I might have done better had I held fire on the repayment.

'The next thing I did was to look at how the team might be strengthened. Certainly, the stand-off between Stan and the board could not continue. One of the first things I did was to meet him at his home. What struck me most when I first met him was his passion for the club and his work here. My instinct was to back him so a good chunk of that £5m went into boosting the team. We brought back Steve Davis, our talisman centre half, from Luton for around £800,000. He had been an inspirational figure during our twin promotions in the early nineties. We also paid a sizeable fee to Tranmere for their scrapping, box-to-box midfielder, Micky Mellon. Graham Branch came in from Stockport too. He was such a versatile player, playing in just about every outfield position. A bit later we brought in Stoke's right back Ally Pickering and Lenny Johnrose, a 'mud and bullets', tough tackling midfielder from Bury.

'There was an immediate impact after the first tranche of new signings. At Bristol Rovers in early January we won a terrific end-to-end game 4-3. Davis, Mellon and Branch were outstanding. But results fell away again after a successive away win at Millwall. Following the humiliating defeats at home by Gillingham (0-5) and Manchester City (0-6), I was pressed by some within the club – and many outside – to remove Stan. But I have never been one for knee-jerk reactions. I took a long, cool look at the situation. I asked myself "If I remove Stan who could I bring in? Would they be any better?" There were only a dozen games left. I knew that any successor would have very little time to bed in, sort out what was needed and put it in place.

'I also spoke with some of the senior players. I knew they were unlikely to tell me much. They knew the dangers of being too open. But as far as I could tell they seemed committed to Stan and the fight against relegation. What I then needed to do was to test Stan's mettle – was he still up for the challenge? He left me in no doubt about that, so we immediately worked together to bring in some key reinforcements. Paul Cook, a gritty midfielder with a left peg like a wand, and Tom Cowans, a swift and skilful left wing back, were signed on loan. Both played important parts in the relegation battle which was eventually won handsomely with an 11-match unbeaten run. The momentum created by that charge to the tape gave us the impetus to achieve promotion at the end of the following season.'

Buoyant at his chairman's unequivocal backing, Stan declared defiantly to the local media:

'Under no circumstances will I resign. I have never packed anything in in my life and I don't intend to start now. I came here to do a job. I have been here eight months and expect to be here for three years or more. The people can keep shouting and bawling until they're blue in the face. They frightened Adrian Heath and Chris Waddle away but I'm mentally and physically tougher than that, and longer in the tooth. I came to do a job and I will do it my way… You don't become a bad manager overnight… I will turn Burnley around. A lot of things have conspired against us but I accept full responsibility and I won't duck a challenge.'

Both Steve Davis and Andy Payton agreed that Stan Ternent was the best manager that they had played under during their careers. Andy Payton said in April 1999, shortly after Stan's position appeared to be in jeopardy:

'We've all got the utmost confidence in our manager. The mood's very good. Obviously wins breed confidence and we've been on this unbeaten run for about seven games. I'm top scorer by miles, so I'd like to think that I've contributed to our improved situation. But that's what I'm paid to do.'

As proof of his importance to his beloved Burnley, Andy Payton netted 20 league goals during that troubled 1998/99 season, almost 40% of his team's final tally.

Payton continued:

'The manager has turned things around. Stan was also my manager at Hull for a while. He's definitely the best manager I've played under. He is better than Liam Brady at Celtic and Brian Horton who were very good managers, too. Coaching-wise, Stan really helped my game as a young lad at Hull… Under Stan every single day was intense. There were no more days off. We had to earn our places.

'It's just a shame that we couldn't have got the right players in earlier in the 1998/99 season, before the takeover by Barry Kilby. The problem was that Ternent got the job last summer when Burnley were about to be taken over. Since then we've got a new chairman, but back then Stan and Sam Ellis were given the job but they weren't given any money to spend. They had to mould their team from the previous season's players who had just avoided relegation.

'The takeover did drag on a bit. That and a bad run of injuries affected the players a little bit. We went to high-riding Bournemouth [where a young Eddie Howe was centre half] and were thrashed 5-0, and then went to

Division leaders, Fulham and were thumped 4-0. If you are going to places like that playing half a reserve team you are going to get stuffed. The takeover eventually went through at Christmas time, halfway through the season, and Stan has started to get the right players in.

'I felt sorry for Stan. But he has spent the money well, bringing in experienced players like Steve Davis, Mickey Mellon, Tom Cowans and Paul Cook, and we are starting to look like a team now… It's a good job we've had this run because if we hadn't we really would be in deep trouble, but we feel as though we can avoid the drop and if we do, we're looking to establish a springboard for next season.'

In conversation with Burnley writer and statistician, Wallace Chadwick, Burnley's commanding centre half, Steve Davis, added:

'I played under a good few managers who had their own ways and styles but Stan Ternent was the best. He was a leader of men who knew when to give his players responsibility and when it was time to lead. He was unpredictable at times which always kept you on your toes.'

Fellow newcomer, Mickey Mellon also said shortly after his arrival at Turf Moor:

'There's only a couple of clubs I would have left my previous club for and one of them was Burnley. It is a big club with a fantastic manager and a great reputation. He's going to attract good players to this club which is good enough for me… I'm sure we are going to go from strength to strength. I've played in the north-west and know about the manager's credentials. He knows how to get teams out of this division… Everything is heading in the right direction. I know that I can continue to improve and know that the manager will help me to do that.'

Club captain, Gordon Armstrong also stated publicly: 'Stan Ternent has the full support of everybody in the dressing room. There's no doubt about that.'

In the 11-match unbeaten run that followed, play-off hopefuls, Stoke City, were hammered 4-1 by Ternent's resurgent side, with Payton once again on target, a mesmerising Glen Little adding two more. Right back, Ally Pickering completed a memorable display by blasting in an unstoppable 30-yard volley against his former club, a goal which he dedicated to his recently deceased father.

On the following Saturday, 'moneybags' Fulham, bankrolled by Al-Fayed's fortune, were out-muscled at a balmy Turf Moor, in front of a basking 13,086 crowd with Ronnie Jepson's brilliant, blistering strike securing the points and Division Two safety. A season which had begun in penury and angry recrimination ended in glorious delight. Burnley were about to rise once more. It was timely, for Barry Kilby was a man in a hurry, reasoning: 'A Premier Two Division will be created eventually. We must be in that Division, for there'll be serious money here. We need to push on. I expect us to mount a serious promotion campaign next season.'

1999 – 2003

Payton's Place

'Rise'

THE new millennium dawned. The dome didn't pull, the river didn't ignite, the Eye didn't revolve but at least the bug didn't bite. On 1 January, the world seemed as it was at the close of the previous millennium. As for Burnley, they shook off their slumbers, and fortified by the Wright stuff, won promotion at balmy Glanford Park, Scunthorpe on 6 May 2000.

Stan pruned his squad radically. Out went 12 players including the disappointing Mark Ford and in came previous loan signing, Paul Cook, 34-year-old central defender, Mitchell Thomas, formerly with Luton and Spurs, and 26-year-old right back, Dean West from Bury.

The new campaign started at a bright, clammy Adams Park in early August. Stan packed the midfield with only Cooke up front. But after Jamie McSporran had put Wycombe ahead in the 27th minute with a searing strike, Burnley were left flat-footed. During the second half Stan strengthened his attack, first bringing on the bruising Irish target man, Alan Lee, and then the predatory Payton. Lee's aerial strength soon paid off. He flicked on for Payton to find space on the left flank and from his cross Cooke headed an equaliser. Burnley had enough chances to have won but Stan was satisfied with a point. Although Manchester City dished out their customary punishment in the League Cup, winning the tie, 6-0 on aggregate, business was quickly resumed with an insipid 2-1 home victory over woeful

Chesterfield. Glen Little's exclusion made more of a splash. Stan's terse explanation was: 'If you are doing the business, you'll be in the side. If not, you won't.' Lenny Johnrose, a midfield 'enforcer' under Ternent, reflected:

> 'Stan was incredibly tough and would hand out unbelievable abuse, some players couldn't put up with him – he would destroy some people and they'd have to go. However, I stood up to Stan and ignored the abuse. I think he quite liked that.' Lenny typified the 'hard as nails' competitor than Stan needed in his teams. As an ultra-tough midfielder, Stan was cast in the same mould. Payton said: 'Johnrose had real attitude and one of the best at taking people out. Stan would say, "Sort f***ing so and so out" and he would.'

After making hard work of beating a poor Oldham side at Boundary Park (1-0) Burnley travelled to Bristol Rovers on a scorching Bank Holiday Monday. There they would find a trigger-happy referee who awarded 42 free kicks and booked 10 players – six from Burnley. In a rare moment of unity both sets of supporters chanted, 'You don't know what you're doing!' Fittingly the game turned on the controversial award of a penalty which Jamie Cureton duly despatched. Stan was incandescent with rage, fuming at the post match press conference: 'The referee was not, repeat not, up-to-scratch. He has a responsibility not just to the players and managers but to Burnley's travelling supporters who've travelled over 200 miles to watch a game of football that's been ruined by a shoddy, not up-to-scratch performance.'

The Clarets took top spot, though, after beating Bournemouth 2-1. Graham Branch, who scored the opening goal, responded to criticism of him by explaining: 'I think sometimes the crowd believe I'm not trying, but I'm very laid back.' While prone to crises of confidence, Branch eventually attained cult celebrity status at Turf Moor. Dubbed 'Graham Di Branchio' after the Italian striker, Paulo Di Canio, his name would be sung heartily, if with an ironic smirk, to the tune of 'O Sole Mio'. His willingness to play in any outfield position slowly gained him deserved respect.

When Preston and Burnley met at Deepdale on 11 September they produced the first 0-0 draw between the clubs in over 100 years. Then Burnley re-took the summit a week later after a 3-0 drubbing of visiting Colchester with Payton notching his first Burnley hat-trick. However, after a joyless 0-0 draw at Ashton Gate; a squandered two-goal lead against Brentford (2-2); an inexplicable home loss to relegation-bound Scunthorpe (1-2); and a frustrating 1-1 draw at the New Den, Burnley slipped to 6th position. The dip in form prompted Stan to abandon his preferred 3-5-2 formation.

At the start of this season, Stan Ternent's 3-5-2 set-up comprised: Steve Davis, Mitchell Thomas and Gordon Armstrong as the back three; Dean West and Paul Smith as the wing backs; Mellon, Cook and Johnrose operating in central midfield with Cooke and Payton up front. At Cambridge on 19 October, Stan reverted to 4-4-2, with Davis and Thomas as the centre backs, West and Smith as conventional full backs, Cook, Johnrose and Mullin in central midfield, Little wide, and Branch and Cooke as the front two. Payton was unavailable. On a chilly evening at the Abbey Stadium, Cooke vindicated his recall by netting an early winner in a dominant team display (1-0).

Ahead of the AGM, chairman Barry Kilby announced a record trading loss of £1.8m, largely brought about by a 30% rise in the cost of playing contracts. Nevertheless, club debts were down by £1m to £3m, helped by the £3.9m raised by a rights issue. Then on a showery 23 October, Burnley turned on a glittering display, beating Bristol City with a thunderous 30-yarder from Paul Cook and a brilliant curler from Andy Cooke.

Burnley's drab 1-0 FA Cup victory at Barnet was covered by the Sky TV. A better result was in the offing, as Burnley went nap against Wrexham on a blowy, wet Turf Moor evening. Graham Branch completed the annihilation with a diving header (5-0).

A narrow loss at Luton (1-2) was quickly corrected with a 1-0 home win against Blackpool in mid-November. Former 'Seasider' Mellon won the game with a vicious, rising 30-yard drive. Having endured a deluge of abuse from the Blackpool fans, Mellon milked the moment. The sponsors duly awarded him man-of-the-match.

Rotherham were comfortably despatched in the FA Cup before Burnley succumbed to the prevalent disaffection at the Madejski Stadium, settling for a tedious 0-0 draw. Surreally, the Reading fans threw underpants onto the pitch in a 'pants for pants' protest at their team's poor performances.

A pulsating contest followed at Wigan on the 27 November. The Division Two leaders Wigan were then managed by John Benson, with John Bond acting as his assistant. Wigan were fortunate to maintain their unbeaten record with a 1-1 draw. Burnley had bossed the first period, with Payton heading the Clarets into a 17th minute lead. However, a rare moment of slackness allowed the home side to level minutes before half-time. Wigan threatened more in the second period, but Alan Lee missed a gilt-edged, late opportunity to win the game. A stubborn Wycombe side then parked the bus at Turf Moor a week later. They reckoned without Payton, though, as the Padiham predator squeezed in a 78th minute winner.

An FA Cup tie at Premier League Derby awaited Burnley in the third round. The result was a major shock. The pride in Pride Park belonged exclusively to the visitors. A Burnley fan described the defining moment thus:

> 'One Sunday paper photo captured Cooke in the act of scoring, rising at least one foot above his marker, a solitary, soaring Claret, frozen in mid-air, among a clutch of grounded Derby defenders. It was the perfect metaphor. Having tackled harder, run faster, passed better and jumped higher, Burnley were literally head and shoulders above Derby. On *Match of the Day*, Alan Hansen said the Clarets were absolutely magnificent.'

Visiting Cardiff were the next side to lose at Turf Moor, although the Bluebirds made the early running. After Mitchell Johnson, a colossus at Derby, had conceded a deflected own goal, Stan took remedial action, switching to a 3-5-2 formation, with Branch replacing West. Almost immediately Davis powered in a headed equaliser, from Paul Cook's fizzing corner kick. The winner came in the 68th minute after Little had turned two Cardiff defenders inside out. His exquisite chip to the far post, was stabbed in decisively by Johnrose (2-1).

There was not much festive joy at Gigg Lane, though, as Bury flew into a 4-0 interval lead. Burnley had several players missing due to injury and illness. Once skipper Steve Davis was dismissed for a deliberate handball offence, his team crumpled (2-4). Stan griped: 'It would have to be Bury, again, wouldn't it? They were a mediocre, mid-table side, but of course they played like Real Madrid against me. At least Warnock wasn't around to gloat!'

Languishing Oxford United arrived at Turf Moor two days later and doggedly held onto a 2-1 lead until Payton struck twice in the closing minutes to seize a hat-trick and the points (3-2). Burnley rose one place to 5th, but that did not last long as Notts County inflicted their fifth league defeat of the season (0-2). Despite creating a host of chances, Stan damned the performance as 'unacceptable.' Burnley then bade farewell to the FA Cup competition after being out-gunned at Premier League, Coventry (0-3). A seven-match unbeaten sequence followed, beginning with a 1-1 draw at Chesterfield, and including home victories over Oldham (3-0) and promotion rivals, Bristol Rovers (1-0). Glen Little scored a scintillating solo winner against Rovers after Burnley were reduced to 10 men, Payton having been red-carded for retaliation. Ian Cox, newly signed from debt-ridden Bournemouth for £500,000, played superbly in central defence alongside the redoubtable Davis.

Before serving his three-match suspension, Payton made sure Burnley grabbed all three points at Bournemouth, heading Burnley into a 32nd minute lead. Burnley's defence then barred the door (1-0). Cox was once again outstanding.

The home 0-0 draw with Wigan on the 19th February was remarkable because it was Ian Wright's home debut for Burnley. Wright explained how this extraordinary event came about:

> 'I just said to my friend, Mitchell Thomas, how I was thinking about blowing it all in at Celtic. Mitchell said, "let me talk to Stan" who was an old friend of mine from our Crystal Palace days. Stan had been a coach there. Every time I speak to Stan he says "when am I coming to Turf Moor?" Vice-chairman, Ray Ingleby, then got involved and the next thing I know, it was happening. I've known Stan since I turned professional and he has been on at me for years to sign for him so I've finally given in. I hope I can make some contribution to their promotion push, but the place has given me a really good feeling. I just want to play. It's a great place to end my career. Hopefully, I will be everything the fans want. It won't be for lack of trying. I've been slaughtered as some kind of football mercenary. That's rubbish! I hope this proves how much I want to play...'

Stan commented:

> 'I'm happy that I've been able to do the deal. I'm happy that Ian feels he wants to come to Burnley and play for us. He's in the twilight of his career now but still a sensational talent. I know Ian from long back when I was at Palace. He's a fantastic character, a great personality, and a lot of the players at Burnley will learn from him. It has taken a lot of sorting out. Ian has taken a mega drop in salary. He could have sat on his backside at Celtic for twice as much, perhaps more. He isn't coming here for a jolly-up. He's an out and

out winner who wants to finish his career on a high... If you stick the ball in the box and give him a chance he will stick it away. You don't lose that. It's like riding a bike.... The place is electric. Everyone is happy that Ian has decided to join. They are exciting times and the supporters deserve a bit of excitement.'

Barry Kilby said: 'I hope we will see an increase in attendances as we are stepping on the gas to get this promotion.' While his star-struck vice-chairman, Ray Ingleby, added, hyperbolically: 'Ian is thrilled to be able to end his career with Burnley. I have always said that we must get Burnley as high up the football ladder as possible. I think attracting Ian increases our stature and credibility in the football world five-fold. We have a world class player at a world class club. It couldn't get any better.' Stan had convinced them that the lift-off in attendances and merchandise sales would ensure Wright's higher wages would be paid for.

Player reaction was generally positive. Captain Steve Davis said:

'I am absolutely delighted. It's a great signing for the club and the supporters. It shows them what the club are aiming to do. It gives everyone a massive boost... You can only learn when you train with players like that. I'm sure he's going to do well and give everyone a lift. He's a bubbly character and will be great to have at the club. I think it's been well documented that we have been after a forward but never in our wildest dreams did we imagine we would get Ian Wright. It's all credit to the board and the manager.'

But while Andy Cooke welcomed Ian's presence, Andy Payton was more reserved, fearing for his position. He had a three-match suspension still to serve. He knew Wright would take his place but wondered whether he would regain it.

Stan allowed Wright to spend most of the week in London where his family lived and where he had media commitments, but while in Burnley he shared a house on the outskirts with his friend Mitchell Thomas. They tried to remain incognito but it wasn't long before their cover was blown, causing Stan to quip: 'They tried to live anonymously with as much success as Bill Clinton attempting to set up home in Emmerdale.' Wright didn't turn the autograph hunters away. He didn't turn anyone down. As Stan said: 'He signed books, programmes, posters and even babies.' He was a superb ambassador for the club, putting his team mates at ease immediately, demanding no special treatment and quickly joining in with the banter. Wright never forgot the fact that he was a working-class lad who had the fortune to make good. Although when he arrived in Burnley one day in a Blue Bentley coupe, Stan chided him with, 'You can't drive that around here. It's Burnley! Anyway, you can see the engine. Don't you get a bonnet with it?'

Wright deserved a better introduction than the dour 0-0 draw that Burnley and Wigan produced. Not many in the Turf Moor crowd of 20,435 complained. Just as Stan predicted, the ticket office was besieged, while the club shop was hard-pressed to meet the febrile demand for Wright-related merchandise. Burnley was suddenly transformed into a boom town. Ian Wright MBE – recast as 'Massive Burnley Enthusiast' – became the first serving Burnley player to appear on a TV chat show.

A week later, Burnley won 2-1 at Colchester, but Wright was unhappy. He was bewildered and angered by the abuse he and his wife received from some home fans. He had allegedly been called a 'black bastard'. Wright hadn't scored yet and this troubled him as well. While furious at Wright's abusive reception, Stan urged him to persevere. Wright complained; 'I have taken a lot of stick in my time which I can handle. But it's not on when fans aim it at my family. I want an apology from the fans.' He wouldn't get one, though. A Colchester spokesman stated: 'Wright is a superstar and he can expect a lot worse when he goes elsewhere with Burnley. The facts are that the chants are offensive but not racist.'

A shattering blow to Burnley's promotion prospects followed, as David Moyes's Preston out-played the Clarets at Turf Moor, winning 3-0. Stan thought that the result flattered Preston. He was confident that his team would recover in the midweek home fixture with Luton. They didn't. On a night of hissing rain, Luton defied the squidgy surface and incessant Burnley pressure to win 2-0. Wright missed three good chances, including a one-on-one with the visiting keeper, while the Hatters made the most of their fewer opportunities. During the second half, the home crowd implored Stan to bring on the benched Andy Payton. After acceding to their wishes, Payton promptly put the ball in the Luton net only to be ruled off-side.

Payton was recalled for the game at Wrexham in place of Wright. At 32-years-old, he was anxious about the prospect of a further contract, and whether it would match those of his higher-paid colleagues. At Wrexham, he made his point. He wasted little time in scoring the decisive goal, then celebrating by revealing a T-shirt emblazoned with

'Natural Born Claret'. Burnley were back on track. While Wright commanded the headlines, in Payton Burnley had a rare jewel – loyal and lethal in equal measure. This was his 20th goal of the season and the 200th of his career.

The next game was at promotion rivals, Gillingham, one of six teams battling for a second automatic promotion place. Preston seemed unchallengeable in top spot. Driven forward by their pugnacious central midfielders, Hessenthaler and Smith, and fed by a marauding wing back Nosworthy, Gillingham tore into Burnley from the off, taking a 4th minute lead through central defender, Guy Butters. With Burnley penned within their own half for much of the first period, Payton was isolated, yet he made the most of a solitary chance to restore parity in the 31st minute. Home strikers, Asaba and Onuora posed the greater threat, though. Only Crichton's agility and his defenders' tenacity kept them at bay. But it came as no surprise when Asaba poked Gillingham into 2-1 lead in the 68th minute, after his brilliant cross-field dribble evaded two floundering Burnley defenders. Burnley were under the cosh and losing.

Stan decided that it was time for 'Ian Wright, Wright, Wright!' Pent up with compressed adrenaline Wright shot off the bench, desperate to join the action. With muscular Ronnie Jepson also thrown into the mix, Burnley reverted to 3-5-2. Payton described Jepson, 'as a big, hard, aggressive bastard who lifted the spirit in the dressing room. When he came on he would rough up opponents, yelling: "Right I'm going to smash this c***!" The defenders were often scared of him which was great for me as I then got more chances.'

With Jepson and Johnrose, putting themselves about, Gillingham's midfield dominance began to fracture. This allowed Little and Thomas more space to bomb forward. With only two minutes left, Thomas looped a centre into the box. In one blinding flash, Wright stunned the ball with his chest and lashed it venomously into the roof of the net. Such was the velocity of his strike, that Gills' goalkeeper, Bartram, could only raise his arms in surrender. Wright charged off to find Stan who embraced him like a long-lost son. The point stolen here would prove critical on the final day of the season. Stan told a *Burnley Express* reporter, 'It was the reason why I brought Wright to Burnley, the reason why I had coaxed him through his doubts, the reason why I bet on one of the most natural goal-scorers I have ever seen.'

A regulation 3-0 home win followed over unadventurous Reading, with both Payton and Wright on target after Davis had out-muscled the visitors' defence to head Burnley into a 37th minute lead. Branch rescued Burnley at Blackpool where Stan complained: 'We should have kicked off at nine because for the last half hour we played OK.' And then Jepson saved Burnley with a last gasp equaliser at home against Bury (2-2). Stan admitted it had been a mediocre display but added defiantly: 'We never jack it in, only that mob that I cleared out last season.' Jepson paid no regard to his goal saying: 'I don't give "a monkeys" about it. The goal belongs to the team not individuals.'

On 'April Fools' Day' in rainy Cardiff, Payton added another, after breaking away and striking his shot between the legs of the advancing keeper. It gave Burnley an unassailable 2-0 lead over the sinking Bluebirds. Cardiff did manage to reduce the arrears with an 'own goal', aided and abetted by Burnley's nemesis, Kurt Nogan, but it was scant consolation. Only Cardiff's 'Soul Crew' exhibited any hostility, recreating scenes reminiscent of the hateful eighties. Burnley remained in 5th spot.

There was no change on the following Saturday, even after Ian Wright's late, late strike proved just enough to subdue the chirpy, yet limited, Magpies. With time almost up and the referee consulting his watch, Steve Davis launched the ball up-field, Wright met it on the edge of the box, controlled it instantly, shimmied around a Notts County defender and blasted an unstoppable drive into the top corner. His glee was uncontainable. Stan said: "I think he kissed me but I've tried to block that from my mind!"

At a wet, cold and dreary Oxford, Burnley again left it late to snatch the points. A remarkable long-range header from Davis and a straightforward one from substitute Weller turned the game on its head. It was a fitting moment of glory for Weller who had bravely survived a debilitating condition and a major operation. Here Ian Wright was the provider, finding the unmarked Weller at the far post (2-1).

With an automatic promotion slot beckoning, Burnley stumbled at home against close rivals, Gillingham, losing 0-3. Stan described it as 'a bad day at the office'. There were unwanted personal repercussions too as his contract talks were put on hold, pending the season's outcome. Gillingham seemed destined to accompany Preston into Division One. Gillingham boss, Peter Taylor, goaded Stan with the parting remark: 'Never mind Stan. Keep going. You'll get it right eventually'. Stan focused his fury on his preparations for Burnley's final four games.

First up was a feisty home contest with Millwall, also promotion challengers, with a huge, hostile, away following. Burnley took a 4-0 lead, thanks to first half goals from Cox, Cooke and Davis, and a stunning long-range effort from Paul Cook, shortly after the break. Incensed by their side's apparent capitulation, the Millwall miscreants took out their anger on the Cricket Field Stand seating, slinging broken fragments into an adjoining enclosure populated by young Burnley fans, forcing their horrified parents to remove them to a safer place.

Meanwhile, on the pitch the Millwall lions belatedly recovered their roar. With nothing left to lose they began counter-attacking with startling energy and menace, led by their skilful centre forward, Neil Harris. Burnley reeled under the pressure pulling everyone bar Wright back behind the ball. Stan raged at this, gesticulating wildly at his players, insisting they held a higher line. With only the isolated Wright offering his besieged defenders an out ball. Millwall had acres of space in which to launch their attacks and pick their passes and crosses.

When Millwall scored their first goal on the hour it was met with only ironic cheers from the away end. When they scored their second, 18 minutes later, there was only a marginal increase in interest. But when they scored a third with still three minutes remaining, the roar from the visiting fans was explosive. Had the game gone on for another 15 minutes, Burnley might well have lost. Afterwards, Stan muttered acidly: 'That's what happens if you try to defend under your own crossbar.' This tense victory lifted Burnley out of fifth place and into fourth.

On Easter Monday at Griffin Park, there was similar mixture of exultation and relief when the final whistle sounded. Lowly Brentford produced a plucky performance, bossing the first period with the gangling Owusu snatching the lead shortly before half-time. Stan reacted by moving Little to the right flank and swapping Mullin to the left. But the masterstroke was the introduction of Wright for Payton. Wright proceeded to tear the Brentford defence to shreds with his powerful running and darting movement, creating gaps which he and Mullin (twice) could plunder. Had keeper Crichton not played a blinder though, Brentford would have taken something from this game (3-2). Burnley rose to third.

The Brentford game featured Ian Wright's final goal for Burnley. He had told Stan that he had been disappointed at making only eight starts. But Stan was concerned that Wright's initial score-less run had put him under too much pressure. By benching him, Stan thought he had thrown those hacks off the scent who were eager to write his obituary. Wright admitted to Stan: 'I was gutted when I wasn't getting a start but I suppose, after I scored at Gillingham, it just kicked in. It was brilliant.'

Although Stan yearned for him to stay, Ian decided his future lie in the media. He joined the end-of-season team 'jolly' in Portugal, though. Wright said: 'Even in London, I've never met people like these Burnley fans before. If I walk down the High Street, they come from everywhere. They are really fanatical, but the thing I'll remember most is the amount of Burnley shirts I've seen on the streets. Everyone wears them. It must be part of the school uniform around here.'

The penultimate game at home against Cambridge resulted in a straightforward 2-0 win for Stan's men, with a brace of goals by Payton, one of which featured a sublime 'Cruyff turn'. These were his 26th and 27th league goals of the season, a tremendous effort that deservedly won him the prestigious 'Golden Boot' award. Elsewhere, Wigan lost at home to Wrexham (0-1), impeding their promotion prospects, while Preston ended Millwall's challenge at Deepdale (3-2).

The season concluded on Saturday 6 May, a day of blue skies and hazy warmth. The calculation was simple. Burnley had to beat already relegated Scunthorpe, and hope that Gillingham did not win at Wrexham. But if both faltered then Wigan, or more improbably, Stoke, could have stolen the prize. Wrexham were managed by ex-Claret, Brian Flynn. It was time to call in a favour.

After 11 minutes, there was wild cheering in the away end. Right back Mark McGregor had blasted Wrexham in front with a 30-yard screamer. Stan would later reward him with a contract. Burnley were then ahead of Gillingham by one point. But 10 minutes later they were in arrears, if only on goal difference, after Scunthorpe's pint-sized midfielder, Lee Hodges, had cracked a vicious, rising drive against the underside of Crichton's crossbar and in. Belying their hopeless position, Scunthorpe immediately raised their game, forcing Burnley onto the back foot. However, almost upon the stroke of half-time, the Scunthorpe keeper made a flailing clearance from a corner, which had neither distance nor power, reaching the unmarked Mellon on the edge of the box. He unhesitatingly, rifled in the equaliser.

Despite being pegged back, Scunthorpe continued to press hard. Two good chances went begging. There was no denying an irresistible force, though. With around 20 minutes left, Glen Little was sent on by Stan. It was an inspired substitution. For almost immediately Little struck a rising half-volley into the top left-hand corner of the Scunthorpe net. The goal had winner stamped upon it. The Wrexham game had not finished when the final whistle was blown and the Burnley fans streamed onto the field. Few doubted Burnley were up. And, so it proved. This time the fans sensed their team was good enough to stay. Burnley were on an upward march. The next day, Stan faxed Gills' boss, Peter Taylor, with a consolatory message. It read: 'Dear Peter. Keep going son, you'll get it right eventually. Best regards, Stan.'

Stan strengthened his side during the summer of 2000, adding former Sheffield Wednesday's full back or midfielder, Lee Briscoe. Stan described the former England Under-21 international as 'a determined left-sided player'. Fellow defender, Mitchell Thomas, quipped: 'Briscoe was the nicest man in the world until he has a beverage and then he turns into a monster.'

Phil Gray, a 31-year-old striker, was recruited from Luton. He had played for Northern Ireland and when he scored in a World Cup qualifier against Malta, in September, he became Burnley's first international goalscorer since Billy Hamilton. However, Stan's prized signing was 'tough nut midfielder' Kevin Ball. Stan believed Ball was his 'best signing', a kindred spirit, for Stan played with similar combative fire. Ball said: 'I had more arguments with Stan than with any manager I played for.' Not that this detracted from Ball's enjoyment of his two years at Burnley.

When Ball arrived at Turf Moor he was 35-years-old, but it was apparent that he had lost none of his trademark aggression with which he had intimidated so many opponents in his Sunderland and Portsmouth days. Ball explained: 'I hated losing. It didn't matter who we were playing. I just wanted to win and if it meant kicking your proverbial granny to do so, then that's just the way I was. I have no regrets.' Against Blackburn in December 2000, Ball launched into a two-footed tackle on Rovers' playmaker, David Dunn, a reckless charge of juggernaut intensity. Ball recalled:

> 'Souness, the Blackburn manager was going bonkers; Stan was going bonkers; the crowd was going bonkers; the referee was fumbling for his card, so I thought "bollocks to this!" and promptly marched off. My lad who had seen what happened on TV stood up for me as always, claiming I got the ball. Not my wife though. She thought I should have been put inside. I saw David sometime after. We had a good laugh about it. I loved derby games. Just like the supporters do.'

Mitchell Thomas told a *Lancashire Evening Telegraph* reporter: 'Kevin is always straight. Serious. Assertive in everything he does.'

No kidding!

As if Stan didn't have enough steel at his disposal, he tried to entice his friend, Vinnie Jones, to join the Turf Moor throng. Although tempted, the former Wimbledon 'hit man' decided it was probably better to stick with the movies. A work colleague who 'moonlighted', almost literally, as a Preston scout had no doubt that Burnley would survive. He confided, though, that while Burnley's back three of Davis, Cox and Thomas was sound, he thought that "Davis's lack of pace might be targeted". The scout suggested that opponents might attempt to exploit Davis's fondness for playing from the back, hoping to pick his pocket, believing his recovery speed to be 'not among the quickest.'

Burnley began the 2000/01 season confidently, holding promotion-bound Bolton to a 1-1 draw in the opening game at Horwich, with Phil Gray prodding in Little's inviting cross. Even more impressively, recently relegated Wimbledon were then beaten 1-0 at Turf Moor with a goal from Paul Weller. According to Mitchell Thomas, Weller was known as 'Mr Angry, because of how easy it was to wind him up in training.'

Although Wolves inflicted yet another defeat on their favourite opponents, Burnley bounced back with an outrageous 'smash and grab raid' at Crystal Palace (1-0). The Eagles manager, Alan Smith, announced breezily beforehand: 'I've known Stan a long time... there won't be any surprises.' His rueful expression afterwards suggested otherwise as his team spurned chance after chance, while the 'admirable' Crichton played a blinder in the Burnley goal.

A subsequent 1-0 win at Huddersfield featured another outstanding display by a Burnley keeper. This time the hero was the lanky Greek international, Nik Michopoulos, who took advantage of Crichton's late arrival to seize the number one position. Stan quipped to BBC presenter and die-hard Claret, Tony Livesey: 'Nik was good... expert at his drills. The problem was he could hardly speak a word of English... just coffee and thank you. I left him with Jeppo [Ronnie Jepson] for two minutes and suddenly he knew five more, 'It's f***ing freezing here, gaffer'." Mitchell Thomas said of 'Nik the Greek', 'He doesn't understand a lot but if he makes a noise when I'm in defence I know I have to get out of the way because he's so big.'

By the second week in November, Burnley were fourth, ahead of bitter rivals Blackburn Rovers. But Andy Payton, a hero of their 1999/2000 promotion campaign, was no longer an automatic choice, nor was his strike partner Andy Cooke, who was transferred to Stoke in December for £300,000. Cooke parted with the gracious words: 'Over five and a half seasons, I have had a very good rapport with the crowd. I've got a lot of good things to take from Burnley. I wouldn't change a day of it...'

Payton was less sanguine about his loss of favour. He told his biographer, Gavin Roper: 'If I'd played the whole season, I'd have probably got at least 20, if not 30 goals... it was a crazy situation with the fans screaming "Get Payton on!" every game when I was on the bench, which was more often than not... it was like Stan didn't want to play me for some reason...'

Arguably, Stan wanted his front men to defend from the front in this more challenging division. Expensive recruit, Ian Moore, met that need, employing his lightning pace and phenomenal stamina to harry opposing defenders deep within their own half, forcing errors and stemming the forward supply. Moore, a former England Under-21 international, was signed on the 20 November 2000 from Stockport County for a club record fee, reported to be £1m.

Chairman Barry Kilby said:

> 'It's a little scary but it's the right move and the right future. We must be careful with our cash despite a £2m increase in turnover during the 1999/2000 season, representing a 56% rise. We didn't do it lightly but we had to step up a gear and look to the future. We bargained down to the last penny.'

Stan added:

> 'Moore's young, 24-years-old, and we've signed him for this year and another four years so he will the future of Burnley Football Club for the next five years... The chairman and the board have backed me on a £1m deal which is a lot of money for this club and I thank them for that.'

Realising he was expected to graft for his new club, Moore said:

> 'It is an excellent move for me. Burnley is an impressive place and the stadium is second to none... I can't wait to get started. I'll chase anything. I'm an honest player and I'll get on with it. As long as I'm up there, getting a few goals, I'll be a happy man and if things aren't going well for me, I'll always work hard for the team.'

At the end of January 2001 'headmaster' Gareth Taylor joined, initially on loan, from Manchester City, replacing the departed target man, Andy Cooke. Taylor's aerial strength was also deployed effectively in defence, notably at set pieces. Like Ian Moore, Gareth Taylor was a hard grafter.

Payton remarked:

> 'Gareth Taylor would have been good to play with... he was good in the air; but I only got the chance to play with him once, when he did his trade-mark flick-ons and I scored a couple... I didn't really get on with Ian Moore. He had pace – loads and loads of it – but I thought he wasn't good enough to replace me.'

But if Payton felt jealous, unappreciated and excluded, Mitchell Thomas commended him on his professionalism, saying: 'Andy keeps himself to himself and just gets on with it.' As for Payton's new rival, Ian Moore, Thomas described him as 'Very quiet, very deep. Never get caught with him when he is having a deep moment or you're trapped. It could be religion, football or home life, anything goes.' New recruit, Phil Gray, was also disenchanted with limited first team opportunities and moved on to Division One, Oxford in November.

While the competition for first team places created some tensions, there was little doubt about the strength of team spirit as Burnley won four games on the bounce during October. Even a 0-5 battering at Nottingham Forest was quickly brushed aside with home victories over Crewe and Sheffield United, and a creditable draw at West Bromwich.

The main jokers in this resilient pack were said to be mesmerising winger Glen Little and elegant yet combative midfielder Paul Cook. Mitchell Thomas described Little as 'the life and soul of every party.' Thomas was convinced that the ultra-chatty Little 'could talk under water'. As for Scouse midfielder and 'dressing room bookie', Paul Cook, Thomas described him as 'A very funny lad, his accent making everything he says even funnier...' Thomas thought Lennie Johnrose was the most confrontational member of the group, claiming 'He is constantly causing trouble. He loves winding people up, loves going against all the rules, like a naughty schoolboy.'

Before the Preston away game on the 9 December, Burnley were strongly placed in in sixth position, having won 11 and drawn five of their opening 20 league games. Home gates were averaging over 15,000, 15% up on the previous season. 12,300 season tickets had been sold, up from 6,800 in 1999/2000, an 81% rise.

Although Ian Moore opened his account at Deepdale with a princely, curling shot from outside the box, to give Burnley an interval lead, Preston recovered to win 2-1. It was a disappointing display. Worse still, recently-relegated Blackburn won 2-0 at a Turf Moor on the following weekend in front of a febrile 21,369 crowd. Kevin Ball's X-rated tackle on David Dunn hardly helped contain the gladiatorial emotions, but neither did a touchline tussle for the ball, late in the game, as Burnley frantically sought an elusive equaliser. Burnley's misery was compounded as Blackburn stole a second goal in the final minute.

Stan remembered how despondent his players were afterwards. Above them, in the Cricket Field stand, the ecstatic Rovers' fans stomped and roared, while along the corridor the raucous whoops from the triumphant Rovers' dressing room were all too audible. Andy Payton took this dispiriting defeat particularly badly. As a lifetime Clarets' fan, he knew how keenly this defeat was felt by the Burnley faithful. Outside the ground the riot police had to battle hard to prevent the Blackburn coaches being attacked. Having had their violent intentions thwarted, a local contingent took out their frustrations in Burnley town centre, where, according to Stan, they smashed 'scores of windows'. Stan concluded: 'We had lost a football match. They had lost their minds.'

Three more league defeats followed in succession, including another 2-0 home loss, this time to Bolton, while Division Two Scunthorpe eliminated Burnley from the FA Cup at the first hurdle. A Boxing Day defeat at Barnsley (1-2) prompted Stan to lay into his players, ranting:

> 'It's not often I have a go at them but I am now… The gloves are off… They might feel a little bit Billy Big Time but we'll see. Our holiday period ended at quarter-to-five. We're training tomorrow and we'll be training right through the holiday period because I'm going to put this right for Burnley fans. They deserve better. Those players are having a laugh. I've stuck up for them but they are having a jolly. That's not good enough… Everything's cancelled. There'll be no time off until I get better performances… When I see Paul Weller going to the line and whizzing balls across the box, and I see one striker and no midfield players, or nobody from the other side of the field getting into the box, that tells me either they've eaten too much turkey and plum duff or they don't have a desire… I don't want Glen Little back until he's right because he's no good to us as he is and I've told the physio that…'

Rumours of Payton's alleged disaffection emerged. It was claimed that he and Moore were involved in a training ground bust up leading to their absence for the Bolton home game on 23 December. The truth was that both players were injured. Then speculation centred upon Andy Payton being transferred to Wigan or Notts County. Exasperated chairman, Barry Kilby, emphasised quickly that there was no truth in either account, adding: 'A lie gets out and is half way around the world before the truth is reported.' Payton was dismissive, too: 'The rumours do not unsettle me at all because there is no truth in them. I don't know where they come from. I think there are only nine players in the history of the club who have scored 100 goals for them, so I want to do that.'

Taking umbrage at the modest clubs he was supposedly linked with, he sniped: 'It's never a decent club, is it?'

Providing a timely reminder of his worth, Payton scored what proved to be the winning goal against Barnsley on 20 January, bringing the eight-game winless run to an end, only for three more dismal defeats to ensue. However, Taylor's arrival on loan sparked a stirring victory over champions-elect, Fulham, with late goals from Moore and Little overturning a 0-1 deficit. A jubilant Stan Ternent gushed: 'The noise the fans made reminded me of the 1960s. It was fantastic, but to be fair we gave them a lot to shout about.' A more attritional home win against languishing Huddersfield came next, although the Terriers were denied a deserved share of the spoils by some brilliant saves by Michopoulos.

Four away games followed two of which resulted in insipid defeats, at Portsmouth and Sheffield Wednesday. Nevertheless, a 1-0 win at Watford, thanks to Gareth Taylor's stabbed effort, took Burnley to 52 points and safety. Then the return game at Ewood Park, played on April Fools' Day, proved more disastrous than the festive fare at Turf Moor. Burnley lost 5-0. Stan refused to shy away from the carnage, positioning himself defiantly at the front of his technical area, oblivious to the plethora of five-fingered gestures from the crowing Rovers' fans. A savaging of this order requires a calm response from the man in charge, and to his great credit, Stan Ternent provided that.

He reflected:

> 'When we achieved First Division status I knew we'd get our backsides tanned from time to time and that's happened today... But overall the players have done really, well. It's just a really bad day, mainly for the supporters. But

the truth of the matter is that we're a million miles away, financially, from Blackburn Rovers and that shows on the football field… If I have a Mini and you have a Ferrari there's only one winner… If you go through the Blackburn side and the people who aren't even stripped you're talking an awful lot of money, probably seven years of my budget… Despite that, there wasn't much between the sides in the first half, apart from the two goals, and when the third went in, the players did remarkably well to keep it to five.

'Afterwards Stan shared a drink with his longstanding friend, the Blackburn manager Graeme Souness together with the Ewood coaching staff. Everyone was on their best behaviour. No-one mentioned the game. Stan quipped later: 'It was a bit like rowing away from the Titanic without mentioning the iceberg.'

As testament of what Stan Ternent described as their 'fantastic character and resilience', Burnley responded by thumping Preston 3-0 at home and Wimbledon 2-0 away. Incredibly, a spirited comeback victory at Norwich (3-2) put the Clarets in with a chance of securing a play-off place. Alas, they fell three points short. The two late equalisers they conceded against sixth-placed West Bromwich proved critical. Nevertheless, as Stan confirmed, seventh place was a fine achievement. He concluded: 'I think I'm close to having a good side. The players are fantastic professionals and all credit to them for a marvellous season.'

Paul Weller and Nick Micholopoulos deservedly won the lion's share of the supporters clubs' player-of-the-year awards, although Stan picked out successful loan-signing, Gareth Taylor for special mention, confiding: 'He's done very well for us and I certainly want to add Gareth to our squad.' Taylor, dubbed 'Golden Bonce' because of his aerial dominance, proceeded to join the end of season trip to Portugal. Stan was also mentioned in despatches having guided his side to a lofty final position. At the player-of-the-year evening, he was presented with a special achievement award in recognition of his efforts.

The 'feel good factor' swirling around Turf Moor was reflected in the 25 per cent rise in average home attendances which stood at 16,234 at the end of the 2000/01 season. Only 14 years before, this figure had been a meagre 3,342! It was small wonder that chairman, Barry Kilby, was so upbeat.

At the AGM Barry said:

'Our club now stands in the top 30 clubs in the country. Once again great credit must go to Stan Ternent and all his staff in improving the standard of the first team squad on what was an average budget for this division... On the commercial side, the new initiatives instigated by our chief executive, Andrew Watson, have started to bear fruit, with the commercial income rising again by 38% to £3.4m to help push our turnover up 28 per cent to £7.2m... Our desire is to maintain and improve our status in Division One. This led the board to authorise a trading loss of £2m as players' contracts were consolidated and additions made to our playing squad. This is imperative for the long-term progress of this club...'

Encouraged by the progress made during the 2000/01 season, by 9 May 2001, 10,000 season ticket holders had renewed their passes for the coming season. But what should have been a time of celebration for Stan Ternent, became a nightmare as he was rushed into Burnley hospital with a suspected heart attack. Much to his and his family's relief, it was a stomach ulcer. He was told very clearly though that he needed to rest. Stan was exhausted not only by his health scare but by his unstinting efforts on Burnley's behalf. Among his well-wishers was the gruff former Manchester City and Sunderland boss, Peter Reid. According to Stan, Reid growled, 'So you've pulled through, eh? F*** me.'

Stan was not idle for long, though. He had a team to build in pursuit of the Premier League dream. Having assembled most of his players on free transfers, Stan approached the board for a further £1m to purchase the gangling QPR centre forward, Peter Crouch whom he described as 'sensational in the air and not too bad with his feet.' Ternent reckoned he had persuaded Crouch to join until Crouch and his wife were unnerved by a 'riot' in Burnley town centre. Burnley MP Peter Pike attributed this discord primarily to poverty, poor housing and segregated schooling rather than innate racism, blaming the local BNP party for exploiting the community and economic malaise in perpetrating their racial prejudice.

Although maintaining his club could not play a leading role in reconciling local racial differences, Burnley chief executive, Andrew Watson, expressed an eagerness to encourage more young, local people from minority ethnic backgrounds to attend Turf Moor matches and join club-run coaching, recreational or learning activities. Funded by a separate grant, Tunisian footballer, Nourredine 'Dino' Maamria became the club's first part-time Ethnic Minorities Development Officer in April 2001. He had a remit to discuss racism in local schools, hoping to break down any aversion the Asian children might have to joining coaching sessions. He also distributed free passes to encourage them to watch matches at Turf Moor.

However, as 'Dino' explained to Burnley author, Phil Whalley he appeared to have a hard task, referring to the lack of interest in football among many Asian families who were primarily interested in cricket. He said that he and his fellow community workers endeavoured to deal with this by introducing cricket sessions within the summer soccer school courses, but added that most Asian parents were unwilling to drop their children off at the club for recreational activities or coaching sessions and then pick them up later.

Another Burnley community worker, Mashuq Hussein, disputed the view that local Asians lacked interest in football. In August 2001, he told *Independent* journalist, David Conn: 'Asian people are passionate about their football. They watch it on TV, they play it, they talk it, the kids love it. But they won't go to Turf Moor. There is still real fear of what treatment we would get...'

Other potential moves collapsed during that summer, although not because of public disorder. According to Stan, he pursued several targets: Sunderland striker, Danny Dichio; Stockport's brawny Finnish/Albanian target man, Shefki Kuqi; and Preston's redoubtable right back or midfielder, Graham Alexander. Although none of these approaches were successful, he managed to sign free agent, Alan Moore. The Republic of Ireland international and former Middlesbrough winger was once dubbed 'the Ryan Giggs of the North East.' That was before his highly promising career was held back by injury. Ivorian born, French defender, Arthur Gnohere was also offered a contract after a successful trial.

In the opening fixture at Hillsborough, new boys, Alan Moore and brawny Arthur Gnohere were on the bench. The starting 11 comprised those who had completed the previous season so impressively. What was unfamiliar was the kick off time of 6.15pm on a Sunday evening. This was at the instigation of ITV Digital who were covering the game on television. It was a dismal introduction to what quickly became a doomed enterprise. During the first half Hillsborough seemed as quiet as the grave. But once Cook had doubled Burnley's lead, in the 79th minute, with a twice-taken penalty, all hell broke loose.

Paul Cook remarked a few days later:

'I'm a football supporter myself and I can understand passions running high during games but you can't have fans running on to the pitch and attacking players. I was grabbed from behind and at first, I wasn't sure if it was a team mate or not, but suddenly there was a commotion. The lad could have been carrying a knife and that's the worrying thing – safety on the pitch should be paramount... He was on the pitch for quite a while. I would have liked to have seen the police or a steward try to stop him – there were enough of them in the ground.'

Ironically, Stan faced the prospect of FA censure for intervening on behalf of his players. In typically combative style Stan retorted: 'If the police and the stewards are not protecting my players, I feel I have to do it. If that offends anybody, I am sorry.' As it turned out no action was taken against him although the fan who assaulted Cook was given a life ban, while others received season-long exclusions.

While Football League new boys Rushden and Diamonds eliminated Burnley from the League Cup, Burnley proudly led Division One at Christmas, after winning 15 and drawing five of their opening 25 fixtures, scoring 48 goals. It was a remarkable feat from a side that Sheffield United manager, Neil Warnock, described as: 'Solid. They don't rip up any trees but they've got that extra bit of quality in Glen Little. The sooner he's sold the better.'

Apparently, Sunderland offered £3m for Burnley's ace winger, who had suddenly discovered a talent for scoring as well as setting up vital goals, tipping the balance decisively in the league victories at Bradford (3-2), Birmingham (3-2), Coventry (2-0) and Preston (3-2). Eying the greater prize of Premier League football, and mistakenly believing that the ITV Digital money guaranteed solvency for the next three years, chairman Barry Kilby turned down the bid. However, the second of two heavy defeats by Kevin Keegan's Manchester City, a 5-1 rout at Maine Road, just before New Year, marked the beginning of a much leaner period. Burnley's final 21 league games yielded just six victories and seven draws with only 22 goals scored. Stan and his team found that their improbable yet magnificent pre-Christmas form became a rod with which to beat them. Heightened supporter expectations soured, notably after a wretched FA Cup defeat at fourth tier Cheltenham Town (1-2), master-minded by future Burnley boss, Steve Cotterill.

In early March 2002, the barracking by what Stan angrily described as the 'mindless few', prompted him to let fly at the detractors:

'The fans here have got champagne tastes on beer money… This football club is fifth in the First Division, that means in the top 25 in England… We are going for the play-offs and still they moan, still they boo. They pay their money and are entitled to their opinion but the booing has a completely adverse effect. These players have done magnificently… I am completely naffed off with the moaners… We've gone from the depths of despair to where we are now and still they are moaning, it is quite incredible.'

Stan was robustly supported by Barry Kilby and his players. Steve Davis, recently returned from a four-months injury, added:

'We do notice the booing and it's not fair. The chairman came in and together with the manager they picked the club off its knees. When I came back here we were very close to going into the bottom division and now we are in a First Division play-off position. It is very easy to lose sight of that. I think the supporters have got to realise we want success as much as them.'

Leading goalscorer, Gareth Taylor commented:

'I can't thank the gaffer enough. I have never had a regular run at another club and hopefully I'm repaying him. I got a bit of luck with my goal against Norwich on Saturday (1-1) as "Crichts" [former Burnley keeper Paul Crichton] went down like an old woman and it bobbled in. It's nice to have 14 goals but there are still 10 games to go… We do understand the fans' frustrations but it is still disappointing. The players here are a great bunch and we are all in this together. If one gets stick from the fans it affects us all. If the fans get behind us it makes a hell of a difference and gives us such a lift. Until Christmas we had a great home record and the pitch was in great condition but it has deteriorated a bit.'

Gareth's remarks spurred Paul Smith of Boundary Clarets to assert:

'I can't believe people are still booing Gareth Taylor. We know he is not the best with his feet but he has got 14 goals this season. If people are going to boo they should not bother coming. It is no surprise that we have got a better record away from home.'

Phil Miller of Accrington Clarets added:

> 'I don't like fans getting on the players' backs. I understand the frustrations but it has been a great season so far. Expectation is so high because of the great start we had. I think some people have got to take a step back and look how far we have come. If you look at the sides at the top, they are bigger and stronger than us.'

The poor state of the Turf Moor pitch was a point of contention with Stan, too. He said:

> 'It is a difficult surface to play on. I have built a passing side and now we need to do something about the pitch… We need a better surface because Pele couldn't pass it on there.'

Sensing that top flight football might elude them, the Burnley board backed Stan's request for reinforcements. After protracted negotiations with cash-strapped Bradford City, inside forward Robbie Blake was signed for £1m with a £250,000 add-on should Burnley secure promotion. Alas, he was impeded by a hernia injury and made little contribution to the promotion push. Consequently, Stan was permitted to bring in David Johnson on loan from Nottingham Forest. Stan said at the time:

> 'Johnson is a class player, a genuine goal poacher. He will bring pace and the ability to hold up the ball. I took him from Manchester United on a 'free', when I was in charge at Bury, and then sold him to Ipswich for £1.1m. From there he went to Nottingham Forest for £3.5m. With Gareth out for two games it is vital we have him in the side.'

Two years later, Stan told Burnley author Dave Thomas:

> 'I wanted to buy [Johnson] from Forest. He was keen to come. Forest were desperate to unload him from their wage bill. He could have come for nothing. He was on £10k a week there. We only had to pay his wages. Over a two-year period, he would not have cost the club much more than £1m. Barry put the proposal to the board but they said "no".'

Johnson's five goals in the final eight games helped Burnley secure eight of the 11 points they gained. But with ITV Digital foundering, the club's financial prospects were unclear, inducing greater caution.

Nevertheless, Paul Gascoigne was briefly added to the mix in the hope that he would emulate Ian Wright in revitalising a promotion challenge. Sadly, 'Gazza' was beset with a serious drink problem, and in no fit state to play football. Having said that, his presence raised home attendances and increased club shop sales, while his wickedly curling free-kick, in the closing minutes of the Coventry game, almost grasped a play-off place.

He was denied, though, by a magnificent save from Swedish international keeper, Magnus Hedman meaning that Burnley had failed again to win a play-off place, this time by just one goal. Stan had good reason to curse the incorrect decision which ruled out Gareth Taylor's 'goal' against Wolves. The consequences were ruinous, for Burnley needed Premier League riches to avert the financial wreckage caused by the collapse of ITV Digital.

ITV Digital was founded upon an agreement struck between the Football League and Granada and Carlton TV companies for exclusive TV rights to cover live matches, principally involving Division One clubs. The deal was worth around £90m a year to the Football League. Burnley's share was almost £3m. The club had budgeted for the full four years of the contract before it was revealed that the contract was not worth the paper it was written on. The financial impact upon First Division clubs was huge. Meanwhile Granada and Carlton, collectively worth around £5b, walked away unscathed.

In April 2002, Barry Kilby said:

> 'ITV Digital has lost £1b [an estimated £1m a day according to press reports] and made a catalogue of mistakes that they are trying to dump on football… I have seen the legal argument… it is not perfect but it is strong. We are going after both Carlton and Granada because they can't just divorce themselves from responsibility for this.'

Unfortunately, the legal case was not as strong as Barry had hoped. Carlton and Granada asserted that they never signed a long form contract. Although subsequently sued by the Football League, the case was lost, with the judge ruling that the Football League had 'failed to extract sufficient written guarantees'. The Football League then filed a negligence claim against its lawyers for failing to press for a written guarantee at the time of the original deal. This action resulted in a paltry award, far less than the £150m damages it was seeking. Consequently, around 600 professional footballers were put out of work while the transfer market nose-dived in value.

Immediately after the Coventry game, Stan announced he would not be renewing the contracts of Kevin Ball, Mitchell Thomas, Lenny Johnrose, reserve striker, Tony Ellis, and deputy goalkeeper Luigi Cennamo. This reduced the annual wage bill from £5m to around £4.5m. The cull might have been more severe given the unaffordability of this wage bill. While Barry Kilby warned that the club could no longer afford to turn down a £3m bid for prime asset, Glen Little, he knew there was no chance of such a lucrative deal being struck in this depressed market. The ITV Digital collapse had not only stripped Football League clubs of essential revenue, it curtailed their capacity to make up the shortfall with player sales.

A year later, Barry Kilby explained to London Claret Phil Whalley:

'What we had been doing, during the 2001/02 season, was securing contracts. We secured Glen Little's early in the season, Paul Weller's too. We brought in Alan Moore. So, our wages rose to £5m. But that was fine, our turnover was £9m. During the season of ITV Digital's collapse, we, more or less, broke even on the year. That annual ITV Digital payment of £2.7m was about 30 per cent of our net revenue. For the bigger Midlands clubs, it was around 20-25 per cent of their revenue... There's no doubt that we were the worst hit because the TV money was a bigger percentage of our income.

The average wage for a reasonable player in our division was then about £4,000 to £5,000 per week... Another factor was when the contracts ran out. We had started to invest to progress, so there was a three-year cycle running through... We've been left with a £5m wage bill that we needed to get down to something like £2.7m...

'As for the Football League, I'm most annoyed, to put it mildly, with the people who negotiated that contract... Our chief executive, Andrew Watson, asked to see the contract but was told he couldn't for confidentiality reasons. The problem was the executive who was then in charge. There were certain directors appointed to the main board but then this cloak of secrecy descended around it. The executive officers who've come in have now all gone and we're left picking up the pieces...

'The Football League needs to improve its communications with the clubs – things like the TV contract need more consultation, the top decisions should be widened out, it can't be left with officers…'

It was small wonder that Barry Kilby was in a glum mood when he addressed the London Clarets AGM in mid-July. He said:

'The recently negotiated Sky TV deal will net us around £500k in the coming season. But we need £2.8m to meet our commitments. What's more, the NTL deal [a cable telecom company] has gone down the pan, too, meaning we will lose another £200k. We will probably be around £4.5m out of pocket… Our first team squad needs be smaller – around 21 rather than 28 as it was during the 2001/02 season.

'Basically, we have three options: obtain a loan to enable the club to meet its immediate commitments and allow time to organise a revised business plan; increase the club's capital by drawing in further investment; and a sale of assets: that is to say selling players and selling the ground, subject to a lease-back arrangement. The first option isn't too appealing given the prospect of interest rates increasing. We will of course try to attract extra financial muscle to the board but don't expect a 'sugar daddy' if we are successful. The reality, though, is that the final solution will involve some combination of all three options.'

Crystal Palace chairman Simon Jordan, warned that seven or eight Division One clubs could go into administration before the end of the season. Among the potential candidates were Coventry with a reported £59.6m debt, followed by Leicester, £30m in arrears, and Derby and Sheffield Wednesday, both with £20m debts.

First Division Bradford City had already entered administration in May 2002, having incurred debts of almost £13m, a legacy of relegation from the Premier League, in the previous year, plus the £5m loss of ITV Digital revenue. Leicester followed suit in October 2002, immediately wiping out ninety percent of their debts to the Inland Revenue and allegedly divesting themselves of £7m in unpaid bills to the construction company responsible for building their new Walkers, now King Power, Stadium. Ipswich then entered administration in January 2003. Like Bradford, relegation from the Premier League had proved ruinous, having incurred debts of £35m, exacerbated, too, by the ITV Digital collapse. Barnsley, recently demoted from

Division One, also entered administration in October 2002. Derby, however, survived another season before being placed in temporary receivership while Coventry and Sheffield Wednesday staggered on for a few more years before emergency intervention became necessary to avert administration. Following growing concerns about clubs using administration to escape their debts, the Football League felt compelled to act. In April 2003, it announced that points penalties would be imposed upon clubs going into administration. It proposed also to impose wage caps to restrain reckless spending. This cap was to be based upon a fixed percentage of turnover.

In September 2002, it was reported that Watford had negotiated a 12 per cent wage reduction with their staff. Tim Shaw their chief executive told an *Observer* reporter that their problem was not only the annual £4.3m loss of ITV Digital revenue. This was compounded by the decimation of the transfer market and the loss of faith from banks and other investors. Among the 24 Division One clubs only Wolves, Norwich and Portsmouth were prepared to guarantee completion of the season's fixtures. It was rumoured that PFA chairman, Gordon Taylor, had suggested that the Football League offer to reduce its allocation of top-flight promotion places to two, if, in return, the Premier League paid the Football League £100m annually to make good its £90m ITV Digital loss. If this was so, the idea was rejected.

As galling as it was, in October 2002, the Football League clubs reluctantly acceded to a £5m bid made by Carlton and Granada to screen match highlights. While some Burnley supporters decried the deal as shameful, Barry Kilby retorted:

> 'At the end of the day we had to go along with the decision. It was a case of either getting the £88,000 or nothing. All the clubs have to face their bank managers! As part of the two-year deal, Carlton and Granada agreed to relinquish their claims to £1m legal fees incurred in the Football League's failed court action against them.'

Burnley Chief Executive, Andrew Watson, added:

> 'If we had signed the alternative deal offered by BBC and Channel Five, their TV money would have been wiped out by us bearing those legal costs... Dealing with ITV again might not be what we would have wanted but when it came down to it they were the only people on the block.' Watson assured Burnley supporters that discussions were being

held with the club's creditors to buy themselves time to seek additional investment.

Burnley's 2002/03 season began with a feeble 1-3 home defeat by newly-promoted Brighton. Ensuing 0-3 losses at Wolves and Reading were separated by a dismal 0-1 Turf Moor reverse against Sheffield United, watched by a crowd of only 12,868, almost 12 per cent below the previous season's average home gate. It was Burnley's worst start to a new campaign in 25 years. With former crowd favourite Marlon Beresford back in goal after agreeing another short-term deal, and Robbie Blake at last demonstrating his pedigree up front, Burnley finally came good at Derby (2-1).

Thereafter their season fluctuated wildly. Impressive victories, notably those in the cup competitions, against Premier League sides Spurs (2-1) and Fulham (3-0), stood in stark contrast with abject home defeats in the league. These comprised thrashings by Rotherham (2-6), Reading (2-5), Watford (4-7) and already relegated Sheffield Wednesday (2-7). After a bewildering 5-6 loss at 'Blunder' Park, Grimsby, on 'fright night', Stan Ternent was asked whether Burnley's under-performing centre-back, Arthur Gnohere, had been substituted because of injury. Ternent snapped: 'If he was injured it was only between his ears'. As poor as some performances were during this season, the lowest point was the killing of a Nottingham Forest fan before Burnley's home fixture with Forest in December. London Claret Steve Corrigan remarked: 'I was ashamed of being a Burnley fan. And the fact that it had little to do with football doesn't make it any better. Shankly was wrong. Football is not that important. It's only a game.'

The final 2-7 humiliation exacted by Sheffield Wednesday, caused Stan Ternent to fume: 'It's back to five years ago and I can't wait for the summer now so I can build a new team, because I have to.' It was inevitable that there would be major changes. Among the former stalwarts released were Ian Cox, Steve Davis, Gordon Armstrong, Lee Briscoe, Nik Michopolous, Marlon Beresford, Paul Cook and Andy Payton.

Some years later, Andy Payton reflected upon his Burnley career with a *Burnley Express* reporter. Putting aside the disappointment of his final years at Turf Moor he spoke glowingly about his former manager, saying:

> 'Stan was a brilliant coach and a proper, players' manager. He was very under-rated – not by us the Burnley players, who went up with him in 2000, obviously. He knew how to

run a football club. He was big on discipline. He may have appeared unfashionable, but he transformed Burnley. He conjured promotion on a shoestring at Bury and continued to perform minor miracles at Turf Moor. Stan was probably the best I played under.

'My greatest moment in football was getting the Golden Boot, the first at Burnley to win it, being player-of-the-year and achieving promotion with Burnley all in the same season (1999/2000). That's better than playing in the 'Old Firm' game or in Europe with Celtic. I got my 200th goal at Wrexham in that season. My only regret is that I didn't get a hundred for Burnley. I could have but I hardly played in my last two seasons there. But I ended up with over 250 goals in my career. I've got to be happy with that.

'When I finished at Burnley I was 37 which is not old in life terms. I had trained every day for over 20 years. Then it was gone, just like that. I suppose it's like coming out of the army. It's hard adjusting. For a while I didn't want to have anything to do with football. I stopped going on the Turf. Then I got myself together, started playing again several times a week, doing circuit training. Life became better again.'

2004 – 2007

Beating the retreat

'Rehab'

WITH Burnley's playing and financial resources so severely stretched, Stan and Barry were exasperated to lose their newly-signed, centre-back, Drissa Diallo, to Ipswich. Diallo had been signed in January 2003, initially on a short-term contract, following the liquidation of his Belgian club, KV Mechelen. Diallo, a Guinean international, had impressed in a faltering Burnley defence, being commanding in the air and quick on the ground. He had been badly missed in the 2002/03 'horror shows' against Watford and Sheffield Wednesday, being absent for six of the final fixtures due to injury.

Stan had hoped to rebuild his defence around Diallo. It was particularly galling to be outbid by a club which had recently been in administration with debts of £35m.

Having cleared these debts with a Company Voluntary Agreement, accepted by 98 percent of the club's creditors, Ipswich successfully petitioned the Football League to have their transfer embargo lifted. They immediately sold Matt Holland to Portsmouth for £750,000, allowing themselves the financial clout to offer Diallo a better deal than Burnley could manage. Diallo had appeared to be happy at Turf Moor, playing alongside his long-standing friend and fellow Guinean international, Mo Camara, who had recommended the club to him.

While Barry Kilby originally believed that clubs entering administration should not be penalised, he thought here that Ipswich had profited from this provision at Burnley's expense. Ipswich already had greater pulling power. Whereas Burnley had just 7,600 season ticket holders by mid-May 2003, 4,000 down on the previous season, Ipswich had almost twice as many at 14,000. Barry also pointed out: 'Administration could have been a lot worse for Burnley than it was for Ipswich or Leicester. It is the old story. If you owe the bank £30m it is the bank which has a problem but if you owe the bank £3m then you have the problem.'

On 31 May 2003, Barry Kilby told a Lancashire Evening Telegraph reporter that he was expecting to bring in nine or 10 players during the summer but insisted: 'We are not going to be paying any transfer fees… The team ran out of steam last season. We need an influx of younger players… I am quite bullish about it.' This suggested that he and his manager were not on the same page in placing a greater accent upon youth. Sensing this, perhaps, Barry added: 'My relationship with Stan is pretty sound. We have had our disagreements for sure, but we have always sorted them and continue to work well together. He is very loyal to me and I hope I am to him.'

Clarifying his intentions, Barry Kilby stated: 'The board has made a decision to try to improve our youth scheme. You must accept that it is not as it was in the sixties when I played in the Burnley 'A' team. We had schoolboy internationals then. We know we can't get academy status yet, although it is an objective for sure. We know, too, that an academy is not a cheap option and that you are not guaranteed success.' He pointed out that talented midfielder, David Dunn, was in the Burnley youth set-up as a 14-year-old before Premier League, Blackburn, with a much larger budget, enticed him to Ewood Park.

Four years later, Stan confided to Burnley author, Dave Thomas:

> 'A youth set-up is fine if the financial circumstances are right. But such a thing was not cost-effective at Burnley at that time. Where are the best players going to come from when there is such competition from other clubs? When I was a young lad at Gawthorpe all the youth team players went on to make first team appearances. Contrast that with the situation now where the failure rate is so high. Today there's just the £1m for home-grown midfielder, Richard Chaplow, and possibly £3-5m for young striker, Kyle Lafferty. Andy Lochhead and Willie Irvine at their

peak would have brought in over £20m each today. Get the club into the Premiership then the best young players will want to come. It only makes sense to think of an academy once the club is in the Premiership. So, what I'm saying is, if the money is tight then the best thing is to use seasoned pros and track the progress of young academy players and use them if there is enough finance to find the quality players.'

With 800 out-of-contract players seeking employment, Barry Kilby claimed:

'The negotiations concerning potential incoming moves are now all about wages. I will be extremely surprised if there are any transfer fees paid outside the Premiership. With supply far outstripping demand, I find it hard to see where the money for transfers will come from. I envisage something like 21 or 22 senior squad players at Burnley for this season, earning on average around £2,000 per week.'

Meanwhile, Burnley's once prized asset, Glen Little, was in limbo. Having been loaned to Reading at the end of the previous season to reduce Burnley's wage bill, his hopes of securing a permanent contract there evaporated with the Royals' play-off elimination. Glen said: 'Reading manager, Alan Pardew is interested in signing me but it is all to do with money and at the end of the day I'm still committed to Burnley where I am perfectly happy if they want me.' It seemed unlikely that any team outside the Premier League could afford to match his wages which were then thought to be around £8,000 per week.

If Little's estimated weekly wage was correct, it underlined the extent of Stan's problem in bringing in essential replacements on his reduced budget of £3.5m. That budget was £1.5m down on the 2001/02 figure of £5m. Besides, 90 per cent of the budget was already committed in meeting the wages of those still on pre-ITV Digital contracts. It was no surprise that Little was loaned out again at the start of the new season, this time to Premier League, Bolton, with their Republic of Ireland midfielder, Gareth Farrelly and centre forward, Delroy Facey, joining Burnley in a reciprocal short-term loan deal.

Barry explained:

'You can't blame us for fighting like hell to maximise our revenues. Looking at past performances, without the windfall of a cup run we have done £2m in season tickets and £1m in gates. We've looked at increasing "walk-ons" but when we've done special schemes and dropped admission prices, we've always ended up worse off. Then there's television money which is at best £600k and commercial activity – the lotteries, catering and shop sales – which is £1.5m at best. This gives us an annual income of around £5m.

'Taking account of wages and other outgoings, this translates into a possible £2m loss for the 2003/04 season. I have put in £3m in capital into the club which I don't expect to see again. We managed to get a suspension of capital payments, we got a commercial loan that we have been able to pay back and the directors have loaned money. Vice-chairman, Ray Ingleby has been a great support to me, particularly, last year. When doing deals with creditors he was fabulous.'

Barry told London Claret, Phil Whalley:

'I want to get us up there even if we now have to fight to stay where we are. We are absolutely punching above our weight just to be in this division. I drove through Burton-upon-Trent last weekend and was surprised to see how big it was. I looked it up and they have double the population of Burnley... Many clubs in the Conference serve much bigger populations than Burnley and a lot are affluent places. In economic terms, we are probably a mid-table Division Two [a third tier] side. There is our history and the size of support to factor in here, then there are other elements you can throw in. Lottery-wise we're one of the best in the country. We're well-organised, we understand it, it's my business as well.

'But shirt sponsors – we can't get one to pay anything like what other teams get because we have no big commercial interests which identify with the town. What industries we have, tend to be branch industries or small firms. It breaks my heart to see how the town, which used to be thriving in the fifties and sixties, when I was a boy, is on a downward spiral, how we export our brains from the area, and there's plenty who would just like to see us waste away and go.

'The lotteries do well but commercially we struggle. It's hard to see we'll ever clear more than £5m-£6m. I have a soft spot for London Clarets. They do fabulously well to come up and support Burnley but what happens to their generation of kids? Is this supply always going to be there or will it dissipate and be lost?'

Meanwhile Stan was telling the local press that he hoped to be competitive despite being reduced to 18 professionals, six of whom were then injured, namely Alan Moore, Robbie Blake, Arthur Gnohere, Mark McGregor, Gareth Taylor and loan signing, Luke Chadwick, while another, Ian Moore, faced a three-match suspension for his indiscretion during the 2-7 debacle against Sheffield Wednesday.

Stan told a *Lancashire Evening Telegraph* reporter:

'It's very difficult, without a doubt, as hard as I've had it. It has been a hectic summer and I've hardly had any time off. The players on big pre-ITV Digital wages have one or two years left of their original three- or four-year contracts. It will gradually work its way out. I've moved a lot out, including Greek under-21 striker, Dimi Papadopoulos for a £250,000 fee, and I might have to move on some more to bring some in. Realistically, as things stand, we are looking to stay in the First Division. That would be massive with what I have got now.'

To add to Stan's woes, 2002/03 player-of-the -year Gareth Taylor was sold to Nottingham Forest for £500,000. He wasn't keen to leave but Burnley could no longer afford him. In the opening game at home against Crystal Palace, on a blistering hot day, Burnley were undone by their suspect defence in which Graham Branch deputised at centre back, alongside the increasingly error-prone Arthur Gnohere. But it was the debutant, full back, Lee Roche, who was at fault for Palace's opening goal, while new goalkeeper Brian 'Beast' Jensen was culpable for the second and third goals. Despite a sparkling debut by Luke Chadwick, on loan from Manchester United, Palace were gifted the points. A heavy defeat at West Bromwich followed (1-4), while further defensive calamities at home against Wigan resulted in a third successive loss (0-2).

Then, at Gillingham on August Bank Holiday, Burnley finally clicked into gear, winning decisively (3-0). It was a magnificent display of swift, perceptive passing, dashing movement, clinical finishing and robust defending. New signing, David May, formerly with Manchester United and Blackburn, was a pillar of strength at centre back. On the following Saturday, Crewe were overcome 1-0 thanks to an outstanding performance by former youth team player, Richard Chaplow. Stan was delighted, crowing: 'It was a fantastic three points for us and we created a lot of chances again. Richard Chaplow was fantastic today. The goal was marvellous for him. He's a player if he can keep his feet on the ground.' Stan was equally fulsome in praising the passing of fellow midfielder, Tony Grant.

At a squally Britannia Stadium, Stoke City were blown away. All three loan signings made impressive debuts: Delroy Facey led the line energetically; Gareth Farelly was composed and incisive in midfield; while Blackburn's Andy Todd helped anchor the defence. Stoke were unable to cope with Burnley's fluent passing and fluid movement (2-1). Thereafter, results were more erratic, not helped by a succession of injuries and Burnley's limited reserves.

Bradford were crushed 4-0 at Turf Moor on 20 September, with another top-drawer performance from two-goal, Luke Chadwick. Walsall were also brushed aside at home two weeks later by Facey's powerful hat-trick (3-1). Although a depleted, flu-stricken Burnley side lost 1-6 at Ipswich, a creditable 2-2 draw was achieved a few days later at West Ham. However, when nemesis side, Reading, were surprisingly routed 3-0 in November, it was Burnley's first league victory in eight games. Sheffield United were subsequently beaten 3-2 in a switchback game in early December but it was a brief respite only as four successive defeats followed.

After a hapless display of defending at Preston five days before Christmas, it was rumoured on Sky Sports news that Stan had been sacked or resigned, whereupon he angrily retorted: 'Under no circumstances will I resign. I would not let this football club down. I wouldn't let the chairman down who has been brilliant or the board of directors. I have never turned anything in during my life and I don't intend to start now.'

The club's AGM, held a few days later, provided little cheer. It was revealed that the 2001/02 wage bill of £7.4m had been reduced to £3.6m in 2002/03 but that figure needed to be trimmed further to £3m. During 2002/03 there was a loss of £2.6m with the figure for 2003/04 estimated to be about the same. New chief executive, Dave Edmundson confirmed it was Barry Kilby who was keeping the club afloat. Barry Kilby said: 'The problem will get worse before it gets better. There's enough money to last until February, but if we don't have a good cup run, the bills or the staff will need to be restructured again.'

Burnley progressed to the fifth round of the FA Cup before being eliminated in a toxic tie at Millwall, sullied by mutual accusations of racial abuse. Had Alan Moore not missed a sitter, Burnley might have reached the quarter-finals where they would have faced Tranmere. Fortunately, Barry Kilby had agreed beforehand with Millwall's owner, Theo Paphitis, to share the proceeds of the tie, whatever the result. He had struck a similar deal with Watford's chairman before their sixth-round tie at Vicarage Road during the previous season.

On the 16 February, Dave Edmundson revealed that the Clarets had avoided administration for this season, at least. The club needed to raise £500,000 by the end of that month and 'thanks to a brilliant response from the fans, plus the proceeds from the FA Cup run, Burnley FC would remain in business for now.' Edmundson added that over £100,000 had been raised because of the 500 Mile Club. This was his fund-raising initiative, comprising sponsored walks, cycle rides, world-wide donations and collections on match days. Meanwhile Barry Kilby strove to agree a stay of execution with the club's three main creditors. He also sought to raise £500,000 from local investors, alongside £1,000 contributions from fans who could afford to donate so much. Alex Ferguson agreed to speak at a fund-raising dinner at Turf Moor, initiated by Alastair Campbell. As a result, there was no need to sell Burnley's star player, Robbie Blake. There was no discussion of players deferring their wages, as was considered at Leeds. Some fans were irritated by this, feeling that the players were contributing less to the cause than themselves.

The club was granted a temporary respite, but the team hovered alarmingly just above the relegation zone. Luke Chadwick began the season well but faded as injury impaired his form, fitness and confidence. The mercurial Jensen was brilliant in some games, as at Sunderland, West Ham and Bradford, while in some others he was a liability, as at Preston. Lee Roche arrived from Old Trafford, highly commended by Manchester United coach and former Claret, Mike Phelan. However, the young full back struggled to assert himself in the bump and grind of Division One. Meanwhile his partner, Mo Camara flattered to deceive. When he bombed forward he represented a threat to opposing defences, and yet his crossing was often woeful.

Troubled by a recurrent Achilles problem, Glen Little failed to make his customary impact leaving Burnley short creatively, despite Tony Grant's and Richard Chaplow's best efforts. Alan Moore was again hamstrung by injury, while Ian Moore felt his striking potency was reduced by playing wide. Nevertheless, Ian Moore chipped in with important goals, none more important than his late headed winner at Bradford.

Of the eight loan signings, only centre forward Delroy Facey and centre back, Andy Todd made much impact. Although decried by some supporters, Lenny Johnrose's brief return during an anxious run-in proved invaluable, as Barry Kilby recognised.

In short, Burnley were too reliant upon 19-goal Blake, Grant, Chaplow, May and Branch, with the latter filling in at full back, centre half and centre forward. It was small wonder that Burnley struggled. Vital victories at relegation rivals, Walsall (1-0) and Bradford (2-1), kept Burnley narrowly the right side of the line. But ultimately, they were indebted to Graham Branch, their often denigrated, yet indispensable, utility player, in scrambling to safety. His goals in successive home games against 'franchise' Wimbledon, and Derby, in late April, enabled his team to gain the six points they needed to avoid relegation.

Barry Kilby then dropped a bombshell, announcing that Stan's contract was not to be renewed. A dire 0-3 defeat at Rotherham in the penultimate game probably sealed his fate. An additional concern to the cash-strapped club was a further 10 per cent fall in Turf Moor attendances. The average gate for the 2003/04 season was 12,541, 3,693 or 23 per cent lower than it had been in 2000/01.

Barry explained his decision thus:

> 'Stan has done a fantastic job for this club, including a promotion and keeping us in the First Division for five seasons. I'm looking to the long-term future of Burnley. With this in mind managerial changes are inevitable. Stan and I have enjoyed a close working relationship; he has always been passionate about Burnley and has been one of the best Burnley managers of all time. I would like to thank him for his devotion and dedication to Burnley. He will always be revered at Turf Moor. I sincerely wish him well with his future plans.'

Stan's last game was a home fixture with Sunderland, the club he had supported as a boy. The sun shone and 18,000 turned up including nine committed cyclists who had completed their 500-mile bike ride, raising £13,000 for the club, a magnificent effort. After the game, a tearful Stan received the rapturous applause of the Burnley supporters with a large Sunderland contingent joining in.

Stan composed the following farewell message to the Burnley supporters.

'I can't quite believe I'm about to take my last walk out of the tunnel as Burnley manager today. I will take a last look at a few familiar places. I will try to take in the amazing atmosphere generated by you, fantastic fans. I will fight – but can't promise – to keep my emotions in check. As a kid, I dreamed of playing for Burnley in the top division. Lately I thought I could take us there as manager. You know how close we came. Now, for me, at least, it is over.

'We've had some wonderful times together during the past six years. I will remember the scenes of sheer joy when we won promotion at Scunthorpe as long as I live, and I won't forget the hangover suffered by half the town the next day either.

'My players throughout these times have all worked fantastically hard. Like me, I'm sure you'll never forget the moment you saw Ian Wright and Gazza walk out at Turf Moor in our famous claret and blue.

'Lately our financial problems, which meant losing some of our best players, have made life tougher. Because of the budgets imposed upon me I stand by the claim that keeping us in the First Division this season has been my greatest achievement so far in management.

'Many people this week have said that I am Burnley's most successful manager for 30 years. That has made me blush, and made me proud. I am pleased to have brought back some credibility, some honour and success to one of the most famous clubs in football. My era is over. Burnley will go on. I have my memories. As my old mate, Vinnie Jones once said, "It's been emotional".'

Stan signed off by thanking Barry Kilby and the board of directors for their support, his team, the coaching and support staff and the fans.

After 300 appearances for Burnley, the Sunderland game was Glen Little's last too having agreed to sign for Reading. He was equally complimentary about his time at Turf Moor, stating he was 'privileged to play for the club and proud to be part of a club with such a great history.'

In referring to Stan's managerial style, he said:

'You have to be mentally strong and I've always been that. I've had my run-ins with Stan over the years at Burnley, but that is part and parcel of football. He's swung for me a few times and you have your rows and square-up, but as long as you don't take it to heart that's the important thing. I've been hit with a bottle, called everything under the sun and even had a right hook, but the day Stan stops shouting in your ear, that's the day you get worried. He might not be everyone's cup of tea and people might not like the way he does things but that's the way it is with him.'

Stan's wife Kath told Burnley writer Dave Thomas.

'He just hadn't seen it coming. He was so wound up in the job. He never thought about the possibility. Even with all those problems he was determined to keep them up. There were no overnight stays even for long distance games. I remember Stan saying: "what preparation is this?" I can tell you now he nearly did get to the end of his tether. It was only his love of the club that kept him there.'

Burnley historian, Ray Simpson commented:

'I firmly believe Stan Ternent was born to manage Burnley. It was his destiny. It seemed to be in his DNA. Surprising perhaps, since he had few opportunities to play for the club's first team when here as a player in the 1960s, and yet despite supporting Sunderland as a youngster and playing many more games for Carlisle than for Burnley, he retained an unyielding loyalty to this club and town. He proved to be the right man at the right time after being appointed as manager in 1998. By 2004, Stan seemed worn down by the struggle, and perhaps a bit like yesterday's man. But how can anyone doubt Stan's passion for the club. He was devastated. At his final game at Turf Moor, he walked around all four sides of the ground bidding a tearful farewell to us all. I don't think there was a dry eye in the house.'

Stan Ternent was replaced with Steve Cotterill, an ambitious young manager who had lifted Cheltenham Town out of Southern League obscurity and into the third tier of English football in a handful of seasons. It was a remarkable achievement given the paucity of resources at this humble Gloucestershire club. Cotterill's next move, to third tier

Stoke City, in the summer of 2002, ended abruptly and acrimoniously. For shortly after his appointment he deserted the Potters to become the right-hand man of veteran manager Howard Wilkinson at Premier League Sunderland. Cotterill believed that he had been chosen as Wilkinson's heir apparent, but became bitterly disappointed. Wilkinson was unwilling to delegate, and with Sunderland careering towards relegation in March 2003, Wilkinson and Cotterill were sacked. Cotterill was without a management post for over a year.

On 3 June 2004, Barry Kilby announced Cotterill's appointment as Burnley manager. saying:

'All the applicants, including Ronnie Moore (father of Ian) and ex-Claret Brian Flynn had impressed but Cotterill, who has signed a three-year deal, was the outstanding candidate to take us forward.'

Cotterill added: 'I turned down eight offers since I left Sunderland but this Burnley job is the right one. There's something about this northwest corridor. Burnley have the tradition, and the chairman is a man I can work with. Everyone here, including the famous old players, have been very supportive and I've been reminded there are wonderful people in our game.'

Cotterill was even more impressed by the local benefactors, who freely offered their time and money in a period of continuing financial hardship for the club. He enthused: 'We have someone who has donated new showers, toilets and wash basins and we have someone who is going to come in and fit them for nothing. How terrific is that? I want it to be a nice place, comfortable, clean and tidy. I want things to be proud of.'

It did not end there. Another supporter donated £9,000 to enable the club to erect nets around the new training pitch to reduce the number of lost balls. With a supporter covering the cost of rail travel for the team's long away trips, and yet one more providing training watches, Cotterill was delighted to find the community and club pulling together.

Cotterill told Alastair Campbell: 'If you walk down the road you don't see Manchester United or Arsenal shirts, they'll be claret and blue... If I was to achieve half here of what I achieved in Cheltenham, I'd get the key to the town...'

A Cheltenham Town supporter posted the following testimonial on the popular Clarets Mad website:

> 'Cotterill's attributes: incredibly hardworking and focused;
> excellent knowledge of other teams and players; gets his
> players very fit and engages with them well; intolerant of

prima donnas; meticulous; top coaching qualifications; self-confident and single-minded; good contacts; gets the best out of moderate players… His greatest skill is inspiring and motivating a team. On taking over at Cheltenham he inherited a squad of talented (by Southern League standards), but flippant, under-achievers. He made them over-achieve hugely, keeping the same first choice back four between 1996/7 when we were Southern League runners-up and 1999/2000 when we finished 8th in Division Three.

'His weaknesses: has obvious "favourite" players – shows arguably excessive loyalty to them during long dips in form; can revert to long-ball game too easily; can create unnecessary difficulty by being uncooperative with the media.

'Stoke fans will naturally be quick to snipe but he didn't do a bad job in the dozen or so games there. They headed rapidly downwards after he left. His move to Sunderland was foolish, motivated by over-ambition, and he himself has publicly regretted it. I would suggest he is too bright to make the same mistake again… He won't be an overnight success but he will do a good job for you in time. Don't be put off by his ridiculous accent.'

Derek Goddard of the *Gloucestershire Echo* described Cotterill as 'a very emotional coach and very sensitive bloke. I first knew him at Cheltenham as an 18-year-old player. He was always a bit tetchy and cocky then. He left to go to Wimbledon where he was plagued with injury. He is not one to get on with the press. He is one of those that if you ask him his name, he would want to know why you were asking.'

Burnley writer, Phil Whalley, once presented Steve Cotterill with a copy of the London Clarets magazine. He had a cursory glance at its summary of a recent team performance, before thrusting it back at Phil, growling: 'This is all bollocks! And if I invited you into the dressing room you would know it was bollocks. But I'm not going to do that because it's none of your bloody business!' Like Stan Ternent before him, Steve Cotterill was no fan of supporter websites. He asserted: 'I don't read websites. I don't think they are actually a good thing. We must stay focused in what we are doing. I certainly don't like the malicious gossip… However, if they raise money for the club, as Clarets Mad has, then that's terrific.'

Upon his appointment Cotterill told the press: 'The first plan is to get three players because we have only eight at the moment.' Nevertheless, he decided not to offer new terms to the four out-of-contract players: May, McGregor, Weller and West, but quickly signed 32-year-old centre back, John McGreal, from Ipswich on a three-year deal. Steve told Tony Scholes who then ran the supporters' website, Clarets Mad: 'The hardest thing is trying to bring players in because the chances are that three or four clubs want to talk with the good ones...'

Cotterill informed the local press: 'We won't be bringing in a lot. That's a sure fact. We've got to put a team together before we can put together a squad... I don't want to be changing the team every five minutes... If we had a budget double the one we have then I could bring in more players but we haven't... What happens when you don't have a lot of money is you end up with team players rather than star individuals...'

As part of a team-building exercise, Cotterill took his players on a short pre-season trip to Austria where they played two Bundesliga division two sides. He commented: 'Trips like Austria are important otherwise the players come in and go home and you don't get to know them. There is so much more to it, they are people not just footballers'. Cotterill's strength as a team builder was illustrated following an FA Cup defeat at Premier League Blackburn in March 2005. At the final whistle, Cotterill drew his deeply disappointed players into an on-pitch huddle, rousing their spirits before presenting them to their fans who gave them the ovation they deserved.

According to a Clarets Mad poll, a majority of fans were pleased with Cotterill's appointment. But the take up of new season tickets remained sluggish with only 8,000 sold by the end of June, just 100 up on the 2003 figure.

Knowing that money was very tight, Cotterill played the transfer market astutely, acquiring five quality players at little or no cost. Not only was McGreal an outstanding, composed and resilient centre back, Cotterill's other signings were equally worthy. These comprised: Watford's pugnacious midfielder, Micah Hyde; Cheltenham's right back or centre half, Michael Duff, who had already been capped by Northern Ireland; pacey ex-Chelsea and Leicester defender, Frank Sinclair; and accomplished Welsh international keeper, Danny Coyne, also from Leicester. Only the transfers of Coyne (£25,000) and Duff (£30,000) required a fee and both were modest payments given the players' calibre.

Coyne represented Wales on 16 occasions having proved himself in a struggling side at Grimsby. While there, he had been the fans' choice as Grimsby's player-of-the-year in successive seasons. Unfortunately, his Burnley career, which began so promisingly, was stunted by a serious injury, whereas Michael Duff's prospects took off at Turf Moor. He would play in 383 league and cup games. Despite sustaining a cruciate injury during the 2007/08 season, Duff recovered to help Burnley seize a hat-trick of Premier League promotions in 2009, 2014 and 2016. He also represented the senior Northern Ireland side on 24 occasions, playing a key role in their memorable victories over England in 2005 and Spain in 2006.

In September, Steve Cotterill added French winger Jean-Louis Valois, to the ranks initially on a 30-day contract. The free agent was unkindly dubbed 'A poor man's Ginola', by a work colleague who scouted for Preston, adding, 'He has some skill but little bottle'. Nevertheless, Valois remained at the club for the whole season, playing a prominent part in the League Cup victory over Aston Villa in October.

Cotterill was equally adept in the loan market, too, signing Aston Villa's fledgling centre back Gary Cahill during November 2004, in a season-long deal. At the outset of his Burnley career, Steve Cotterill seemed as sceptical as Ternent in selecting youth players, although he, too, considered Chaplow to be an exception. Cotterill questioned: 'Some of the youngsters might be good enough technically but are they tough enough mentally to go out in front of crowd, and do it?'

And yet he had no qualms in blooding the inexperienced Cahill, playing him in all but one of the 28 league games remaining. Cotterill's trust was richly rewarded. It was readily apparent that Cahill had the necessary maturity, might, technique and mentality to go far. He starred in a debut 1-0 home win over Nottingham Forest, helping Burnley keep seven clean sheets in his first nine games. Such was his commanding presence, that he and his centre back partner, John McGreal, snaffled most of the player-of-the-year awards at the season's end.

With Cotterill's already small squad shrinking to unsustainable levels, because of injuries and departures, several other loan deals were struck. Tussling midfielder James O'Connor spent two spells with the club; the first on a short loan, the second as a prelude to a £175,000 transfer, after he had lost his way at West Bromwich. Ipswich reserve striker Dean Bowditch, also came in during March on a month-long loan, scoring the opening goal in a 3-1 home win over Watford. Cotterill described him as 'a good, young, exciting player.'

Aston Villa's Peter Whittingham and Portsmouth's Richard Duffy performed filling-in turns, as well. While Whittingham showed little of the attacking verve and set play acumen, that marked his later displays for Cardiff, the latter distinguished himself in a brief stay by scoring the winning goal at Leeds in early November 2004. That unexpected 2-1 victory, with a heavily patched-up side, epitomised the fierce battling spirit and defensive nous which Cotterill instilled in his players. Arguably, Cotterill was at his best when the odds were onerous, as was the case when his side overcame Premier League teams, Aston Villa (3-1) and Liverpool (1-0) during this season's cup competitions. Lest it be forgotten, he had also orchestrated Cheltenham's FA Cup victory over Premier League-chasing Burnley, in 2002.

In a *Times* article in September 2004, Cotterill made a rare disclosure of his chosen methods. He said:

'When defending corners and free kicks against taller players, I ask my players to stay on their feet and not give away more set-plays than necessary. If you keep the ball better than the other team, you will tend to concede fewer corners than you earn. Once facing a set-play, there are two ways of defending: zonal, which I'm not keen on, and man-to-man. I also have a spare man who is free to chase the ball. So, if the opposition have a player who is head and shoulders their best header, then we'll have done our scouting and get our spare man to lock up the area where he is most likely to attack.'

While Cotterill remained alert to bargain deals, skill improvement was his priority. The fruits of this were realised in the better performances of Mo Camara and Frank Sinclair. The poor quality of Camara's crossing had been a source of exasperation to Stan Ternent throughout the 2003/04 season. With his playing resources so limited, Steve Cotterill could ill afford such wastage. So, during pre-season, he had Camara repeatedly practising crosses, not letting up until the left back could routinely attack with intensity and accuracy. Similarly, he tasked his coaches with removing the careless aberrations in Frank Sinclair's game. The result was equally impressive as Sinclair was transformed into a rock-solid centre half or full back, bringing about his re-birth as 'the Power'.

After extending his one-year contract in December 2004, Frank Sinclair said: 'Initially I came because of the gaffer, because I needed to play for someone I trusted.' Reflecting upon the stringent demands of his personal training plan, he added with a beaming smile: 'I had a hard summer but it was an opportunity to start afresh. I've enjoyed it so much here that I had no hesitation in signing for a further two years.'

Steve Cotterill's first competitive game was at home to Sheffield United in what had become re-branded as the Coca Cola Championship. Although Micah Hyde deservedly snatched a first half lead, the hosts had to scrap thereafter to remain on terms. On an afternoon of scorching heat, a 1-1 draw was a commendable return.

Adopting a tightly disciplined 4-5-1 formation, Cotterill's Burnley side were equally hard to beat in the games which followed. Despite its slender resources, Cotterill's Clarets reached 11th position by early December, well in sight of a play-off place. Of their first 23 league games, eight were won and nine drawn. While only 20 goals were scored, just 19 were conceded. Lone striker, Blake, contributed 50 percent of his side's goals.

The October 2004 edition of the London Clarets' magazine, *Something to Write Home About,* contained this entry:

> 'How other clubs must hate playing host to us now. Before, we were the most generous of guests, bearing extravagant gifts of easy goals. Now we are the Division's meanest machine. We draw our opponents' sting, confound their creativity, denying them time and space, utterly frustrating them with our iron curtain defence and our phenomenal work rate, driving their managers and supporters to distraction. Entertainment may be in short supply but sod that. We're competing with Premiership contenders and doing alright.'

Jimmy Robson, a prolific striker during Burnley's glory days and a highly-experienced coach, was surprised by the success of Cotterill's tactics, notably his use of Blake as a lone striker. He questioned: 'If you stop the service to Blake, surely you stop Burnley? If the opposition puts two players on Blake, one in front and one behind, his supply is cut off. Blake hasn't the stature to compete for high balls and hasn't the pace to get away from his markers if the service is on the ground.'

But while Blake lacked pace, he had consummate skill. His first touch was deft and sure. His nimble dexterity, his quick feet and sudden twists and turns, often confounded the tightest of markers, creating space for himself where, it seemed, there was none. Although he offered little in an aerial contest, he was rarely out-powered on the deck. With his strong back and muscular legs, he regularly held off burly defenders pressing from behind. In addition, he had an array of penetrative passes. Moreover, as Preston found in a 2-0 defeat at Turf Moor, in December 2004, Blake had a ferocious shot, too.

Cotterill took little time in choosing Blake as first team captain, arguing:

> 'Robbie came back for pre-season leaner and fitter than ever before. He looks hungry and wants to do well. He is a fantastic, top player and his attitude in pre-season was first class. We know all about his skill and ability, but his industry in training has been excellent too.' As for Blake, he confirmed: 'Training has been very difficult but enjoyable. I can improve and I'm sure the Gaffer will help improve me as a player.'

Having been impressed with Burnley's 0-0 draw at Reading on the 2 October, a Sky reporter wrote.

> 'Steve Cotterill has assembled a superb rear guard in a summer of wheeling and dealing... While Reading had two goals disallowed, it could have been Burnley that stole the points, especially in a second half that saw them sit back, soak up the pressure and counter attack superbly... If Burnley can find a natural goalscorer to play off the sublime Blake, they may well have a shot at the top six.'

What followed became an unwelcome annual pattern. A promising pre-Christmas promotion tilt degenerated into a New Year slump, occasioned by the loss of Burnley's premier striker. On the 5 January Robbie Blake signed for Premier League Birmingham for £1.5m. 'Crown jewel', Richard Chaplow, departed soon after, signing for West Bromwich, also for £1.5m.

Undaunted, Steve Cotterill congratulated chairman Barry Kilby on achieving an 'excellent deal, having held his nerve right until the last minute.' Even when confronted by the temporary losses of Branch and Duff through injury, Cotterill wasn't given to complaining. He asserted:

> 'I know we won't be buying anyone, though. A lot of the Blake money is going towards the Turf Moor pitch, to prevent waterlogging in front of the Bob Lord stand. The pitches at Gawthorpe training ground need improvement, too.' He added, wryly: 'I've never had so many agents on

the phone now that we have sold a couple of players for big money.'

Despite his thin reserves, Cotterill was unwilling to stand in the way of his players' ambitions. He said:

'Everyone here would like to wish Richard Chaplow all the very best and hope he continues to further his football career. I met his parents in the summer and we said if the right offer came in at the right time from a Premiership club, we would allow him that opportunity and we've been true to our word.'

With Burnley reduced to 14 fit senior professionals, Cotterill was permitted to sign 26-year-old, disgraced midfielder John Oster. Oster had played in 40 Premier League games for Everton and 59 first team matches for Sunderland, as well as representing Wales in 11 full internationals.

Cotterill described Oster as:

'Very good technically. With his play-making ability, he will help restore some of what we lost with Robbie Blake's departure.' Oster commented: 'I've been put out on a limb and it hurts. For a long-time my name had "bad boy" written next to it but it's up to me to sort that out. The only way to do that is on the pitch.'

Oster had been sacked by Sunderland after allegedly committing an offensive prank while on loan at Leeds.

A much bigger surprise came on 24 February when Burnley beat Sheffield United in the race to sign 30-year-old Stoke striker, Ade Akinbiyi. He came in a three-and-a-half-year deal, once a transfer fee of around £600,000 had been agreed. Cotterill said: 'Ade's an infectious character, a leader who has had some big money moves that now top £12m. He's very charismatic and has time for everyone. He's a very popular lad who is very fit and hard-working, so he'll fit into the dressing room very well.'

Unfortunately, Akinbiyi was so pumped up for his debut appearance against Sunderland that, within three minutes of coming on as a substitute, he became involved in a violent altercation with a Sunderland defender which resulted in his instant dismissal! Akinbiyi's apologies were sincere and profuse when Steve Cotterill asked him, after the game, whether he had anything to say to his team mates.

Because of a thigh injury and a three-match suspension Akinbiyi had only nine games in which to make an impact. His four goals garnered four points but this came far too late for Burnley to revive their pre-Christmas momentum. Nevertheless, Steve Cotterill and Barry Kilby were delighted with the overall progress made.

Cotterill said:

> 'This has been a remarkable season. We have more than cemented ourselves in the division and yet sold £2.75m of players, brought in over £1m from the FA Cup run, which included a 1-0 victory over Liverpool, and over £250,000 from the Carling Cup competition, in which we beat Aston Villa... When I was appointed, Barry Kilby told me my brief was to keep Burnley up but said if we got relegated I wouldn't get the sack...
>
> 'I have found this area to be very hard-working. It's very, very working class which I warmed to, having grown up on a council estate. The only thing against it is the constant bloody rain. If we had better pitches at the training ground and the ball rolled in the right direction, the weather might not bother me so much.'

At the end-of-season awards night, Steve Cotterill was rightly awarded an outstanding achievement commendation for helping his team achieve two prestigious cup victories, and for guiding them to a respectable position of thirteenth, despite losing two key players and having to juggle with a small first team squad.

Barry Kilby said:

> 'Steve's established himself here very well, and I'm not claiming credit for that... We have had a bumper year, making a profit this time but what that money is going on is to fund wages for the next two years... It is getting tougher and tougher for a club like Burnley in the Championship with its revenues. We're about eighteenth in the table of revenue... You have got to remember that we're playing clubs that take £250,000 more than we do in every home game.'

Chief Executive, Dave Edmundson claimed that the club had ridden out the financial storm caused by the implosion of ITV Digital, thanks to ruthless cost cutting. However, the average gate remained almost static at 12,466, although Edmundson claimed that 'one of the greatest performances off the field was getting 8,500 season ticket holders, a phenomenal achievement when there was no optimism.'

Given the welcome cup booty, and the savings accruing from the departures of three high-earners – Blake, Grant and Ian Moore – Cotterill was given a £500,000 war chest for the 2005/06 season. Cotterill commented:

> 'I think the situation has got worse from the last year. I don't think we have improved as regards numbers. There's only so many good free transfers out there, and you can't get every one of them. We were very, very fortunate to get the ones we got. It gets increasingly difficult once the free transfers run out, you're after Tommy trialist and nine out of 10, they end up being foreign. They may look good on video tape but I've yet to see a bad video! It's a bit different when you bring them over.'

With Grant's contract ending, Camara moving to Celtic on a 'Bosman', and Ian Moore switching to Leeds for £50,000, the club saved around £100,000 in wages. Goalkeeper Brian Jensen and Graham Branch were the sole surviving first team players from the Ternent era. Brian had covered Coyne's five-month absence capably, encouraging a delighted Cotterill to award him a further three-year contract.

Cotterill explained:

> 'Brian has worked very hard this season and reformed his reputation [for inexplicable gaffes]. He is a great lad, a good character to have in the dressing room, always ready with a funny line. He is popular not only with his team mates but with the supporters, too. Phil Hughes has helped him and Danny with their coaching, and arguably we now have the best two goalkeepers in the Championship. Brian was very realistic in his demands and so was his agent. It was all sorted out in a couple of hours.'

For the final seven games of the 2004/05 season Cotterill rotated Jensen and the recovered Coyne. Jensen said:

> 'I can see what the gaffer wants to do. He explained it to us and it gave Coyney a boost. Me and Coyney have always been really supportive of each other. I supported him earlier in the season and then when I was in, he was really behind me.'

Having only nine first team players at his disposal at the start of the summer Cotterill returned to his former club Bournemouth, to bring in winger Wade Elliott and midfielder, Garreth O'Connor. Elliott had excelled in Bournemouth's luckless 0-2 FA Cup defeat at Turf Moor in 2005, having run Mo Camara ragged. Cotterill also signed Stoke striker, Gifton Noel-Williams on a free transfer.

Cotterill said:

> 'Gifton will be a good asset in both boxes… He is a good lad, an intelligent footballer, and come in on the right pay structure, as all the players have… He's not always easy on the eye but he will do what he is very good at – holding the ball up and heading it. I'm not expecting him to outrun centre backs – that won't happen. But he will help us keep the ball and bring midfielders into play. If he gets the right service from the wingers, and I'm thinking Wade Elliott here, he will score a lot of headed goals. He is a big, strong, physical presence, and you need that'

What Steve discreetly omitted to say was that Gifton was not troubled by an arthritic knee as had been widely rumoured. Gifton later told Burnley communications [now media] manager, Darren Bentley:

> 'There was a time at Watford when I had an arthritic condition after I got a kick on the knee cap. I was out for about a year with the injury. I developed rheumatoid arthritis, but that has been in remission for almost six years now. I've had to carry that tag and it frustrates me immensely. I actually have a dropped arch in my foot and that's what perhaps make me look a little leaden and cumbersome.'

Cotterill made a further swoop upon Bournemouth to sign 22-year-old, former Arsenal midfielder, John Spicer for £35,000, and then flew to Florida to persuade Wayne Thomas to join his side. Thomas was a burly central defender, previously with Stoke. Former Chelsea left back, Jon Harley, was also signed from Sheffield United for £75,000 to plug the gap left by the departed Camara.

The 2005/06 season began badly, though. Only one victory – a 4-0 home drubbing of Coventry – was recorded in Burnley's first 10 games, which included five defeats. Thomas incurred a serious knee injury in the 1-2 defeat at Reading on 29 August, ruling him out of the next 17 league games. To compound their woes, Jensen's nasty injury at Watford was culpably ignored by the referee, allowing the Hornets to score a match-clinching third goal with Jensen prostrate in pain. Following a 1-0 reverse at Plymouth on the 17 September, Burnley were second from bottom.

However, Cotterill's men suddenly turned the corner on 27 September with a 3-0 home victory over Ipswich. Former trainee Chris McCann, a Republic of Ireland midfielder, netted late in the game. A rare victory was then achieved at Molineux, thanks to dogged defending and Garreth O'Connor's brilliant long-range, free-kick. Despite subsequent losses at home to Leeds (1-2) and at Crystal Palace (0-2), Burnley embarked upon a four-match winning run which lifted them into a play-off place on 19 November.

The outstanding victory in this winning sequence came at Luton on 5 November 2005. It was particularly impressive given that Burnley had to play for an hour without a recognised goalkeeper. Before Jensen was dismissed for handling outside his box, rampaging Akinbiyi had blasted Burnley into a two-goal lead. His second was a 20-yarder, that veered past ex-Claret, Marlon Beresford, at blistering speed.

Having no reserve goalkeeper on the bench, midfielder, John Spicer, put on the gloves. He had no previous experience, but performed heroically behind his gritty defenders. Although Luton twice reduced the deficit, either side of Akinbiyi's hat-trick penalty, Spicer and company kept their hosts at bay for a nail-biting final half hour, winning 3-2.

At the end of the game, the exhausted Burnley players and their hoarsely ecstatic fans shared a euphoric celebration. Even the Luton fans applauded. Cotterill hailed the win as the greatest of his career, enthusing:

> 'It was fantastic character by the boys. I'm proud of them. Luton are a good side. Ade is a gem. There were a few eyebrows raised when I signed him. I told him at half-time to make sure he got the match ball. I love him and so do the players.'

Ade was indeed a gem, coveted by others, notably Neil Warnock manager of promotion-bound Sheffield United. Akinbiyi's twelfth league goal of the season was sufficient to defeat his former club Stoke on Boxing Day, lifting Burnley into fifth spot – their highest position under Cotterill. Another post-Christmas slump set in, though, accelerated by the sale of Akinbiyi to the Blades on the 25 January 2006 for £1.75m.

Akinbiyi told the press at his departure:

'I am definitely sad to leave. I will always remember Burnley as a great time in my career. I know Steve was almost in tears as we talked. I've never seen a manager so devastated to see me leave. I felt Burnley got the best out of me. Steve has told me he wants me to go to Sheffield United and be the top scorer in the league. That's the kind of honest guy he is. Steve is an out-and-out winner. He's helped me so much, pushing me further than anyone has ever done... Steve needs three or four players and, obviously, I hope my fee helps.'

Chairman, Barry Kilby explained that it was too good a sum to refuse for a 31-year-old, but insisted that the sale did not reflect a lack of ambition. He said:

'We have done five straight seasons at this level. In the previous 20 years, we had just one. I would argue that for Burnley to be back in this company is a success story. Premiership clubs coming down now, have parachute payments of £8m, whereas before they came down laden with debt. This distorts the market... Leeds sold 150,000 duplicate shirts with a £20 mark up. This earned them more than we take in gate money... We have plenty of ambition but unfortunately not enough money to fulfil that yet...

'We're forever asked, where is the money? The truth is we made a profit of £1.8m last year and after spending around £800,000 on Akinbiyi and James O'Connor and £100,000 on agents' fees, what was left enabled us to keep the wage bill at £3.5m, the nineteenth highest in the division. Steve will get well over £1m of the money from Ade's sale to rebuild, while the arrears are being met by the profits we made last year. Eventually that will run out... We are really fortunate to have directors who, between them, have put something like £8m into the club in the past four or five years. I have put £5m of my own money in and have pledged to put in another £750,000 to cover us until February of next season. That's when the money runs out again unless we have money from cup runs, or try to get someone to put capital in or trade players. The only alternative is cutting your wage bill. It's that simple.'

At the November 2005 AGM, Barry Kilby confirmed that the sale and lease back of Turf Moor and Gawthorpe was imminent. It transpired that Longside Properties, a company in which Barry Kilby owned 51 per cent of the shares, was the purchaser.

Barry Kilby reflected upon this momentous occasion in an interview held 10 years later. He recalled:

> 'We were in a big mess after the ITV Digital fiasco. The £3m hole we were left with couldn't be filled no matter how hard we tried with cost cutting and fund-raising. On several occasions during the years that immediately followed, it was touch and go whether we would have to enter administration. We got by with the skin of our teeth, but only after we had agreed to mortgage Turf Moor and the Gawthorpe training ground in 2006. Without that we would have had to cut the player budgets down to the bone, probably drifting down the divisions to where we were in the late eighties, and seeing support dwindle as a result.
>
> 'Nevertheless, this deal didn't solve everything at a stroke. Money remained very tight for a few years after. In 2001/02, we were strong contenders for promotion to the Premier League. But after 2003, we were forced to battle to preserve our second-tier status. Steve did a really good 'backs to the wall' salvage job – picking up players at low cost, and yet consistently putting out competitive sides. I am proud that we managed to "hang in there" under him. But the task of keeping us in the division on such slim pickings eventually told upon him. It was perhaps a good learning experience, albeit a particularly harsh one, for he appears to a better manager now.'

At the time of this interview Steve Cotterill was successfully guiding Bristol City back to the Championship.

This £3m purchase deal that Barry Kilby arranged for Turf Moor and Gawthorpe in 2006 was crucial. Without this, Burnley's future would have been grim. It was not as if the deal was financially advantageous to him. The combined development value of the two sites was estimated to be £1m. The deal would not have happened had Barry not been a devout Claret, something he had inherited from

Roy, his father. This purchase helped future-proof Burnley's proud heritage.

The sale of Turf Moor and Gawthorpe was expected to clear all external debt, although £1.6m of directors' loans remained. Barry agreed to consider a proposal whereby each supporter investing £1,000 as part of the chief executive's '500 Miles' fund-raising scheme would be reimbursed with shares. In response to a supporter's suggestion, he said he would also look at creating a cheaper share than the £200 'ordinary share' to incentivise investment in the club by less affluent fans.

The affordability of football in Burnley had been called into question once more following the publication of the national social and economic statistics for 2004. While the unemployment rate in Burnley had fallen to four per cent, lower than the national rate of five per cent, and much lower than its mid-eighties figure of 15 per cent, local wage levels in 2004 were well below the national average. More than half the local population had an average annual income of less than £15,000 (The national average was then around £25,000.), with only 6.5 per cent earning more than £40,000. Twenty-five per cent of Burnley's population lived in the most deprived neighbourhoods in the country.

Meanwhile, there was an unsettling suggestion circulating among Burnley fans that Cotterill was about to be poached. Barry Kilby confirmed that Leicester had made a bid for him, but that it had been rejected. After his chastening experience at Sunderland, Cotterill's head was not so easily turned. He told the local press: 'I'm staying at Burnley. I'd like to thank Leicester for approaching me, but a lot has been built here in the last 18 months. I have a great relationship with the chairman and supporters. I would like to thank everyone who sent me cards and letters this week. I have been overwhelmed.'

Former England and Bolton striker Michael Ricketts then arrived from Leeds on a loan deal, just as Ade was departing. Cotterill had been a great admirer of Ricketts when the ex-Bolton striker had been in his prime, as had many others.

At Bolton, Ricketts had initially impressed. Tall and muscular, he was a target man with thunderous power. He then had the world at his feet, courted – it was said – by Spurs and Liverpool. Having scored prolifically for Bolton during their successful 2000/01 promotion campaign, Ricketts adapted quickly to Premier League football. He netted 37 times in 98 league games for Bolton, 19 in 2000/01 and a further 12 in 2001/02, snatching a late winner at Old Trafford. However, a dismal debut for the senior England side in February 2002, appeared to derail him. Thereafter, his career unravelled at breakneck speed. Even an exasperated 'Big Sam' Allardyce was powerless to arrest Ricketts' tailspin. A £3.5m move to Middlesbrough was arranged in 2003. It was expected to be a renaissance. Instead it was a lavish calamity – he managed just three goals in 32 Premier League appearances at the Riverside. His subsequent two-year spell at Leeds was an unproductive flop. Ricketts' desire was called into question, notably by a *Daily Mail* journalist who described him as a 'waistful (sic) talent', mocking his mounting poundage. Cotterill's penchant for restoring under-performing players to form, fitness and confidence would stand the severest test with Ricketts. Cotterill thought he should begin by working on Ricketts' self-image.

Cotterill argued:

> 'Everybody keeps talking to Michael about being an England international. He has probably had that rammed down his throat more times than he cares to remember. I've tried to take him back to the days when he was hungry and desperate to get into the Walsall team…. People say he's a difficult character. I don't see that in him. I see a laid back Brummie. Sometimes that can be misconstrued that he doesn't care… It will be an interesting couple of months… He wants to do well having been in the wilderness for a couple of years. We'll try our best to help him.'

Ricketts began promisingly. On debut, he scored the goal which defeated Plymouth on 4 February 2006 (1-0). Having neatly averted a challenge at the edge of the Pilgrims' box, he dispatched a low drive into the left-hand corner with the nonchalance of a master craftsman. His nimble winner ended a seven-game win-less sequence. There was brief hope that he would fill the gap left by the departed Akinbiyi. But apart from finishing clinically at Portman Road, a week later, Ricketts contributed little thereafter as Burnley racked up six successive losses, imperilling their Championship status. His 12 league games produced only two goals.

Just in the nick of time, Sunderland striker, Andy Gray, and Wigan's Irish playmaker, Alan Mahon were signed on loan deals, both with a view to permanent transfers. Gray was signed for a £750,000 fee while Mahon cost £200,000. Eleven points were accrued from the final eight games, easily sufficient to secure safety, but not enough to exceed seventeenth position, four down on the previous season. Gray opened his account in a debut victory over Norwich, and seized the match winner against Queen's Park Rangers. Gangling

Northern Ireland striker Kyle Lafferty, a former Burnley trainee like Chris McCann, scored his first goal for Burnley with a late equaliser against Luton.

Ex-Burnley captain and talismanic centre half, Steve Davis Mark II, was appointed as first team coach after another former Claret player, Mark Yates, moved to Shrewsbury. Davis was delighted with the signings of Gray and Mahon stating: 'We're not talking about two extra bodies to fill a few spots; they're two quality players...' Cotterill was similarly excited, notably over the acquisition of Mahon, saying: 'I couldn't believe it driving home after signing Mahon... He will make us play more football than we play and that is vital.'

Having strengthened the side with the addition of Gray and Mahon, Steve Cotterill was infuriated by his team's dismal display in a 0-1 defeat at Millwall in the penultimate game. He ranted:

> 'We were poor, especially in midfield. Their full backs had too much time on the ball. It was just poor and I'm pretty much fuming. You motivate players by trying to train them properly, by bringing them down the night before and by making sure they eat all the right things. If we had to come down Saturday morning and it took seven hours we might have had an excuse... Here we didn't. It doesn't happen very often, but when it does you feel let down and disappointed because the minimum requirement is maximum effort...
>
> 'All those people who came to see us who were probably up at six o'clock on Saturday morning, enduring the motorway, bless them. They do that and we don't put on a performance for them. We've been on a good run and it's come to an abrupt halt... Even with the few chances we created in the second half we deserved to get nothing... The only player who can come out of this with credit is Andy Gray. From minute one to minute 90, he played exactly the same and unfortunately didn't have enough players to join him. I thought that when John Spicer went on he was our best defender and he doesn't play right back... He did okay against Marvin Williams who has great pace.'

This was Ricketts' last start for Burnley. He looked overweight, unfit and uncommitted. Steve's Cotterill's efforts had been in vain.

But Steve was more upbeat two weeks later, when reflecting upon the 2005/06 season. He told a *Burnley Express* reporter:

'When I first came here, there were eight players, and in the following summer we had nine – and that culminates in a disaster really because you end up with players having you by the short and curlies, maybe inducing you into giving them longer contracts than you would otherwise. We are not in that predicament this year which may make this easier.

'The big thing is when you sell people you are always chasing, and for two years we have been doing that. We formulated a team around Robbie Blake and that changed, then another around Ade Akinbiyi and that changed. It disrupts you a little and coincides with a loss of form, although to be fair to the lads on the turnover from Ade to Andy, I feel they adjusted quite well. It would just have been nice to have had Andy in quickly after Ade left... That's what happens with these transfer windows.

'As for other positives, Chris McCann has come on, and at the start of the season we didn't have a left back. I think we end it with one of the best in the league in Jon Harley. The other success stories would be Michael Duff going in at centre half, and John Spicer who ended up playing everywhere. We saw a revitalised Garreth O'Connor. Graham Branch has played everywhere and the signings of Gray and Mahon will be good ones. There's also been the re-emergence of James O'Connor in the past two months after having had a very quiet season, so there have been lots of positives to take forward.

Graham Branch easily the longest-serving player at the club, having been signed in December 1998, was delighted to receive another one-year contract. He said:

'I'm really happy. The boss has been brilliant. He is one of the best managers around and for him to want me for another year is great for me personally... The legs might not be what they were 10 years ago but I still feel that I have something to offer.'

Although Crewe's Northern Ireland striker Steve Jones and their central defender Stephen Foster joined on free transfers, there was an unusual lack of summer transfer activity. Encouragingly, former trainee Kyle Lafferty won two Northern Ireland caps, as did Michael

Duff and Steve Jones. Meanwhile, Steve Cotterill surprised the fans in awarding the captaincy to his imposing central defender, Wayne Thomas. Thomas took over the arm-band held previously by Frank Sinclair. Cotterill announced:

> 'I think there is more to come out of Wayne and, in giving him the armband, he has to be responsible and mature. These are things that are missing from time to time and if he puts this right he can grow into being a top player'.

Burnley writer, Phil Whalley wrote in in the London Clarets' magazine:

> 'Let's hope the manager has called this one right. The defender's disciplinary record is certainly poor... One can only hope that this decision hasn't been met with resentment and incredulity among the squad.'

But whatever doubts existed over Thomas's appointment, these were soon set aside as Burnley's 2006/07 season started well with victories over Queen's Park Rangers and Leicester, only for them to stutter, losing successive home matches against Wolves (a long-standing habit), Hartlepool, in the League Cup, and newly-promoted Colchester. Just when a slip was turning into an embarrassing slide, Barnsley were beaten 4-2 win after the visitors had taken an early two-goal lead. The unlikely hero in this impressive turnaround was Gifton Noel-Williams, who recorded his first Football League hat-trick.

A self-deprecating Gifton admitted:

> 'I can't really blame the fans for not fancying me. If they are looking at people who have been performing at the club, I would not be up among the top five. But I have broad shoulders. I've got on with it and I get paid to do a job. Hopefully, I've shown the Burnley fans what I can do and it's up to me to continue that and to kick on and score a few more.'

Gifton's reward came with his abrupt removal from the transfer list. With Gray's first minute goal proving sufficient to defeat Stoke at the Britannia Stadium, Burnley rose to third place, amid rumours of a bid made by West Bromwich for Steve Cotterill. Barry Kilby was sufficiently concerned to state:

> 'Absolutely no approach has been made. The story is a non-event. The last time I spoke with Steve he was very

happy. He's doing well at Burnley and we might go top on Saturday. He's our manager. He's just signed a new contract and as far as I'm concerned, he'll be our manager for some time to come.'

Disappointingly, on 23 September, Burnley failed to beat Southampton in a winnable home game. Shortly after Jones had given Burnley a fourth minute lead, captain Wayne Thomas felled Southampton's Viafara in the opponents' box while awaiting a Burnley free-kick. Thomas was dismissed. Just two minutes later, Southampton equalised. Although Gray restored Burnley's lead, Southampton came back to win.

Cotterill fumed:

> 'A moment of unthinkable stupidity has cost us three points. We were the better team and they knew it. We showed great character to go 2-1 up. The lad might have made a meal of it, but I don't blame him for going down. Nine times out of 10 I stick up for my players, but I can't do that because people will think I'm an idiot.'

October began with renewed hope, as Burnley crushed Norwich 4-1 at Carrow Road, captured live on Sky TV. Having received a boardroom ultimatum, Norwich manager Nigel Worthington, was under extreme pressure, not helped by this hapless performance. Norwich failed lamentably to crack Burnley's solidity at the back or cope with their devastating counter attacks. The outstanding features of Burnley's victory were Wade Elliott's dazzling wing play and Steve Jones's bustling promptings. Gray scored twice, assisted by Elliott, just before half-time, and by Jones, just after. A scurrying James O'Connor set the ball rolling with a smart shot after half an hour and substitute Alan Mahon finished the game off with a screamer from the edge of the box. Enjoying their Sunday dessert of schadenfreude, the large Burnley contingent chanted: 'Worthington out'. Burnley moved up into third place, while the dignified Worthington stepped down.

Hull were then despatched 2-0 in an unremarkable home win on the following Saturday. Steve Cotterill commended his new centre-back partnership of Duff and Sinclair for the 'immaculate' way they dealt with Hull's constant stream of crosses. Duff also chipped in with a headed goal. Burnley rose to second spot, causing chief executive Dave Edmundson to appeal for more support. The 11,530 attendance for the Hull game had been the third lowest in the division.

Edmundson revealed that, while Burnley's home attendances remained around this level, the club would continue to lose £30,000 per week. He urged more to attend, stating:

'If there are to be funds made available for the manager, those funds have to be generated from other sources and that includes supporters coming down on the day… This is probably our best chance of promotion. When we were in trouble just a few years ago, the fans rallied round to ensure we didn't go out of existence. Surely those same supporters are now delighted that we are second in the league and would want to be a part of that success?'

Two hard-fought goal-less draws with Southend and Plymouth followed, causing Burnley to slip a couple of places. Steve Jones told a *Lancashire Evening Telegraph* reporter:

'I think there's a lot of managers in the division that must feel we shouldn't be up there, but we feel we should be with the results we've got. We're quietly confident… I think we've got our feet on the ground, though. All the lads are tremendous. We all work hard for one another, and it's going really well for me. The way that Gifton Noel-Williams and Andy Gray are linking up front probably means I might remain on the left wing for some time, but as long as I can get into the team, I'm not bothered. It's a team ethic and that's installed in all of us. I knew this was the place to come to. I really needed a fresh challenge. The strong Irish connections help. I'm delighted with my choice.'

But just as the supposed West Bromwich raid fizzled out, yet another arose as Sheffield Wednesday sacked their manager Paul Sturrock and requested permission to speak to Steve Cotterill. Barry Kilby refused, stating with rare irritation:

'When any management job becomes available now we have come to expect that Steve, one of the division's brightest young managers, will become a target. Steve is clearly an ambitious man who wants to manage in the Premier League and I believe he can do that. But we see our future there, too. We are going for promotion this season and we can do without these distractions.'

Cotterill responded:

> 'It was quite nice of the chairman to tell me… I did not spit out my dummy. I have not had a lot of time to think about it as I have been concentrating on the next game… It is flattering and probably a measure of how well we are doing at Burnley. But I've got my feet on the ground. I'm honest and hard-working and that will never change.'

Burnley vice-chairman Ray Ingleby then gave a press interview a day before the televised home game with Preston on 27 October. He emphasised:

> 'We do not want to lose Steve Cotterill… We want him to take us to the promised land… I would like to think the supporters can show what he means to Burnley Football Club. The best way they can do that is to turn up en masse tomorrow night to show Steve is wanted. This is all about Steve, not about the directors or money. It is about supporters chanting his name, making a lot of noise and making sure we out-sing Preston…
>
> It's very gratifying that we chose a very good manager. But it is very unnerving, too. We've backed him and he's got the team he wants. So, to think that he might leave, especially in a season where we have very high hopes, is very scary. Yes, one day we will lose him. Because of his talent, there will be a club big enough knocking on our door that Steve will want to talk to and have every right to. It will have to be the right club, a Premier League club. But we think we can be in the Premier League. We want him there… The current directors are committed to get Burnley in the Premier League, but not at any cost because we are not going to bankrupt the club. If we are there or thereabouts with the play-offs by the turn of the year and the club does not happen to be losing any more money, the directors will do all they can to make sure additional resources are made available.'

Thankfully, the Preston game was a scorcher, watched by a raucous crowd of 14,871. Man-of-the-match James O'Connor put Burnley into the lead on the stroke of half-time only for Preston to hit back strongly after the break, helped by two key substitutions. Their second goal was scored with only 10 minutes remaining. But Burnley were not done. The irrepressible Frank Sinclair then stepped up to the plate. Rediscovering the elixir of youth, Frank zipped down the right flank, producing a sizzling, low cross which Preston's central defender, Sean St Ledger could only divert into his own net. Back on terms, Burnley smelt blood. Pouring forward, they won the game in the final minute when an exquisitely-flighted, left-wing cross from Jones was deftly glanced past the flailing Preston keeper by Andy Gray. Pandemonium broke out on three sides of the ground. A relieved, hoarse and exhausted Steve Cotterill uttered: 'God shone down on us today because we deserved that!'

Interviewed after receiving his Sky 'Man-of-the Match' award, an exuberant James O'Connor declared:

> 'The spirit has been really good this year, right through the squad and management. We have got a nice rhythm and everybody seems to be enjoying their football. Preston got two very quick goals against the run of the play but it was great spirit from the lads to come back. It's very important we stay level-headed...'

Dispiritingly, Burnley's facilities manager, Doug Metcalfe, reported that major repairs were required to the Cricket Field Stand after 355 seats had been vandalised by Preston supporters. This amounted to almost 10 per cent of the stand's capacity. Damage had been inflicted too upon the toilets and concourse. A gloomy prospect of potential reprisals at Preston lay ahead.

Gray's high-class finishing then enabled Burnley to snatch all three points at Luton. He followed up his deft lob over Beresford with a powerful back-post header from Wade Elliott's superb cross. Burnley were third, but the clouds were gathering.

McGreal and Thomas were out with knee injuries, Noel-Williams and Garreth O'Connor had succumbed to illness and Foster faced suspension for his dismissal at Kenilworth Road. Cotterill demanded more reinforcements:

> 'We need these before we get to Christmas because by the time we get there we'll have only 11 players and no sub at all... Everyone knows we've got the smallest squad and I'm sick and tired of saying it. Tonight, at Luton we were down to our last 16 players... If we want to stay there or thereabouts, we need to strengthen. The boys have given their all again and they really are first class.'

Having received the Championship manager of the month award for October, Cotterill dedicated it to his team, stating: 'I take the little personal pat on the back, but it is very much a collective effort.' However, he singled out Andy Gray for special praise. Gray's brace at Luton took him to the top of the division's scoring charts with nine goals. Cotterill said:

> 'It will give Andy confidence. He's very low maintenance. He never asks for anything. He trains fantastically well, like he plays – full of effort and honesty. He's an absolute top lad… The forwards have been together a little while now. They are intelligent and struck up good partnerships, whatever pairing we've had, so we're delighted because we need that to happen.'

Although Chris McCann's last-minute header, from Mahon's pin-point cross, was sufficient for Burnley to overcome Ipswich, three successive defeats were inflicted by Cardiff, West Bromwich and Birmingham respectively. Winning ways were restored on 28 November 2006 when lowly Leeds were beaten 2-1 at Turf Moor. Gray was once again on target against his family's club. However, he sustained a metatarsal injury in this game, ruling him out for at least 10 weeks.

Steve Cotterill put on a typically brave face for the press, announcing:

> 'There are opportunities now for others, namely Kyle Lafferty. That's the only way we can look at it… Andy is going to be missed but it's a big chance for Kyle… We must remember he's only a kid. He is not really ready for this, but now he is having to be… We'll continue to work with him… Everybody knows what I'm like with a young player coming through a club, because I've had them wherever I've been. Nothing gives me greater satisfaction than to see Chris McCann and Kyle Lafferty out on the pitch because they will give everything they've got.'

Lafferty made an immediate impact, curling a beauty into the bottom corner to give Burnley an 86th minute lead at Ipswich on 2 December. Exasperatingly, Burnley then conceded a soft equaliser four minutes later. The error was repeated in the following home game against Sunderland. Lafferty's brace of clinically-executed goals had given Burnley a two-goal advantage but in the final 10 minutes, the Black Cats struck twice to earn a draw. A loss at Coventry on 9 December, was followed by others at Barnsley and Hull during a cheerless festive period. By New Year, Burnley were eleventh and falling. Between 28 November 2006 and 31 March 2007, Burnley failed to win a single game in 18 league matches and one FA Cup tie, sliding from fourth to nineteenth in the table.

The start of this barren run coincided with a row between chief executive Dave Edmundson and a *Lancashire Evening Telegraph* reporter. Edmundson accused the journalist of distorting his comments concerning the recently-released club accounts for the year ending June 2006. Edmundson was quoted as saying that the club suffered an annual £2.1m loss, mainly due to low cup revenue and declining attendances. This was despite the sale of Akinbiyi, which had yielded around £1.4m up front, and the £3m sale of Turf Moor and Gawthorpe.

When asked whether the club might need to sell another player in January 2007 to reduce the loss, Edmundson allegedly said that this was possible, while emphasising that, 'selling a player is not the only option'. He pointed out that the club was desperately trying to help the manager increase the size of his squad, not reduce it. The reporter understood though that the chances of realising this ambition rested upon a good FA Cup run and other unspecified funding sources. Edmundson was also quoted as saying: 'The club sits in the top three of the Championship, but in wages terms we are in the bottom three – that's in an area where 600 people a year move out of town, and an area where the average wage is actually going down.'

The club immediately attempted to quell the fans' anxieties, aroused by this article, by stating:

> 'Burnley Football Club wishes to reassure supporters that, while player sales are inevitably "an option" for a majority of Football League and Premiership clubs, current boardroom discussion surrounds the need to actively seek investment to strengthen the squad, not weaken it by selling a major asset. The £2.1m loss is factual but significant losses were inevitable with match-day revenues being affected by league position and the lack of a lucrative cup run. However, such losses were budgeted for. The Burnley board of directors are looking to redress the deficit, and options such as future private investment and director loans are ways of doing this. So, too, are increased attendances, which we saw for the visit of Ipswich last weekend when 700 more supporters

'walked-up' on the day to give us an above-budget gate return.'

The facts seemed not so much in dispute as the tone.

Ray Griffiths had recently joined the Burnley board of directors, having made an outstanding success of his warehousing and distribution business. He, too, was locally born and bred and a lifetime Clarets' supporter. When questioned by Burnley author Dave Thomas about the club's finances, he replied:

> 'Where does the cash go? Largely it goes on players' wages. The irony is that with a successful team, there are the win bonuses to factor in. The club is already over budget on player salaries and Steve Cotterill was given a higher salary with a new contract. Already this year, three directors have each put in half a million. A new director has put in half a million and a tenth director will soon join the board. This does not buy new players; it simply keeps the club afloat and makes up budget deficits.

> 'There are the incidentals to contend with, too. For example, Barry Kilby and I put £17,000 together to fund the youth team's summer trip to Germany. Is there an answer? You could put £3 on the admission price and that would clear the weekly losses immediately. Concession prices are too low. But how do you do this in Burnley, a dying town? Getting to the Premiership would attract new investors, re-vitalise the club and retain Steve Cotterill. But it's all luck. A goal line clearance, a penalty... Top two? I can't see it. I worry about the size of the squad...

> 'The biggest frustration is fans not being better informed and more conscious of the constraints. All they have to go on is what is fed to them by the press. If only they knew... There's no black hole. It can all be accounted for. Just on a match day there is the police to pay for, the stewards, the security, gate staff, referee, linesmen, ticket printing, advertising, telephones, ticket office salaries, St John's ambulances and computer costs...'

> 'We receive regular briefings on what cash comes in and what goes out. I have the memo here for July/August. It explains the overspend on players' salaries. It refers specifically to "huge spend on kit issues" and details the impact of a slow start in commercial and catering income,

higher than budgeted match costs because of the poor Carling Cup revenue [Burnley were eliminated at home in the first round by lowly Hartlepool] and a downturn in lottery income. The players' wages budgeted for in July and August amounted to £699,142, and yet the actual cost was £807,965. And the shortfall is not made up from matchday receipts... The lowest point I ever felt was at the Orient game in 1987. I thought we were finished and would end up playing my home town club, Bacup Borough. Look where we are now. I just wish the fans knew what it costs to run this club.'

Nevertheless, in his local newspaper column, former Claret star, Andy Payton, urged the club to 'really go for it... If ever there was a time to speculate to accumulate then surely this it,' he claimed. 'If the board of directors or anyone else from outside the club could come up with a few million quid to give the manager then I'm sure he would cement a place in the play-offs and possibly even better.' But not all Clarets' fans were so gung-ho.

For example, Burnley writer Phil Whalley opined in the London Clarets' magazine:

'Edmundson's comment that the Championship was becoming like the second tier of the Premiership indicates the pressure of wage inflation in our division... The even more lucrative Sky deal about to begin for the Premiership will continue the trend and will also ensure that clubs coming down will be even richer, better-resourced and more advantaged than they are now.'

Hence Barry Kilby's aversion to parachute payments, which he denounced as distorting the market, at least before his club became one of the chosen few.

Phil Whalley continued:

'From next season, just one year in the Premiership will net £50m. It's certainly enough to tempt a gambling man, but Burnley would face administration and almost certain relegation if they went for it in January 2007 to the tune of Payton's "few million quid" and failed.'

Ray Griffiths' sobering account appeared to substantiate largely what the *Lancashire Evening Telegraph* had reported. However, as a result of additions to the board, which Ray had discreetly referred to, suggested that additional investment was being made. Although their names were not disclosed to Dave Thomas, the new directors were: Mike Garlick, a 42-year-old managing director of a highly successful, London-based, IT recruitment firm; and Brendan Flood, managing director of Modus, a thriving property development company, specialising in property investment and shopping mall development. Once again, the new directors were long-standing Clarets' fans and brought up locally. Garlick was born a mere 200 yards from Turf Moor. It was understood that both men had invested £500,000 each in the club.

Mike Garlick has been the sole chairman of Burnley FC since May 2015, having previously shared the role with Nelson-born director and international businessman John Banaszkiewicz after Barry Kilby resigned in May 2012 because of ill health. Reflecting upon his five-year association with the club in 2012, Mike recalled:

'It felt like a dream coming true when I first joined the board of the club I had always supported. My roots are firmly established in Burnley, although I now spend much of my time working in London. I was educated at Burnley Grammar School. My family have lived in the town since the 1850s, when they arrived among the growing throng of textile mill workers.

'Burnley is as important to me as it was to preceding members of my family. I believe in this town and its people. So many owners have no connection with the town or club. That's not my story.

'I first considered buying shares in the club in 1999, but back then I was very hands-on in my business and the time didn't feel right. My business has expanded widely since then with bases in several European countries. However, in the summer of 2006, I heard about the share issue, met Barry Kilby and things went from there. I thought he [Barry] and the board of directors had done an excellent job in taking the club forward and building up the infrastructure, notwithstanding the resource constraints of that time.'

When Brendan Flood joined the Burnley board of directors in early December 2006, it was rumoured on the fans' message boards that he might have considerable wealth, raising hopes of a significant investment. Brendan Flood recalled that he was quickly collared by Steve Cotterill who was worried by his depleting resources, and declining results and brooding over his frustrated ambition. Cotterill, like so many supporters, possibly espied a potential 'sugar daddy' in the newly-arrived Flood. Despite being warned against putting any money into a football club by a world-weary Barnsley director, Flood ignored him. At the opening of the January transfer window Flood funded the return of Ade Akinbiyi for £750,000. All but £100,000 of the fee was paid up front.

A very grateful Steve Cotterill stated:

> 'I don't think we would have been able to bring Ade back without Brendan coming on board. He's not only a fan, but a big fan of Ade's, and I think he was quite pleased with how his money was spent. I have thanked him personally for that... With the loss of Andy Gray we have struggled to win a game, as hard as we have tried. Another striker was therefore a must. The prices quoted for younger strikers were unbelievable and certainly not something we could get into. We have got someone who is 30-plus, but Ade didn't do too badly the last time he was here and he was 30-plus then. Only the pessimists will say you shouldn't go back. The optimists will be delighted.'

In his book *Big Club, Small Town and Me*, Brendan Flood wrote that he found some board members doubtful of Burnley's sustainability as a Championship club. He was concerned, too, that Akinbiyi had lost his zip, despite scoring with a deft lob in an FA Cup defeat at Reading in January. It transpired that Ade had spent too much time on weight training while side-lined at Bramall Lane, bulking his physique but impairing his speed and dexterity. It took him nine more games before he scored again, equalising against Crystal Palace on 3 March. By then Burnley were eighteenth.

As explained in his book, Flood invested £2m in the club, most of which was made available for transfers. Steve Cotterill told Flood that the first team could not be successful without more experienced players, although he continued to select Lafferty and McCann. So, Flood funded the signings of two battling midfielders; Cameroon international, Eric Djemba-Djemba, on loan from Aston Villa, and Icelandic international, Joey Gudjonsson, from AZ Alkmaar for £150,000. Flood also bought Sunderland's Scottish international centre half, Steven Caldwell, with half of the £400,000 fee paid up front. Reserve goalkeeper, Mike Pollitt was brought in, too, from Wigan, as cover for Jensen. Before wages were reckoned with, Flood had shelled out a further £1.3m in these four deals, £1m of which was paid immediately. This was a bold measure.

It was anticipated that Caldwell's firm leadership and organisational ability might tighten the defence. Before his arrival, there had been discontinuity in the club captaincy, with it passing quickly from Thomas to McGreal and on to Sinclair. These incoming transfers gave Cotterill the scope to release Frank Sinclair, Micah Hyde and Gifton Noel Williams.

The ever-popular Sinclair left for Huddersfield, initially on an 'emergency loan', but with a view to a possible permanent contract. Frank said:

> 'I leave in good spirits and on good terms with the manager. We have always been honest with one another and he didn't stand in my way. He was the reason I joined the club in the first place. I have had some wonderful times.'

Micah Hyde moved to Peterborough for a fee of £100,000, a quarter of which was contingent upon 'Posh' being promoted. Although falling out of favour latterly, Hyde's magnificent, looping volley at Ewood Park in March 2005 had become immortalised in Burnley folklore. Meanwhile, Gifton Noel-Williams signed for Spanish second division side Real Murcia for £50,000, but Burnley rejected a £500,000 bid from Celtic for Lafferty, an offer which Cotterill described as 'nowhere near acceptable'. Both McCann and Lafferty then signed contract extensions until 2010.

Despite the deeply disappointing results, John Harley told a local journalist: 'We're a good team. Steve Cotterill has got together the best team ethic I have come across. Once we get one win we'll be OK'. This offered scant solace while Burnley remained three places above the relegation zone. It was not what Brendan Flood envisaged when he splashed out almost £2m in transfer fees. His conversations with Steve Cotterill became increasingly tense. Flood recalled an agitated Cotterill ringing him to demand: 'Look Bren, if you're going to bloody well sack me, just sack me, okay!' Flood reassured him that this was not what he wanted. What he wanted was to help him figure out what was going wrong. Barry Kilby then sanctioned two emergency loan signings: Graham Coughlan, an intimidating centre half, from Sheffield Wednesday; and Paul McVeigh, a striker or winger from Norwich who had previously played for Spurs and Northern Ireland.

On the eve of a crucial midweek home game with Plymouth, Steve Cotterill gave a pumped-up interview to the local press asserting:

'As regards the chairman and the board, I think the job I've done here in two-and-a-half years, and what it's been done on, probably earns myself time and credit with them. There have been three or four occasions when I could have left the club, but I didn't. I've committed myself here, so maybe things even out, if you see what I mean. I've never had anything like this before, but I think there have been a few really good managers who have been on uncomfortable runs this season. You just have to get on with it.'

Roared on by a slim but stoked-up crowd of 9,793, Burnley tore into Plymouth from the start, scoring three times without reply in the first 40 minutes, with Duff, McVeigh and Jones on target. Plymouth could not cope with the Clarets' aggression and intensity. Burnley eventually won the game 4-0, after Elliott lashed in a fourth on the hour. Burnley author Dave Thomas remembered:

'Around 9.45, the manager walked around the touchline, very slowly, punching the air and applauding the fans. The players had gone. As he approached the tunnel he turned once more to face the Longside and pointed at his heart. Something had happened. We'd won!'

Cotterill told the waiting press:

'The lads played angry tonight. I think for the first time there was a little bit of stick which they got at the weekend and they read those things. I suppose the key now is to keep angry! They wanted that result for a long time. We have had a big cross to bear. I'm delighted for the players, for the chairman and the directors and the supporters who have stood beside me because it's probably the toughest time I have had to face.'

He subsequently praised Brian Jensen, revealing that the 'Beast' was off the transfer list. Cotterill said:

'I felt Brian hadn't been keeping us in the game long enough. After I left him out in one game, where I felt he deserved to be taken out of the firing line, he had the hump about it, but he's off the list now because he apologised and wanted to come off, so that's fine. To be fair to him, he has absolutely trained his socks off since he's been out of the side.'

In a later interview, Jensen described how stressed Cotterill was, how he picked on him and other players, 'slagging them off for no reason', undermining their confidence. However, Steven Caldwell recognised the depth of passion Cotterill had for the club commenting: 'He wears his heart on his sleeve and he cares.'

As glib as Harley sounded in his press interview, he was right. Following that emphatic victory over Plymouth, Burnley proceeded to beat promotion-bound Birmingham at St Andrews, just four days later, thanks to a wonderfully cool finish from John Spicer. Cotterill dedicated the victory to the recently deceased Brian Miller, a Burnley hero not only during the club's glory days, but at its nadir in May 1987. Cardiff, Norwich and high-riding West Bromwich were then overcome, lifting Burnley well clear of the relegation places. A final position of fifteenth represented an improvement of three points and two places on the previous season.

A relieved Steve Cotterill responded to this abrupt uplift in fortunes by showering his players with plaudits, not only Jensen, but Wayne Thomas and Andy Gray, too, both of whom had struggled to recover their form following injuries. Cotterill said:

> 'Thommo's ended up being the player I signed him for… He's defended first and foremost and earned rave reviews while Andy Gray is one of the top strikers in this league. Anybody can play with him… He's intelligent and does all the horrible work, holding the ball up, the aerial stuff and the fighting with the centre halves… Paul McVeigh has helped here, allowing us to play a bit differently, and taking some of the weight off Andy.' He complimented Djemba-Djemba, too, describing him as 'mightily impressive in the heart of midfield.'

The previously muscle-bound Ade Akinbiyi was mentioned in dispatches as well. Cotterill said:

> 'Ade has been out of the team. When he came back from Sheffield United he wasn't as fit as he should have been. He'd bulked up which lost him a yard of pace. He was desperate to come back and score goals and do well again. But he needs to be loved. Because people see him as a big, bruising figure, they don't think he can have a loss of confidence, but he can, like anyone. I had to take him out of the side but he doesn't sulk and he was the first one to

his feet when we scored against Plymouth. He's a good man and deserved his headed goal in the 3-0 win over Norwich.'

A Burnley star of the future was unveiled at the beginning of May when local lad Jay Rodriguez signed his first professional contract with the club. Whereas, 14-year-old starlet John Cofie moved to Manchester United for a £1m fee. While this was a substantial fee, the transaction highlighted the difficulties of scouting for young talent when the most promising recruits could be picked off by richer clubs.

Cotterill's squad for the 2007/08 season was enhanced by several notable signings. Robbie Blake returned from relegated Leeds for a £250,000 fee. The Kosovan Albanian forward, Besart Berisha, was signed from Hamburg for £340,000 following a brilliant display at Turf Moor in a 'B' international, and Manchester City's left back, Stephen Jordan, arrived on a free transfer, providing competition for Jon Harley.

As for the other full back berth, Cotterill was permitted to spend a further £200,000 on Preston's highly competitive right back, Graham Alexander. This seemed a lot to pay for a 35-year-old but Cotterill argued:

> 'We've got probably the best right-back in the Champ-ionship over the last eight years... He's a very good, experienced professional who looks after himself impeccably well. He's a fit lad, still playing international football for Scotland. Plus, he's played in central midfield before, which may be a possibility for us.'

With the injury-prone keeper, Danny Coyne, released, Cotterill found an apparently worthy replacement in Hungarian international, Gabor Kiraly, formerly with Crystal Palace. But Cotterill's best deal of the summer was selling Wayne Thomas to Southampton for £1.2m, and replacing him with Watford's elegant, quick and doughty centre back, Clarke Carlisle, for £200,000. Carlisle had been troubled previously by alcohol addiction, but had sought help in overcoming this. The former Everton and Wigan defender, David Unsworth joined, too, on a one-year deal to provide additional cover at the back. Although Cotterill would not remain in post long enough to witness the fruits of his recruitment, he had assembled the nucleus of a side which would win promotion to the Premier League in May 2009, under his successor, Owen Coyle.

Among the others leaving the club were centre half, Stephen Foster, midfielder, Garreth O'Connor and utility player, Graham Branch, who had served Burnley well in a stay of nearly eight years during which he had made 232 senior appearances. There were changes behind the scenes too, with former chief executive, Dave Edmundson moving to a new role as Head of Strategic Development which focused upon the club's community activities. Chairman Barry Kilby and operational director Brendan Flood took on a more 'hands on' responsibility for the everyday running of the club, jointly sharing the functions previously held by the chief executive. Barry Kilby pointed to the need to 'drive up the club's revenue streams.'

If Steve Cotterill was uncertain about the club's heightened ambitions, Brendan Flood left little room for doubt in his June interview with BBC Radio Lancashire. Flood said:

> 'The immediate plan is to get a good, entertaining team and we are doing our best to do that now. Steve Cotterill has been out there shopping and is very careful who he goes for. This is his, big, big chance. His heart is definitely in the club and he's massively ambitious… I think he's got the brains and willpower, and with the right people around him, we'll get the best out of him and he'll get the best of the players. I'm confident that he's as good as you get and he just needs the breaks to come his way and he'll grow into it.'

Flood also referred to a radical overhaul of Turf Moor to,

> …get the economy of the club better and bring in revenue other than on a Saturday afternoon.' Flood added: 'We need to be more analytical of where we are going wrong and put it right and do it in a professional way. The standards we expect of ourselves have got to be higher. Barry is a good balance for me, because he's probably older and wiser in football terms. I've got to take from him as much knowledge as I can to make the right decisions and between us we can be good leaders of the club.'

A month later, Barry Kilby announced a five-year re-development of Turf Moor comprising an upgrade in facilities. There were to be new dressing rooms, spaces for small businesses and entrepreneurs, and retail, hotel and leisure facilities, to generate greater revenue, and contribute to the regeneration of the town. Gawthorpe was identified for development also, as the club sought youth academy status. Barry Kilby described this as 'another brick in the wall, building us towards the Premiership', adding 'clubs like Burnley need kids coming through.'

It was then estimated that the entire project would cost around £15m to complete. It depended upon Burnley Cricket Club being persuaded to co-operate, though, for the outline plans envisaged building on adjacent land currently occupied by them. It was understood that Longside properties, who owned Turf Moor and Gawthorpe training centre, would allow the club to sub-let the retail outlets, permitting rental income to flow into the club.

Meanwhile, the club had to prove its worth on the pitch. Steve Cotterill remarked on the eve of the 2007/08 season:

> 'We've had a tough two or three years with injuries to players at important times and hopefully we won't get that situation any more. The one thing we have got is a bit more strength in depth.'

With the club allegedly turning down a £2m bid from Fulham for young striker Kyle Lafferty, Cotterill added: 'We're delighted we've got four strikers now.'

Unfortunately, new signing Besart Berisha would not be among them, having sustained a serious knee ligament injury in an international friendly against Malta. After spending ten months on the side lines he was loaned to Rosenborg and then AC Horsens, before being sold to Bundesliga side Arminia Bielefeld, in August 2009, for a fee believed to be around £75,000; he did not make a single senior appearance for Burnley.

Although stronger up front, Cotterill fretted over his back four, particularly after Michael Duff suffered a cruciate knee injury. Nevertheless, Burnley made a flying start defeating West Bromwich in the opening home game in front of a healthy 15,337 crowd, but as autumn arrived that early momentum became lost. According to Brendan Flood, Cotterill became progressively jumpy. Cotterill told Flood: 'Expectations are higher now, Bren. You're here, we've bought a few players and the fans want glory now don't they?' Cotterill seemed equally disturbed by the ground redevelopment plans, remarking: 'The crowd are more anxious this year than they have before because of all the hullabaloo that's gone on off the pitch. That's a definite fact. There's less patience with the boys at home now, and I don't think that's fair. We shouldn't be edgy about playing at home.'

With the team spluttering once more, Turf Moor attendances began to decline. Only 9,978 turned up on a chilly November evening for the home game with Hull. Burnley performed abjectly, allowing the toothless Tigers to win an awful game with a late, scuffed effort.

The club was about to announce an annual loss of £4.3m to the end of June 2007, almost double that in the previous financial year. The wage bill had risen to £7.1m against a £6.7m turnover. This deficit would have been higher had Brendan Flood not have bought over £3m worth of shares, making him the club's second largest shareholder. Other directors had made loans to the club as well. Flood was not only worried that the new investment was foundering, he was concerned about Cotterill's demeanour, noting how snappy he was with his players.

Flood believed that it was time for a change of manager. After he had spoken at length with Cotterill about his concerns, at what Cotterill wryly described as the 'Last Supper', Flood put the proposition to Barry Kilby. It was then mutually agreed that Steve Cotterill's period in charge should come to an end, two days later, on 8 November 2007. Cotterill had been at the club for three and a half seasons, longer than that served by any other Championship manager of that time. Cotterill confirmed to a *Burnley Express* reporter:

> 'If ever there was mutual consent, this was it. There are no problems at all, no bitterness with the board of directors. It is a big shame that it has happened. I have had a great time here. It has been a tough couple of days for me, but that is something I will just have to come to terms with. It's a great club, I have loved every minute of it and I will miss it.'

In a strident act of loyalty, Andy Gray told the local press:

> 'The performance on Tuesday night was not good enough, neither was it in the Southampton game, and this wasn't the manager's fault. We've got to take responsibility; we have to hold our hands up. When you go out onto the pitch, it's up to the players, the only thing the manager can do is prepare you. I've worked under a lot of managers and I've never come across anyone as hard-working as Steve was, or thorough. We've been prepared all season. The squad we've got is more than good enough. We've been unlucky with injuries, but we've still got a good enough team.'

Barry Kilby told the assembled press:

> 'Let me first say that Steve Cotterill has all the capabilities to be a Premiership manager. However, what has happened in the last 10 games and the slide down the table, maybe

the directors thought it was time for a change. We played poorly against Hull and bad home defeats never help. That was a defining moment. I think we are the fourth lowest in the division in terms of attendances, and last Tuesday we had a gate lower than 10,000. It's not necessarily about performances but people want winning teams and we still have ambitions to get into the top six.'

Brendan Flood added:

'Maybe Steve has done everything he can here and his opportunity lies elsewhere. He has already done a lot and I think those extra yards might feel too much for him now… We must entertain. We have been entertaining in some games but have been fragile in others… Perhaps with greater freedom and different tactics, we might see a team that is consistent every week and does attack teams from the off. They are good footballers and we just have to see if a better team can be got by having a different person leading them…'

Burnley director, Clive Holt, added:

'Although Steve kept us up on slender resources and appeared to be very knowledgeable he struck me as very restrictive in his methods. There was little flair in Steve's teams although they were tightly organised. It was very apparent that after Owen Coyle came in, Cotterill's players were able to express themselves more and show how good they were.'

Capital punishment

'In for the Kill'

O PERATIONAL director, Brendan Flood set out the following person specification for the post of Burnley manager:

'Familiarity with Burnley or similar club'; 'a good knowledge of the Championship'; 'a good track record'; 'possession of modern coaching skills'; 'a passion for the academy'; 'an ability to bring in gifted young players who are sufficiently capable to join the first team squad immediately.' Flood expressed a preference for a 'young, hungry manager.'

These criteria seemed to rule out Joe Royle, who was Steve Cotterill's nomination, and the heavily tipped Peter Reid – but appeared to support the case for the club's preferred candidate, Brian Laws. Laws had begun his career at Burnley, representing their youth team in an FA Youth Cup semi-final in the late seventies. He was also an integral member of the Third Division championship-winning side of 1981/82. However, Laws was still under contract with Sheffield Wednesday and the Owls chairman refused Burnley permission to speak with their manager.

Caretaker manager Steve Davis hadn't ruled himself out of consideration exclaiming, after an impressive 1-0 victory at Leicester:

'It's a proud moment for me to manage the club I love. It's where I live; it's my home. I don't really need to say more.' But Flood was dubious, stating: 'I think it'd be a lot of pressure for Steve to take on the post of manager... In time, I think he would be capable. Who knows? We don't want someone using this as their learning zone.'

Other candidates were touted including Simon Grayson, who had done such a fine job at Blackpool on limited resources. Paul Jewell was favoured by one Clarets website. But it was a leftfield nomination that suddenly attracted Flood's interest. This concerned St. Johnstone manager Owen Coyle. Sports journalist Alan Nixon and Bolton chairman Phil Gartside backed his candidacy enthusiastically. Having sounded Coyle out, Flood was instantly impressed and sought to persuade Barry Kilby that this was the man they were looking for. He succeeded, for on 22 November 2007 Coyle was confirmed as Burnley's new manager.

Flood explained:

'When we first spoke with Owen he struck me as a young Bill Shankly. That's a big label to give him but there are definite similarities. He's tee-total and has the same steely determination. We were trying to be open-minded with the interviews, with Peter Reid and Paul Jewell as possibilities, but I thought Owen was head and shoulders above the lot. He's a hidden gem and a natural winner who's probably been overlooked a little bit. If you look at his background, he's a Glasgow boy. He's one of nine children and part of a big family. Nothing is too big a challenge for him. He wants the pressure of Saturday afternoon. He likes pressure and if you are going to be successful in football, you are going to have to handle the pressure and, in a way, enjoy it. He's been in management for four years. He knows the pressure of buying and selling players and man-management. He knows how to get the best out of the resources available...

'He's Scottish and a Republic of Ireland international. We probably need to source players from outside our own backyard. We can't get good lads on our own doorstep, and maybe need to get into that connectivity with Scotland and Ireland. Owen's an ideal door-opener for that...'

Saints' midfielder, Paul Sheerin, and a cluster of their fans gave Coyle a glowing reference, despite his departure on the eve of a cup final appearance. Coyle's motivational skills were highly commended. However, one warned: 'He's a shrewd guy with impeccable timing to ensure he does the best for himself.' Less than two years later, his warning began to resonate at Turf Moor.

At Coyle's inaugural press conference at Burnley he stressed:

> 'We are only one step away from the Premier League, and that's where we want to be. I'm not going to make big claims saying we are going to do this or that. What I will ensure is that we leave no stone unturned to try to deliver that kind of success to Burnley... I like to think I have a good knowledge of football and my teams have always prided themselves on having a real spirit about them. It is important that the fans are part of that too because the players are representing them and the fans must see that they are giving every ounce of effort they have to achieve results...'

Club historian, Ray Simpson remembered:

> 'When he arrived, Owen Coyle was such a breath of fresh air. He seemed to arrive from nowhere and clearly regarded Burnley as a big step up from St Johnstone where he had previously managed. I met him almost as soon as he joined the club. He was accessible, friendly and so enthusiastic. It was captivating. There was no doubt that he talked a good game.
>
> And look what he achieved, so quickly, mainly with the players that had stuttered under Steve Cotterill's management... In 2007, the club decided to have a commemorative shirt of blue and white vertical stripes in recognition of its 125th birthday. The Football League granted us permission to use these in the home game against Stoke City. Coincidentally, this was Owen Coyle's first game in charge.'

Against Stoke, Burnley played with fluency and verve, although unable to break down the visitors' rugged defence (0-0). London Claret, Brent Whittam, spoke for many home fans when he wrote:

> 'The biggest difference here, despite the fact we didn't win, is that we looked as though we were desperate to win. We

really went for it… It bodes well. If we continue to play like this, the wins will come…'

Three days later, Burnley won 2-1 at table-topping Watford with goals from Gray and Gudjonsson. Fellow London Claret, Andrew Firmin commented:

'At the end of this match I found myself feeling something I had to search a bit to name. Ah, that was it: I'd actually enjoyed this game… Remember enjoyment? After three and a bit years of being told we should welcome dour, sterile football because it gets results, even though it so often failed to do so, we might be about to discover there's no contradiction between playing good football and winning games…'

Burnley then won 3-1 at fourth-placed Charlton with Blake and Elliott in devastating form. Coyle commented:

'Our sense of spirit and camaraderie was evident for everyone to see. Even when we were under pressure each player knew that there was a colleague at their shoulder giving everything for him and that augurs well.'

After a frustrating 1-1 home draw with Leicester, Burnley turned in another impressive performance on the road, defeating their nemesis, Wolves, 3-2 and lifting themselves into seventh place. Here ended the Coyle bounce, though, as Burnley lost four and drew two of their next six league games, reducing them to twelfth place.

Then on the 18 January, leading goal-scorer, Andy Gray, was transferred to Charlton for an initial fee of £1.5m with potential add-ons taking the total figure up to a possible £2m. Coyle expressed his disappointment with Gray after he requested not to be selected while his transfer was being negotiated. Coyle reacted by sending Gray home, emphasising, 'I only want players who are totally committed and focused as we prepare for a big match.' Ade Akinbiyi performed well in Gray's place, however, scoring the opening goal in a 2-1 victory at Coventry.

Coyle exclaimed: 'Ade led the line brilliantly. I can't speak highly enough about him as a man… He is still prepared to knuckle down and await his chance.'

Brendan Flood explained to the local press the decision to let Andy Gray go, stating:

'The popular players get tempted by agents and other clubs, and have more power than the board. If they want to go, it's almost like they are going on strike because they won't give you the productivity you want. They attempt, I think, in a genuine way to hold you to ransom, and I think that's almost where it got with Andy. The defining moment for me was when Andy's dad, ex-Leeds defender, Frankie Gray, rang me several times on Thursday. If he'd stayed we would have had a very unhappy player on our hands, plus I think Charlton would have continued to work away at him. That would have jeopardised any value we got in Andy Gray. It's sad, but that's how players operate these days. They are very streetwise... I've invested £5m in the last 12 months and we will be reinvesting every penny we get for Gray and some more. We've got serious offers in on four players and we are expecting some success on two or three.'

However, bids for Celtic striker, Derek Riordan, Sheffield Wednesday midfielder, Glen Whelan, and Dundee United's goal-scoring midfielder, Barry Robson failed, leaving Flood to promise Coyle he would have the £2m for summer deals. In the meantime, former Celtic centre back, Stanislav Varga and fellow Sunderland 'exile', Andrew Cole were signed on loan.

Cole was a free-scoring former Newcastle and Manchester United centre forward and an England international. An exultant Coyle said:

'I'm absolutely delighted to have a player of his calibre at the football club. I did my homework and what I was really taken by, when I sat down with Andrew, was his hunger and desire. He still wants to show people he can play and score goals. He has bought into what we are trying to do and I'm delighted he was of the same mindset... You only need to look and see he has been a top-class player all his days... It gives the whole club a lift.'

On a chilly February evening at Loftus Road, Cole treated us to a master class of finishing, emphatically vindicating Coyle's assessment of him. Not that he made his presence felt during the first 30 minutes, when newly-enriched QPR took a two-goal lead. Cole was subjected to the merciless derision of the smug home fans. However, four minutes before the interval, Cole expertly flicked Gudjonsson's fiercely-struck but wayward free kick past Camp in the home goal. Burnley were back in the game. At half-time Coyle astutely replaced tricky Blake with barnstorming Akinbiyi, rightly believing that Ade could punch greater holes in QPR's hesitant defence. Within six minutes of the restart, Burnley were level. Cole located a pounding Akinbiyi on the right with a defence-splitting pass. Akinbiyi's instant cross found Cole in space, who volleyed home with unstoppable power, the ball clattering against the underside of the bar before flashing into the net. Burnley were in the ascendancy, swarming all over their reeling hosts. On the flanks, Elliott and Lafferty continually tormented their markers with pace, power and trickery. An Elliott drive smacked against the woodwork, but Coyle's men were not to be denied. In the 77th minute Akinbiyi headed home from Caldwell's flick on, to put Burnley in front, and with four minutes remaining Cole seized the game and his hat-trick, sweeping in Alexander's low, quick free-kick at the near post. At the final whistle, Cole held the ball aloft for all four sides of the ground to admire. It was a perfect riposte.

A delighted Coyle said:

> 'I thought Andrew Cole was superb, and Ade Akinbiyi again. Ade was unfortunate to be left out of the starting 11 but came on at half-time and summed up the spirit in the whole football club. Tonight, was about our spirit and sense of togetherness. It would have been very easy at 2-0 down to fold and end up getting a hiding, but nothing could be further from the truth.'

Cole was equally buoyant, exclaiming:

> 'I am very pleased, not just by the hat-trick, but by the way the lads came back from 2-0 down to win. That gave me great pleasure because when QPR went two-up, they were giving it the big "ole". Every goal feels good. I have not played too many games this season, but to score goals now gives me the same feeling as it did when I was a kid. I still have the same appetite to play and win games. The manager played a big part in getting me to the club. He said he thought I could bring a lot to the club, playing week in and week out, helping others. When managers have that belief, it makes you feel really good and he has that belief in me. We are all playing for the manager. He gives us the enthusiasm to want to carry on playing and he makes me feel as if I am 21 again.'

Off the field, the re-development plans for Turf Moor and Gawthorpe were under-pinned by the appointment of former Burnley centre forward, Paul Fletcher, as development director. His CV read impressively. For after spending 16 years as a professional footballer at Bolton, Burnley and Blackpool, Paul Fletcher had acquired considerable experience in the development of football stadia, eventually becoming one of Europe's leading experts in this field.

Fletcher's commercial career began at Colne Dynamos during the late eighties. He then became chief executive at Huddersfield Town where, over a six-year period, he oversaw the construction of the award-winning Alfred McAlpine Stadium, declared to be the RIBA 'Building of the Year' for 1995. In 1996, he returned to his parent club, Bolton Wanderers, as chief executive. After two years at the Reebok stadium, he was invited by the FA to become Commercial Director of the £500m Wembley National Stadium project. With costs escalating, though, he left, becoming the chief executive of Arena Coventry Limited. Here, he was in charge of the construction and delivery of the proposed £64m Ricoh Arena in Coventry, which was to comprise a 32,000 seater stadium for Coventry City, potentially the largest casino in the UK, two hotels, an exhibition centre, a health and fitness club and a wide range of community facilities. In January 2006, he was invited to join Coventry City Football Club as managing director. However, in October 2007, he resigned in protest at the stadium's owners, Arena Coventry Limited, for refusing to accept a purchase proposal from an American consortium for both the Ricoh Arena and Coventry City FC. Two months later he became development director at Turf Moor, subsequently becoming the club's chief executive. In 2007, he was awarded an MBE for services to football.

On the 5 February, Paul Fletcher announced that the projected costs for the re-development programme would rise to £30m. He explained:

> 'It is a costlier project than before. The exhibition space has been included to make the development more profitable. I don't think the first proposal made enough money for the football club... We need to make sure every square foot of this building is profitable and operational. The business element and usage will attract more funding. The plans for the cinema and the redevelopment of the Bob Lord stand might be brought back if we make it to the Premiership... The building needs to be a community building which is

not just owned by the football club. The new facilities can regenerate the area and help increase the value of people's houses. We are clearly not sitting back and waiting for the future to happen – we are creating one.'

With the global economy engulfed by a growing fiscal crisis, some supporters became worried about the viability of this project, fearing that the scale of borrowing involved, exposed the club to potentially ruinous risks. London Claret, Phil Whalley, was one among many to voice their doubts. He wrote in the April 2008 edition of *Something to Write Home About*:

> 'How viable is a £30m facelift for a club like Burnley, already losing over £80,000 a week with an unsustainable wage bill?... If this extra £10m is also borrowed that puts the club £20m in debt at a stroke... The lending climate now is not a benign one.'

Phil then compared Fletcher's estimable vision of how the Turf Moor redevelopment would benefit Burnley's people, with that articulated by him about Coventry's prospects before the Sky Blues' financial collapse. Phil was concerned whether Burnley might suffer a similar fate if the redevelopment project went ahead as planned.

The stunning victory at Loftus Road raised hopes of winning a play-off place. But this optimism was dashed quickly. Only four of the remaining 14 games were won with seven lost. The solitary bright spot came at a sodden Turf Moor on 29 March when Kyle Lafferty performed superbly as a spearhead striker. His capability in this role should have been apparent from his Northern Ireland displays. Sure-footed on the saturated surface and ruthlessly dominant in the air, he bullied the Barnsley defenders from start to finish, scoring a memorable goal in the process, lashing the ball into the far top corner from an acute angle. Under Coyle he had played mainly on the left flank. Little more was seen of his prowess as a central striker, though, at least at Burnley, after Rangers made an astonishing £4m bid to take him to Ibrox, £3m of which was to be paid up front plus various add-ons.

Just prior to his departure, Lafferty was quoted in a Belfast newspaper as saying he was 'desperate to end his hell at Turf Moor', although his statement which followed was more measured and appreciative of his time at the club.

He said:

'I've enjoyed my time at Burnley, and learnt so much at the club, but now I feel it's time for me to move on. I need a fresh challenge at this stage of my career. I have given my all to Burnley but don't feel wanted. No player is going to stay where he is not wanted. I was happy under the previous manager, Steve Cotterill. Things have changed though and to be honest I don't feel the same way. If I'd been given the opportunity to leave during those last two transfer windows I would have left – however those bids were turned away by the club. I understand Wolves and Rangers wanted to sign me and I would have been thrilled to move to either club... I understand that it will be the club who agrees the best deal with Burnley who gets my signature... It's always been an ambition of mine to play in the Premier League and I feel if I moved to Wolves then I'd have an excellent chance of reaching what many believe is the greatest league in the world. It would also help my international career. Playing for Northern Ireland is very important to me and, if I want to secure my place alongside David Healy for the World Cup qualifiers, then I feel it is imperative I make a move now. I feel the sooner a deal is done the better for everybody concerned.'

Both Coyle and Lafferty attempted to quash any impression that there was a rift between club and player. Coyle remarked that 'Lafferty's comments came as a major surprise to everyone as Kyle is in here every day with a big smile on his face which is evident from his play.' Coyle said that he understood Lafferty's disappointment about not moving on when bigger clubs were coveting him, but emphasised that these clubs had not met Burnley's valuation. 'At the end of the day, Kyle is under contract to Burnley.... He has been a major part of our plans and I reiterate that Burnley Football Club will not be forced into selling players.'

Lafferty distanced himself from any suggestion that Owen Coyle was to blame for his unhappiness, identifying a small section of carping fans as the cause of his unhappiness, alongside his sadness at the departures of close team mates. He said: 'I feel some of my comments were taken out of context. In no way were my comments aimed at the present manager because I feel, under the previous manager and Owen Coyle, I have been treated really well... However, I feel that there is a small section of supporters I will never win over. That in turn was affecting my performances which dipped in mid-season when I let some comments get to me. Certain people who I was close to have left the club and it no longer feels like home. I just feel a fresh start is what I need...'

The season came to a calamitous end with a 5-0 defeat at Crystal Palace. A dejected Coyle told the press: 'It reinforces what I knew we needed, in terms of personnel, and we will endeavour to do that in the summer. Defensively we've not been good enough. Albeit with 10 men we've given away real soft goals. I thought young Alex MacDonald did well. If there's anything you can take from it that's probably the only thing. I'll speak to the players on Tuesday... There will be some we make offers to and some we won't.'

Brendan Flood was true to his word. Owen Coyle was given the financial backing to bring in: striker Martin Paterson, from Scunthorpe for a fee potentially rising to £1.3m, inclusive of add-ons; versatile midfielder Chris Eagles from Manchester United for £1.5m; and midfielder Kevin McDonald from Dundee United for £500,000. In addition, Chilean goalkeeper Diego Penny, Dutch holding midfielder, Remco van der Schaaf and rugged Norwegian left back Christian Kalvenes also joined. However, Coyle's £500,000 bid for Hearts left-winger, Andrew Driver was rejected, Andrew Cole turned down a permanent deal, presumably because of wages, and David Unsworth rejected a player-coach role at the club, having expressed the wish to extend his playing career. Meanwhile, midfielder James O'Connor departed for Sheffield Wednesday, left back Jon Harley joined Watford and midfielder, John Spicer, the goalkeeping hero at Luton, went to Doncaster.

Coyle said of Paterson:

> 'There is a premium you pay for goalscorers...last season he played 36 games, scoring at just under a goal every two games... There is no doubt we are getting a player who is hungry and scored 15 goals in the Championship for a relegated side... He's lightning quick and has a great work-rate. He's 20 and a Northern Ireland international. He can only get better. We want younger types to boost the team.'

But it seemed that Burnley's Kosovan Albanian signing, Berisha, did not fit in with Coyle's plans as he was sent on loan to Rosenborg.

Coyle justified his purchase of strapping, 19-year-old McDonald thus:

'I have known Kevin since he made his debut at 16… I couldn't have been more impressed by a young man who has developed each year into a fine footballer. He has progressed to such an extent that we felt we wouldn't get him at one point. There were some big clubs courting his services – Celtic, Liverpool and West Bromwich… Last year he took his game on and scored plenty of goals from midfield. He's six-foot three inches, mobile, has a great physique and we feel we can make him even better in a good Burnley team for years to come.'

McDonald confirmed there may have been bigger, better offers but he valued the link he already had with Coyle.

And of Eagles, Coyle had this to say:

'To get a player of this stature shows what we are trying to do. He can play anywhere but I see him playing in a very attacking role for us, to get forward at every opportunity. He's a creative player, scores goals and capable of taking players on. He has an array of talent and we are delighted to get him.'

Eagles commented:

'I met up with the gaffer just for a chat because I didn't know what I was going to do. I've been at United for seven years, since I was 14, so it's been long. But when I met him I was so impressed, and so was my agent, really there was only one club in my mind. I'm just delighted to be settled now and just want to concentrate on playing for Burnley. I need to be playing competitive football, and the English league, is, I think, the best there is.'

Brendan Flood also announced the club's intention to sign a partnership deal with an American club. He explained:

'We feel there is an exciting opportunity to tap into that pool of talent before other clubs and hopefully, through an affiliation with one partner, start to build a relationship that will ultimately benefit both clubs. That may even entail us ultimately taking a franchise on as a partner and that particular club being re-branded as 'The Clarets'.

Barry Kilby added:

'We're not expecting it to be a major cost – it's more a co-operation between clubs. Now, they are looking to incentivise us to join with them. That may change – as they get stronger, they might see the value of what they've got… We have got the whip-hand now, but I do think that American soccer is going to be enormous in the future, and that's why we're making the effort.'

As for Youth Development, Flood thought that there needed to be a re-think after Manchester United's successful raid on their 14-year-old starlet, John Cofie. He said:

'Our best prospect is to focus on the 16-upwards age group, both here and abroad, because with under-16s we are always going to get them stolen off us. The John Cofie thing certainly made me aware of what the risks are in relying on that pipeline.'

The 2008/09 season kicked off at Hillsborough, not that the Burnley defenders seemed aware of this as they found themselves two-down after only four minutes play. Wednesday eventually won at a canter 4-1. An aggravated Coyle told the press conference:

'The defending was nothing short of naïve. I can accept being beaten and I can accept somebody working really hard to score a goal against you, but I don't think Sheffield Wednesday had to work particularly hard for any of their goals and I left the players in no uncertain terms about that… Clarke Carlisle was a big miss at the back. I thought Martin Paterson did well, Stephen Jordan did well and Wade Elliott played well. But you are not going to win games with three players doing well.'

Coyle was ruthless. Neither keeper, Penny, nor midfielder van der Schaaf played in another senior game that season, the latter loaned immediately to Brondby. Jensen was recalled in goal with Gudjonsson becoming the holding midfielder before the superior Alexander was chosen for the part. But these changes did not plug the leaks. On the following Saturday, suspect travelers Ipswich plundered the gifts offered by their over hospitable hosts, winning 3-0. With a Red Devils' parachutist failing to deliver the match ball, having landed mistakenly on a fragile stand roof, and his rescue team struggling to retrieve him, the occasion smacked of Fred Karno's Army. The game had to be postponed for 45 minutes, while the parachutist remained stranded on his lofty perch. Pauline Pratley was one of several London Clarets facing an arduous, much-delayed journey home. With understandable lugubriousness she posed the rhetorical question:

> 'What's rubbish in the air, has no sense of direction and probably shouldn't be anywhere near a football pitch? No, not the parachutist: I'm talking about the Burnley defence. Today's rooftop spectacle has attracted all the headlines, but the real circus was on the pitch.'

A pained Owen Coyle commented:

> 'I thought we had total control of the game and probably had three or four real opportunities; it just looked like a matter of time until we'd score, but we really shot ourselves in the foot… Ultimately, I'll take responsibility because I pick the team. But I would never envisage losing the sort of goals we've lost again.'

Burnley were bottom with a minus six goal difference. One supporter drew a parallel with the Waddle era, remarking: 'Again, we have vastly inflated expectations alongside much laudable talk of creative, attacking football, undermined by insufficient attention to the workaday detail of sound defence.'

Coyle realised that he needed a more redoubtable formation, headed by an uncompromising, combative target man. He partially addressed this need by signing Cardiff City's Scottish international centre forward, Steve Thompson, who had become surplus to the Bluebirds' needs. Thompson said on arrival:

> 'I'm delighted to be here at Burnley and linking up with Owen Coyle, because he was a big reason for me joining the club. I was his boot boy at Dundee United when I came through the ranks and I remember him as a real character and top-notch striker… I'm quite sure we'll be climbing the league very shortly. There are 12-15 teams trying to get into the play-offs. It's a very difficult thing to accomplish if you look at some of the teams up at the top with parachute payments and some of them getting 29,000 supporters a match. But would you have tipped Hull last year? I know I wouldn't have, so it's there for anybody and there isn't a great deal of difference in quality. Maybe one or two clubs

have got one or two players who have that bit extra, but I like to think we've got players with exceptional quality as well, with the likes of Chris Eagles. I'm aware of Wade Elliott's quality, so it would be foolish to underestimate us… It's about getting on a good run and sustaining it.'

Speaking with surprising candour, Burnley winger, Wade Elliott told a *Lancashire Telegraph* reporter:

'You do a pre-season, and you're never sure how the season is going to go. I don't know whether, when we played Inverness, it went too well for us. I know it sounds silly, but we played a new formation against them, and we were knocking it about, and it all came very easily. I don't know whether we thought it was just going to happen for us again at Sheffield Wednesday, and we got there and it was a completely different game. It was a shock to everyone. But you can't just go out and expect to play. Maybe the Inverness game lulled us into thinking we could, a little bit of complacency, perhaps. Before we knew it, we're getting steam-rollered and it's a horrible start to the season. We almost went back to basics at Palace (0-0) and at home to Plymouth (0-0). To come off the back of a 4-1 and 3-0 beating, you're never going to stroll around playing brilliant football, have a big win and things suddenly drop for you. You do it in small steps, and we've done that in the last couple of games.'

However, the baby steps suddenly morphed into huge strides at the City Ground, Nottingham where Coyle's 4-1-4-1 formation worked like a dream. With Alexander robustly protecting the back four and Thompson holding the ball up well in advanced positions, Burnley were transformed. Coyle earned his win bonus by taking off the disappointing Paterson and the tiring Thompson, re-uniting Blake and Akinbiyi up front. Blake was superb, linking defence with attack, displaying splendid passing and movement, while Akinbiyi pulled the Forest defenders around, creating space for his partner. Burnley won 2-1, moving up to nineteenth place.

A delighted Owen Coyle was quick to praise the contribution of Alexander.

'I felt in the first 10 minutes Grezza got nicked a couple of times in possession. But he's probably better versed to deal with it, so he began to move the ball quicker and had an influence on the game. We know what we get with him. After losing the first two games he's acted as a defensive screen. We know very well that when he gets the ball he's capable of passing it.'

Further victories over Blackpool (2-0), Watford (3-2), Preston (3-1) and a draw at Swansea (1-1) took Burnley up to eighth place by the end of September. In addition, Premier League side, Fulham were beaten (1-0) at Turf Moor in the Carling (League) Cup. There was little doubt that Coyle deserved to win the Championship's Manager of the Month award for September.

Fulham were the first top London side to experience the Clarets' capital punishment meted out during this glorious season. And Burnley's surprising executioner was rising home-grown star, Jay Rodriguez. With only two minutes remaining, Eagles produced an exquisite defence-splitting pass, putting the alert, young Rodriguez through on goal. Instead of snatching at the opportunity, Jay coolly shimmied past the flailing Fulham keeper and planted the ball in the back of the Cottagers' net. Coyle said: 'I'm just delighted for young Jay to come on and show that level of composure… We do that in training but to replicate that in a game against a Premier League team is magnificent.'

Jay's coaches, Geoff Smith and Vince Overson were impressed, too. Three years later they made these observations about his progress. Geoff Smith said:

> 'He always had something – good touch and movement and the willingness to work so hard, too hard perhaps. There was a time when he got very anxious about his finishing, causing him to break into tears when, on one occasion, he rounded the Bradford keeper and missed the target. There was some doubt then whether he would succeed because he got so down. But he managed to come through this setback which was brilliant because he has such a great appreciation of players around him. That's what the pro's want…'

Former Burnley centre half, Vince Overson, added:

> 'Jay isn't a natural finisher. He's had to work particularly hard at it. But he's got a fantastic attitude. He's such a down-to-earth lad, respectful of his coaches, colleagues,

family and roots. Despite winning an England under-21 cap, he knows he's not yet the finished article but remains determined to succeed. He was deservedly awarded the Burnley players' Player-of-the-Year at the end of the 2010/11 season after scoring 15 league goals, but that didn't turn his head either.'

As Burnley began to prosper on the pitch, Brendan Flood continued to probe further opportunities for investment. In mid-September, a publication named *Arabian Business* quoted his desire to have an Arabian royal splashing cash at the Turf. Flood told the *Lancashire Telegraph*:

> 'While we have a strong board, the club will always be open to financially stronger, strategic investors who may give us an advantage over our competitors... In discussing our ambitions with the Arabian business press, we are making sure that Burnley is a forward-thinking club and a viable option for strategic investors.'

Meanwhile, Paul Fletcher in his new role of chief executive admitted that the ever-escalating fiscal crisis was affecting the club's ability to borrow money to fund the proposed Turf Moor re-development. A more cautious progression on a down-sized project was proposed with the assurance given that 'we won't press the button on the project until we have the funding.'

On the eve of the home clash with top-of-the-table Birmingham (1-1), Robbie Blake gave a forthright account of his views in an interview with the local press. He said:

> 'The games coming up at home against Reading, and at Wolves and Coventry could determine our season... If we've got aspirations of being in the top six we've got to take points off these teams... I'm not getting any younger. I'm frustrated that I'm not playing but I must knuckle down and get on with it. When you're a manager and you know your four strikers can do a job, you're going to rotate if they haven't scored in successive games or the team hasn't won or drawn a couple.
>
> 'It's nice for a manager to have that problem. It's more of a squad game now. I don't think you can win the league with just 11 players picking themselves all the time. There's a lot of quality players who aren't even in the 16. I think

I'm good enough to take the chance when it comes. I've just got to be patient.'

Blake would get his chance at Coventry on 21 October 2008 where he came off the bench to score a late winning goal, deftly lifting the ball over the Coventry keeper. Then against Reading Blake once again came on as a late substitute, striking the decisive goal with a moment of magic. It allowed a patched up and besieged Burnley side to escape with all three points, thanks also to Jensen's heroic performance between the sticks. Having been restored to the starting 11 at QPR, Blake scored the crucial opening goal, a shot which was so powerful and precise that Rangers' keeper Cerny was left rooted to the spot. Blake would retain his first team place for the rest of the season.

Up until the end of November 2008, results were mixed. There were comfortable home wins against Norwich (2-0) and Derby (3-0) but disappointing losses at Wolves (0-2) and Barnsley (2-3). However, the outstanding result was the defeat of Chelsea in the Carling Cup, albeit 5-4 in a penalty shoot-out.

Over 6,000 Clarets turned up to bellow Burnley on. Drogba's goal shortly before half-time only served to crank up their volume. Undaunted by this deficit, Coyle had the prescience to replace the hard-working, but largely shackled, Paterson with a bounding Akinbiyi who immediately put himself about, giving McCann and Gudjonsson more options and treading on a few Chelsea toes to boot. In the 69th minute Eagles and Blake combined in a flash of brilliance. Eagles darted for a gap in the inside-left channel. Anticipating his run, Blake located Eagles with a perfectly weighted pass. Eagles latched onto it, turned quickly, wrong-footing his marker and unleashed a stinging shot that Cudicini could only parry into the path of the onrushing Akinbiyi. The Burnley fans clustered at the Shed End held their breath as Akinbiyi quickly steadied himself before calmly poking the loose ball into the unguarded net to spark a cacophony of unhinged celebration. Akinbiyi tore off his shirt in exultation, roaring his defiance as his delirious team mates engulfed him. Thereafter, the game became an attritional battle with the rattled Chelsea players resorting to pumping unproductive high balls into the visitors' box. While Chelsea fashioned a few openings that fortunately fell to the profligate Di Santo, Burnley held firm.

And so, this hard-fought contest went to penalties, Jensen making the crucial save at the death to seize the tie. A tabloid paper captured that moment of triumph as the great Dane hurled himself to the left to push away a goal-bound spot kick. 'Jensen Interceptor!' read the caption. Capital punishment – 2 had been administered. Burnley were in the quarter-finals.

An ecstatic Owen Coyle picked out Jensen and Akinbiyi for a special tribute. He declared:

> 'Brian has been outstanding all season and we said if it got to a penalty shoot-out we felt he'd save a minimum of one. I'm delighted for him because it's a reward for how hard he's been working in the games and training. Aside from scoring the goal, Ade led the line, brought us up the park to get others on the ball, and that was a big turning point in the game. The backing we got from 6,100, you'd have thought there were 30,000 there! Hopefully it gives everyone in the town a lift!'

But as exciting as this cup run was, promotion was of greater importance. The club's latest accounts underlined this. The annual operating loss was down from £4m to £1.8m, but this hid a twenty-four per cent rise in the wage bill, which had increased to £8.8m.

The club partly bridged the gap with a £1.6m increase in match income and other commercial activities, but the most substantial income came from player sales. Lafferty's departure contributed the lion's share of the £5m profit in transfer dealings. Chairman, Barry Kilby told the shareholders:

> 'It was particularly pleasing to see Owen Coyle step in and make a positive impact on and off the pitch. Under his stewardship, the club is actively pursuing a policy of investment in younger players and developing our youth system, thanks to the sterling work of Vince Overson, Terry Pashley, Jeff Taylor and their backroom team, now under Martin Dobson, Director of Youth Development.'

Chief Executive Paul Fletcher added to the upbeat mood with his enthusiastic account of his recent link up with Cary Clarets, Burnley's new American partners. Fletcher said:

> 'They realise the value of linking up with a Championship club, where young players have a good chance of progressing into the first team. This is something that people around the world are cottoning on to. One of the worst places to send young players is the Premier League.'

Meanwhile, Burnley director John Sullivan professed to be using his Russian and Hungarian business contacts to pursue similar links there.

Back at Turf Moor, the Burnley players were flexing their muscles in readiness for Arsenal's visit on 2 December 2008, in the quarter-final of the Carling Cup. Martin Paterson said:

> 'Going away to somewhere as massive as Chelsea was a wonderful experience. But we weren't there to enjoy it and rub shoulders with them, we were there to beat them, and it will be the same tomorrow. We're not there to take people's shirts and be glad to have played against them – we are aiming to get into the semi-finals of the Carling Cup.'

Ade Akinbiyi added:

> 'Arsenal have probably the best kids that most people have ever seen, but they are not going to like coming to Turf Moor on a cold Tuesday night. We've come this far, we have nothing to lose, and everyone has confidence in themselves. When we went to Chelsea we didn't lie back and we are not going to do that against Arsenal.'

The Burnley lads were as good as their word, as Kevin McDonald plundered two goals in a brilliant display of skill and power, while the Arsenal players – particularly Bentner – squandered chance after chance with Jensen once again magnificent in the Burnley goal. A triumphant Coyle said:

> 'The last thing I said to the players before they went out for the second half was to come in with no regrets. If we got to our maximum and were beaten by a better team, then we could accept that. We just didn't want to feel we had let ourselves down, but with this group of players there was no chance of that happening.'

As for Arsene Wenger, he was less magnanimous in defeat than he had been in victory earlier in the year, when Arsenal had won an FA Cup tie at Turf Moor. No surprise there, then! The Burnley contingent in the 19,045 crowd, had hollered their approval throughout. Capital punishment – three threatened to become four as fellow semi-finalists, Spurs, came within range.

Four days later, Burnley faced a tough contest with promotion rivals, Sheffield United, at Bramall Lane. But with Michael Duff injured in the warm-up, Chris McCann already succumbing to sickness and Carlisle suspended, Coyle was forced to play left back, Jordan at centre half, winger Elliott at right back and right-footed Alexander at left back. However, Coyle's makeshift team did him proud, winning 3-2 with Eagles scoring a terrific goal to seal the game. Against Cardiff at home on 9 December, Burnley looked understandably 'leggy' and were fortunate to escape with the 2-2 draw earned by Thompson's late equaliser. Visiting Southampton appeared to be an easier proposition as Burnley racked up a 3-0 interval lead, but they were left hanging on anxiously as the Saints retaliated strongly in the second half. Burnley remained in fourth place. Then, with Christmas only five days away, the Clarets celebrated by coming from behind, at Ashton Gate, to win 2-1 with goals from Paterson and Thompson. At this point Burnley appeared odds on to secure at least a play-off place. Then the wheels fell off. The next five league games were lost. The downward spiral was finally halted on 31 January when Thompson's 90th minute goal was just enough to defeat visiting Charlton (2-1). Burnley rose to eighth.

Notwithstanding Burnley's spluttering league form, on 6 January 2009, they put on a scintillating first half performance in the Carling Cup at White Hart Lane. Sadly, a calamitous second half display gifted Tottenham four avoidable goals (1-4). The semi-final tie seemed dead and buried but Coyle's indefatigable men thought differently.

Spurs arrived in Burnley for the second leg two weeks later. It was a cold, drenching, dog of a night. Shrouds of insurgent rain swirled in the glare of the floodlights, saturating the thousands of fans queuing at the turnstiles. The gusting gale rattled the stand roofs ominously. As Burnley author, Dave Thomas, wrote, 'It couldn't have been worse on the deck of a North Atlantic trawler.' Spurs' manager, Harry Redknapp, complacently selected a hybrid 11 to defend their three-goal lead, and nearly came a cropper. In the 34th minute Burnley were awarded a free-kick 30 yards from the Spurs' goal. Novice Spurs keeper, Ben Alnwick, took up a position left of centre in anticipation of a cross. Blake espied the gap to the keeper's left, took aim, and blasted a curling shot into the unguarded top right-hand corner. Turf Moor erupted. Alnwick hung his dripping head in disappointment.

Burnley pressed forward relentlessly but to no avail, at least until the 73rd minute when Blake went on a twisting, turning run on the left, bamboozling Gunter and Bentley, before whipping in a low cross which McCann stabbed in at the far post. Hope turned instantly to belief. The roar from the 19,500 crowd was shuddering. Rodriguez was brought on for Gudjonsson. Akinbiyi replaced the exhausted

Paterson. Burnley piled forward. With just two minutes left, Alnwick tried to claim a high cross but failed, the greasy ball slipping from his grasp. Rodriguez volleyed it home. Rarely has Turf Moor experienced such a tumult. It was all square, but with Burnley in the ascendancy. Regrettably, a gilt-edged chance to finish off reeling Spurs was missed in a moment of indecision. It proved fatal. With Burnley almost played out, first Pavlyuchenko, then Defoe scored the late extra time goals which took Spurs to Wembley. While Spurs lost on penalties to Manchester United in the final, the Burnley players resolved to reach and win the Championship play-off final at Wembley. That night of disappointment was converted into an unshakeable ambition. Their promotion surge began here.

Before that, there was an FA Cup campaign to contest. Following victories over QPR and West Bromwich, both after replays, Burnley were paired again with Arsenal once again, this time at the Emirates. It proved to be a round too far for them as the Gunners ruthlessly took their revenge (0-3).

In readiness for the promotion push, Coyle sought to bolster his faltering defence. But the once plentiful well had dried up. Flood's chain of perfume shops had gone into administration and Modus, his property development company was in difficulty. It was unsurprising that Coyle's request for more cash was met with a guarded response.

Coyle's impatience was palpable. He stated:

> 'We can't stand still. We must keep striving to improve, and that's the difficulty we've got just now with the credit crunch everywhere. Everyone's been hit hard by that… Everything we'd put in place to develop the whole football club has had to be put on hold. I've identified three or four targets which I hope nobody else has. I can't do anything on it just now but maybe come the summer, when things change financially, I might be able to make inroads. We're not able to purchase anyone in terms of a fee. We've asked about a few on loan and been priced out of them.'

In late February, a Sunday tabloid speculated that Coyle was about to return to Bolton as their manager. If true, was this his irked reaction to being thwarted in strengthening his side? On the following Saturday, Sheffield Wednesday crushed Burnley 4-2 at Turf Moor. Once again, the case for the defence was found wanting. No-one managed to shackle Leon Clarke, Wednesday's powerful, marauding centre forward or their probing playmaker, Tudgay. Burnley dropped two places to ninth. Returning to his broken record, Coyle exclaimed: 'We cannot keep shooting ourselves in the foot. Defensively we had a really poor day.'

In response to the mounting speculation about his impending departure, Coyle had this to say on 3 March 2009:

> 'There's been all sorts of speculation but I've no intention of going anywhere. I didn't bring players into this club, to leave at the first opportunity. That's never going to be the case. I'm here for as long as the club want me and they know that, so much so that Brendan, the chairman and I have had a chat about it, about making my contract a bit longer. We have ambitious plans to take this club on. I don't want anybody to be distracted. We want to develop a team that will serve the club well in years to come. I fully understand how a football club runs, and if the money is tight, it's tight. We still have tremendous scope for improvement. Brendan and the chairman know that, and that's why we'll look to sit down and add to what we've got.'

On that evening, though, Burnley put their promotion chase back on track at squally Blackpool. The conditions were atrocious, with a howling gale accompanied by slanting rain. There was considerable doubt whether the game would be played. But with the endorsement of the Blackpool management, it was agreed that it should. Christian Kalvenes decided the outcome with a late, winning goal of high quality. Venturing down the left flank, Kalvenes reached the edge of the Blackpool box, before exchanging a sharp one-two with McCann and calmly slotting the returned ball past Rachubka. Burnley rose to seventh.

A relieved Owen Coyle said:

> 'The goal was a fantastic move and such a cool finish, but the biggest thing that summed us up was character. The desire to come back from Saturday was immense and to come and get a shut out after how poorly we defended on Saturday was pleasing. I believe that this is a game we would have lost when I came to the club last season. It really was a must-win game for us.'

Later that week, the *Lancashire Telegraph* published an interview with Andrew Cole. While Cole complimented Coyle highly, he was reproachful of the Burnley board. Cole said:

'Owen Coyle was probably more like Sir Alex than any of the managers I worked with. I could talk to him. He understood me. Owen treated me like a grown man and I wish my time had worked out for longer. It is terrific the way they have played this season, especially given their limited resources. Owen is still a young manager but he has every chance of going on and managing at the highest level. He knows how to get the best out of his players. He makes it clear what he wants from them and how he wants to play. Burnley should be doing everything to keep Owen at the club.

'Who knows what is possible when you have a manager of his quality in charge? It would have been great to have played my last year at Burnley. Owen and I had spoken and agreed on a contract, then the board withdrew it and started trying to change it. It was nothing to do with Owen, he wanted me to stay and I wanted to stay. Perhaps we both deserved a little better, but that has gone now and I wish the club all the best because the lads, the manager and the fans were different class.'

The choice, timing and purpose of Cole's words were curious.

Nevertheless, Burnley's results continued to improve. Crystal Palace were defeated 4-2 at Turf Moor, on 11 March, with Burnley recovering from a two-goal deficit. Neil Warnock was apoplectic at the controversial award of an 83rd minute penalty from which Burnley equalised, setting up their late victory. A relieved Coyle exclaimed:

'Again the lads have shown real courage and bravery, to go with physical fitness and mental strength to see it through. I don't want to be chasing games every week, but we know that when we do, we're still in every game we play. It's a tremendous thing to have in your armoury...'

Then three days later, on 14 March 2009, Burnley thrashed Nottingham Forest 5-0, lifting them into fifth place. A bubbling Owen Coyle stated:

'Some of the finishes were exquisite and fit to grace any game. A few of them deserve to win a match in their own right. It doesn't happen very often when you win 5-0 that your left back's the man-of-the-match, but Christian Kalvenes was outstanding, as was right back, Rhys Williams [a loan signing from Middlesbrough] and Carlisle and

Caldwell because Forest's McSheffrey, Tyson and Earnshaw are very good strikers. It's very much a team effort.'

Burnley then drew at Ipswich 1-1 and won 2-1 at Plymouth with another magical goal from Blake. Shortly afterwards, Ade Akinbiyi completed a move to Houston Dynamo in the USA. Coyle said:

'Ade has had a massive impact at this club and I cannot speak highly enough about him. He has been a model professional and a big part in what we are doing, on and off the park. He is going to America for a lot less money than he earns here. He is going for a lifestyle change and I just wish people would be aware of the facts before commenting on them.'

Burnley reached the play-offs having squeezed past QPR and Sheffield United, and thrashed Bristol City 4-0 in their final game at home. Their semi-final opponents were Reading, strongly tipped at Christmas for automatic promotion. However, the Royals' side which arrived at Turf Moor was a pale shadow of the free-scoring outfit that had previously terrorised Championship defences. Their leading scorer, Kevin Doyle, started the game but was clearly unfit.

It was a typical play-off contest, taut and tight, with few chances, seemingly destined to end in stalemate. But with six minutes left, Reading's sturdy centre back, Andre Bikey, unaccountably tugged at Thompson inside their box. A penalty was awarded which Alexander dispatched nonchalantly, whereupon Bikey 'lost it', histrionically haranguing referee Atkinson before assaulting Robbie Blake. The errant defender was dismissed immediately. Although Burnley had only a slender lead to take into the second leg, the melancholy demeanor of Steve Coppell, the Reading manager, suggested that the tie was already won.

And so it proved. In the return game, Coppell blooded 20-year-old debutant Simon Church, while inexplicably leaving his experienced strikers, Dave Kitson and Noel Hunt, on the bench. Although Reading had the better of the first half, Paterson and Thompson each hit spectacular goals after the break to take Burnley to Wembley. However, the wild celebrations in the away end were not replicated by the Burnley players or their manager. Coyle emphasised: 'We acknowledged the fans' tremendous support but we haven't yet achieved our goal. There's so much work to be done because Sheffield United are a quality side.' A grizzly Graham Alexander growled: 'We've won nothing yet.'

The Blades' manager, Kevin Blackwell, was a Sky TV pundit for the second leg at the Madejski Stadium. His mood darkened as Burnley took control, first with Paterson curling a 30-yarder into the top left-hand corner, and then with Thompson finding goal with a volley that clipped the underside of the bar. As the Sky camera focused on Blackwell for his post-match reaction, he looked ghastly. Clearly, Burnley represented the greater threat to him, having already performed the double over his side. He later rebuked the Football League for choosing Mike Dean as the play-off final referee, citing his shortcomings in a recent Sheffield derby. Blackwell's consternation was very encouraging.

Burnley chairman Barry Kilby believed that one season in the Premier League would clear his club's considerable debt. And with the prize so agonizingly close, the pressure was ramped up enormously. Meanwhile, the pessimists on social media predicted administration, and a fire sale of its top earners, if Burnley failed to win.

But Barry made light of this, assuring Burnley fans:

> 'I'm fine. I'm quietly confident. Everything is in order and we are ready for the big game. It has been one of the best seasons ever and we want to cap it off on Monday. Once the game has started I'm like any ordinary fan, but you do have in the back of your mind the massive financial implications. It would certainly be like an atom bomb going off in the club's finances – something like eight to 12 times the earnings that we draw now. It would literally set the club up for years to come, so there's a big prize to fight for that's for sure. But if it doesn't go for us on Monday we will sit down and plan to do this again in the Championship. I'm confident we'll do it sooner rather than later... Our faith in Owen has been vindicated. He's been a breath of fresh air at the club.
>
> He's brilliantly positive and realistic at the same time. Obviously, it would be great to win but we have next season if it doesn't come off. It's unbelievable how something like this can lift a place, particularly Burnley, which identifies very strongly with its football team... I didn't know whether we would sell our full quota but we have, having drawn Clarets from all over the world, so it's great to know that we are meeting a big city club like Sheffield United on equal terms.'

As it happened, the Blades' performance at Wembley was as dismal as Blackwell's mood. Burnley should have won more comfortably, having squandered several good chances to add to their narrow lead. Only Sheffield United's wing backs, Kyle Naughton and Kyle Walker, distinguished themselves in their side's largely plodding display. It was left to Burnley's midfielder, Wade Elliott, to win the game with an eye-catching goal, a superb, curling, 25-yard effort that keeper Paddy Kenny hadn't a hope of stopping. Sheffield United might have saved themselves had Mike Dean not waved away an apparently just claim for a late penalty. It was when Kalvenes shoulder-charged Walker clumsily inside the Burnley box. Otherwise the Blades seemed blunt. Burnley fully deserved their victory, that returned them to the top flight after a 33-year absence, during which the club almost expired.

Afterwards, a surprisingly restrained Coyle commented:

> 'We were worthy winners. From start to finish we got the ball down and played. We knew we would come under some pressure when Sheffield United put the ball into our box but we stood up to that. Caldwell and man-of-the-match, Carlisle were imperious in central defence, limiting them to very few goal-scoring opportunities. We have used the fewest players and don't have quantity, we know that, but I believe we have real quality... The goal typified the way we play, the passing and movement, culminating in a great finish. We looked dangerous on the counter-attack... We have had around seven ties with Premier League clubs this season and we have shown that we can stand up to the best, although it's easier to play in one-off cup ties than it is to play weekly in the Premier League. There's no doubt we'll need to add to the squad but we do have terrific spirit and that will never go away.'

Coyle's was credited by his players for helping them to remain confident and relaxed, enabling them to play at their best when under pressure. Robbie Blake said:

> 'Owen was so relaxed around the players and made the place so relaxed, you'd think you were just going out into the car park for a kick-about...He was so enthusiastic and positive. He never brought anything negative to the club... He improved my game, too. I had always been a striker, never having to track back much, but he got me playing

wide on the left in a three-man attack, tracking back to help the full back, when needed. He deserves massive credit for believing I could do this. I never thought I was capable of making tackles in my own box.'

First team coach Steve Davis added:

'Owen's just very relaxed, he fills everyone with confidence, gives the players licence to go out and express themselves and play with no fear, which I think is vital. You need to go on the pitch and know that if you make a mistake, if it is an honest one, that you're not going to get slaughtered for it. They players are allowed to make honest mistakes which any human being should be allowed to do. If you put the graft in, which the supporters expect, the manager and his assistant expect, the coaches expect and the players expect, you'll be fine. The manager's been great from the point of view of just letting everyone play. The squad is set up to play attractive football.'

Full back or centre half, Michael Duff remembered:

'We had some good characters back then with people like Blakey, Stevie Jordan, Stevie Caldwell. It was a unique group. We were the most unprofessional group of footballers you've ever seen. Somehow – by hook or by crook – we produced. We used to eat doughnuts on a Friday and drink cans of coke but whatever the formula, it worked.'

The play-off final 'Man-of-the match', Clarke Carlisle added:

'Owen told us week in, week out, that it didn't matter what other teams were doing or who they'd got in their side. It was all about what we did and how we performed, because he believed – and this filtered through the club and the squad – that if we played to the best of our ability we'd be more than a match for anyone. There was a freedom to go and express ourselves and play the game in the right manner. It was instilled into us that if we, as a team, played to our strengths and abilities, we could win the game… On the other hand, Steve Cotterill was a set-play man. He'd instill in us the routines, the disciplines, the ruses. He told you exactly what he wanted you to do. There were no grey areas. If you didn't comply he'd give you grief. He was in total control. Owen didn't bother much with positional play practice, set-plays and corner routines, so much so that when it did happen we would look at one another in amazement. What he encouraged was spontaneity, thinking on your feet, ad-libbing whenever the opportunity arose.'

Clarke Carlisle, allegedly 'Britain's most intelligent footballer', was selected by *The Spectator* for special praise:

'In a short, graceful interview Carlisle gave every sign of being one of the most impressive human beings. Moved to tears, he spoke with wisdom, articulacy and passion about the game, players, supporters and his own personal journey through a host of injuries as well as alcoholism. If anyone should carry a torch for all that is great and good in the beautiful game it is Clarke Carlisle.'

In his biography, Brian Jensen described how Coyle would participate in five-a-side games, using the opportunity to coach his younger players. Rising star striker Jay Rodriguez remembered how Coyle had helped him in this way. Jensen remarked that Coyle's commitment and enthusiasm was highly infectious, making training sessions a delight. Jensen said Coyle was highly protective of his players, often rebutting any outside criticisms of them.

However, away from the rejoicing Burnley fans, many sporting Owen Coyle masks, it was being rumoured that their 'messiah' was about to join Celtic. Barry Kilby commented:

'I heard in the post-match press conference that Strachan had gone at Celtic and that Owen was mentioned. It is a big distraction and we've lost valuable time that we should have been putting into other matters. The Glasgow press have been stoking this up and both Owen and I have been annoyed with it all. Owen is adamant that he's happy here.'

And yet Coyle seemed to equivocate about his future. When Alastair Campbell publicly questioned him on the subject, on the town hall balcony during the home victory parade, Coyle's unease was palpable. Burnley fans were left holding their breath for several weeks, until the club announced, on the 19 June, that Owen Coyle had extended his contract with Burnley until July 2013.

With business as usual resuming, Brendan Flood told the local press that he was seeking other clubs' advice in managing the Premier League money. He indicated that wages would be kept low in Premier League terms. A figure of around £15m per year was mentioned, nearly double Burnley's existing wage levels but with income set to soar to £40m, £30m of which was TV money alone, the ratio of wages to income would be reduced to much healthier levels than hitherto.

Flood said:

> 'We've not finalised the details of the budget yet. We'll have agreed a business plan by the end of June, once we have fully understood what needs to be done.... We must look at it as a three-year process, considering parachute payments. We have brought in a lot of young players and are very hopeful of adding new signings. We're not going to sign anyone who is demanding £30,000 per week [It was reported on 19 June that a wage ceiling of £15,000 per week had been established]. If they're chasing the money then it turns Owen off... There'll be six or seven players, tops, not all bought, probably in the 20-24 age bracket. I think our club will be very attractive because we can give incoming players the chance to play at the top level, which might not be possible if they were at Manchester United and Liverpool... I'm confident we can do okay... We think we can be successful with British players and perhaps some Scandinavian lads like Jensen, Gudjonsson and Kalvenes. They seem to settle better in England. The best thing we have is the team and club spirit. If we break it, it would be breaking the hidden secret... We've got to keep everyone nice and grounded but believing in themselves.'

On 1 June it was announced that Modus Ventures Ltd., Brendan Flood's commercial property company, had been placed in administration, reviving speculation about whether the football club would have suffered a similar fate had promotion not been won. At the end of July, the local press reported that KPMG administrators had reclaimed a £3.7m loan made to the club while Modus was a going concern. Burnley FC made a statement denying that the repayment would adversely affect the football side of operations, while former Burnley MP Peter Pike, asserted: 'The investment by Brendan Flood was crucial to the club at the time he made it. The squad could not have been strengthened in the way it was without that investment. The club is now in a strong position to repay the loan.'

While Steve Jones, Gabor Kiraly and Alan Mahon were released, and van der Schaaf and Berisha deemed surplus to requirements, Coyle splashed out a club record fee of £3m to capture Hibernian's Scottish international centre forward, Steven Fletcher. He also signed Derby's pacey, attacking right back Tyrone Mears for £500,000 and Newcastle's Canadian centre back, David Edgar, who was a free agent after rejecting a new contract with the recently-relegated Magpies. Twenty-year-old Manchester United right back Richard Eckersley joined too for a £500,000 fee, determined by tribunal. Hamilton were also persuaded to part with their promising Scottish under-21 international left back, Brian Easton, for an initial figure of £350,000. Having extended his search to South America, Coyle acquired on loan Fernando Guerrero, a 19-year-old Ecuador international winger with blistering pace.

Unfortunately, Coyle's pre-season preparations were interrupted by some strangely timed international fixtures which robbed him of seven members of his first team squad for several days just prior to the opening game. Coyle's irritation was magnified once he learnt that Caldwell had sustained a groin injury while representing Scotland, ruling him out of first team action until early October. Coyle reacted quickly, bringing in the burly Cameroon international central defender, Andre Bikey, from Reading for a £2.8m fee. Despite Bikey's indiscretion in the play-off semi-final, he had been a physically imposing defender in Coppell's side, totalling 62 appearances at Premier League and Championship levels. Coyle said: 'He has loads of pace and power – he is a very good player.'

When asked by members of the press whether he had been surprised by Burnley's recent success, Coyle replied: 'I don't pinch myself now that we are in the Premiership. We've earned the right to be here, having played over 61 games last season. We want to get the ball down and play with a smile on our faces. We gained a lot of goodwill after our League Cup semi-final performance against Spurs. We looked a decent club and became many watchers' second favourite team.'

However, after a disappointing home display against Leeds in a friendly, Coyle admitted that the summer preparations had not gone entirely to plan, commenting: 'Results in pre-season aren't important, but it's always nice when you get them along with performances. We got neither on Saturday against Leeds. There's plenty to work on, but that's what we like doing. We've got a tremendous work ethic.

We've done the longer fitness stuff, we'll look to add that sharpness, to progress the speed and movement of the ball, which we didn't manage against Leeds.'

Alastair Campbell reminded the media: 'Promotion to the Premiership is probably worth around £60m to the club, but to the supporters it is priceless.' While BBC broadcaster, Tony Livesey, also a lifetime Claret, said: 'At other clubs, football is more like entertainment to local supporters, but for Burnley supporters it is the town.'

Burnley's season started at Stoke where they lost 0-2, not helped by a makeshift centre back partnership of Carlisle and left back Jordan. Brian Jensen said: 'We played quite well at Stoke at the weekend but conceded two poor goals, quite unlike ourselves.' But then came two stupendous 1-0 home victories over Manchester United and Everton with Blake scoring with a ferocious volley against United and Wade Elliott adding one of his own against a subdued Everton side.

Coyle observed:

> 'Our movement and passing were good against Manchester United. We got our blocks in. I wasn't surprised by our goal. I know what Robbie Blake is capable of. The place was rocking. Against Everton we started the game at a terrific pace. They didn't cut us open too often. I thought we were the better team. We've had a great week but that's all it is. We have a long way to go. We train at high intensity and that shows on the pitch. We have honest, hard-working players. Thirty-five more cup finals ahead.'

Robbie Blake added:

> 'I have watched my goal against Manchester United about four times now and I still can't believe it. What a tremendous atmosphere there was. You are not conscious of it when you are playing, you're too involved in the game but at the end you are! The Gaffer won't let us get our feet off the ground, though. We need to press other teams like we did against Manchester United to have a chance. We know we must play at our best and hope that the other teams don't. The Gaffer is so upbeat. It is very infectious.'

Brian Jensen reflected:

> 'My penalty save was pure instinct. Last season Ronaldo took the penalties so we didn't have a clue which way

Carrick would hit it. We squeezed Manchester United in the centre, pushing them out to the wings... However, they didn't pressurise us as much as I thought they would. It was a brilliant atmosphere, the best it's been since I've been here. We need this support in every single game, whether winning or losing, and we need the team to work so hard in every game. In our favour, we have an unbelievable work ethic.'

Just as the transfer window was about to close, Portsmouth and former Preston and Bury striker David Nugent was signed on loan. Upon arrival, he expressed the hope that he would be deployed in a spearhead role, saying:

'I'm looking to play as a striker here. At Portsmouth, I was playing mainly as a winger. I didn't get much opportunity to play – 10 minutes here, 20 minutes there. It wasn't enough time to get into the game.'

Nugent did not have to wait long to make an impact. His thumping 67th minute header from Elliott's sumptuous cross gave Burnley an unassailable lead at home against Sunderland. Then nine minutes later, he danced around the Sunderland central defenders, on the edge of their box, before curling the ball into the top, left-hand corner. It was a stunning finish. Up until Christmas he was used as an impact substitute, but having headed Burnley level in the Boxing Day derby with Bolton, he started in 17 of the remaining 20 league games, scoring four more goals.

Nugent's goal against Bolton enabled Burnley to climb one place into thirteenth position, comfortably above the relegation zone. However, the man who helped them rise so spectacularly was about to desert them for the club they had just played.

Five years after Owen Coyle's sudden departure from Turf Moor, Barry Kilby reflected:

'We had made a good start to life in the Premier League, winning all four of our opening home games against Manchester United, Everton, Sunderland and Birmingham. We also beat Hull at home in late October and should have beaten Arsenal (1-1) and Aston Villa (1-1) here, too, before the festive season began. Despite enduring some heavy defeats on the road, notably at Spurs (0-5) and Liverpool (0-4), after the Boxing Day game we had 19 points from as many games. If we could have maintained that form, I knew we had a realistic chance of survival. Then Owen shocked us by leaving early in the January transfer window, after pledging to us that he was committed to completing his work with Burnley. The players had bought into his upbeat message. We all had. But he thought Bolton offered a better prospect of survival, believing them to be five or 10 years in advance of ourselves, despite their lower position then.

'I thought I had persuaded him to stay but by the next day he was gone. His departure had a devastating effect upon the players he had inspired with his spirit and drive. We were prepared to go with Owen's assistant, Sandy Stewart and first team coach, Steve Davis, but they both insisted that they were leaving with Owen. The backroom staff went as well. Phil Hughes, the goalkeeping coach and chief scout, Cliff Roberts, and crucially the important signings we had lined up, such as Arsenal midfielder, Jack Wilshere, on loan, and North American winger, Stuart Holden, went with them too...

'Despite what the fans liked to think, there were not many ready replacements out there. The team was down because Owen's abrupt departure. I thought Brian Laws was a decent call but he had an invidious task trying to fill Owen's shoes. He had little time to strengthen the team because of the timing of Owen's departure. The crowd got on his back, particularly when the results deteriorated. When Owen jumped ship he probably sealed our fate. We never recovered the verve we had shown at the start of the season.'

Immediately after Coyle's departure, Barry Kilby lamented:

'Obviously, it is a trauma for the football club to lose our manager and our entire coaching staff within a week. Anybody would have had a rough time coping with that. We have had little time to negotiate the appointment of a new manager, particularly if he was already with a club, and try to bring in the players to keep us in the Premiership. We fully expected that he would move on eventually, but upwards not sideways. He was very emotional about leaving the club, claiming that only an offer from Celtic or Bolton would have induced him to depart. It's come at a bad time for us… We have now got to get going again…'

Club captain Steven Caldwell was equally upset at Coyle's departure commenting to Burnley author, Dave Thomas:

'To us, as players, it was a huge moment in our season. I always felt it was a possibility, but when you are such a tight-knit group any major change hits you much harder. I don't blame him for that in the slightest but it had a huge bearing on our season… And it wasn't just the fact that the gaffer left; Sandy Stewart, Steve Davis, Phil Hughes and Cliff Roberts went, too. All Cliff's scouting knowledge, disappeared as well. That shocked us. It was a very strange situation to be in. Usually some staff are left behind.

'Brian Laws, the new manager, had to bring in all new staff and that takes some getting used to. Things didn't go to plan, confidence went and the things we were good at, at the beginning of the season, stopped happening. We didn't seem to be playing as freely as we once did. We stopped playing to our strengths… One or two things happened with Brian Laws. I had it in mind that I'd be leaving. I suppose I felt that way since Owen left. I had a fantastic relationship with him. He is a top-class manager and we would have stayed up if he had remained in charge. That's how good Owen was. He got the best of players and built a great dressing room spirit so he's second to none. But I totally understand why he left. The transfer kitty he had at Bolton was much bigger than what was on offer at Burnley. Burnley could or should have backed him more to get to the next level. I suspect that is why he left. I was bitterly upset. It took the sting out of us. The team was in shock. Everybody was gutted.

'The group had a couple of meetings trying to keep things going, trying to rally the club, but it was an unstable time and maybe people started to think about themselves, not the club. I'm better for working with Owen. He brought a lightness and enjoyment. He brought over-achievement, changed the way I thought about football. For 18 months, we over-achieved… Brian Laws wasn't impossible to work with. I'd hoped we would have a good relationship. A few things happened with that relationship that caused problems. I wasn't fit for a start and was sitting on the sidelines. There were no run-ins, it was just unfortunate I wasn't fit and wanted to play. I felt Laws should have pushed me into the team to help them even though I wasn't fully fit. Nevertheless, the best decision I ever made was coming to Burnley.'

Clarke Carlisle recalled:

'Stevie Caldwell said to me that when he moved to Wigan, the players there couldn't believe some of the stuff Owen had said to us. It was simply the power of positive thinking. It's a confidence thing. You fake it to make it. You give people confidence, from that you play better, and from that comes more confidence and then you become a better player. He could make an average player good, and a good player excellent. If he had a secret, this was it.'

Ade Akinbiyi reflected in a later interview with the local press:

'Coyle had a drive about him. He got mad in the dressing room and if things weren't right kicked things. He did quite a lot of it to be honest when he wasn't happy. He had a false tooth that used to come loose so you knew he was mad. But I enjoyed working for him for his motivation. He knew what he wanted and he just drove it through the team. He lifted everyone. Obviously, it wasn't a good ending but he got the club up.'

Shortly after Coyle left, Graham Alexander admitted:

'I was gutted to be honest. Most of the players were disappointed by Owen's departure. We had two fantastic years with him. But there were players and people behind the scenes who had a lot to do with that, too, and they were still there. I hoped we could have carried that on. We hadn't played for him, we'd played for Burnley Football Club and that's what we needed to take on, for ourselves, each other, the fans and the people who paid us. There was an incredibly strong group of players there. As much as Owen did a great job, it wasn't down to one man… We can't think about Owen Coyle because he will not be thinking about us. Hopefully, we can stay in the Premier League.'

In his biography, Jensen described how deflated the Burnley first team squad was at Coyle's abrupt departure. It was said that their attempts at recovering the 'Coyle spirit' foundered quickly amid mutual acrimony. Jensen concluded: 'The magic had gone.'

Unabashed, operational director, Brendan Flood tried to assure the players and the fans:

> 'We are very happy with our squad. It's a fantastic squad. The job is now twice as attractive than when Steve Cotterill left. We don't need to advertise. Twelve candidates have rung about the job straightaway... It's fair to say that we're not the best of pals with Bolton at the moment. These things happen in football. Owen Coyle's move to Bolton probably represented his best bet of remaining a Premiership manager...'

2010 – 2013
'What goes down'

'Harder Than You Think'

CONTRARY to what some fans thought, or what Brendan Flood hoped, there was not a legion of eligible candidates, eager to replace Coyle. Neither Alan Curbishley nor Steve Coppell seemed interested. If Paul Lambert was, Norwich soon scrubbed that by offering him a new, presumably better, contract. Paul Fletcher said he was keen on Ian Dowie but nothing came of that. In the end, it seemed to be a choice between free agent Brian Laws and Doncaster boss, Sean O'Driscoll, although it wasn't entirely clear whether O'Driscoll was really interested in the post or whether anyone on the Burnley board was captivated by his candidacy. Finally, Barry Kilby announced to the local press that Brian Laws had been appointed as manager, saying:

> 'We are delighted to welcome Brian Laws back at Turf Moor. Deloitte and Touche looked at how well he managed on a limited budget at Sheffield Wednesday, where they rated him top of the tree if results are put against available resources. He was a success at Hillsborough and has all the credentials to be successful here. I'm sure the fans will relate to him. He has had to work quickly because of the transfer window. As the manager, he has to make the decisions about incoming transfers and get the team organised for the rest of the season.'

Brian Laws responded:

> 'I'm delighted to be here. Owen Coyle did a magnificent job. Hopefully I can carry on with the baton. I'm not a novice. I've been in the game for a long time. It feels like coming home. Everyone is pulling in the right direction. I work well with the players and the supporters.'

Laws immediately faced the small matter of a return league game at Manchester United, although club elder statesman Martin Dobson and youth team boss Terry Pashley were entrusted with the team preparations, given the abrupt departure of Coyle and his backroom staff. Nevertheless, Burnley acquitted themselves well in the first half during which they should have taken a two-goal lead.

Brian Laws commented:

> 'I'm very proud of the players and supporters. For an hour, I thought we were comfortable. We attacked with venom, defended with purpose and counter-attacked so well. Clear chances fell to Steven Fletcher and David Nugent. We should have got something out of the game. If we can be as creative as this against the best then we have a chance. Sometimes we have been too "gung-ho" this season, allowing us to become overstretched. While it's showing that you've got no fear, it's not quite as simple as that. You should slow the game down and keep possession better and for longer. We were too cavalier in the last 20 minutes of the game at Old Trafford. I will be working on that. David Edgar and Michael Duff were excellent in central defence, while David Nugent was exceptional. His game has moved on a lot since I last saw him... I still want the players to play good football. I don't want to snuff it out... I might be putting the reins on a little bit but I won't be pulling too hard.'

Clarke Carlisle made the following observation about Laws' change of emphasis:

> 'The new manager is trying to implement a new plan, a new focus within the side. I think we saw that in the FA Cup defeat at Reading, a big swing from one focus to another. It's marrying the two, and that's what makes a successful team and that's what we're trying to do.'

This seemed to be a balanced, even-handed view of Laws' new approach. Indeed, experienced professional, Graham Alexander, who was granted a player/coach role under Laws stated: 'I've enjoyed the training sessions with Brian Laws. He offers a fresh voice.'

However, sports journalist Alan Nixon, a firm friend of Coyle, suggested that Laws had difficulty in bringing about his shift in focus, stating:

> 'Laws was unsure what to do at times, changing the system, changing the way players thought about trying to win games. Obviously, some of the old guard were not keen on that and one or two made their views known. Things always look worse when you are losing and Laws did not know how to stop the trend. But it wasn't entirely his fault.'

Certainly, Robbie Blake remained committed to Coyle's attacking mentality. He told London Clarets Jane Pike and Pauline Pratley:

> 'Under Owen Coyle we only played one way: we weren't a team to put 11 men behind the ball and sit back, because we didn't have the players to do that. We've got players who attack, and he knew we could attack teams and score goals. Look what we did to Manchester City away (3-3). We made them look very average in the first half... but we were capable of conceding goals at the same time because we left ourselves open as well. I think as manager, Owen didn't want to change the way we played.'

With Burnley losing their first five games under Laws, including a toxic relegation tussle at Bolton, the pressure mounted upon him. When West Ham arrived at Turf Moor on a bright 6 February, Burnley were occupying the final relegation place. Brian Laws realised this was 'a must-win game.' His new signings – centre back, Leon Cort, a £1.5m acquisition from Stoke, and Danny Fox, reputedly a £1.8m buy from Celtic were in his starting 11. Much to the relief of the club and its fans, Burnley won – just!

Laws concluded:

> 'The players were magnificent in dealing with that pressure. They were assured, competitive and creative. A terrific goal from David Nugent put us ahead. Danny Fox had a fantastic debut, setting up Nugent's goal with a long, raking pass, also scoring with a cracking free kick. He stopped

one as well. New signing, Leon Cort showed composure and firmness at centre back. He showed no sign of panic. However, it was a very nervy last 10 minutes. We lost a bit of shape and dropped too deep but managed to hang on to win.'

The corner was not turned, though. An abject 0-3 defeat at Fulham followed. Worse still, relegation rivals Portsmouth and Wolves, snatched maximum points on their visits to Turf Moor. Only a home draw with Stoke on 10 March interrupted an eight-match losing sequence. Nevertheless, player/coach Graham Alexander was upbeat about the point gained here, insisting: 'Stoke are a hard team to play against. We forgot to play our own passing game in the first period but were happy to get something out of the game with a good second half performance. It showed how well we are coping with the pressure of relegation.' The Easter home losses just about sealed Burnley's fate, though – a controversial 0-1 loss to Blackburn and a 1-6 humiliation by a rampant Manchester City. Despite winning 4-1 at Hull a week later, helping ensure that the Tigers accompanied them down, Burnley duly returned to the Championship. Burnley had won three, drawn one and lost 14 of the 18 Premier League games played under Laws' management. Under Coyle, Burnley had won five, drawn five and lost 10 of their first 20 league games.

As relegation loomed, Barry Kilby put a brave face, claiming:

> 'We kept to our plan with our budget. We are going down strong. The Owen Coyle factor had a big impact upon our season. We go down in a healthier state than Hull and Portsmouth. It's given us the chance to bring through younger players. We have sold 10,000 season tickets for next year. This is way above many clubs in the Championship. We still want to end up above Hull because this will give us £800k more that we can spend very well.'

A remarkable 4-2 home victory over Spurs in the final game of the season ensured that this consolatory prize was gained, Burnley having bravely recovered from an early two-goal deficit. Barry concluded: 'The final game against Spurs was on the twenty-third anniversary of the Orient game. It provides a timely reality check, demonstrating how far we have come.'

One of the few bright elements in Burnley's catastrophic collapse were the energetic and skilful performances of loan signing Jack Cork, the son of Wimbledon's FA Cup winning striker, Alan Cork. Chelsea's young midfielder enjoyed his stay at Turf Moor, saying: 'The fans were brilliant and the players great despite the results. I've loved it here. It's very easy to settle, one of the best places I've been at...' Brian Laws added: 'Jack is such a popular player. He's been a big plus after the bad news we've had about Chris McCann's injury.'

With McCann still side-lined, Cork returned for a season-long loan in 2010/11. He was joined by tall, burly, Scottish international striker, Chris Iwelumo, who arrived from Wolves, with Steven Fletcher moving in the opposite direction for a £7.5m fee. Preston's Scottish winger Ross Wallace joined for an undisclosed figure, as did Hull's combative midfielder, Dean Marney. Marney told a local reporter: 'I was getting a bit stale at Hull. Burnley is a club on the up. I want to get back in the Premiership. It's a strong squad here. I like to get the ball down and play. I've a good engine but need to work on my goal-scoring.' Laws also signed the Owls' keeper, Lee Grant, for around £1m. He was expected to challenge strongly for the number one slot.

Although Robbie Blake left for Bolton, Chris Eagles and Tyrone Mears remained – as did Jensen, Bikey, Fox, Cort, Edgar, Duff, Carlisle, Alexander, Rodriguez, Paterson, Thompson and Elliott. On paper, this seemed to be a team good enough to challenge for promotion. The pressure was on Laws to bring about a swift revival. He acknowledged this stating: 'This is my team. I'd like to think I'd be judged on that, more so than last season... The summer has given me a clean slate and the time to enforce what we want to do and how we want to do it. That's given me a huge lift because the players have been so responsive...'

The 2010/11 season began well, with Iwelumo's header defeating Nottingham Forest in the opening game at home. A satisfactory point was gained at Ipswich before an out-of-sorts Leicester side was brushed aside easily (3-0) at Turf Moor. However, this encouraging start was undermined by a poor first half display at Swansea where Burnley were undone by Scott Sinclair's eighth minute goal (0-1). A pulsating home derby with Preston followed, covered live on BBC TV. A switchback contest ended in a 4-3 Burnley win.

Brian Laws exclaimed:

> 'What a derby! It had everything. Seven goals. Tackles going in with a passion. Both sides giving it a real go. The sending-off of Preston's Billy Jones was possibly the turning point, though... I was very disappointed with our first half display. Preston went man to man. They didn't give us an

inch of space and every time we lost the ball they counter-attacked us. The introduction of Jay Rodriguez and Chris Eagles later in the second half gave us more impetus. We became sharper and quicker in our passing too, penning them in for longer periods. The crowd then got behind us. In the end, we won the game because of this. It was a great hat-trick by Chris Iwelumo. It showed he's not only good with his head but with his feet too. There were many mistakes, though. We got away with it, a bit. It showed us how hard this division will be. I sensed we would get a third to put us back on terms, but it was Jay Rod who got us off the hook with that late headed winner.'

Laws was commendably honest, for Preston had looked the better side for much of this game with their marauding Republic of Ireland winger Keith Treacy creating havoc on the left flank. At Middlesbrough, Burnley had no such luck, losing 1-2. Laws was critical of central defender Carlisle for his defensive lapses, stating:

'We went with a positive approach at Boro' but Carlisle was too Gung Ho and it cost us. Instead of capitalising on our set pieces we gave away too many soft free-kicks. It was very disappointing, particularly to get within three minutes of a decent result.'

However, this set-back was quickly forgotten after Burnley came out on top in the grudge match with Bolton in a third round Carling Cup tie at home. Brian Laws reflected:

'The pleasing thing was we focused on the game, not what surrounded it. It was nice to put to bed the acrimony concerning Owen Coyle's sudden departure from here last January, and to focus on the future. The atmosphere was terrific. It drove the players on from the first whistle. The momentum never dropped. There was no holding back. Chris Eagles was outstanding, working hard in defence too. Despite facing an experienced Bolton team, we were the better side.'

The ill-feeling felt by many Burnley fans towards Coyle enticed 17,602 to attend the game – a remarkable attendance figure for an early round, League Cup fixture. After the game, a delighted Jay Rodriguez commented:

'I learnt a lot while on loan at Barnsley. Their manager Mark Robins was very helpful, staying behind with me after training, helping me with my game. Now I am playing on the flank in a front three with Chris Iwelumo as the central striker and Chris Eagles on the opposite wing. I'm happy with this role as it extends my learning. The team are playing well away but have yet to get that first win. I'm sure it's not far off, though.'

However, Burnley would not record their first league away win of the season until Boxing Day, frustratingly surrendering two-goal leads at Sheffield United (3-3) and Norwich (2-2), during October and November. Nevertheless, young Rodriguez proved to be the 'real deal', fully vindicating Laws' faith in his ability to trouble defences with his pace and nifty footwork, his powerful shooting and aerial strength. Laws deserved great credit not only for sticking with Rodriguez, but also in recognising that his starlet was much more effective facing goal, having the opportunity to run at defenders with the ball, rather than having his back to goal as a target man.In Rodriguez's inaugural season as a first team regular he became Burnley's 'top gun', scoring 14 league goals in 37 starts and five substitutions. It was just as well that Rodriguez's performances were so impressive, as Paterson continued to be plagued by injury. Brendan Flood commented: 'We want to get the Academy up to scratch, so we can produce another Jay Rod. It may be not like the sixties but it should be good enough to grow our own talent.'

But it wasn't Burnley's attack which caused Laws grief, so much as the fragility of his defence. After Sheffield United had twice come from behind to earn a 3-3 draw at Bramall Lane, snatching a 94th minute equaliser, Laws griped: 'We're not looking to get plaudits for being an attractive side, we want to be professional and organised… We were sitting so deep at one point, I thought our defence was behind our goalkeeper…' While Laws complained about his players' lack of discipline, many fans blamed Laws' supposedly inadequate tactics. A subsequent 3-0 home win over Barnsley on 19 October 2010 briefly subdued the re-emerging discontent. Afterwards, a relieved Brian Laws praised the contributions of Chris Eagles, Brian Easton and Leon Cort, the latter being selected as the 'man-of-the-match' for his two critical tackles when the game was still in the balance.

But four days later, Burnley were thrashed 0-4 at home by 10th-placed Reading. Shell-shocked Laws said:

'We lost our unbeaten home record today with our poorest display of the season. We weren't good enough. So many performances were below par. Half the team weren't with it. Our key players were snuffed out. After Cort was dismissed for two rash tackles we tried to be positive but then conceded two more sloppy goals. We missed Carlisle – his organising ability and leadership. Hopefully this is just a blip.'

Too often, Burnley centre back, Leon Cort, was left alone to deal with Reading's Shane Long, one of the fastest strikers in the Championship. As in their abject 1-6 home defeat by Manchester City in April, Burnley's swifter visitors were allowed too much space in which to probe, accelerate and pick their passes, resulting in the slower and poorly organised home defenders being by-passed at will.

On 30 October Barry Kilby announced a boardroom re-shuffle with Nelson-born John Banaszkiewicz joining the board of directors. Barry said:

'John is a real identikit for what we want as a Burnley director. First and foremost, he is a businessman… His experience in building up an international business is an invaluable asset to the club. His heart is with the club. He is a genuine supporter who comes from the area… The board has been reduced to five directors. We have decided this streamlining is necessary to reach more efficient decisions on sales, purchases and capital matters.'

John Banaszkiewicz told the local press:

'Like the other directors, I'm passionate about this club. In fact, all directors here are as passionate as any supporter. We have got to make the club more global if it is to grow. I can help here with my international business experience… One of my early objectives is to get Gawthorpe and the academy up to scratch… Maybe we can't afford a £35m player, but we can find a new Jay Rodriguez.'

While plans for the re-development of Turf Moor were put on hold because of the possibility of a double-dip recession, Philip Wilson, was appointed as chief executive of the proposed university of football at Burnley. It was reported that a BA (Hons) degree in football administration was to be awarded with a curriculum comprising football finance, stadium management, commercial matters, accounting and law. Club chief executive Paul Fletcher confirmed: 'We are not just targeting students from Burnley. We want to reach out to people in India, China, Dubai, Australia and all over England. I think this is a first for a British football club.'

As for the annual accounts for the year ending in June 2010, the club reported a £14.4m pre-tax profit. Because of the club's promotion to the Premier League, its income went up from £11.2m n in 2008/09 to over £44m with TV and match day revenue contributing £40m of that. Retail turnover was up by 43 per cent; ground advertising revenue up by 40 per cent; while corporate hospitality income doubled. On the debit side, the wage bill continued to soar. In the 2007/08 season, £9.76m was spent on wages. With the club investing heavily in a promotion bid during the season which followed, that figure rose to £13.4m. This outlay then went up by another 60 per cent during the club's solitary Premier League season, when wages totalled £22.37m, much higher than Brendan Flood's originally estimated figure of £16m.

Nevertheless, the cost of wages, as a proportion of turnover, reduced from an alarming one 119 per cent in 2008/09 to a much more sustainable figure of 51 per cent in 2009/10. The club also paid all but £1m of its debt, repaying its directors' loans and settling the outstanding bills from the 2008/09 promotion season which had carried a £11.7m loss. The bottom line was that the club emerged from its one season of Premier League sun with all debts cleared and £14m in the bank. Moreover, the club's average home attendance in the Premier League was 20,654, its best since the glory days of the early sixties, and 58 per cent higher than that in its promotion year of 2008/09 when the Turf Moor gate averaged 13,082.

However, the upbeat financial news was undermined by a further calamity on the pitch as on 11 December 2010, visiting Leeds overturned a two-goal interval deficit to beat Burnley with a crushing second half display. Although well placed at the break, thanks to a poked effort from Easton and a fine breakaway goal from Rodriguez, the Clarets had ridden their luck. Before taking the lead, Leeds' left-winger, Max Gradel had twice burst through Burnley's flimsy defence, leaving him one-on-one with keeper, Grant, only to spurn both gilt-edged chances.

Leeds' boss, Simon Grayson, strengthened his midfield for the second half, adopting a higher line of defence and a more intense pressing game. Leeds immediately overran Burnley. Brian Easton's limitations at left back were ruthlessly exposed by the tricky Snodgrass, while Gradel continued to run riot on the opposite flank. Leeds poured forward at will, with their Argentinian striker Becchio leading the line with darting menace. As in the Reading game, it seemed as if Laws had been out-thought appearing to offer no tactical response to Leeds' change of game plan, although once again his defenders allowed their opponents too much space.

Laws looked both angry and baffled at the post-match press conference, where he again denounced his team's lack of profession-alism. He said:

> 'A few words have been said, and rightly so, because that's not acceptable... We should be winning that. It's about being professional. It's about being switched on and organised... The manager will always take the rap, but the players must also take a portion of it because of the way they went out in the second half... I'm disappointed that we didn't continue to do what we did in the first half when we were 2-0 ahead.
>
> 'Their winning third goal came from our corner! Howson was allowed to run the length of the field. In the first period, we troubled their centre halves with our attacking formation but after the break they had it easy... I said at the break, "Don't be complacent because you haven't won the game yet" but one or two maybe thought they had. That's not good enough!'

Although Burnley won well at Barnsley on Boxing Day (2-1), recording their first victory at Oakwell in over a generation, it seemed as if Laws was on borrowed time. Sure enough, after another dismal home defeat, this time at the feet of languishing Scunthorpe (0-2), Laws' unhappy period in charge came to an end. As in previous press conferences, following a defeat, Laws seemed bewildered, blaming his players' attitude. Here he said:

> 'It is difficult to understand how the same players who turned in such a good performance at Barnsley on Boxing Day should be so below par against Scunthorpe. It is difficult to put my finger on it. It must be complacency, expecting Scunthorpe to be an easy ride. Our passing skills were off. I can understand the supporters' frustration.'

The reality was that the players had lost their 'Band of Brothers' mentality which had served them so well under Owen Coyle.

Barry Kilby was generally cautious about ditching his helmsman after a run of poor results. His instinct was to give his managers time, backing their attempts at bringing about necessary improvements. Despite making a shaky start, Stan Ternent's subsequent success had vindicated his chairman's faith, as had Steve Cotterill's successful defence of Burnley's Championship status during the mid-noughties. But in January 2011, Barry felt bound to take decisive action if his club was to find a way back to the Premier League before their newly-found wealth disappeared. In regretfully announcing Brian Laws' departure, he said:

> 'I have telephoned Brian from America, where I am now, and have asked him to step down as manager. Everyone is naturally disappointed and frustrated that recent results have not gone as we would have hoped. The board of directors has therefore decided that we need a fresh approach to achieve our goal of returning to the Premier League... Brian had a difficult time coming in when he did, not helped by not having the best of luck, but coming to this critical point of the season, when our objective of promotion remains a priority, it was thought it was time for a change.'

Clarke Carlisle's observations seemed to reveal his deep misgivings about Laws. He said:

> 'It is important to get the right appointment. It shouldn't be rushed. First team coach, Stuart Gray, who is standing-in, is well respected. Youth team coach, Terry Pashley, has brought charisma and drive to training. It has been sorely needed. It's old school but there's nothing wrong with that.'

The club decided to replace Laws with Bournemouth's 33-year-old manager Eddie Howe, who had turned around his home club's fortunes spectacularly since his appointment in 2008. At the start of the 2008/09 season the Cherries were saddled with a 17-point deduction for entering administration, but Howe guided them to safety and then won promotion to League One in the following year. Confounding all expectations, Howe had then overseen another promotion tilt with Bournemouth, finishing third in League One. It was reported that Burnley agreed a £300,000 compensation package with Bournemouth for Howe and his assistant, Jason Tindall.

At his appointment at Turf Moor, Eddie Howe told the local press:

> 'The ambition of the club matched mine... I'm very impressed with the stadium, crowd and players. The players are good technically, skilful with flair. We have already enjoyed a good, sharp training session. That's what I enjoy being involved in – games and training. I'm a coach, more of an enabler, an encourager rather than a shouter or screamer... I don't relish having the spotlight on me. I would much rather the focus was on the club and the players rather than on any one individual. I am part of the coaching team. It is not about me, it is about the team behind the team... I know I have to do the media side but football is what excites me. I'm here to build not just for now but for the future. I have goals but these are best kept for myself and the players.'

As promised at his appointment, the club backed Howe with additional funds. Howe wasted little time in bringing in lightning quick 25-year-old, central midfielder, Marvin Bartley from Bournemouth, in January for around £350,000. He also signed Swindon's prolific goal-scorer, Charlie Austin, for a reported £1m fee. Howe said of Austin:

> 'Charlie learnt his trade at Poole Town. He didn't lose hope after being released by Reading as a 15-year-old. He has always had a knack of scoring goals. He is a very good finisher but works hard, both on and off the ball. He is strong in the air. Importantly, he wants to improve... we beat off a lot of competition when signing him for Burnley. He wanted to come here.'

A delighted Barry Kilby commented:

> 'Eddie Howe is a breath of fresh air. We needed a new broom and with Eddie we believe we have a very thoughtful and intelligent manager. Austin is an excellent signing – exactly what we need, younger players like Austin and Bartley whose value will appreciate.'

Unfortunately, Austin sustained a shoulder injury at the end of January 2011, ruling him out for the rest of the season. While Howe's Burnley flirted with play-off ambitions, prompted by a six-match unbeaten run, they were undone by barren spells, notably during mid-March and early April when six fixtures, yielded just one point.

In March 2011, Barry Kilby addressed the parliamentary select committee for culture, media and sport. The select committee was investigating football governance following the catastrophic financial collapses of clubs which had 'bet the ranch' in a mistaken pursuit of unsustainable glory. Unusually, the committee convened at Turf Moor to give themselves a better understanding of how and why Burnley FC had bucked the trend in not spending lavishly once in possession of the Sky TV booty.

Barry Kilby explained:

> 'Yes, we have been accused of a lack of ambition. That issue always crops up, usually in the phone-in programmes. It was easier when a team came up with Championship players. You could improve their wages but it was still very manageable. However, if you get to a second year in the Premier League, you start swimming in the waters of established players in that league, and the costs start to rise. Fans want to win matches. We all should have prizes for good government – we don't, and that what sets the theme. The pressure is enormous.
>
> 'If you want to keep a club like Burnley in the Premier League you need between £40-50m put in every year on top of gate receipts, prize and TV money to compete, and even that figure doesn't make a big impact. With a Championship club that might be achieved with director loans, but once you get into the Premier League, it is about getting exceptionally rich people who can put their personal money in.

Barry continued:

> 'When we got up, it was a bit easier at first. We hadn't been in the top flight for 30-odd years, so perhaps it was easier to manage the fans' expectations. It was easier to get across the message that we were being sensible, we were clearing our debts, so that if we went down we could handle it. I think the fans understood this but had we stayed up for a year or two, the pressures to spend more would have grown... When we lost heavily in a Premier League game, some of the pundits on *Match of the Day* accused us of being "clowns

or jokers" – this adds to the pressure to spend.

'The big problem is that players' contracts don't just last for the season in which they were signed. You have a three-year commitment, and that's the big difference between the divisions. It's been said that we should insist on a player taking a wage cut in the event of relegation from the Premier League. It is possible to do this with a player that is already contracted to the club, but not with new recruits with Premier League experience.

'Last season, we came up from the Championship and the players got an increase. It's easy to say, "Well, if we go back down, it comes back down". That's a logic that's easy to enforce. But if you're trying to get an established Premier League player, that's not an easy one to pull off. If some other club is in the market for that player, they might not operate that clause. Some clubs do not appear to care about the economics. Most clubs have quite big debts. Clubs of our size now have benefactors who are owed quite a lot of money. You can afford a wage bill of £45-50m, the way the Premier League is set up with the TV money and the normal trading… The big problem is if you come back down. Parachute payments do distort the competition somewhat, but I would say it's not guaranteed that the ones that come down with these payments are then able to go back up because they are invariably shedding players. They've got to try and get their house in order, to get back to an even keel. The gap is massive. Premier League clubs now have an average wage bill of £50m.

'However, I am slightly wary of wage restraints and determining everything by diktat. The season we went up, we increased our spending with directors' loans. We knew what we were doing and how we would cover it, if it didn't come off. There's a bit of flexibility there. 60 per cent seems a sensible marker for clubs to follow in setting their wage bills in relation to their turnover… However, it's always happened that someone funds a new centre forward from their own resources. I am wary of a straight-jacket imposed from above that says, "Whatever the circumstances you can't do X" This tends to reinforce the status quo, impeding the ability of the smaller clubs to better themselves.'

John Banaszkiewicz, then the newest Burnley director, also reflected upon the club's financial situation when he addressed the London Clarets' AGM in July 2011. He was candid and forthright, admitting that the club had made the mistake of 'resting upon the laurels of Premier League money, rather than re-doubling its efforts at generating more income.'

With new Financial Fair Play rules, due to come into force for the 2012/13 season, he expected the wage bill to drop substantially. He pointed out this would place a tight curb on all Championship clubs, given that they were currently spending, on average, 88 per cent of their annual turnover figure on wages. Such expenditure was said to fall foul of the new rules. With former loan signing, Jack Cork, expected to move to Southampton, John Banaszkiewicz thought that, with hindsight, the club should have attempted to buy him in January 2011 when his wage demands were more manageable. The young Chelsea midfielder had played superbly in an erratic Burnley side for a season and a half.

After completion of the 2010/11 season, Barry Kilby described the club's financial situation in these terms:

> 'In 2008/09, we made a £11m loss; in 2009/10, we made a £14m profit; in 2010/11, we made a £4m loss, when we were in the top quarter of Championship clubs for wages. This was covered by the £17m parachute payment we received following our relegation from the Premier League. Our one-year stay in the Premier League, enabled us to clear the £10m debt incurred by loans made to the club by the Burnley directors during the 2008/09 season.
>
> 'In a normal Championship season, without the cushion of a parachute payment, we would expect to achieve a £10-12m turnover. With the Football League Financial Fair Play regulations now in place we need to ensure that wages amount to no more than 60 per cent of our turnover. So, after the parachute payments expire, we will be looking at a maximum wage bill of £6-7m.
>
> 'With these regulations in force, clubs will have to break even on trading or face financial penalties. This is a big deflationary factor. We can no longer carry the losses we have had before, as incurred in the 2008/09 season, for example, when we made a strong push for promotion.

'The Financial Fair Play regulations obviously favour the bigger clubs who can rely upon bigger gate receipts and other revenue, so don't have to carry so many losses. There's a lot of new money coming into the Championship now, particularly foreign money. There are now only seven clubs in the Championship which are not owned by foreigners. The Championship is attracting more foreign money because of the potential financial incentives given by the Premier League. We always need to be aware of our size.

'We are planning on having a £11m wage bill in 2011/12, taking account of the continuing parachute payment. We are also committed to developing Gawthorpe training centre and placing a greater accent upon youth by expanding our scouting network and bringing in younger players. This is to negate the financial disadvantage we face, because younger players are generally on lower wages.

'We wanted to sign Jack Cork permanently at the end of the 2010/11 season, but his wages had become unaffordable. We took the £3m offered by Bolton for both Mears and Eagles because there was only one year left on their contracts and both wanted to play in the Premier League. Chris Iwelumo was also allowed to move to Watford for around £50,000 during the summer of 2011.'

The average home gate in 2010/11 was just under 15,000. This represented an annual fall of 28 per cent, placing additional pressure upon manager, Eddie Howe, to divest his team of their higher earners, and place a greater accent upon youth. Therefore, Clarke Carlisle also left, on loan to Preston, as did Leon Cort who was moved to Charlton, ultimately in a permanent deal. Meanwhile, Graham Alexander, Steven Thompson and Kevin McDonald were released. Much to his chagrin, Eddie Howe was compelled to accede to Danny Fox's transfer to big-spending, Southampton. The deal was apparently worth £1.8m, which the Burnley board said, 'was too good to turn down.' Finally, Wembley hero, Wade Elliott, moved to Birmingham for an undisclosed sum.

Howe then brought in England under-21 internationals, Junior Stanislas and Zavon Hines from West Ham, the latter having his £250,000 transfer fee set by tribunal. Preston's 22-year-old, Republic of Ireland international winger Keith Treacy, was signed too, for a fee around £750,000, while young Manchester City defenders Kieran

Trippier and Ben Mee were signed on season-long loans. Both players had represented the England under-21 side and had experience of playing in the Championship; Trippier with Barnsley and Mee with Leicester.

Howe introduced Mee thus: 'Ben is a fantastic young player. He has a fantastic attitude, a winner who is an England under-21 international. He is rated highly at Manchester City. He is a left-sided centre half but can play at left back. He is comfortable on the ball. He is very aggressive.' As for Trippier he was described as an attacking right back with an impressive crossing ability and a fearsome shot. He seemed an ideal replacement for the departed Mears.

In addition, midfielder, Chris McCann, was persuaded to sign a further two-year deal while Portsmouth's £2.5m offer for Martin Paterson and a separate unnamed bid for Rodriguez, apparently worth £4.5m, were both rejected.

Howe also placed his stamp upon youth development, appointing Jason Blake, another former Bournemouth colleague, as head coach for the younger professionals and reserves. Blake had never played football professionally, but he was a UEFA 'A' licence holder. Howe told the local press:

> 'He's someone I'm delighted to bring to the club. He will bring enthusiasm and dedication to the job. He has had experience of running the centre of excellence at Bournemouth and was a big part of the team down there. Jason's main strengths are working with and developing young players.'

Blake faced an immediate challenge. On 20 October, the Football League voted to accept the Premier League's 'Elite Player Performance Plan' (EPPP), which comprised a reform of the rules governing academies and the transfer of youth players. Previously, the transfer of youth players was subject to a tribunal system, where no agreement could be reached between the buying and selling clubs. In its place, a formula was introduced which determined a youth player's value. This denied the selling clubs the opportunity to negotiate a fee. Under these new rules, a club buying a youngster, aged between nine and 11 years, would have to pay his parent club £3,000 for each year of his development.

The fee for players aged between 12 to 16 years, ranged, according to age, from £12,500 to £40,000 per year of development. Under this new regime, Burnley could not have commanded a fee higher than

£40,000 when selling John Cofie, their 14-year-old Ghanaian prodigy, to Manchester United in May 2007. As it was, United coughed up £1m for Cofie. Peterborough's director of football, Barry Fry, predicted that smaller football clubs would abolish their youth systems altogether, with famous lower division 'nursery' clubs, such as Crewe, left struggling to survive in this hostile market.

Moreover, top clubs were no longer restricted in where they scouted youngsters. This removed a curb that had been introduced previously to prevent 'over fishing'. Henceforth, any club could sign a youngster from anywhere in the country.

It was also determined that Football League clubs with academy status would only qualify for EPPP, if their academies maintained an annual budget of £2.3m a year and employed at least 18 full-time staff.

It seemed as if the Football League had voted in favour of these proposals because a 'no vote' would have resulted in the Premier League withdrawing its £5.4m 'solidarity payments'.

In late October 2011, Martin Dobson, left his role as Director of Youth Development, having fulfilled his contract, while Vince Overson, head of the club's centre of excellence, left with immediate effect. Estimable youth coach Ashley Hoskin left too. Their loss of dismayed many Burnley supporters, notably those with an active interest in Burnley's youth development. They were concerned that well-regarded and experienced Burnley coaches were being replaced by Howe's former Bournemouth colleagues, ostensibly without good reason. Doubts were expressed, too, about the dismantling of an apparently successful recruitment network.

The 2011/12 season began disappointingly as visiting Watford, under the management of future Burnley boss Sean Dyche, coasted into a two-goal lead, helped by an unfortunate error by Ben Mee. Hornets' striker Marvin Sordell ran Burnley's newly-assembled defence ragged with his pace and power. However, thanks to Howe's late introduction of Austin and Treacy, the game was saved with two goals in the last 13 minutes. Howe said:

> 'I feel frustrated more than relieved after pulling back a two-goal deficit. New signing Keith Treacy was excellent. He gave us real impetus providing an indication of what he is about. Regarding the interest being shown in Jay Rod and Danny Fox, it's not ideal.'

With a lucrative deal with Southampton in the offing, Fox made it clear that his ambitions lay southwards.

Because Charlie Austin was still finding his feet and Paterson was injured once again – he would be out of action until December 2011 – Howe was permitted to buy Bournemouth's highly promising, 19-year-old striker, Danny Ings. Howe's assistant, Jason Tindall told the local press:

> 'Danny Ings is a fantastic talent. He had a very good season with Bournemouth last year prompting various Premier League sides and three Championship clubs to show a keen interest in him. He's a 110 per cent player, a very intelligent young man, who scores and makes goals. I have worked with him for some time. He works hard and listens well…'

Regrettably, Ings sustained a knee injury in his second training session, ruling him out of contention for five months. Tindall remarked:

> 'It is a great blow to lose Ings to injury in only his second training session at the club. We are a bit thin on the ground at present, with Paterson injured once more. But Danny's attitude is fantastic. He's in every day at 8-30am ready to work on other parts of his body, increasing his upper body strength.'

Burnley's injury woes were compounded when Michael Duff suffered damage to his knee ligaments in a League Cup victory over Barnet. He was expected to be side-lined for six weeks.

Tindall added:

> 'We have a nice bunch of lads here. Twenty-one-year-old Junior Stanislas has joined from West Ham, encouraging his friend, Zavon Hines to join him. Junior had been at West Ham since he was ten so it was quite an upheaval for him to move so far away but he arrived with a really positive attitude, wanting to do well here. He likes to attack and score goals but he has the versatility to play on the left, where he offers a good crossing ability, or alternatively just behind the main striker. We have high hopes of him.'

Austin and Rodriguez quickly established a formidable striking partnership. Nottingham Forest found out the hard way on Tuesday 27 September 2011, when Burnley thrashed them 5-2, Rodriguez scoring with two headers and Austin nabbing the fifth. Stanislas was the architect of this impressive victory, supplying a succession of devastating crosses that the Forest defenders struggled to combat.

Blackpool were also beaten 3-1 at Turf Moor, while Derby (2-1), Millwall (1-0) and Coventry (2-1) were overcome away. Either Austin or Rodriguez were on target.

However, as autumn turned into winter, Howe's men were struggling on the brink of the relegation zone. Eddie Howe stated: 'We need to improve in all departments, but particularly at the back.' He suggested that he had extracted all he could from the current players and needed to bring in fresh legs. Howe's plea did not fall on deaf ears. During the January window, the club allowed him to shell out £150,000 on Derry City's left back Daniel Lafferty, and to sign ex-Cherries striker Josh McQuoid on a three-month loan from Millwall. In addition, permanent deals were agreed for Trippier and Mee, the former costing around £400,000 and the latter a little more.

But before these reinforcements could be made, a remarkable late recovery took place at Hull on 26 November 2011. Here, Burnley overturned a two-goal deficit, by scoring thrice during the final 12 minutes. It proved to be a turning point. Five of the next six league games were won, including a prestigious victory at West Ham (2-1) on 3 December, clinched with a thumping header from loan signing, Sam Vokes. After a fortuitous home win over Hull (1-0) on New Year's Eve, sealed by the newly-returned Paterson, Burnley were in seventh place and eyeing a play-off spot. However, just six of the final 22 games were won, meaning that Burnley achieved only thirteenth position, five places lower than in the season before. Home form was particularly frustrating – seven wins, nine draws and seven defeats.

It was announced on the 18 November 2011 that chief executive Paul Fletcher was to leave the club. Fletcher explained:

> 'I genuinely thought I couldn't contribute more, apart from making Burnley's University College of Football Business a real success… There are a few frustrations I won't go into… The club needs to be looking for new initiatives and to change the way it does things. Hopefully, the new chief executive will have a bit more success with that than I have.'

American Lee Hoos was chosen to replace Fletcher, having served Fulham, Southampton and Leicester in a similar capacity. While at Leicester, Hoos oversaw the purchase of the club by a consortium from Thailand, and the subsequent appointments of Sven Goran Eriksson and Nigel Pearson as managers. News of this led some supporters to question the club's intentions in recruiting Hoos. However, Hoos addressed their concerns quickly, stating in the local press: 'I don't believe my remit is to find investors for the club. It's about evolution not revolution.'

It came as shock, though, when Barry Kilby announced in May 2012 that he was standing down as chairman because of ill health. His place was to be taken by John Banaszkiewicz and Mike Garlick, who had agreed to share the chairman role.

John Banaszkiewicz said:

> 'Mike and I will chair board meetings alternately, with the casting vote alternating too. In light of the FFP regulations, youth development has become more important here. We can't stop talented young players like Jay Rod from moving on. Incidentally, he has been an excellent ambassador for this club. What we need to do is find and bring in more young players like him...
>
> 'The Championship is probably the most competitive league in the world with around 15 teams vying for a place in the Premier League. According to an analysis conducted by Deloittes, during the 2011/12 season Championship clubs incurred a combined loss of £189m contributing to an overall debt of £720m. The clubs with the greatest debts were said to be Middlesbrough with £98m, Nottingham Forest with £75m, Leicester with £48m and Preston with £38m. In all, Championship wages represented about 90 per cent of its collective income. We don't have to bet the ranch, though, if we continue to invest in young talent to sustain us, acquiring and developing young, up-and-coming players like Austin and Ings. As for the transfer fees, we obtain from sales, most of the revenue has to be put into the club to sustain its continued running.'

Mike Garlick added:

> 'In 2011/12 we made a loss of £4m. We need more non-matchday revenue, and to do this we need to become more proactive in seeking commercial sponsorship. This is of paramount importance. Both John and I have international businesses which give us the opportunity to promote Burnley FC abroad. We must be ambitious on and off the field. If we're not, we will go backwards. If we remain competitive in the Championship we'll get another shot at the Premier League.'

As expected, Jay Rodriguez was transferred to Southampton in June 2012 for a fee of around £7m. He represented the Burnley youth system's most lucrative product. This year was a time of celebration, as the Burnley youth team progressed to the semi-final of the FA Youth Cup before being eliminated by Blackburn.

Yet, despite Eddie Howe's reforms of youth development, not one member of this talented squad became a first team player in the top half of English football.

With the 2012/13 season just one month away, Eddie Howe reflected:

> 'It's been a very busy summer. We've signed centre back, Jason Shackell from Derby for £1.1m. I've admired him for some time. He will fit in as a leader. In fact, he has everything you want in a modern centre half. We had to be patient, though, in negotiating his transfer… We have also brought in George Porter, a very quick young winger from Leyton Orient who brings exciting promise to our Development squad… We have added right back Luke O'Neill from Mansfield as cover for Trippier, and acquired Reading left back Joseph Mills on a season-long loan. We have paid £500,000 to Wolves, too, for their centre forward, Sam Vokes… The board have also been very receptive to my ideas about what improvements we need in training… Here, we do very little running without the ball. As far as training facilities are concerned it is important to keep on the move as a club.'

Shortly after his arrival, Jason Shackell commented: 'I like training here. It's based upon attacking football which I enjoy. It's a massive honour to be awarded the captaincy.'

The 2012/13 season began well with an emphatic 2-0 win over Owen Coyle's recently relegated Bolton side. Eddie Howe concluded: 'It doesn't get much better than this. It was pretty much the perfect performance. I thought we were well on top for most of the game. The decision-making was good throughout. We knew we needed to improve our defensiveness after last year…'

Owen Coyle had to endure an unpleasant afternoon. His team played dreadfully and he was constantly jeered by the Burnley fans, notably when a small plane trailing a recriminatory banner circled overhead. The banner read: 'Judas Coyle you reap what you sow.' In his post-match press interview, Coyle preposterously claimed credit for assembling the victorious Burnley team when only two of its players had served under him!

Having scored the opening goal, injury-jinxed Martin Paterson exclaimed to the press: 'I always said that when I'm fully fit I'll score goals and work defences.'

But the euphoria of this impressive victory soon dissipated. A 3-2 defeat at Middlesbrough followed, causing Howe to say:

> 'In the first half we were excellent, passing and moving well and getting a lot of balls into their box. However, we scored twice only to concede almost immediately. Stanislas was excellent – his best game for the club. But Boro' played well between our lines as we defended a bit too deep.'

Another defeat at Huddersfield followed. An increasingly exasperated Howe said:

> 'We didn't keep it tight at the beginning as planned. We never really opened them up either. It was a disappointing display. We gave Jordan Rhodes too much time in the box for the second goal. Pato is out again as well, having sustained a tiny tear in his hamstring, leaving us thin on the ground with strikers.'

Brighton then rammed home Burnley's shortcomings in a decisive 3-1 victory at Turf Moor on 1 September 2012. Howe conceded:

> 'Brighton dominated the first half. We gave away three goals from set plays which was particularly disappointing. There were two great finishes but we should not have allowed Mackail-Smith the space to produce an overhead kick in our box. Because of injuries we were forced to play one up front so it was difficult to make an impact. We need Pato back.'

With Burnley then languishing in twenty-second position, Howe was grateful to play a side without a point thus far. Peterborough packed a surprising punch, though, despite eventually losing heavily by 5-2. Howe commented:

> 'Peterborough at home was a crazy game. After scoring first and being well on top, suddenly we were 2-1 down. Although we eventually won 5-2 we could have scored more for we created enough chances to win three games. Once

again there were defensive lapses with our midfielders letting runners go. But Junior was excellent again – very positive, showing pace and running at people. This ability has been evident in training for a year but he hasn't shown it enough in games. Technically and athletically he's got the lot. Now he needs to be more ruthless.'

Although Charlie Austin embarked upon a prolific goal-spree, notching hat-tricks against Peterborough and Sheffield Wednesday (3-3) and producing a winning brace at Derby (2-1), Burnley continued to concede too easily. A first-half lead at Leicester was frittered away by poor defending. Swindon were gifted three avoidable goals in a League Cup defeat. Then both Millwall (2-2) and Sheffield Wednesday (3-3) grabbed late goals to deny Burnley victory in games which should have been won. Charlie Austin fumed that his goal rush was not reaping better rewards.

Then to cap it all, Burnley blew a two-goal lead at Crystal Palace to lose 4-3. Howe's post-match comments were becoming repetitive. After the Palace fiasco, he said: 'We had a plan to cope with Palace's wide men but once Zaha switched wings we couldn't cope with it. This performance was nowhere near good enough. We defended well for 30 minutes. We were two up but then fell apart. When we concede we look nervy. We don't look as good in the second half of games as we do in the first.

'Charlie's goals are fantastic, but the ones we are conceding are not.' Club captain, Jason Shackell added: 'We're doing a lot of talking but there's not enough action. There is a lack of discipline. Collectively we are not defending well enough.' Shortly afterwards, Howe and Tindall left Turf Moor at their request, returning to their former club, Bournemouth. It was reported in some national papers that Bournemouth chairman, Eddie Mitchell had offered Burnley £1.4m in compensation for them.

Co-chairman, Mike Garlick told the local press:

'John B and I are surprised and disappointed that Eddie is leaving a great club like Burnley so soon in the season. However, we understand that his decision reflects his personal circumstances rather than any matters at Burnley Football Club, be that supporters, the players or the Board. We agreed with Eddie that quite a lot of things have gone well. The infrastructure has been improved and that remains as we move forward. He left for valid family reasons... There's 80 per cent of the season left so there's plenty of time in which to turn things around.'

Eddie Howe said:

'I'm pleased Burnley have been well compensated for our services. That was important from my respect... Hopefully that will help them make the right appointment... Burnley treated me very well. I can't speak highly enough of the club, the people who work for it, the players and the supporters, who have all been brilliant to us since we walked through the door... Hopefully we've played our part in a rosy future for the club... We've done our best to try to promote a long-term plan for the best for the club. But it's for other people to judge our time in charge. There's stability in the boardroom, and they have been fantastic with me and my team and helped us to implement what we wanted to do. To leave is incredibly difficult, but it is a decision I must make for my family and for personal reasons, which I can't go into detail on.

'There is only one club I would contemplate leaving Burnley for and that is Bournemouth. Whoever takes the job of manager here will be taking over a fantastic football club.'

In reviewing the interest shown in the managerial vacancy, co-chairman, John Banaszkiewicz said:

'There have been 15 to 20 applicants for the vacant manager post so far. We want someone like Eddie, but with a bit more aggression with the players. Mike and I are going to take our time. It's a massive appointment. We need to get it right for the long term. In the meantime, youth team manager, Terry Pashley will take over the running of the first team.

Various managerial contenders were mentioned including Mick McCarthy, Ian Holloway, Michael Appleton, Billy Davies and, surprisingly, Owen Coyle. At least Lee Hoos was quick to scotch that rumour stating:

'I just couldn't see how that one would happen. Obviously, I wasn't there when the whole Owen Coyle saga happened but I got enough feedback to know that there was a very bitter aftertaste and I just couldn't see a way back for that one.'

On the pitch, Charlie Austin extended his purple patch by nodding in the winner against Blackpool. He said:

> 'I've been told that my goal today means that I've equalled Willie Irvine's 1966 club record, having scored in seven successive games... This is nice but the win counts for more. Lee Grant made two great saves to make sure we got all three points... "Pash" has been brilliant for us in training, leaving smiles on all the players' faces. He's so enthusiastic. It rubs off on all of us.'

Recent signing, Brian Stock added

> 'Pash deserves a lot of credit. He's got us to be more professional on the pitch, alongside "Faz" and "Blakey". It's been a good atmosphere since Eddie and Jason left. It's also given me the opportunity to play in my favoured holding midfield role.'

Youth team manager Terry Pashley made an impressive start as caretaker first team boss, winning both of his initial games in charge. In netting a brace of goals in the midweek 4-3 win at Bristol City, Austin trumped Ray Pointer's 1958/59 club record in which the 'Blond Bombshell' scored 12 times in eight successive games. Just as fans' thoughts were turning to Pashley as an eligible candidate, Burnley were hammered 4-0 by promotion-bound Cardiff.

On 30 October 2012, co-chairman, John Banaszkiewicz announced:

> 'After two weeks of interviews we have decided to appoint Sean Dyche as Burnley's new manager. He impressed us with his pride, passion, motivation and hunger. He is a strong character who, as a player, won four promotions with four different clubs. He is a leader, who is extremely ambitious, more so we thought than any of the other candidates we considered. He came across as very good on the technical aspects of the game who has the qualities needed for bringing club and community close together... Sean has loyally served Watford for eight years whereas we have had three managers in as many seasons. We need greater continuity and stability if we are to move forward...

> Consequently, we will do our best to hold onto Charlie Austin in the January window.'

Sean Dyche chose ex-Nottingham Forest midfielder Ian Woan as his assistant, while Tony Loughlan was appointed as first-team coach. He commented:

> 'The players were immediately very responsive, receptive to realigning the way things need doing. We want to be flexible in our thinking. It's a case of adding to the defence not taking away the scoring. All players have the will to win. But sometimes it needs re-igniting.
>
> 'One of the first things I did with the players here was to hold a feedback session which involved asking each of them to complete a questionnaire. This called upon their ideas for improvement and enabled me to gauge how clear they all were about what needed to be done. What I emphasise is the framework, the shape of the team, rather than the individuals, although I try to develop the players as much as the framework.
>
> 'My emphasis is upon how the CLUB can move forward. We need to develop the connection with the people of Burnley. A Burnley supporter told me that Burnley people support the club. That's music to my ears. It's a fantastic club. If they phone you, you take notice... My background has been in youth development. I want to see this club being as successful as Watford were in that regard.
>
> 'I don't brand myself. As manager, I'm at the front of the club but no more than that. As for my rasping voice, it's a family thing. My boy has it, so did my dad. It does have its uses, mind!'

The players soon found out how determined their new boss was, insisting upon a culture of 'minimum requirement: maximum effort.' Dyche demanded a higher level of fitness than had previously been attained, stating: 'I want to see honesty, integrity, pride and passion. I want to see a team who puts sweat on their shirts. When I was a supporter, the one thing I wanted to see was a team which gave everything for the club.'

Midfielder Dean Marney was enthusiastic about the regime Dyche had introduced, saying: 'Sean Dyche's training is intense. His game plans are good too.'

Co-chairman, Mike Garlick outlined to the local press the board's ambition for the rest of the season, stating:

> 'Ultimately, we want to try to get promotion but we don't need to go up this season... Sean has just over a two-and-a -half year deal so we'd like to think he's got time to improve things and take us one step further... The target we set Sean for this season is to get above thirteenth position, which we achieved the season before, and to stop shipping goals and improve home performances, which have not been good enough over the last two years.'

Sean Dyche made an immediate impact, presiding over impressive home victories against Wolves and Leeds in his first two games, achieving clean sheets in both. A delighted Charlie Austin said after the Leeds victory: 'We kept it tight. Everyone put in a real shift. We deserved the points. Chris McCann provided Tripps with a superb ball which enabled him to produce a great cross that I nodded in.'

Dyche's tactics succeeded in bolting the back door, halving the number of goals conceded. On debut against Wolves Dyche set out his stall, playing Marney and Edgar in central midfield, with Stock operating in a holding role in front of a back four of Trippier, Shackell, Duff and Mee. Wide-men Paterson and Wallace were instructed to support Austin as the solitary striker, when in possession, but to track back swiftly to cover the full backs when not. Playing an energetic pressing game, Wolves were squeezed, and restricted to few chances, the best of which fell to the muscular raider, Sako. The recipe was successfully repeated against Leeds when the recovered McCann replaced Edgar.

Dyche experienced his first set-back in a 2-1 defeat at Ipswich. He observed: 'Against Ipswich we deserved something but we gave it away by attacking with gusto without making sure we had enough balance behind. We will be working on that. We didn't create as I hoped either. We need to shift the ball quicker because teams bank up swiftly.'

His first high-profile challenge came on a sparkling, cold, Sunday lunchtime on 2 December 2012. This was the feisty, home derby with arch-rivals Blackburn. A crowd of 21,341 watched a pulsating, no holds barred, physical contest that began with Burnley pushing forward energetically and ended with Sam Vokes' late headed equaliser. Dyche said: 'We came across two fine centre halves and a goalkeeper on form... I really enjoyed the impact the subs made though... To give the fans that goal at the end is important because it would have been a bit of a travesty to have come away from that with nothing...' He quipped with a smile: 'It also showed up that chap who shouted out "What's Vokesy going to do in five minutes?"'

The annual accounts for the year ending 30 June 2012 revealed that a profit of £3.16m was made in the last financial year, which would have been an operating loss had it not been for Rodriguez's transfer fee of £7m. In a statement which smacked of the past 'Sell to Survive' policy, the co-chairmen pointed out that 'player trading remains a cornerstone of how the club balances its books.'

One surprise, however, was the size of the wage bill. Despite the strict economies introduced at the start of the 2011/12 season, wages remained high at £16.9m. Given the impending new Financial Fair Play regulations, this was a cause for concern, particularly with the parachute payment having halved to £8m.

Howe's restructuring of Burnley's youth development system had raised staffing costs. The impact of the Elite Player Performance Plan (EPPP) was a factor in this, but with Jason Blake replaced as development coach by Simon Weatherstone a year after his appointment, there were further doubts raised about the success of these reforms. Nevertheless, Blake continued as academy director and resumed his former duties once Weatherstone returned to Bournemouth as their first team coach. Lee Darnbrough, a Howe signing, too, joined the club in November 2012 as Head of Recruitment and Analytics. He had previously served West Bromwich in a similar capacity. Burnley's chief executive, Lee Hoos, confirmed that Darnbrough would not dictate which players Dyche should sign, but assist 'in terms of tracking and landing those players, helping myself and the board ensure we are getting value for money.'

Dyche was positive about Darnbrough's appointment stating:

> 'It's a similar model to what I had at Watford. It's the way a lot of clubs are looking now because as manager you are very time-bound. We do DVD analysis, pre-hab programmes, weights programmes and all different things. We want as much information on targets as we can. It's still not an exact science but the more you can put into the process, the better chance you have of a better outcome.'

While Dyche made Burnley harder to beat, the goals dried up at both ends. Only 12 goals were scored in his first dozen games, almost half the number achieved under Howe in two fewer matches. After a 0-1 home defeat by Leicester on 29 December, Burnley were in thirteenth place, no better off than in 2011/12. Nevertheless, the defensive disciplines Dyche instilled served Burnley well in their subsequent upward surge.

In January 2013, the board decided to re-purchase Turf Moor and Gawthorpe training centre via a new company, Turf Moor Properties Ltd. by means of a bond issue. Co-chairman, John Banaszkiewicz, explained:

> 'This arrangement enables us to protect Turf Moor and Gawthorpe from the uncertainties of the football industry and its finances. Having examined all the options, the board is confident that a bond issue represents the most cost-effective finance option and enables a section of our fans to play a part in bringing our spiritual home back under the control of the club. Additionally, buying both Turf Moor and Gawthorpe back makes sense financially and operationally for our long-term future. It will eventually see an end to rental payments and put the club on a firmer financial footing.'

On 5 July 2013, the club proudly announced that its ground and training complex were once again back in its ownership following the completion of a buy-back campaign developed by the co-chairmen. John Banaszkiewicz said: 'Despite concerns that it would be tough to raise the funds we needed, this innovative scheme has been very successful, bringing us £3.5m.'

During February and March 2013, Burnley struggled. Dismal home displays against Middlesbrough (0-0), Huddersfield (0-1) Barnsley (1-1) and Hull (0-1) caused dismay in the stands and on the websites. However, a spirited performance at Ewood Park helped allay relegation worries. Here, Burnley were robbed of victory by a poor refereeing decision late in the game. Nevertheless, a subsequent 3-1 home win over relegation rivals, Bristol City, appeared to signal safety only for lacklustre defeats at Blackpool (0-1) and Leeds (0-1) to suggest otherwise.

Demotion was ultimately averted, thanks to Edgar's late headed equaliser against champions elect Cardiff on 20 April, and to winning strikes by Ings and Paterson at Molineux (2-1) a week later. While the victory at Wolves removed the threat of relegation for Burnley, it almost sealed their hosts' successive drop. A spectacular shot from Stanislas and a tap-in from Paterson were then sufficient to beat Ipswich in the final game of the season. Burnley rose to 11th place, ensuring Dyche met the board's immediate objective of achieving a higher position than in the season before.

Dyche concluded: 'We have finished 11th in arguably the toughest ever Championship, certainly in my lifetime. Next season will be even tougher given the profusion of cash-rich opponents. But as Burnley has done in years before, we'll punch above our weight and come together as a community and a team.' And how!

2014 – 2017
'Eyes on the prize'

'Times Like These'

HAVING secured safety by a comfortable margin, Sean Dyche's next headache was to form a competitive team for the 2013/14 season. The contracts of six members of his first team squad were due to expire in June 2013. Dyche had already told the press that the club must play hardball with new contracts. He said:

> 'There are players – who were deemed to be good players – on contracts that were agreed when we were trying to get back into the Premier League immediately. That doesn't mean we aren't trying to do that now, but those contracts now must come down because the cost base must come down. So, the negotiation process becomes obviously more difficult. We can't just give them what they want. It's not perfect, but it is what it is.
>
> 'I don't think as a club there will be massive investment. Burnley is a club that pulls together and that's important because if there's money for investment it won't be millions. Burnley wants to be a club that is solvent, it wants to be a club that moves forward, it still wants to be competitive. But if competitive means rolling out millions of pounds and then a year later finding it is in absolute trouble, I'm not sure that Burnley fans really want that.'

Four high-profile squad members left the club before the start of the 2013/14 season: former prized asset Chris McCann, who was surprisingly not offered a new contract; £1m-plus striker Martin Paterson, who left the club after dismissing a new deal offer as 'derisory'; goalkeeper Lee Grant, who elected to return to Derby, nearer to his family; and Charlie Austin, who was transferred to Queen's Park Rangers for around £4m, after his proposed move to Hull collapsed because of an allegedly suspect knee.

However, midfielder Dean Marney and centre back Kevin Long signed new contracts, while Dyche moved quickly to plug the gap left by the departing Grant by signing Bristol City keeper, Tom Heaton, on a free transfer. Heaton had begun his career at Manchester United, as had creative Wigan midfielder David Jones, whom Dyche also signed on a free transfer. Jones had previously helped Derby and Wolves achieve promotion to the Premier League, seeming to be an ideal replacement for the departed McCann. Versatile Scottish midfielder Scott Arfield was added to the squad, too, having impressed during a trial period. He had been mystifyingly released by Huddersfield. The Terriers' negligent loss would become the Clarets' enormous gain.

With Austin moving on just before the new season started, Burnley were left with only two recognised strikers, Vokes and Ings. Ings had already suffered two serious knee injuries. In the previous season he had managed only three goals in 32 league appearances, 17 as a substitute.

Vokes had been no more prolific managing four goals in 46 appearances, albeit 33 as a substitute. It was small wonder that Burnley were listed among the bookies' favourites for relegation. As for the fans, their expectations were mostly modest. Here is what a collection of London Clarets thought:

Barry Heagin reckoned:

> 'Mid-table and I'd be very happy. We have a good defence, but we're going to lose our senior strikers and we need some solid midfielders. I don't think we'll play particularly decent football, we'll play percentage football, because I don't think we can compete playing expansive football. There are too many teams in the Championship who can play expansive football better than us. We're going to be dragging out results all season.'

Patrick O'Neill said:

> 'I'm not looking forward to the new season. I can't see any prospect of doing better. Dyche must mould his own team. It's 6 July and I'm hoping he'll bring in some of his own players, so we can have something to look forward to in August, but I can't see it. The likes of Keith Treacy and Marvin Bartley just aren't good enough.'

Lee Firmin commented:

> 'The idea of youngsters coming through hasn't worked out as we've released a majority of those we were most confident about two or three years ago. After all that talk about the development squad there isn't anyone you can see playing 15-20 first team games for Burnley for the next couple of years. From January onwards, we played dreadful football. You can't really have much hope that the manager can build anything from what will be a weaker side. All we can hope for is that we will stay up and a couple of youngsters come through"

John Pepper added:

> 'I'd settle for finishing above Blackburn again and beating them at least once. I'd like to see some attacking football. I wasn't sorry when Eddie Howe departed, in fact, I was quite glad to see the back of him. His mantra was that he was trying to build something here, but I couldn't for the life of me see what it was. We've assembled something like five so-called wingers, none of whom could beat an egg, let alone a full back, and three left-backs of varying quality. That's part of Dyche's problem, he's inherited an unbalanced squad with not enough players of real quality. Perhaps he is more of a players' manager than Howe who came across as slightly detached and remote. I won't be sad to see McCann go and I've never rated Paterson. It depends on who he can bring in, so we can't make any judgements yet'

Ian Wood concluded:

> 'I think it will be unbelievable if we could finish above where we finished last season. The division won't be as

tight. The teams coming down will be better that the ones in the previous year, and the teams coming up from Division One won't be as good. So, it won't be as tight but I don't think it will be a pretty season. It'll be hard work. I don't know what happened to young striker, McCartan. Obviously, he's gone. He looked a good player. But other former youth team players like Hewitt and Howieson are key in that they can save us money in the transfer market, and if Dyche can build those into the team while bringing in experienced players where we need them, then maybe it could be something towards the future.'

Yet by tea-time on 21 September, Burnley had won five, drawn two and lost just one of their opening eight league fixtures. Away from home, Sheffield Wednesday had been cut open, then stubbornly resisted (2-1), while Derby were thumped (3-0). At Turf Moor, Birmingham had been brushed aside (3-0) and Yeovil eventually shrugged off (2-0) although both Bolton (1-1) and Blackburn (1-1) came from behind to claim a share of the spoils. Only Brighton had dented Burnley's flying start, helped by the dismissal of keeper, Heaton (0-2). At Elland Road on 21 September, Burnley's dazzling away performances continued with another deserved victory (2-1). On a glorious, early autumn afternoon, Burnley swarmed all over Leeds straight from kick off, establishing a two-goal lead through Arfield and Vokes, then, as at Hillsborough, they skilfully thwarted their hosts' desperate attempts at recovery.

Astonished London Claret, Pauline Pratley, recorded:

'Somehow last season's mediocre collection of misfits, donkeys and lightweights – further weakened by the loss of once-key players – have been transformed into a top-two football club. Our team is slowly but surely being created in Sean Dyche's image. If he were a dog, he'd be a Rottweiler. I don't think there's been this level of team unity since – whisper it quietly – the Owen Coyle days. There's another similarity to the Coyle era, too. During the run-in to promotion, there were games I never doubted that Burnley would win. That feeling soon departed once we were in the Premier League and didn't return under Brian Laws and Eddie Howe – St. Bernard and poodle respectively. It's early days but could that feeling be returning?'

An elated Sean Dyche reflected:

> 'In the first half we were really, really good and opened
> Leeds up to create so many chances. We looked like we had
> that real air of confidence. In the second half, we started
> brightly and Paddy Kenny made a fantastic save from
> Danny Ings. Had it been 3-0, that would have been job
> done, but they settled and in the last 20 minutes we've had
> to hang on. I would say that was controlled, but of course
> Tom Heaton deserves massive credit. You must make big
> saves in games and the two he made in the second half were
> as good as goals. I think we have kept him reasonably quiet,
> on the whole, this season, but when he's needed he has made
> big, big saves.
>
> 'It's not that easy to get things to work immediately,
> but we have galvanised a group of people who want to play
> for Burnley Football Club and I think that is a massively
> important thing. The fans can see their will to win a
> football match and it's hard not to gush about them at the
> minute because they have been terrific. They are delivering
> every week and that is a fantastic feeling for everyone
> connected with the club.'

Burnley proceeded to flatten Charlton (3-0) at home and outplay
Doncaster (2-0) away. But the star performance came in a 2-1 home
win over Reading on a radiant afternoon on 5 October. Burnley flew
at Reading from the off, pressing them hard all over the pitch, not
giving them any time to settle or pick their passes, catching them in
possession and forcing a litany of distributional errors. From front to
back, Burnley were ruthless and relentless.

Dyche was uncharacteristically, yet understandably, euphoric after
the game, hailing his team's performance as a brilliant display. He
enthused:

> 'I am thrilled. I think that is one of our best performances
> since I've been at the club. Reading are a big club, just out
> of the Premier League and highly fancied, with a very good
> manager and good, experienced players. But I thought
> some of our football was terrific. We opened them up at
> will at times in the second half, and arguably deserved to
> win more comfortably. It got a bit nervy in the final five
> minutes, with the mayhem that can sometimes happen

from putting balls in the box, but we thoroughly deserved to hang on to win.

'I am waxing lyrical for the first time and rightly so. I spoke to the group this week about expectations and whether that changes you as an individual and as a team. I spoke to them about Ed Moses, who was not beaten over ten years in 122 races. I said, "imagine getting to 50, then 70, then 90. What were his thoughts about the challenges, his opposition and all the science allowing everyone to get better and stronger?" But he just kept winning. Now I'm not suggesting it's a given and I am not suggesting we will win forever, but you must be open-minded and push away that thought that we're due a defeat because we're not. If you think about it statistically, you can win every game. It's not a probability, but the mindset has to be, forget the past and look to the future.'

On the following Saturday, the Ipswich hoodoo was put to bed with a ragged 1-0 victory, thanks to a late header from Arfield. Once again Dyche had warned his players not to be distracted by the club's poor record at Portman Road – Burnley had not won there since January 1970. Dyche insisted that what happens in the past has no impact upon the present or the future.

Dyche told the waiting press:

'All credit to everyone. The players put so much effort into that performance again today, and although there were quiet moments in our display, we still found the wherewithal to go and win it 1-0. Within all that, I am really pleased that we have turned around what could have been a negative situation.

'There were people questioning why we sold Charlie Austin, and then about the funds and all of that, so I am so pleased. The board came out and were very honest, and we came out and said we were believers in the people we work with. So, I am really pleased for the players and the supporters who looked beyond that.

'Of course, results galvanise it all, but I believe there is a positive energy and feel about the group. All noses are pointing in one direction. I always say that results cement that, and if a couple don't go our way, that is when we really need to show there are no cracks and no doubting questions, but in the meantime, that is another fantastic win at a tough place to come.'

The scintillating victory over promotion rivals Queens Park Rangers, came a week later. Sean Dyche said:

'We are still looking to support the group the best we can, within the finances that are available, but the challenge of football is not to say you can't do this or that. You can do anything you wish and I have made that clear to the players. We have good players in a tight group and it will need support at some point, but we can only do that one step at a time, and today was another big step forward in what we are trying to achieve here.

'I think you have to say that the QPR result is the best of our season, given the quality in their ranks, the manager and the resources they have. To come to Turf Moor and for us to give a performance like that, to win, was terrific and I am so pleased so many were here to see it [16,074 attended]. I thought we were fantastic from the first whistle to the last. I thought the energy, discipline, application and, most of all, the quality was excellent, culminating in a great result. They had only conceded four goals before today and were unbeaten. It was Danny Ings who got the goals this week, with an excellent finish to a superb move, and then converting a late penalty.

'I spoke to Danny on Thursday and said he looked like a young man enjoying his training and his performances. He said he was and that will do for me, but credit to all of the players. We have spoken to the lads about having a freedom to play, no matter who that is against. The players have a framework, but within that they have immense freedom to express themselves. I believe in them and trust them to deliver performances.'

Danny Ings complimented his strike partner Sam Vokes, telling Burnley Media Manager Darren Bentley:

'My first goal against QPR gave me satisfaction because of the preceding passage of play, which included the sharp one-two with Big Sam that put me through on goal. I'm not sure people realise how good he is. He is not just a big, typical English striker who can head it; he can slide other people in as well. He's done that on many occasions this season.'

Full back, Kieran Trippier also gave his perspective on this crucial victory:

'We have no fear of any team in the league. Our spirit this year is unbelievably high. The difference comes from our superior fitness. We ran non-stop for 98 minutes against QPR. The gaffer's first pre-season training laid the foundations for this.'

Centre forward Sam Vokes and goalkeeper Tom Heaton then gave their opinions on why Burnley were then topping the table. Vokes said:

'Dyche is the reason that Burnley are currently doing so well. He is very high on different types of psychology. He is a good motivator off the pitch and in the changing rooms. Coming here with his extensive playing experience has helped, as has his relatively youthful age. He understands the lads and gets on with them off the pitch. We know how good we are as individuals and what a great team spirit we have. It's why we are able to keep up with those clubs that have spent millions.'

Goalkeeper, Tom Heaton agreed:

'I think most of the credit can be put Dyche's way. He sets the standard, the expectation, the format of what he wants. He simplifies it for players. We knew from pre-season there was something special and we managed to keep it going. He's been fantastic to play for and he should be very proud. I think once you get that physical conditioning, we certainly got in pre-season, it simplifies things. We know we've got the quality, so if you can put in the work ethic and application as we have done in every game this season, you are already giving yourself a chance, especially in the Championship where fine margins can make big differences. There are some great sides in the Championship this year and we're one of them. It helps that the manager is so approachable. There's a great camaraderie with him but there's also an authoritative line that you don't cross. The ground rules are simply his expectations: smartness is one – being in club tracksuits and club-issued trainers when we are in public.

Forget that, and it's a fineable offence. He likes smart
haircuts. He doesn't want people slouching around with
headphones on when in public. We don't wander around
texting either.'

Republic of Ireland international, Keith Treacy credited Dyche in
helping him with his personal issues, saying:

'There have been a few ups and downs since I came to the
club, but I'm trying to put everything behind me now.
Everything off the field is starting to fall into place, and
my football is hopefully going to see the benefits of that.
That's mainly down to the gaffer, to be honest. He cares,
that's the bottom line! Football isn't the be-all-and-end-
all with the gaffer. He actually cares about the players as
individuals and their off-field problems and tries to help as
best he can. I can't speak highly enough of him.'

In reflecting upon his apprenticeship at Nottingham Forest, Dyche said
that his manager, Brian Clough, ensured that each player understood
how a Forest team should play and behave, irrespective of their position,
status or experience. Dyche recalled Clough telling him and his fellow
centre halves to: 'head it; kick it; pass to someone better.' Dyche
maintained that once the Forest players had grasped Clough's basic
instructions, they had a freedom to play. In turn, Clough attributed his
managerial success to the example set by Alan Brown, his former boss
at Sunderland, whom he regarded as royalty. Brown had once been a
morally strict and uncompromising centre half, captain and manager
at Burnley. He was arguably the architect of Burnley's League triumph
in 1960, achieved under Harry Potts. As a player at Turf Moor, Brown
had served under the ascetic, demanding and shrewd manager Cliff
Britton. Like Britton, Brown insisted upon the highest standards of
conduct on and off the pitch. Brown also focused on the details of how
his teams should play, being a brilliant coach, strategist and innovator,
who devised a vast array of mesmerising set play ruses. With Dyche
arriving at Turf Moor, exhorting the Brown/Clough mantra, it was as
if the wheel of time had turned full circle.

Dyche's pressing game, which had been employed so decisively
against Reading and QPR, was derived from Barcelona who he
regarded as the finest exemplar of this method. Dyche remarked
that, while it was Barcelona's passing skills which garnered the
plaudits, it was their pressing game which impressed him most of

all. He said that when he took over at Burnley, he and his players looked at replicating their approach. Dyche said that at Burnley the tactic starts with forwards, Sam Vokes and Danny Ings, who harry the opposing defenders and goalkeeper, and then extends through the midfielders to the back four. He expected everyone to do their bit to deny their opponents time and space and continually strive to get the ball back.

Dyche's influences extended beyond football. He referred to his interest in leadership styles formed outside the game, referring to winners in other sports. He cited the huge impression made upon him by the dedication, determination, fitness levels and collective spirit of the Oxford University rowing team, with whom he spent some time while completing his Pro-licence coaching qualification. He said:

> 'There is no confusion in their journey. They focus fiercely upon the Boat Race they are driving to win. Within the boat you have the reserves, who train as hard, if not harder, than the elite crew, even though they know they might not get in the boat for the big event. There was also a simplicity, a rawness of vision, just a blackboard with a date and a time when the Boat Race is going to be. I took a lot from that. The coach, Sean Bowden, was brilliant. He took me on the water in the launch boat at six in the morning and I was with them right the way through until they were on the rowing machines at eight at night. It's still a team game, but they work six months for one event – we, of course, do it every week.'

Although Burnley's subsequent results up until New Year were less impressive – two victories, six draws and two losses, they still went into Christmas in pole position, following a 2-1 home win over Blackpool. Dyche wryly reproached his detractors, saying, if this had been a mini-slump, as was claimed by some, it was a remarkably productive one.

But the club's financial situation was less healthy than their mid-season points tally. A £7.6m loss was announced for the year ending the 30 June 2013. This comprised a sobering £146,000 loss per week. The fall in turnover from £23m to £15.2m was a direct result of a £7.4m reduction in the FA parachute payment. It meant that core turnover – money generated outside of the Sky TV contributions – had dipped below £10m, that had been the norm before promotion in 2009. Co-chairman, Mike Garlick indicated that the £8m shortfall had been covered for this year, but drew attention to the much-reduced turnover expected in the following year, with the FA parachute payments ceasing.

Better news came with the appointment of Terry Crabb to the board. He was the founder of Dorset Cereals and, like other Burnley directors, was locally born and bred. He stated his willingness to contribute to the club's unexpected tilt at promotion, saying: 'It was the homespun culture of the Burnley board that swung the deal. That's probably the most important thing, alongside the fact that the club is run properly by people who are either born in Burnley or who are local to it now.'

Despite the hugely impressive start made by Dyche's men, the case for reinforcement had become overwhelming by Christmas – particularly given the small size of Sean Dyche's first team squad (just 19 players) and the mounting risk of injuries to key players derailing the team's upward momentum. Michael Kightly had already been brought in from Stoke in a season-long loan, but there were no obvious replacements for Vokes or Ings should either or both become injured. Consequently, Dyche was permitted to sign a belligerently industrious Brighton striker, Ashley Barnes, for a fee of around £750,000.

Barnes said shortly after arrival: 'I have never had such a welcoming feeling before at any club. From the moment I walked through the door, it was just brilliant. This is a club unlike any other that I have been at. The training is so intense. You must be sharp every single day. I love that intensity. It can only help you on a match day.'

Meanwhile the Clarets pressed onwards and upwards. Despite a 1-0 defeat at Middlesbrough on Boxing Day, they embarked upon a 16-match unbeaten run in the Championship, which featured 10 wins, the most important of which were probably those against promotion-chasing rivals, Nottingham Forest and Derby County.

In reflecting upon his side's 3-1 defeat at Turf Moor on 22 February, Forest manager, Billy Davies, said:

> 'In the first half, we played against a side that looked like promotion contenders. They bossed us all over the pitch and we gave away three soft goals with some silly mistakes at the back. We didn't play anywhere near well enough to contend with them in the first half and we got what we deserved. The second half was much better and much more like us. We hit the bar, had two efforts cleared off the line and scored late on. We were more aggressive, more energetic, but it was too little, too late. Burnley play a very

direct game that puts you under pressure and quite simply we never handled it.'

Dyche then gave his impression:

'As a manager you never get that perfect half, but that first 45 minutes is certainly as good as I've seen from our group. Some of the football was absolutely first class. We have a belief in the team and you saw today we were majestic in the first half. We scored three and it could have had more. I thought it was total domination. Our passing and movement were exceptional, we played through the units quickly and we hurt them in so many ways.

'When you are up against a strong Nottingham Forest side full of class players, with massive resources, expectation and finance, that only adds to the quality of this performance. We have seen signs of what we produced in that first half many times this year, but to dominate so powerfully for 45 minutes is rare in any game. Goalscorers often get the headlines but, to a man, everyone delivered today.

'Once you are 3-0 up, it turns into a different game and in the second half, as teams with nothing to lose do, they rained balls into our box from every area of the pitch. Tom had to make one big save but I never really thought we looked in trouble and could have had more on the break. We have set that mantra of one game at a time, so now we prepare for next week's game against Derby. At this stage of the season, points from wherever you can get them are valuable, but we are on another good run and are looking forward to the next one.'

Burnley beat Derby 2-0 on 1 March, establishing a five-point lead over their dangerous rivals in third place. When asked about the crucial dismissal of Derby's Chris Martin, Dyche said:

'There are fine lines but we've had seven penalties not given this season, including one today. I must say, I felt they should have had one in the second half, but so should we for the foul on Ashley Barnes. What put Martin in trouble were the previous incidents. He had been lively, let's say, and he got away with one with Jason Shackell, and another with Ben Mee. He then got booked with the third one and the referee is then under pressure. In the incident, I think he lost his footing, but once he does that he appeals very quickly. If you do that, it's hard for the referee to decide. In a tough call, he felt it was a second yellow and Martin went.'

'For once it wasn't Danny Ings and Sam Vokes on the goal sheet. David Jones and Dean Marney picked up a goal apiece and it's always pleasing for the players and staff when a set play comes off. I am pleased for them because they have been in the right area several times and it's just not fallen to them, but it's a group effort and we were outstanding again today.

'Sometimes the toughest fight you have is against someone with nothing to lose. They were 1-0 down and with 10 men, so in the second half they had four at the back, one in front and the rest running everywhere. That can be awkward to play against, as it was in pockets, but overall, I felt we deserved the win. I thought the football in the first half was terrific.

'I talk a lot about the fact how the lads go about their business daily. If you do it there, you don't need to change anything, or flick a switch on a Saturday.

Individually, you just go and deliver and I thought in the first half, after a slow start, we soon started to play. Some of our movement and the way we shifted the ball through the units was excellent. Several teams have come here and have looked to contain us this year and I'm pleased to say they haven't fared that well. There was another sign of that today, but that's great respect to our players.'

Probably the most important result, though, for long-suffering Burnley fans, was the 2-1 victory at Ewood Park on Sunday 9 March. For a generation, they had endured the haughty derision of their local rivals, whose club had been consistently much richer and stronger thanks to Jack Walker's millions. Here, the wheel turned around.

Dyche proclaimed:

'Today is about the supporters. I'm delighted for them because before today Burnley had not defeated Blackburn in the past 35 years. The players and staff were desperate for things to change, so I am really pleased for them and for the board, as well. All the board members have been Burnley fans since they were boys. It is certainly an enjoyable feeling to win, particularly after coming from behind. I think the mentality has been there for all to see.

'I said to the lads at half-time that they were on the cusp of making history and that we should keep going forward. I told them that the marker is one goal, score that goal and the game will change. And it did. After we scored they found it difficult. We were always on the front foot and always looking to nick another. I've made it clear throughout our journey so far, that I believe in the players. Not just the quality they've got but I believe they understand how we are trying to play as a group. The physicality today was again exceptional. They'll go hard this group, for however long it takes to achieve what we can achieve.

'Shacks has done brilliant for the equaliser. He's thrown his head in where it hurts and he's got his reward for the team. He got one here last year and that was a very brave header, too, just his natural reaction. I must say it was a fantastic cross from Ross Wallace. We know he's got that quality. The cross is a horrible one for keepers because it is one that just sucks them off their line. As for the winner, I thought Ingsy was exceptional with his work ethic today, he just kept going and going and going. The demand that he's placed on himself, and for us as a group, is absolutely first class. Some strikers, if it's not quite happening for them, will switch off, but he doesn't. He keeps going and I thought he got his rewards today. He is a fantastic person as well as a player.'

Despite losing at home to champions-elect Leicester, on 29 March, a game in which Sam Vokes was carried off with a cruciate injury, Burnley built up an unassailable lead over the chasing pack. On Monday 21 April, promotion was duly achieved with a fluent victory over Wigan. Fittingly, the game was won with two goals of sublime quality. In the 22nd minute, centre back Duff pinged a long, lofted pass towards Kightly on the left flank. The former Wolves and Stoke winger immediately found Arfield who, in turn, fed Jones. Jones then chipped the ball to Ings who unhesitatingly flicked it over his head into the vacant inside right channel. Anticipating Ings' intention, Marney fastened onto the ball, and instantly crossed into the box for Barnes to race forward and smash home the opener. Turf Moor shuddered with the resulting roar, while Barnes, berserk with elation, slipped and fell on the adjacent advertising hoardings as he hurled himself at the adulatory crowd. Twenty minutes later, the game was sewn up as Kightly rifled a left-wing free-kick inside the far post. At the final whistle, most of those in the 19,125 crowd, charged onto the pitch to acclaim their heroes.

The Clarets' triumph comprised a string of new records: It was Burnley's best start to a season since 1897/98; their first victory over Blackburn Rovers in 35 years; their first win at Bolton in 29 years; and their first double over Leeds in 87 years. The 89 points they gained in finishing second to Leicester, was the most the club had achieved since 1981, when three points were first awarded for a win. The 35 goals Burnley conceded during this season were the fewest in the Championship, making them the meanest defence in the division. Twenty clean sheets were maintained in all competitions. Burnley lost only five league games, the lowest number of defeats since the club's Second Division championship-winning season of 1972/73. Before being beaten by Leicester in March, Burnley had maintained an unbeaten home record in the league for 23 matches. Right back, Kieran Trippier was credited with an incredible 14 assists. Vokes and Ings clearly benefitted from Trippier's prowess at crossing. Having managed just seven league goals between them in the season before, Vokes and Ings shared 41 league goals this time around. It was a phenomenal transformation.

Dyche attributed his side's success to three factors: meticulous planning, a team always willing to go that extra yard or mile and a highly dedicated backroom team. He explained to a *Burnley Express* reporter:

> 'My backroom team comprises my assistant, Ian Woan, first team coach, Tony Loughlan, goalkeeping coach, Billy Mercer, medical physiotherapist, Alasdair Beattie, and sports scientist, Mark Howard. They are all different. This works well because if you have only "yes men" then you will never achieve a better outcome. We often come up with different ideas and opinions, whether it is about training, team preparation, planning or players. It's up to me to make the final decision, but it is good to have their support.
>
> 'Alasdair and Mark are vital workers behind the scenes. Mark learnt his craft with Sam Allardyce at Bolton. It was Mark who advised me that although only Walsall

and Morecambe had used fewer players than Burnley, in this season's league games, we were still out-running our opponents, even after 30 games. Moreover, his statistics also proved we were then still full of energy and quality. So, added to the players' obvious belief in themselves and one another, these statistics underlined the advantage we had gained over our closest rivals.

'Helped by Alasdair's considerable expertise, we have tried to guard against soft tissue injuries. The game is changing in terms of severe contact injuries. So now, it is more about building muscular strength. We think we have good support from our science and physiotherapy staff but their work depends upon the players taking responsibility for the sessions they lay on. The players have grasped that here, and long may it continue.

'And, of course, there's more to do in improving analysis, sports science, players' dietary needs, strength and conditioning, athletic performance and so on. We're not yet the finished article…

'I didn't get carried away when promotion was won, despite having that pent-up anxiety of getting over the line when you're so close. I don't get too high with the highs nor too low with the lows. It's an internal celebration for me, though. I can assure you I'm more delighted than you will ever know. I'm extremely proud. The players have achieved so much this season.

'There are words we've used a lot, relentless, limitless. It's just a mindset. The hardest thing is to contend with all the noise on the outside. But it's only noise if you stay focused on what you do. Real achievers, I believe, stay focused on the job in hand, whatever job that might be. They don't get caught up in all the noise around them. They stay focused on that role and responsibility. The players have been exceptional. Next season, all we can do is what we can do. I'm always reality-bound.'

Right back, Kieran Trippier was less cautious, remarking with unreserved joy:

'I want to play against the best teams and the best players. I'm looking forward to playing at the Etihad. City let me go without me having the opportunity to prove myself but I came here and enjoyed myself. This season has been unbelievable. What a set of lads! Look at Tom Heaton. Last year he was relegated with Bristol City and now he's part of the defence with the best record in the Championship. You must cherish these moments. I've always said to myself, my dad and mum, I'll never make a better decision in my career than that in signing for Burnley.'

Goalkeeper Tom Heaton believed the rudiments of success were set before the season started, maintaining:

'It was the pre-season period in Cork that was critical. The time when we knew it had all come together was after a day of incredibly strenuous work, hard labour in fact, which ended with us split into three teams. Each team had to complete a lap of the pitch in less than 60 seconds. If one team member failed, then the whole team had to do it again. Not one person from any team failed. It was then when we knew we had something special going. It left us feeling really fit and ready to go, fresh and energised.

'Our fitness is science-based. No stone is left unturned; be it diet, nutrition, weight, heart-rate, hydration, supplements or pre-habilitation programmes which are designed to prevent injuries. The chef at Gawthorpe makes sure that food selections are of the right kind. Breakfast is optional. Lunch is not. And let's say you won't get bacon, sausages, a full English. Salads, soups, fruit are the norm at lunchtime along with varied hot food, different options of meat, vegetables and potatoes.

'Lunch is an example of where the manager's little ground rules come in. If anyone sits there texting, that's a "no" and a fine. Fines aren't always money and Friday is the day when they are imposed in a fun kind of way. Anyone can nominate someone for a fine, whether it's being late or using a phone when we shouldn't. A fine can sometimes be a forfeit, having to sing or dance.

'The daily training depends on whether there is a Tuesday game but it is always high tempo and the application from everyone has been incredible. At some clubs, you get slackers but not here. No-one has tailed off. In fact, everyone has put even more into it as the season has gone on. All of us have pulled in the same direction and that's rare. It's been a pleasure to come in every day.'

Captain and centre-half Jason Shackell remarked:

'I've played in every game this season. It's been my biggest involvement, so for me, this is the best promotion by far. You see some of the clubs and the money they've spent, so to do it with such a small squad is an incredible achievement. I can't give the gaffer and his staff enough credit. We stay together. People doubted us from the outside and maybe that galvanised us more. The lad's will always have one another's backs and that's shone on several occasions. From day one we knew we were a good team and a good squad and when the results started coming that just bred confidence. The gaffer gets us working day in, day out and the lads have really bought into what he wanted and believes. We've been a real tight-knit group from the start. The gaffer wouldn't let us lose focus, whatever happens. From being fourth favourites to go down and then getting automatic promotion with the likes of cash-rich QPR and Wigan below us, just makes it an incredible achievement.'

Long-standing Burnley supporter, Tony Scholes was deeply affected by Burnley's momentous triumph. He conveyed this in an article entitled, *My Unshakeable Belief.* Tony wrote:

'I'm not sure when I got this belief. I suppose I'm like Barry Kilby. He attributed his pessimism to what his mum drummed into him. She insisted: "If it's that good, it won't last".

'Pre-season started with a 1-0 defeat at Morecambe. Dyche spoke of the barracking he received there. But then we got off to a decent start. I think we all sat up and took notice of how well we played at Derby, where we won 3-0. Then we beat QPR 2-0, everyone's favourites for promotion. It was still no more than a good start, though. We'd notched 44 points by the half-way stage. That led me to think we had a chance, but what was to come was often difficult to take in.

'So, when did this worrier finally realise that something very, very special might be on the menu? It was at Blackburn: what a day! So many Burnley fans had never witnessed anything like it. Many hadn't even been born when we last beat them. I came home and watched it again, and again, and again. I love Sky+. We came home with an eight-point lead over Derby and from that day my belief never wavered. After we drew at Watford I referred to the light at the end of the tunnel. It was done and dusted at the seaside. No way was Dyche not going to allow us to get the necessary points. Are you nervous?" a friend asked before the Wigan game.

'I'd experienced Shackell scoring at Ewood, then Ings scoring at Ewood and the hysteria at the final whistle. Then I'd gone to the Turf all relaxed. I still find it hard to believe I was so confident. It's just not me. Had this ginger bloke somehow got inside my head? We brushed Wigan away, just as we'd done with QPR in October and Forest in February. The after-match celebrations were wonderful. The tears came three days later as I suddenly realised the enormity of what we'd achieved.

'When I first started watching the Clarets, we were managed by Harry Potts. I adored him. No-one will touch Harry for me, but Sean Dyche now runs him a close second. I think most people agree that this team has out-done that of five years ago. Steve Caldwell, the captain of that 2009 promotion-winning side, agreed. I believe this is our club's finest achievement since my dad first took me to Turf Moor in October 1960. The manager's one-club mentality has got everyone pulling in the same direction. I'll stand alongside thousands of Burnley fans watching OUR team playing Premier League football. I really can't wait. I have that unshakeable belief.'

Sean Dyche was unable to keep Burnley in the Premier League, despite strengthening the defence with the addition of young Manchester United centre half, Michael Keane. However, four points were taken from champions, Manchester City, and a courageous draw was snatched at champions-elect, Chelsea. Dyche's unshakeable belief persisted, despite the departures of the outstanding Ings, Trippier and Shackell. Once back in the Championship, Burnley thrived. Joey Barton, James Tarkowski and Andre Gray were drafted in, the latter for a club record fee of £6m plus. After a Boxing Day defeat at soggy Hull, Burnley remained unbeaten in their final 23 league games to take the title in front of stiff opposition. It was a truly remarkable achievement.

When asked about how he managed Joey Barton, Sean Dyche replied:

> 'One of the first questions I was asked, when I signed Joey Barton, was "How are you going to handle him?" And I told them exactly what I told Joey, that I wasn't going to handle him. He's a man not a boy and he's enjoyed that openness. We have respect, we have honesty, and he thrives on that. Sometimes you must interview someone to know how they are feeling. With Joey, you just look at him and you know he's in a good place. His conduct, the way he's been around people in Burnley. He's been a credit to the club.

Barton responded:

> 'The staff and players have made me feel part of the group from day one… It's been easy for me, playing in such a good team with good people and I'm enjoying every minute of it.'

Barton's contribution was crucial: his astute reading of the game; his fierce competitiveness; his composure; the range and vision of his passing; and his remarkable stamina; his sharp anticipation and grasping of 'second balls'. Dyche recognised and utilised his leadership strengths, too. At Milton Keynes and Charlton, Dyche allowed him to berate his team mates after sloppy first half performances. Barton's angry interventions prompted immediate improvements after the break. MK Dons were thrashed 5-0 while Charlton were thumped 3-0. During half-time at the Valley, Barton demanded that his team mates tell him who came second when Usain Bolt won his first Olympics gold medal. Not one of them knew. Barton snapped, 'See! No-one remembers those who come second. To make history we must take the title! Promotion is not enough.' Soon after the resumption, George Boyd and Andre Gray scored the goals that deservedly secured the Championship title for Burnley.

Dyche continued:

> 'I don't do screaming at players. I don't do names. If I use expletives it's to enhance a moment. It's not directed at anyone. And despite how I look, I don't do teacups either. Why would I do that? Everybody is just trying to do a job. A footballer's job is to learn. In helping players to improve, first,

you should work out how they learn; visual, kinaesthetic, written or discussion. With footballers, the usual three are: kinaesthetic, that's showing them things out on the grass; discussion; and visual. Very rarely do footballers write things down. Not because they're thick, but they're not in school anymore. People put a lot of stock in what managers say in moments before you go out onto the pitch, but that's not where the real work is done. If the players don't know what they're doing by that stage then, trust me, you haven't had a good week. It's just about reminding and prompting. We focus on ourselves not anybody else. The key core values are respect, good manners, good time-keeping, pride, passion, hard work, belief and integrity. This is the glue that holds everything together.'

Andre Gray and Sam Vokes led the charge to the Championship title, sharing 38 goals, with pacey Gray winning the Championship player-of-the-year for his 27 league goals. Vokes and Gray formed a solid partnership both on and off the field, although their regular car-sharing arrangement failed to bring about a convergence in their musical tastes. Sam Vokes said: 'We have an argument every morning because Andre's not having my music at all. He calls it "hillbilly music" and I'm not having his, to be honest, as you can't understand a word of what is going on.'

But Burnley's Championship goals weren't just left to Gray and Vokes. A midfield fortified by pugnacious, yet polished and composed, Joey Barton, added 21. Arfield contributed eight while the tireless Boyd scored five. Even the defence managed 10. Two critical, late strikes were landed by imperious centre half Michael Keane, denying hot rivals Brighton and Middlesbrough, vital victories. Meanwhile, the meagre number of goals conceded (35), and their 20 clean sheets, identified Burnley's defence as one of the tightest in the division.

Keane commented:

'This club has helped me massively. At United they make you a technical player, but coming here you must defend. I learnt a lot in that first season in the Premier League because there was a lot of defending to do. I've gone from strength to strength helped by the consistency of playing in the same back four and the reminders from the manager each week in training – he just drills it into you, so when it comes to matchdays it all comes naturally. My centre back partner, Ben Mee, has been brilliant, going from strength to strength like I have. It's dead easy playing with him. He talks to you all the time and puts his body on the line for you. He likes to play as well, but the first thing for Ben is to defend, and he's brilliant at it.'

Republic of Ireland left back, Stephen Ward, added:

'I feel I have improved a lot here. The manager's attention to detail, especially with the back four, is something I have not always had at other clubs. Here, the detail is brilliant. It might be the smallest thing, a yard here or there, but it makes a big difference in a game. I don't think I've been at a club where we have worked so hard.'

Once again, the watchwords were: 'framework', 'discipline', 'togetherness', 'resilience' and 'relentless' plus a new one, 'strong jaw'. Some names had changed but the mantra remained the same: 'Minimum requirement: maximum effort'.

Sadly, Ian Britton, one of the heroes of 1987, succumbed to prostate cancer shortly before his former club were crowned as Championship winners in May 2016. However, this is a football club that respects and celebrates its past and honours its heroes. Ian will never be forgotten. His goal against Orient in 1987 helped keep the club alive. Without that goal, this incredible journey would not have started.

Back in the Premier League for a third time in seven years, Burnley finally had the resources to strengthen in depth. Turf Moor was being improved. State of the art training facilities were being created at the Barnfield Training Centre, Gawthorpe. All remaining debts were cleared. It was, therefore, time to develop a team capable of holding its own in the top flight.

Icelandic international winger, Johann Berg Gudmundsson, was the first to arrive, in July 2016, alongside Charlton team mate, goalkeeper Nick Pope. However, it was the £8m, club record signing of Anderlecht's Belgian international midfielder, Steven Defour, which first demonstrated the club's new intent. Defour made an instant impact, setting up match-winning goals against Liverpool and Watford, and scoring with a blistering long-range strike against Hull. Steven said:

'I've scored a few nice goals in my career but I think the whole action makes this the nicest for me. I still have to fully adapt to the Premier League. I am used to playing with a lot of possession, whereas here there are games when you do not have so much possession. Here, the game never stops! There is no pause in play, so you can be 2-0 up and the game is never finished. In Belgium, the intensity is a bit lower.'

Sadly, this bright beginning was not sustained, not helped by niggling injury. There was little doubt about Defour's class, though. His disappointing experience seemed to underline how physically demanding it is to play in Dyche's Burnley side.

The club's record transfer fee was then broken twice more with the signings of Republic of Ireland internationals, Jeff Hendrick and Robbie Brady. The acquisition of central midfielder, Ashley Westwood took the club's total spending on new players up to an astonishing £40m for the season. With Tom Heaton and Michael Keane winning senior England caps, the number of full internationals in the Burnley squad rose to eight, the highest figure since the early sixties. There was certainly no lack of ambition here. Turf Moor became a fortress as Burnley took over 30 points from their home games. Sean Dyche reflected: 'Only once this season, following the opening day defeat, have we been in the bottom three, so nobody can argue that we haven't deserved to retain our Premier League status.'

Burnley's most impressive victory was at home against Liverpool on 20 August. This game was won 2-0 despite the Clarets having the lowest percentage of possession (19.6%) attained by a winning side in the Premier League for 10 years. It was a model counter-attacking display, combining energetic pressing from front to back, disciplined defending in depth and swift, decisive raids which yielded two fine goals. Whenever possession was lost, Burnley's two wide midfielders reinforced the back four. Burnley consistently squeezed the space between their lines, ensuring Liverpool's gifted play-makers had little room in which to operate, forcing their attackers into wider positions where their movement and passing became largely lateral. Having barred their direct route to goal, the visitors resorted to unproductive long-range shooting.

Champions Chelsea were held too at Turf Moor, thanks to Robbie Brady's sumptuous free kick, on his debut. Burnley confounded Chelsea with their resolute and tireless defending in depth, while their probing long balls interrupted the Londoners' pressing game. Although visiting Manchester City and Arsenal teams were victorious, Burnley deserved at least a share of the spoils. Only Manchester United, and Spurs, after an inspired tactical change, merited their wins at Turf Moor. Burnley showed too that they had the mental and physical strength to win games while under the cosh. Their home victories over Everton and Crystal Palace illustrated this, both games being decided by last minute goals. Although Dyche successfully employed a 4-5-1 formation in several games, mostly he favoured the 4-4-2 or 4-4-1-1 set up that had yielded previous success. Despite operating in a much more challenging league, his three strikers Gray, Vokes and Barnes did him proud sharing 25 goals, while the defence remained largely redoubtable, as recognised by the international selections of Heaton, Keane and Ward.

A home draw with West Bromwich on 6 May 2017 gave Burnley their fortieth point, thereby securing their Premier League status for a further season. The club's 30-year journey from rags to riches had reached an incredible, lofty milestone.

Mike Garlick, the club's largest shareholder, assumed the sole chairmanship of the club on 28 May 2015 following three years as co-chairman alongside John Banaszkiewicz, who had stepped down to devote more time to his family and his diverse international business interests. However, John continues as a director. Recently, Mike Garlick, his vice chairman, Barry Kilby, and long-standing director, Clive Holt, looked back over their club's sometimes bumpy, yet amazing 30-year journey.

Mike reflected:

'In the 2014/15 season, the club made a record profit of over £30m, but, way back in 1985/86, the finances here were so precarious that Burnley FC was close to folding. The prospect was so real that extra programmes were printed so that souvenirs would be available for the final home game of the season. The club survived only by the skin of its teeth. The following campaign, 1986/87 was the "Orient Season" when the team had to win its final game to stay in the Football League. For a second consecutive year, the club was close to extinction. It seems inconceivable that a club once so powerful and successful in its golden years was so close to disaster just 30 years ago.

'On desolate nights in 1986/87 some crowds were less than 2,000. We were short of everything. The groundsman had to collect the soil from the molehills at Gawthorpe to fill the holes in the pitch at Turf Moor and level the goalmouth. The 1988 Sherpa Van Final was the turning point, and in 1992 there was promotion at last as Burnley left the wilderness years of the old Fourth Division under Jimmy Mullen. This was followed by another promotion, this time into the top half of English football. It lasted only a year, but then Stan Ternent got the bus on the road again and won us promotion back to the second tier in 2000.

'And in 2009, despite the club being under severe financial stress, we were back in the top division. Our investment to get us there was described then as a "calculated gamble", an understatement, perhaps. When we were immediately relegated how many thought we would be back again? But we did return. Could we get back a third time, we wondered, after a second one-year stay? The statistics were against it, but Sean Dyche and his team were up for it, and there we were at the pinnacle again.

'In 2015/16, we were champions of the Championship; we had the Championship's top scorer and its player-of-the-season; we were top of the fair-play league; we had four players in the PFA team of the season; Michael Duff became the first player to be promoted three times to the Premier League with the same club – a true reward for a great club servant – and we had an award-winning Community Department. What a season this was!

'I had high hopes we could remain a Premier League side following our magnificent Championship-winning season but I think it's fair to say that we have exceeded all internal expectations. And with the two other sides promoted with us in 2016, Middlesbrough and Hull City, both making an immediate return to the Championship, I think that further emphasises the scale of our feat.'

Barry Kilby added:

'I believe our club commands considerable respect. I'm sure this owes something to our durability. As with Portsmouth, Bradford, Plymouth, Brighton and Swansea we have endured and yet triumphed over almost suffocating financial adversity, and like these other clubs we have had to pull ourselves out of the mire without the assistance of rich benefactors. This respect we now enjoy has been hard-earned.

'Our first tilt at the Premier League in 2009/10 ended disappointingly, as did the managerial careers here of Owen Coyle and Brian Laws, for very different reasons. In came Eddie Howe. You could see his potential but perhaps he wasn't ready for that step up. He resigned in the autumn of 2012 to be re-united with his family in Bournemouth. Sean Dyche replaced him. He's certainly the right man for us – bright, straight talking, calm and confident, placing a strong emphasis upon a team ethic. He never gets too high or too low. The players respond to him so well.

'Our second experience of the Premier League opened our eyes to the widening margins of the haves and have nots. During that 2014/15 season, only eight per cent of our revenue came from gate money. This is the impact of the massive hike in satellite TV fees. The consequences are interesting because now, for the first time perhaps, the lesser lights in the Premier League can afford to rebuff raids on their star players by having the financial clout to keep them sweet at home. Obviously, this cranks up the inflationary wheel, and we have seen in past seasons how difficult it is for us compete in this market irrespective of our enhanced wealth. With gate money being less essential at the top of the pyramid perhaps more top clubs will make offers that will undercut what we charge to see a game.

'In 2014/15, our annual turnover grew to a figure of more than £50m, small beer when compared to Manchester United's £400m, but it gave us some strength in the market, albeit time-limited. Our purchase of Brentford striker Andre Gray was evidence of that. But once the parachute payments, earned in our second Premier League season in 2014/15, ceased, our turnover would have fallen to around £13-14m, had we not been promoted again at the end of the 2015/16 campaign.

'Now that so many Championship clubs are sustained by lucrative backers we are facing inflationary demands for players, both in transfer fees and wages, that we would not have believed possible four years ago. Agents, too, are very sharp in operating within this environment, quoting a price, only to crank that figure up exorbitantly at the drop of a hat, creating auctions. We must be savvy and tough in the present market place. Fans are sometimes frustrated by the apparent lack of action. They need to realise that doing deals in the top two divisions of English football is now unbelievably hard.

'When I look back at my life in football, I guess I might be unique among English club directors, in that I once played for this club that I now help run – albeit as a Burnley junior. In fact, I was in the same Burnley youth side as former Turf Moor star, Martin Dobson. But whereas Martin went on to play for England I went on to play for Padiham.'

Clive Holt reflected:

'If we think about the club's recent history of success, I suppose we should start with Eddie Howe. For Eddie could certainly spot a player. Let's take Ings, Trippier, Mee and Shackell for example. They have all played important parts in Burnley's rise. But I didn't think Eddie's heart was in the job, particularly after his mum suddenly died. He wanted to be in Bournemouth and throughout his time here, he kept going back and forth. It wasn't working for either party so a split was amicably agreed in autumn 2012, enabling him to resume the management of his home town club.

'Once Sean Dyche replaced Eddie, he immediately tightened up the team's defence which had been shipping too many goals. One thing that strikes me about Sean is that he appears very cautious about who he brings in lest it upsets the team dynamic. However, I think we would have stayed in the Premier League in 2014/15 had Danny Ings not signed a pre-contract agreement with Liverpool, which, I thought, turned his head. Had that not happened he might have scored sufficient goals to have kept us up.

'Despite that setback, we've developed so strongly since those dark days of 1986/87. Firstly, we have created and sustained a competitive Championship side without spending the earth, although if it were not for the 'parachute payments', it is doubtful whether we could have competed as well as we have at this level. During the 30-year period I have been directly involved in running the club we have improved the ground enormously, providing covered seating for over 20,000 supporters. We have also installed a superb, all-weather playing surface at Turf Moor that is fit for Premier League football, although a prolonged dry spell during September 2014 meant that it wasn't at its best for much of the 2014/15 season. That drought caused the surface to disintegrate, resulting in the ball not running quite as smoothly as before.

'We have covered the entrance to the Bob Lord Stand so that supporters are protected from adverse weather when buying food or drink before and during a game. We have introduced tighter access control arrangements with cameras installed in the turnstile booths to ensure that tickets are not being used fraudulently – say, by adults attempting to gain admission with concessionary tickets.

'And perhaps most significantly of all, we have upgraded the training facilities at Gawthorpe, restoring it to a state of the art standard as it had been during the late fifties and early sixties. The £10m developments taking place there have required some tough negotiations though.

'We have had robust exchanges with the contractors in ensuring that the flood defences were adequate. We discovered that the foundations for the new buildings and the construction of the new pitches had not complied with the recommendations set out in the DEFRA flood report. Both the buildings and the pitches needed to be raised above their original height. At their previous levels, both the foundations and the new pitches were overcome with flood water during the deluges of 2015/16.

As was the case in constructing the two stands at Turf Moor, it is imperative that we keep tight oversight of the detailed building specifications, challenging any departure from these. My job is to hold the contractors to account ensuring that the development is fit for purpose and that we do not incur unnecessary costs because of contractors not complying with the agreed specification. We have also been in some tough negotiations with the National Trust who own the land around Gawthorpe Hall. This has resulted in a re-siting of the gas pipe serving the training facilities so that it does not interfere with preserved bushes and trees. And as with other historic sites, we must ensure that any new development, including road access, does not damage any historic remains.

'It has been some journey but one that I'm proud to have helped the club to make. We know that without the resources that recent team successes have delivered, we would have had a major challenge in preserving our competitiveness at Championship level, let alone at Premier League standard. But we remain ambitious. Given the progress we have made since 1987 it is right that we are.'

Epilogue
'The medium is the message'

WHEN Burnley were struggling for survival in May 1987, dozens of journalists, radio and TV reporters descended upon Turf Moor to cover the drama unfolding for this imperilled, once famous club. News was then principally conveyed by the press, radio and TV broadcasters. The digital age radically changed all that. News became an instant commodity. The wait for the daily paper or evening broadcast was a thing of the past. The internet enabled all purveyors of news, official and unofficial, accredited or not, to provide immediate coverage of common, minority or parochial interests. Then along came social media with its flurry of opinions, both fair and unfair; information, both accurate and inaccurate, genuine and fake; and a torrent of comments, demands and criticisms, whether reasonable or not, borne and recycled by incessant on-line chatter. The immediacy and vast breadth of social media shapes the form and content of its messages, often reinforcing a misplaced sense of personal entitlement that can be harmful and at odds with collective responsibility.

This is the environment in which a media manager of a modern football club must operate. And because the market for top flight English clubs is now a global one, thanks to satellite TV and the growth in overseas investors, media savviness is mandatory requirement for all staff situated in the public eye. This is the challenge facing a media manager, such as Burnley's Darren Bentley. Like so many others involved in running this club, Darren is a dyed-in-the-cotton Burnley fan, having followed his side since his early youth during the mid-seventies, when Leighton James was his hero. Here, Darren explains how he and his club cope with this challenge.

'The current manager Sean Dyche appears self-assured in his dealings with press and TV reporters, adopting an honest, open and authoritative demeanour. My job is to offer him and his players advice on issues that might arise during these interviews. For example, when current right back,Matt Lowton was selected for interview, we offered our advice about how he might deal with some potentially tricky questions about his former club, Aston Villa. As for the club chairman, Mike Garlick, I will sometimes present him with some options about which he may wish to comment, fleshing out the issues involved. But he chooses the topics he wishes to focus upon and the approach to be used. These interviews are never stage-managed. The chairman, manager and players conduct their interviews in the way they see fit. At our weekly senior managers meeting, I may bring to my colleagues' attention any relevant interviews that might take place during the week ahead.

'Of course, there is always a danger that what is said by the chairman, manager or player in an interview is deliberately or inadvertently misinterpreted, arousing an unintended controversy. This happened when Sean Dyche made a wry comment about Pep Guardiola's pronouncement on his players' diet, pointing out that such provisions about healthy eating had been in place at Burnley for some time, but had perhaps not been considered newsworthy because the club had a lesser standing with the media than Manchester City.

'His comments were not intended to be critical but were nevertheless represented by some as a gripe. Not that Sean is fazed by such occurrences. He is adept at defusing any fall out from such misunderstandings. However, he takes the precaution of ensuring that whatever he says at a press conference, for example, is fully captured on camera, so there is less risk that what he says will be taken out of context. This way his humorous asides will be seen for what they are. The dangers inherent in this process were underlined recently in an incident involving former Sunderland manager, David Moyes, when he was heard to chide a female reporter off camera. Irrespective of whether Moyes should have said what he did, arguably, his remark might not have been quite as offensive had the viewers seen Moyes' ironic expression when he delivered it. My cameraman was present, as it was directly after Sunderland's home game with Burnley.

'With the Premier League having gone global – 80 plus countries receive live coverage of EPL games – there is a constant call upon clubs to provide TV interviews with their managers and players each week throughout the season. On Thursdays, the manager is required to participate in a televised press conference concerning the weekend game. In addition, the manager and one of his players are expected to be available for one-to-one interviews. Sky and BT also require an interview with a player on arrival at the ground before a televised game, stipulating that the player chosen must be participating in that game. It is my job to co-ordinate these interviews, agreeing a rota with the manager for the selection of his players. Some discretion is applied, however, in making players available for interview. For example, it was decided to exclude Joey Barton from the rota after an FA charge was brought against him for his alleged betting activities. Andre Gray was excluded too after his historic tweets were exposed.

'We have one of the smallest media teams in the country. Given Burnley's currently prominent profile at home and abroad, this presents us with a significant challenge in meeting all demands placed upon us, particularly with the prodigious growth in social media. I try to respond to every tweet we receive, providing it is politely worded and free of expletives, but it can be frustrating to repeatedly receive tweets asking questions that are easily answered if only those submitting them looked first on official club channels. One of the most trying aspects of social media can be responding many times to those who opt for this short-cut approach.

'As we know with the controversy created by Andre Gray's historic tweets, care needs to be exercised in using social media. Notwithstanding this incident, Sean Dyche insists that his players remain personally responsible for their private tweets, as befits their status as adults. However, he demands that they should not send any tweet concerning football, steering them away from potential trouble and recourse.

'Apropos Andre Gray's historic tweets, he and his advisers prepared an immediate personal response once his tweets were exposed. The apology was essentially his own work. All I did was to tidy up the grammar and punctuation. He rightly saw that it was necessary to issue an authentic personal statement distancing himself from the person he once was. Here we believe it is important for everyone to exercise responsibility for themselves. While Sean Dyche has clear expectations about how his players should behave while representing the club he also insists that they remain personally accountable for their conduct when outside the club.

'Probably the greatest highlight of my career with Burnley FC was when we I joined the exultant Burnley players on the winners' podium at Wembley in May 2009. It underlined to me just how inclusive this club is.'

References

Beast: Brian Jensen – From Norrebro to the Premier League: Hans-Gerd
    Crabbed and Dan Hirsch Sorenson: Dabber Publishing (2010)

The Best Ground in the Fourth Division: A Recent History of Burnley
    Football Club (1960 -1988): Andrew Proctor: Janus (1992)

Big Club, Small Town & Me: The Epic Story of Burnley's Meteoric Rise to
    the Premiership: Brendan Flood: TH Media (2009)

Burnley: A Complete Record: Edward Lee & Ray Simpson: Breedon
    Books Sport (1991)

Burnley: The Glory Years Remembered: Mike Presage: Breedon Books/
    DB Publishing (2000)

Burnley Football Club 1882-1968: Images in Sport: Ray Simpson:
    Tempus Publishing Ltd. (1999)

Burnley FC Matchday Magazines 1973 – 2017: Burnley Football Club

Burnley Were Back: Stephen Cummings: Janus (1996)

Champions: How Burnley Won Promotion 2015/16: Dave Thomas:
    Pitch Publishing (2016)

The Clarets Chronicle: The Definitive History of Burnley Football
    Club 1882-2007: Ray Simpson with Darren Bentley, Wallace
    Chadwick, Edward Lee & Phil Simpson: Burnley Football Club
    (2007)

The Clarets Collection 1946 – 1996: A Post-War Who's Who of Burnley
    Football Club: Ray Simpson: Burnley Football Club (1996)

Entertainment, Heroes and Villains: Success and Failure at Burnley FC':
    Dave Thomas: Vertical Editions (2011)

The Football League Directory 1985-87, 1993-94: Tony Williams (Ed):
    Nunes / Hamlyn / Harmsworth / Burlington

Forever & Ever: A Rock 'n' Roll Years Diary of Burnley Football Club: Tim Quelch in collaboration with Burnley FC and the London Clarets (2000)

Inverting the Pyramid: The History of Football Tactics: Jonathan Wilson: Orion (2008)

It's Burnley Not Barcelona: The Search for Champagne with Beer Money: Dave Thomas: The Parrs Wood Press (2003)

My Fight for Football: Bob Lord: Stanley Paul (1963)

Never Had It So Good: Burnley's Incredible 1959/60 League Winning Triumph: Tim Quelch: Know the Score Books (2009) Re-printed by Pitch Publishing (2015)

Left Foot Forward: A Year in the Life of a Journeyman Footballer: Garry Nelson: Headline (1995)

Living the Dream with Andy Payton: Gavin Roper: Bruce Publishing (2011)

No Nay Never: A Burnley FC Anthology: Dave Thomas (2004)

No Nay Never: A Burnley FC Anthology Volume 2: Dave Thomas: Burnley FC (2008)

No Nonsense: The Autobiography: Joey Barton: Simon & Schuster (2016)

The Official Burnley FC Yearbook 1992/93, 1993/4, 1994-95: Ray Simpson: Burnley FC

The Pride and Glory: Official 120-Year History of Burnley Football Club: Edward Lee & Phil Whalley: Burnley Football Club (2002)

The Rothmans & Sky Sports Football Yearbooks: 1973/74 to 2017/18: Headline

Russians Don't Land Here: 2006/2007 at Burnley Football Club: Dave Thomas: Hudson and Pearson (2007)

Something to Write Home About: London Clarets' magazine 1983-2017

Stan the Man: A Hard Life in Football: Stan Ternent with Tony Livesey: John Blake (2003)

Thanks for the Memories: Roger Eli with Dave Thomas: Vertical Editions (2012)

Underdog! 50 Years of Trials and Triumphs with Football's Also Rans: Tim Quelch: Pitch Publishing (2011)

Up the Clarets: The Story of Burnley Football Club: Rev. David Wiseman: Robert Hale (1973)

Who Says Football Doesn't Do Fairy Tales: How Burnley Defied the Odds to Join the Elite: Dave Thomas: Pitch Publishing (2014)